T0330538

Foreign Investment and Dispute Resolution Law and Practice in Asia

Edited by
Vivienne Bath and Luke Nottage

Routledge
Taylor & Francis Group

LONDON AND NEW YORK

First published 2011
by Routledge
4 Park Square, Milton Park, Abingdon, Oxon OX14 4RN
605 Third Avenue, New York, NY 10017

Routledge is an imprint of the Taylor & Francis Group, an informa business

British Library Cataloguing in Publication Data
A catalogue record for this book is available from the British Library

Library of Congress Cataloging in Publication Data
Foreign investment and dispute resolution law and practice in Asia / [edited by] Vivienne Bath, Luke Nottage.
    p. cm. – (Routledge research in international economic law)
    Includes bibliographical references and index.
    1. Investments, Foreign–Law and legislation–Asia. 2. Dispute resolution (Law)–Asia. I. Bath, Vivienne. II. Nottage, Luke.
    KNC747.F668 2011
    346.5'092–dc23
                                                                2011021923

ISBN: 978-0-415-61074-2 (hbk)
ISBN: 978-0-203-15553-0 (ebk)

Typeset in Garamond
by Wearset Ltd, Boldon, Tyne and Wear

Contents

Figures and tables

Figures

Tables

Contributors

Editors

Vivienne Bath (BA (Hons)/LLB (Hons) *ANU*, LLM, *Harv*) is Associate Professor, Faculty of Law, University of Sydney (Sydney Law School), and Director of the Centre for Asian and Pacific Law at the University of Sydney. Prior to joining the Faculty of Law, she was a partner of international firm Coudert Brothers, working in the Hong Kong and Sydney offices, and specializing in commercial law, with a focus on foreign investment and commercial transactions in the People's Republic of China. She previously practised as a commercial lawyer in New York and Sydney. Vivienne specializes in Chinese law and cross-border commercial law and has published widely in these areas. She is a co-author with Robin Burnett of *Law of International Business in Australasia* (Federation Press, 2009). Vivienne speaks Chinese and German.

Luke Nottage (BCA/LLB/PhD, *VUW*; LLM, *Kyoto*) is Associate Professor at Sydney Law School, founding Co-Director of the Australian Network for Japanese Law, and Program Director (Comparative and Global Law) at the Sydney Centre for International Law. He lectures, writes and consults world-wide in the fields of contract law, product liability and safety regulation, civil dispute resolution (especially arbitration), corporate governance, and cyber-law, mostly comparing developments in Japan or transnationally. Luke has produced eight books and over 100 chapters or major articles, mostly in English and Japanese, and contributes to three looseleaf commentaries. Luke serves on the Rules Committee of the Australian Centre for International Commercial Arbitration (ACICA), has lectured and written for the Chartered Institute of Arbitrators (CIArb), and was a founding member of the Australasian Forum for International Arbitration (AFIA). Since 1990 Luke has worked closely with law firms and companies in New Zealand, Japan, Australia and the US in cross-border dispute resolution and transaction planning, and he is a founding Director of Japanese Law Links Pty Ltd.

Contributors

Simon Butt (BA (Hons)/LLB (Hons), *ANU*; PhD, *Melbourne*) is Senior Lecturer, Sydney Law School, and Associate Director of the Centre for Asian and Pacific Law. Prior to joining the University of Sydney, Simon worked as a consultant on the Indonesian legal system to the Australian government, the private sector and international organizations, including the United Nations Development Programme (UNDP) and the International Commission of Jurists (ICJ). He has taught in over 70 law courses in Indonesia on a diverse range of topics, including intellectual property, Indonesian criminal law, Indonesian terrorism law and legislative drafting. He is fluent in Indonesian.

Govert Coppens (Cand. Laws/MLaws, *Leuven*) is completing a PhD at the University of Leuven, Belgium. His research focuses on jurisdictional matters in investment law and international investment arbitration. He holds a Diploma in Legal Studies with Distinction from King's College, London, and a Certificate of Public International Law from The Hague Academy of International Law. Govert has also worked as an intern for various international law firms.

Hop Dang (BA/LLB, *Hanoi*; LLB, *Bond*; LLM, *Melb*; DPhil, *Oxon*) is a partner in the Hanoi office of Allens Arthur Robinson, a leading regional law firm in South Asia. Hop practises mainly in Vietnam where he has extensive experience and expertise in representing foreign investors in negotiating internationally enforceable agreements with Vietnamese partners and the Vietnamese Government. Hop's doctoral thesis focused on international investment law and he has published widely. He has taught courses at law schools in Vietnam, Singapore and Australia, and is a Visiting Senior Fellow at the University of New South Wales and at the National University of Singapore. He is a Fellow of the Singapore Institute of Arbitrators and an Arbitrator at the Singapore International Arbitration Centre, the Kuala Lumpur Regional Centre for Arbitration and the Pacific International Arbitration Centre in Vietnam.

Nils Eliasson (LLM/PhD, *Lund*) specializes in international commercial arbitration and investment treaty arbitration. Based in Hong Kong, Nils is responsible for Mannheimer Swartling's Asian dispute resolution practice. He has acted as counsel in disputes encompassing energy, oil and gas, real estate, construction, engineering, licence disputes, mergers and acquisitions, insurance, and other areas. Nils has represented clients before arbitral tribunals in various jurisdictions, and has experience in conducting arbitrations under the auspices of most major arbitration institutes as well as ad hoc proceedings under the UNCITRAL Arbitration Rules. He has also acted as counsel for investors and states in a number of investment arbitrations under bilateral investment treaties as well as under the Energy Charter Treaty. Nils has written many articles and other works on international arbitration and investment arbitration. He is a frequent speaker at international arbitration conferences and a guest lecturer on international arbitration and international investment law at universities in Lund, Stockholm, Beijing and Shanghai.

Salim Farrar (LLB (Hons)/LLM *London*; Dip in Sharia Law and Practice, *IIU Malaysia*; PhD *Warw*; PG Cert in Teaching in Higher Education *Coventry*) is Senior Lecturer, Sydney Law School, and Associate Director of the Centre for Asian and Pacific Law. He first graduated in Law from King's College London in 1991 and was called to the English Bar in 1992. He worked in Malaysia from 1994–6 before completing a doctorate in comparative criminal justice at the University of Warwick as a British Academy Scholar. Salim went on to teach at the Universities of Coventry, Warwick and Manchester before appointment as an Associate Professor at the International Islamic University Malaysia in 2004. His principal research and teaching interests are in Islamic law, criminal justice and human rights, with a particular focus on Southeast Asia and the Middle East. He speaks English, Arabic, Bahasa Malaysia and French, and wrote *The Criminal Process in Malaysia* (Pearson, rev. edn 2008).

Shotaro Hamamoto (LLB/LLM, *Kyoto*; docteur en droit, *Paris II*) is Professor at the Graduate School of Law, Kyoto University, Japan, and was *professeur invité* at the Université de Paris I (Panthéon-Sorbonne) in 2009. He publishes in Japanese, French and English on the theory of international law, recognition, law of treaties, law of the sea, human rights, investment law, sports law and European Union law. He was assistant for the Government of Spain in the *Fisheries Jurisdiction* case (Spain v. Canada) before the International Court of Justice and advocate for the Government of Japan in the *Hoshinmaru* case (*Japan* v. *Russia*) and the *Tomimaru* case (*Japan* v. *Russia*) before the International Tribunal for the Law of the Sea. He also represents Japan in the UNCITRAL WGII (Arbitration and Conciliation), working on transparency in treaty-based Investor-State Arbitration since 2010. He is an arbitrator at the Japan Sports Arbitration Agency and member of the Board of Editors of the *Japanese Yearbook of International Law*.

Akira Kawamura (LLB, *Kyoto*; LLM, *Syd*) is the current President of the International Bar Association, and a partner at Anderson Mori & Tomotsune based in Tokyo. He has an extensive general corporate and litigation practice with numerous large multinational domestic and foreign clients, and long experience in the legal aspects of investment in Asia. He specializes in corporate, M&A, intellectual property, international trade, entertainment, publication, energy and real property law. Mr Kawamura is a corporate auditor and board member of a number of Japanese companies, and is also an experienced arbitrator/mediator. He is executive director of the Japan Arbitrators Association and a councilor of the Japanese Society of International Law. He is also an influential member of the Japanese Bar, having served as Executive Director of the Japan Federation of Bar Associations (Nichibenren) and in other roles. He was a Visiting Professor at Kyoto University's Faculty of Law, and serves on the Advisory Board of the Australian Network for Japanese Law. His numerous publications in English and Japanese have included *Australian Law and Business* (1979) and *Law and Business in Japan – New Edition* (2nd edn 2000), as author and editor-in-chief.

Joongi Kim (BA *Columbia*; MA *Yonsei*; JD *Georgetown*) is Professor of Law and Associate Dean for International Affairs at Yonsei Law School in Seoul, Korea, having previously held visiting professorships at Hongik University and the National University of Singapore. He has published and lectured widely around the world in the areas of international trade and investment, dispute resolution and corporate governance. He serves as a director of the Korea Council for International Arbitration and the Korean Arbitrators Association, served on the KOSDAQ Dispute Resolution Commission and was the Founding Executive Director of the Hills Governance Center at Yonsei. He previously practiced law at Foley & Lardner in Washington DC, and is an accredited member on the panel of arbitrators of CAA, DIAC, HKIAC, JCAA, KCAB and KLRCA.

Prabhash Ranjan (BA (Hons) (Economics) *Delhi*; LLB *Delhi*; LLM *SOAS*; PhD Candidate *King's College London*) is Assistant Professor at National University of Juridical Sciences (NUJS), Kolkata, India. Prabhash is a Chevening scholar and has been awarded the King's College School of law doctoral scholarship. Prior to joining NUJS, Prabhash worked as a Research Consultant to the UNDP Regional Centre in Colombo; Research Assistant to Professor Valentine Korah at UCL; Consultant to Oxfam Great Britain in India; and as Legal Researcher at CUTS International, India. Prabhash has published in many widely-read journals as well as in edited volumes published by Oxford University Press (UK) and Wiley (India). Prabhash has also presented papers at major international conferences.

Sita Sitaresmi (BA (International Studies) *Warwick*; LLM *Adelaide*) is a legal consultant to the State Secretary, Indonesia. She previously served as Deputy Director for America and Pacific Affairs in the Coordinating Ministry for Economic Affairs. From 2005–9 she was a member of the negotiation team for the Japan–Indonesia Economic Partnership Agreement and for treaties with the NAFTA states, such as the Canada–Indonesia Foreign Investment Protection and Promotion Agreement, the US–Indonesia Investment Support Agreement, the Mexico-Indonesia Investment Protection and Promotion Agreement, as well as others with European countries. She is a British Chevening scholar and an Australian Leadership scholar. Her research interests are in International Investment Law and Arbitration, International

Trade Law, International Energy Law and State Responsibility in relation to state contracts. Her most recent research is on the implication of certain BIT provisions on fiscal security.

Muthucumaraswamy Sornarajah (LLM, *Yale*; LLD, *London*) is CJ Koh Professor at the Faculty of Law of the National University of Singapore and the Tunku Abdul Rahman Professor of International Law at the University of Malaya at Kuala Lumpur. He was previously Head of the Law School of the University of Tasmania in Australia, and has been a Research Fellow at the Centre for International Law in Cambridge and at the Max Planck Institute for Comparative Public Law and International Law in Heidelberg, and Visiting Professor at the American University, the University of Dundee, Scotland, the World Trade Institute of the Universities of Berne and Neuchatel, Kyushu University and the Georgetown Centre for Transnational Legal Studies, London. He is the author of *The Pursuit of Nationalized Property* (Martinus Nijhoff, 1986); *International Commercial Arbitration* (Longman, 1992); *The Law of International Joint Ventures* (Longman, 1994); *The International Law on Foreign Investment* (Cambridge University Press, 3rd edn 2010) and *The Settlement of Foreign Investment Disputes* (Kluwer, 2001); and he co-edited *China, India and the International Economic Law* (Cambridge University Press, 2010). Professor Sornarajah was the Director of the UNCTAD/WTO Programme on Investment Treaties, Pretoria and New Delhi. He is a Fellow of ACICA and on the Regional Panel of the Singapore International Arbitration Centre. He is an Honorary Member of the Indian Society of International Law.

J. Romesh Weeramantry (BA/LLB, *Monash*; LLM, PhD *London*) is an Associate Professor at the City University of Hong Kong. He recently completed a doctoral thesis on investment treaty arbitration through the Queen Mary School of International Arbitration, University of London. His professional experience includes work in international arbitration, dispute resolution and public international law at the Iran–United States Claims Tribunal (The Hague), the United Nations Compensation Commission (Geneva) and at a leading Swiss law firm. He has also practised as a barrister at the Victorian Bar. Additionally, as an independent consultant he has provided several legal opinions on public international law and has worked with international organizations including UNCTAD and UNITAR. Romesh has published in a variety of law journals including the *American Journal of International Law*, is a contributor to the Oxford University Press investment claims database, and co-authored *International Commercial Arbitration: An Asia-Pacific Perspective* (Cambridge University Press, 2010). He has been a Special Associate and Rules Committee member for ACICA and was a founding Chair of AFIA. He has designed and taught courses on international and investment arbitration at various Asia-Pacific universities.

Preface

Akira Kawamura
President, International Bar Association

It is a distinct honour to provide a preface for this valuable book on 'Foreign Investment and Dispute Resolution Law and Practice in Asia'. It also happens to commemorate the final stage of my long career as a lawyer practising international business law, and as a humble student of this area of law and practice.

When I first saw the title of this book, edited and partly authored by legal academics at the University of Sydney, I was instantly reminded of the thesis I had submitted to Sydney Law School for my LL.M degree nearly 35 years ago. My topic was 'A Comparative Study of Laws on Foreign Investment in Australia and Japan'. My thesis supervisor was Professor Ross Parsons, whose academic achievements are now honoured by the Ross Parsons Centre of Commercial, Corporate and Taxation Law established within Sydney Law School. I remember the days I spent with my family, my wife Masako and our two daughters, on the beautiful beachfronts around Sydney Harbour during the two years I studied at Sydney Law School. Now I look back and realize that it was the happiest time in my life. Hence, I am writing these short words with very personal and happy sentiments.

It seems to me that foreign investment law had become less of a critical concern for international legal practice, and that the subject had been attracting less interest from academia, compared to when I was writing my thesis on this topic in 1970s. At that time, the foremost policy priority for foreign investment law in Australia was the protection of Australian companies and natural resources, through ownership and other restrictions, from takeovers by foreign interests. Likewise, in Japan, foreign investment policy was concentrated almost exclusively on the protection of domestic industries.

The world has changed and this timely book on 'Foreign Investment and Dispute Resolution Law and Practice in Asia' ambitiously surveys contemporary issues in foreign investment and dispute resolution law throughout the Asian region. The study reveals that the current policy priority in most of the countries in Asia is the promotion of foreign investment in the region, rather than the old-fashioned policy of protecting domestic companies.

The twenty-first century appears to be an era in which globalization can have a broad impact on people's lives. Although we are not yet able to see clearly an ideal image of the global society that many aspire to, which still lies for us beyond the horizon, we have many alternative legal and political means to reach towards the ultimate goal of a free society world-wide, where the well-being of citizens and sustainable economic growth can be realized.

This book deals with the international legal frameworks for promoting foreign investments including those established by the World Trade Organization, bilateral investment treaties and free trade agreements, as well as the domestic regulatory frameworks of major capital exporting or capital importing nations in Asia. The impact of the Trans-Pacific Strategic Economic Partnership Agreement (TPPA) on those domestic regulatory frameworks may prove to be more important than the existing regulatory frameworks themselves for those nations, like Japan, which are now considering joining the TPPA. This book is therefore a very important instrument for lawyers in both the public and private sectors to stay up to date about developments in foreign investment and dispute resolution law and practice in Asia.

The International Bar Association (IBA), which I presently head as its President, is the world's largest organization for the legal profession. It is composed of the bar associations and law societies of 137 countries. It is literally the global bar for the global legal profession. Since the collapse of Lehman Brothers and other major financial institutions, it has become apparent that the GFC could not have been addressed as effectively and as quickly as required without the critical thinking and hard work of a highly organized global network of legal, accounting, financial and other professionals. The legal profession responded very effectively to this challenge and proved itself worthy of being called a global profession. After the GFC, it has often been said that economic power has shifted from the West to the East. The Asia-Pacific region is now the centre stage for world economic growth, and naturally the laws of foreign investment and dispute resolution in the region should be critically important topics for the global legal profession.

I wholeheartedly welcome, on behalf of the global legal profession, the painstaking international and comparative study of the laws and practices in these fields, epitomized by this book.

Acknowledgements and note on style

This book is partly derived from an international symposium on 'Investment Treaty Law and Arbitration: Evolution and Revolution in Substance and Procedure' held at the University of Sydney Law School over 19–20 February 2010, for which Nottage was a co-organizer. From the 65 presentations, we solicited seven of the thirteen chapters in this book (from Hamamoto, Bath, Eliasson, Sitaresmi, Butt, Farrar and Coppens), and also prevailed on one of the Distinguished Speakers at the conference (Sornarajah) to provide a new concluding chapter reviewing foreign investment law developments across the Asian region. The editors are grateful for the financial support offered by Sydney Law School (including its Sydney Centre for International Law, the Centre for Asian and Pacific Law, the Parsons Centre for Commercial, Corporate and Taxation Law) and the University of Sydney's Institute of Social Sciences ('new capacity project' grant). We also acknowledge sponsorship for the conference from Allens Arthur Robinson as well as our media partners, the International Arbitration Reporter and the Transnational Dispute Management Journal. We also thank the co-organizers of the conference, our colleagues Chester Brown and Kate Miles, for their subsequent collaboration as they too brought together another book from this major antipodean event (*Evolution in Investment Treaty Law and Arbitration*, Cambridge University Press, 2011).

We are very grateful to our other contributors, who stepped up promptly to fill out our geographical coverage of both international and domestic law regimes affecting foreign investment in Asia (Weeramantry, Ranjan, Kim and Dang), as well as to the President of the International Bar Association (Kawamura) for adding a Preface to this book. We also acknowledge the research and editorial assistance of Wan Sang Lung, Andrew Cong and Eriko Kadota, supported by a grant from the Law School's Legal Scholarship Support Fund.

Figure 6.1 is reproduced with permission from 'Figure 1.1. FDI Liberalisation in Indonesia and The Foreign Investor Response' in Organisation for Economic Co-operation and Development, OECD Investment Policy Reviews: Indonesia 2010 (OECD Publishing, http://dx.doi.org/10.1787/9789264087019-en). Data extracted as Table 8.1 is reproduced with permission from the International Bank for Reconstruction and Development/The World Bank, *Doing Business Report 2011* (2010). Chapter 2 is a shorter version adapted, with permission from Kluwer, from a longer article published in 28(1) *Arbitration International* (2012).

We should also mention some editorial decisions regarding style. First, due to the large numbers of investment treaties mentioned throughout this book, we do not provide their full titles or treaty series references. Instead, we refer to each of them by their country or region names and (the first time it is cited) the year in which the agreement was signed, such as the Japan-Korea BIT (2002) or the China–New Zealand FTA (2009). For consistency, we also generally refer to an 'FTA' (free trade agreement) even if the particular treaty uses different nomenclature (such as 'Economic Partnership Agreement'); and to a 'BIT' (bilateral investment treaty) even if the treaty is entitled an 'Investment Promotion Agreement' or has a similar title. Although collectively there now exist thousands of such investment treaties world-wide, many can now be accessed in English text through the UNCTAD website (www.unctadxi.org/templates/Startpage_____718.aspx) or via the websites of individual countries or organizations (such as: www.meti. go.jp/english/policy/external_economy/trade/FTA_EPA/index.html or www. aseansec.org/4920.htm). Hundreds of international investment arbitration rulings can also be freely accessed via the International Centre for the Settlement of Investment Disputes (http://icsid.worldbank.org/), or the 'Investment Treaty Arbitration' database (http://italaw.com) and the UNCTAD website (www.unctad.org/), both of which also include rulings and other information related to arbitrations resolved outside ICSID procedures.

Second, authors have chosen their own conventions regarding transpositions of foreign words into the English alphabet, and any translations are their own (unless otherwise noted).

Vivienne Bath and Luke Nottage
March 2011

Abbreviations

AANZFTA	Agreement establishing the ASEAN–Australia–New Zealand Free Trade Area
ADR	Alternative Dispute Resolution
AFC	Asian Financial Crisis
ANZCERTA	Australia New Zealand Closer Economic Relations Trade Agreement
APEC	Asia-Pacific Economic Cooperation
ASEAN	Association of South-East Asian Nations
ATS	Australian Treaty Series
BIT	Bilateral Investment Treaty
CECA	Comprehensive Economic Cooperation Agreement
CIETAC	China International Economic and Trade Arbitration Commission
CIL	Customary International Law
EMR	Energy and Mineral Resources
EPA	Economic Partnership Agreement
EPZ	Export Processing Zone
FDI	Foreign Direct Investment
FET	Fair and Equitable Treatment
FIA	Foreign Investment Agency of Vietnam
FIC	Foreign Investment Committee
FIZ	Free Industrial Zone
FTA	Free Trade Agreement
G-20	Group of Twenty
GATS	General Agreement on Trade in Services
GATT	General Agreement on Tariffs and Trade
GFC	Global Financial Crisis
GGU	Government Guarantees and Undertakings Agreement (Vietnam)
GLC	Government-Linked Companies
GOC	Government-owned Corporation
HKIAC	Hong Kong International Arbitration Centre
ICA	International Commercial Arbitration

ICC	International Chamber of Commerce
ICSID	International Centre for Settlement of Investment Disputes
IIA	International Investment Agreement
IISD	International Institute for Sustainable Development
ILM	International Legal Materials
IMF	International Monetary Fund
ISA	Investor-State Arbitration
JIEPA	Japan–Indonesia Economic Partnership Agreement
KORUS	Korea–US FTA
LDC	Least Developed Country
LNG	Liquefied Natural Gas
M&A	Mergers and Acquisitions
MAI	Multilateral Agreement on Investment
MDTCA	Ministry of Domestic Trade and Consumer Affairs
METI	Ministry of Economy, Industry and Trade (Japan)
MIDA	Malaysian Industrial Development Authority
MFN	Most Favoured Nation
MHS	Malaysian Historical Salvors Sdn Bhd
MITI	Ministry of International Trade and Industry (Malaysia)
MNC	Multinational Corporation
MOFA	Ministry of Foreign Affairs (Japan)
MOFCOM	Ministry of Commerce (PRC)
MOJ	Ministry of Justice (Vietnam)
MTP	Monetary Transfer Provision
NAFTA	North American Free Trade Agreement
NDRC	National Development and Reform Commission (PRC)
NEAC	New Economic Advisory Council
NEM	New Economic Model
NEP	New Economic Policy
NIEO	New International Economic Order
NGO	Non-Governmental Organization
NT	National Treatment
NYC	New York Convention on Recognition and Enforcement of Foreign Arbitral Awards 1958
OECD	Organisation for Economic Co-operation and Development
OIC	Organisation of the Islamic Conference
PCA	Permanent Court of Arbitration
PIA	Promotion of Investments Act
PTA	Preferential Trading Agreement
PTS	Preferential Trading System
PRC	People's Republic of China
SAFE	State Administration of Foreign Exchange (PRC)
SASAC	State-owned Assets Supervision and Administration Commission of the State Council (PRC)
TPPA	Trans-Pacific Strategic Economic Partnership Agreement

UNCITRAL	United Nations Commission on International Trade Law
UNCTAD	United Nations Conference on Trade and Development
UNITAR	United Nations Institute for Training and Research
UNTS	United Nations Treaty Series
VCLT	Vienna Convention on the Law of Treaties
WTO	World Trade Organization

1 Foreign investment and dispute resolution law and practice in Asia

An overview

Vivienne Bath and Luke Nottage

1.1 Introduction

This book critically assesses patterns and issues in both the substantive law and the policy environment impacting on foreign investment flows in major Asian economies, and international dispute resolution law and practice related to those flows. The main focus is foreign direct investment (FDI), although we also touch on (typically shorter-term) portfolio investments. There are a number of different definitions of FDI. This book adopts that used by the United Nations Conference on International Trade Law (UNCTAD 2009: 35): 'FDI can be defined as an investment made by a resident of one economy in another economy,... of a long-term nature or of "lasting interest"'.[1] As well as inbound FDI, the book examines the recent growth in investments undertaken abroad by states in the Asian region (especially China) that have traditionally been net capital importers. FDI flows have generally accelerated since the Asian Financial Crisis of 1998, paralleling the strong economic growth in Asia that has kept the world economy afloat following the Global Financial Crisis of 2008 (GFC). However, the GFC has led to shifts in FDI and other capital flows, as well as reassessments of FDI restrictions and broader concerns about maintaining appropriate regulatory capacity and discretion over market activity.

The book is also timely and distinctive in paying particular attention to the burgeoning number of Bilateral Investment Treaties (BITs), as well as investment chapters increasingly incorporated into bilateral and regional Free Trade Agreements (FTAs), concluded by Asian states. (In this book, we have included Australia and New Zealand, which have become active participants in this treaty-making process across the Asian region.[2]) Such investment treaties have increased in both number and scope particularly over the past two decades. Their purpose is not only to protect foreign investors against illegal host state activity (the traditional concern of BITs) but also increasingly to introduce substantive liberalization to facilitate foreign investors' access into host state markets (through FTA investment chapters). Both types of treaties increasingly extend protections such as non-discrimination to the pre-establishment phase (that is, when investors are applying for host state approval), and in some cases present the promise of broader pre-establishment liberalization of investment, as well as protecting foreign investments once made. These commitments are typically backed up by the agreement of states to allow foreign investors to bring arbitration claims directly against host states, rather than having to persuade their home states to bring 'diplomatic protection' claims on their behalf.

Yet there are growing concerns world-wide, particularly but not exclusively among developing countries, that the system created by these predominantly bilateral agreements – and its enforcement through the investor-state arbitration (ISA) processes and substantive principles – fails adequately to balance the private and public interests involved. This has been most noticeable in South America, with Bolivia and Ecuador withdrawing recently from the framework 1965 Convention on Settlement of Investment Disputes between States and Nationals of Other States (establishing the World Bank affiliated International Centre for Settlement of Investment Disputes, and therefore known as the ISCID Convention). The ICSID Convention facilitates enforcement of ISA awards resulting from arbitrations administered under ICSID Arbitration Rules (last revised in 2006), if the host state has given 'consent' to arbitration – a consent which is typically now provided through bilateral or regional treaties (Dolzer and Schreuer 2008). In North America, Mexico still has not acceded to the ICSID Convention, while Canada has signed it, but not yet acceded to it or incorporated it into local law. This means that ISA disputes involving these states arising under the North American Free Trade Agreement (NAFTA 1994) must be conducted under other Arbitration Rules. The United States of America (US) has acceded to the ICSID Convention but has faced growing concern from citizen groups and others about adverse rulings and lack of transparency in ISA proceedings (Kelsey 2010). It agreed to omit ISA from the Australian–US FTA (2004), for example (Nottage and Miles 2009). No investment chapter was included at all between Australia and New Zealand when those countries concluded a FTA with ASEAN (AANZFTA 2009), and they omitted ISA in an investment protocol added on 16 February 2011 to their long-standing bilateral FTA (ANZCERTA 1982). More generally, the Australian Government's Productivity Commission recommended in December 2010 that treaties concluded by Australia should not provide foreign investors with better procedural and substantive rights than those available to local investors (PC 2010).

In addition, reservations about the ISA system have also been evident in Asian countries such as the People's Republic of China, as outlined in Chapters 4 (Bath) and 5 (Eliasson). China has long been careful to restrict its obligations under its BITs (Bath) while working successfully to attract substantial amounts of FDI. China acceded to the ICSID Convention in 1993, well after it commenced signing BITs. Despite its willingness to enter into BITs, China's earlier treaties substantially restricted the scope of its consent to ISA. It was only when China embarked on a program of exporting

FDI itself that it began to conclude 'new generation' treaties (dating from the late 1990s) which allow for a much wider scope of ISA (Eliasson). More recently, the Philippines succeeded in having ISA consent omitted from the FTA it concluded in 2005 with Japan. As explained in Chapter 3 (Hamamoto), Japan had otherwise included ISA in almost all its treaties since 1977, with noticeably more pro-investor substantive protections added to its own 'new generation' treaties (especially FTAs) from around 2002. The latter trend was partly triggered by the collapse of negotiations in the World Trade Organization (WTO), and earlier in the Organization for Economic Cooperation and Development (OECD), on a new multilateral investment treaty. However, the wording of ISA provisions provided particularly in some of Japan's older generation BITs may not provide clear consent to arbitration, at least through ICSID (Hamamoto and Nottage 2010).

This backdrop of treaty practice may help to explain another interesting phenomenon in this region: Asian states appear disproportionately less likely to be formally involved as respondents in ISA proceedings, and only 13 known claims have ever been filed by Asian investors (including two recent cases by Chinese investors discussed by Eliasson). Nonetheless, as outlined in Chapter 2 (Nottage and Weeramantry), further 'institutional barriers' deterring ISA filings (such as costs and availability of suitable arbitrators) and other factors need to be considered as well.

An assessment of such patterns and questions necessitates detailed comparative study attentive to socio-economic context and competing theories of the role of law in Asia. Our book aims to fill this gap in the existing literature, which mostly comprises shorter works aimed at legal practitioners. It is also distinctive in combining comparative law analysis on host states' domestic legal systems with commentary on the increasingly significant international treaty obligations impacting on those regimes. Contributions from both senior and up-and-coming academics with extensive country-specific expertise (and often considerable practical experience), as well as interests in international law, critically analyse the law and practice of investment treaties and FDI regimes in Asia and tie this to domestic law on investment in the case of a number of important Asian jurisdictions.

As well as the overviews provided in this chapter and the next, the concluding chapter (Sornarajah) draws extensive comparisons across the region. The book also focuses on developments in major destinations or sources of FDI in Asia: Japan (Chapter 3 by Hamamoto), China (Chapter 4 by Bath and Chapter 5 by Eliasson), Indonesia (Chapter 6 by Butt and Chapter 7 by Sitaresmi, taking as a case study the 2005 FTA – or 'EPA' (Economic Partnership Agreement – with Japan), Malaysia (Chapter 8 by Farrar and Chapter 9 by Coppens), India (Chapter 10 by Ranjan), the Republic of Korea (Chapter 11 by Kim) and Vietnam (Chapter 12 by Dang). For China, Indonesia and Malaysia, one chapter focuses on treaty-related issues and another on FDI regime developments more generally. Summaries of key issues and trends covered in each chapter are set out in Section 1.4 below, after our more specific introduction to economic development and regulatory regimes (Section 1.2) and dispute resolution more generally (Section 1.3) throughout Asia.

1.2 Economic development, investment flows and regulatory regimes in Asia

Over the past 30 years, the Asian region has developed as a major economic force and, by 2006, Asia accounted for more than 35 per cent of world gross domestic product (GDP) (IMF 2006). The development of the region is illustrated by Figure 1.1 below, which shows the remarkable growth of exports of merchandise and services from Asian countries since 1980.

Notwithstanding the Asian Financial Crisis (AFC), most of the countries of the Asian region were in a strong economic position in the first six to seven years of the twenty-first century. China and India were particularly strong, but other Asian countries showed high rates of GDP growth backed by substantial increases in merchandise exports. The GFC had an effect on the economies of Asian countries mainly through its impact on trade and investment, rather than through their financial systems (Chia 2010). As a consequence, the growth of the export-oriented economies of the region slowed markedly in 2008 and 2009, with the economies of Malaysia, Singapore, Thailand, Hong Kong and South Korea suffering from negative GDP growth in 2009 and other economies showing a marked slow-down in GDP growth and merchandise export growth. The rate of GDP growth in China dropped from 13 per cent in 2007 to 9 per cent in 2008 and 8 per cent in 2009.

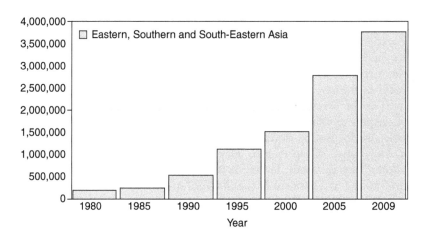

Figure 1.1 Total trade in merchandise and services, Eastern, Southern and South-Eastern Asia: Exports (US$ millions) (source: created (March 2011) from data at http://unctadstat.unctad.org/TableViewer/chartView.aspx).

By 2010, however, the region was showing strong signs of recovery (Chia 2010: 6, Table 1) – to such an extent that Anoop Singh of the International Monetary Fund (IMF) commented that the Asian region was moving into a leadership role in the world economy, with an economic importance which is 'unmistakable and palpable' (Suriyanarayanan 2010). Recovery from the recession was led by China, which had GDP growth of 10.3 per cent in 2010 (Li 2011), and India, which rebounded to a growth rate of 8.9 per cent (Trading Economics 2011). Indeed the IMF has predicted that Asian GDP (a calculation in which the GDPs of Australia and New Zealand are included) will exceed that of the G7 countries (the United States, Canada, Great Britain, Japan, Germany, France, and Italy) by 2030 (Suriyanarayanan 2010).

The growing importance on the international stage of the major economies in the Asian region is reflected in the creation of the Group of Twenty (G-20) in 1999, and the strengthening of its role in 2008 in the aftermath of the AFC. Its purpose is to bring together 'systemically important industrialized and developing economies to discuss key issues in the global economy' (G-20 2011). The members of the G-20 jointly account for approximately 90 per cent of global GDP and 80 per cent of world trade. The membership includes the major Asian economies of Australia, Indonesia, Japan, China, Korea and India, as well as Russia, the United States, Canada and Mexico.

1.2.1 Historical overview of economic development and foreign investment in Asia

Japan has emerged and remained as a major outbound investor in the region and world-wide, despite – and, to some extent, because of – its domestic economy's 'lost decade' of economic stagnation over the 1990s. From the late 1960s, Japanese companies began investing in natural resource projects abroad, for example in Australia. This aspect of its activities remains important as Chinese (and to a lesser extent Korean and Indian) companies now also compete for increasingly scarce resources. Particularly over the 1980s, Japan also began investing heavily in manufacturing capacity in South-East Asia. This was partly to circumvent still high tariff barriers but mostly to create production networks for exporting finished goods to Europe, the US and then Japan itself. However, an increasing percentage of such goods are also now being exported to other parts of Asia which are characterized by a rapidly growing middle class. The 1980s also saw more speculative investment into Europe and the US, fueled by the rise of the yen and loose monetary policy, but that eventually led to the collapse of an asset 'bubble' in Japan in 1990, a serious non-performing loans problem for Japanese banks, and minimal growth until a partial revival over 2002–7. Nonetheless, Japanese investment accelerated into China particularly from the mid-1990s, and the last few years have seen large investments into South Asia and Vietnam (Drysdale 2009: 5–6, 13–16). By 2002, thanks to decades of active investment abroad, Japan's balance on income had exceeded its balance on goods – one factor identified by Hamamoto (Chapter 3 in this volume) as contributing to the development of a more active investment treaty program from around that time.

By the late 1990s, the Japanese government's attitude towards inbound FDI had also become more positive. Access to the telecoms sector had been liberalized in the wake of WTO commitments, but the belated collapse of major financial institutions over 1997–8 (amidst a broader deregulation program for financial markets initiated in 1995) generated an influx of foreign investors in this sector as well – mirroring, albeit on a small scale and off a low base, a surge in FDI world-wide, particularly in those sectors. The Koizumi administration (2001–6) also began actively encouraging inbound investment more generally, in another attempt to free up the domestic Japanese economy. The government announced plans and measures first to double the stock of inbound FDI, and then its percentage compared to GDP. The latter goal had almost been achieved by 2011, when stocks reached 5 per cent of GDP. However, as in Korea (discussed by Kim in Chapter 12), this ratio remains very low by OECD standards – attracting ongoing concern from policy-makers domestically and especially abroad.

However, Japan's still comparatively low level of inbound FDI is driven primarily by economic rather than legal factors (GAO 2008). At a macro level, foreign investors were put off by Japan's inflated asset prices through the 1980s, and its stagnant domestic economy through the 1990s. At a micro level, hostile takeovers and even other mergers and acquisitions (M&A) or 'greenfield' investments were constrained by the existence of a cadre of 'lifelong employees' – a phenomenon that emerged in the 1950s, particularly in larger firms. Another impediment came from cross-shareholdings and other links within large corporate groups (*keiretsu*), replacing the pre-war *zaibatsu* which had been centred much more on family-based shareholdings (still the case in many parts of South-East Asia). In contrast, legal restrictions on FDI had become much less important even by the early 1990s, especially when compared to the policies of most ASEAN countries. The 'prior licencing' scheme enacted in 1950 was replaced by 'prior notification' legislation in 1980, after Japan joined the IMF and OECD in 1964 and opened up more and more sectors over the 1970s. From 1991 the law changed to an 'ex post notification' system for most investments. The government retained the power to block large investments on national interest grounds, but did so on only one occasion, in 2008 (in respect of an English investment fund's proposed 20 per cent stake in an electricity wholesaler). Japan has also never expropriated any foreign investment (Hamamoto and Nottage 2010)

Turning to *South-East Asia* (Dixon 2010: 108–27), this sub-region's economies emerged rapidly from various crises in the early 1980s (compared, for example, to the situation in South America), thanks in part to the generous treatment of the Bretton Woods institutions in the shadow of the Cold

War standoff in Asia. FDI inflows accelerated as Japan, then Korea and Taiwan, expanded their regional production chains and began to free up their own financial markets. Economic growth, centred on exports of finished manufactured products to developed countries, accelerated particularly in Thailand, then Malaysia, Indonesia, the Philippines and ultimately Vietnam. This led to some liberalization of domestic markets, but a 'South-East Asian Chinese business model' remained strong until 1997, revolving around family-owned corporate groups and considerable state involvement in business activity. Other than in Singapore and the Philippines, foreign investment was generally limited to non-controlling levels (as in Malaysia, the ASEAN country most heavily dependent on FDI, along with Singapore) or to various export and other priority sectors.

Although this meant that countries remained relatively insulated from regional and global developments, large-scale shifts particularly in short-term capital flows contributed to the AFC in 1997. The international community (notably the World Bank and the IMF) called for major changes in the business environment throughout South-East Asia (and indeed Korea), but responses varied. Thailand liberalized its foreign investment regime dramatically over 1997–2000, generating a major surge in M&A-related FDI over 1998–2001. There was more resistance to the changes proposed by the IMF in Indonesia, although investment in insurance and banking services was partly liberalized, and FDI flows turned negative in 1998 – with high levels of disinvestment until 2003. The drastic effects of the AFC on Indonesia are summarized by Butt (Chapter 6 in this volume). Malaysia also liberalized some sectors but rejected IMF assistance, reimposed controls over cross-border financial movements and advanced support for the local banking and corporate sectors (Farrar, Chapter 8 in this volume).

By 2003, significant liberalization had occurred in ASEAN as a whole, but some major regulatory barriers remained to foreign ownership. Broader impediments to FDI included relatively ineffective bankruptcy laws and M&A procedures as well as resistance to change among local enterprises, which often still maintain high levels of 'blockholdings' or state involvement. Despite this, and in contrast to sharp declines in export and GDP growth for several years after the AFC, FDI inflows remained strong in South-East Asia overall. However, although East Asia remains a major source of FDI and a key partner in regional production networks, its relative share is less than in 1997. This reflects the increased attraction of China as a destination for FDI, particularly over the last decade, and China's rapid integration into regional trade as well as investment flows.

China is a major success story in terms of FDI, despite its relatively late start (Sornarajah 2010a: 132–7). Foreign investment was encouraged from 1979, with the inception of the Open Door policy instituted by Deng Xiaoping, but began its current exponential rate of growth only from the 1990s. In 1980, FDI in China was US$57 million, rising to US$3.4 billion in 1990. By 1995, however, it was US$37.5 billion, increasing to

US$40.7 billion in 2000, US$72.4 billion in 2005 and US$95 billion in 2009. This growth reflects changes in China's investment policy aimed at encouraging FDI, and, in particular, the commitments and changes made by China to its investment policies when it acceded to the WTO in 2001 (UNCTAD 2011). Notwithstanding this, as Bath describes (Chapter 4 in this volume), investment in China continues to be highly regulated, and subject in each case to government review and approval. Liberalization in the Chinese context extends to the areas in which foreign investment is permitted or encouraged and to facilitation of approvals by modifications to the regulatory process – it does not extend to allowing foreigners access to the Chinese market as a matter of right. As noted by Bath (Chapter 4) and Eliasson (Chapter 5 in this volume), the past ten years have also seen considerable growth in China's outbound investment activities. This in turn has focused attention on Chinese policies, such as the restrictive provisions in many of its extensive range of BITs and the encouragement given by the Chinese government to the overseas expansion of Chinese enterprises, particularly state-owned enterprises and sovereign wealth funds.

India, on the other hand, was considerably slower to welcome FDI, and this is reflected in the amount of FDI in India (GAO 2008). In 1980, FDI in India was US$79 million, which by 1990 had increased to only US$237 million. By 1995, following the introduction of more liberal investment policies designed to attract FDI (and a consequent increase in the number of BITs and FTAs entered into by India, as described by Ranjan in Chapter 10) this amount had risen to US$2 billion (still well behind China). By 2000 it had increased to US$3.5 billion, rising to US$7.5 billion in 2005 and finally expanding substantially by 2009, when it had risen to US$34 billion (UNCTAD 2011).

Foreign investment regulation in India had historically been very restrictive, reflecting socialist economic policies adopted since its independence in 1947 and arguably also its earlier colonial history (Sornarajah 2010a, and in this volume). In 1991, in reaction to its balance of payments crisis and IMF bailout, India initiated an economic liberalization project under Prime Minister Narasimha Rao and Finance Minister Manmohan Singh. Economic reform included reducing tax and tariff rates, easing licensing requirements and regulations on corporations and opening the economy to foreign investment. Initial reforms also saw the creation of the Foreign Investment Promotion Board, established to liaise with international firms over investment clearances. The liberalization of the FDI regime continued throughout the 1990s, with the creation of the Foreign Investment Promotion Council (to promote foreign investment) and the Foreign Investment Implementation Authority (to streamline the foreign investment application process). From 2010, India has been moving towards reform of FDI restrictions in the retail, real estate and insurance industries.[3]

The rise of India as a location for FDI is demonstrated by the results of a 2010 survey of countries considered attractive destinations for FDI by senior corporate executives, in which China ranked first, and India third (after the US), with Australia (7th), Vietnam (12th), Hong Kong (14th), Indonesia (19th) and Malaysia (20th) all in the top 20 (ATKearney 2010). Like China, India is also now becoming a source of outbound investment, although the total of Indian outbound investment in 2009 was US$14.8 billion, a relatively low amount compared to China (US$48 billion) and Hong Kong (US$52 billion) (UNCTAD 2011).[4]

1.2.2 Recent trends in Asia

Globally, flows of FDI are now increasing rapidly again, despite a short-term drop in 2008–9 resulting from the GFC. In 1970, total FDI on a world-wide basis was $13.3 billion, increasing to $56 billion in 1980, $207.6 billion in 1990, US$1401 trillion in 2000, with a slight drop to US$1114 trillion in 2009 (UNCTAD 2011). UNCTAD estimates that this trend will continue, with total flows of FDI in 2010 envisaged to be approximately US$1.2 trillion; in 2011, US$1.3–1.5 trillion; and in 2012, US$1.62–2 trillion (UNCTAD 2010: 19).

A substantial amount of this investment flows both into, and increasingly out of, developing countries. Developing countries attracted half of all FDI in 2009, and were the source of approximately one-quarter of outbound FDI. Investment outflows and stocks of FDI from China and India, but also Russia and Brazil, have increased substantially over the last decade – again apart from a dip in 2008–9 reflecting the impact of the GFC (UNCTAD 2010: 5–7). China, and to a lesser extent India – the largest developing countries in Asia – have begun to play a significant role as investors. The increasing importance of developing countries as investors has had, and can be expected to continue to have, an impact on the investment treaty framework (including attitudes towards ISA) adopted by those countries.

Collectively, countries from the Asian region now play a significant role in terms of FDI. In 2008–9, five countries from the region were in the top 20 recipients of FDI: China was the second largest recipient (US$95 billion); Hong Kong was fourth (US$48 billion); India was ninth (US$35 billion); Australia was seventeenth (US$23 billion); and Singapore was nineteenth (US$17 billion) (UNCTAD 2010: 4). An UNCTAD survey of transnational corporations asking which countries will be the top priority for investment over 2010–12 identified China, India, Vietnam, Indonesia, Thailand, Australia, Malaysia and Japan among the top 20 host economies (UNCTAD 2010: 25).

Australasian countries are also now significant investors. In 2008–9, Japan was the third largest source of FDI outflows (US$75 billion); Hong Kong was fifth (US$52 billion); China was sixth (US$48 billion); and Australia was the fifteenth largest (US$18 billion) (UNCTAD 2010: 6). Perceptions about (direct or indirect) state involvement in Chinese outbound investment, however, have been generating concern, sometimes with remarkable parallels with patterns from Japan's emergence as a major investor in the 1980s (Milhaupt 2008). Asian countries also increasingly invest in each other. Since 1980, the sources of investment in Asia have demonstrated greater intra-regional investment. In 1981, for example, the European Union (EU) countries accounted for 18.3 per cent of investment in South, East and South-East Asia; the US accounted for 23.3 per cent; Japan accounted for 19.5 per cent; and Hong Kong, Korea, Singapore and Taiwan collectively accounted for 17.8 per cent. By 2008, investment from the EU had decreased to 14.3 per cent; from the US, to 7.9 per cent; and from Japan, to 8 per cent. Investment from China, however, had increased to 13.3 per cent; and from Hong Kong, Korea, Singapore and Taiwan, to 22.2 per cent (UNCTAD 2010: 41).

Despite many Asian countries being geographically quite close together, there is wide divergence historically, economically and socially among countries in this region. This is reflected in different approaches to law and political economy as well as, of course, in relative economic development and success. Although living standards have generally increased across the region, sometimes dramatically, Asian countries retain significantly different histories, religions, ethnicities, legal systems and economic strengths and interests.

Some are common law countries, such as Singapore, Malaysia and Hong Kong. Others have legal systems more similar to continental European civil law systems, although with their own distinctive local elements. For example, the legal systems of Japan (influenced by a US-led Occupation over 1945–52) and Indonesia (a former Dutch colony, then a dictatorship until 1998) are markedly different in a number of important respects. China and Vietnam are developing their own legal systems, drawing on socialist, civil and common law elements. In addition, Asian states such as Bangladesh, Indonesia, Malaysia and Pakistan are members of the Organisation of the Islamic Conference.[5] Others including China and India also have substantial Muslim populations, although the Muslim influence in Asia does not, so far, appear to have had a major impact on state practice relating to investment or free trade treaties. Overall, typologies based on conventional 'legal families' can still provide a head start to understanding Asian legal systems. Yet other comparative lawyers propose different classificatory schemes (such as the nature of the background political system: Taylor and Pryles 2006) or simply more recognition that most legal systems world-wide – not just in Asia – nowadays represent 'hybrid' or 'mixed' legal systems (Oruçu 2007).

Fortunately, however, there are many and growing similarities among countries world-wide – even within the diverse Asian region – in terms of their regulatory approach to FDI. The US Government Accountability Office found this pattern, despite some local variations and unique approaches to particular issues, including often a formal review process for investment and a process for dealing with concerns about national security and related issues (GAO 2008: 14–24).[6] Yet periodic studies by the Asia-Pacific Economic

Cooperation (APEC) forum indicate that there are also significant differences across Asian countries in both the content of investment laws and in the ways in which these laws may be applied to foreign investment.[7] In his concluding chapter, Sornarajah points to a legacy of colonialism and a more state-centric conception of economic development in Asia. This book's case studies of the actual operation of the investment regimes in China (Chapters 4 and 5), Indonesia (Chapter 6) and Malaysia (Chapter 8) provide a further indication of the widely different approaches which can be taken to the regulation of FDI and to the practical implementation of rules which affect FDI in different administrations across Asia, even where FDI is formally now welcome and indeed strongly encouraged.

Asia is also part of a world-wide trend whereby developing countries invest both in other developing countries and developed countries. Increasingly, countries in the Asian region such as China and Australia are both recipients of investment and hosts of companies that invest abroad. Asian countries are active participants in the international investment community and are parties to a large number of different international treaty regimes touching upon international investment law. Most Asian countries are parties to the WTO agreements, with some exceptions such as Laos, the Democratic Republic of Korea and Timor L'Este.[8] Most are also parties to the ICSID Convention, with some notable exceptions such as India, Vietnam, and Thailand (which has signed but not ratified the Convention).[9] In particular, states in the region are often parties to both BITs and bilateral or (increasingly) regional FTAs, many of which contain provisions relating to investment.

Over time, as the discussion in the chapters in this book indicates, many states in the Asian region have become more willing – at least in theory – to make commitments as to the liberalization of their investment regimes. The comparison between the terms of the BIT between Australia and China (1988) and the investment chapter of the New Zealand–China FTA (2008, discussed by Bath in Chapter 4 of this volume) provides a good example of this process of development. There can be, notwithstanding this, a considerable gap between the objectives of international agreements relating to investment and the terms and implementation of domestic FDI rules. For this reason, this book looks at the law and practice of a number of important domestic regimes, as well as considering international obligations through BITs and associated implications for ISA.

Within the region, there are different degrees of enthusiasm for BITs and commitments on investment, despite the fact that overall Asian countries are active participants in the system of international investment agreements.[10] At one extreme is China, which as of mid-2010 had signed over 120 BITs (of which 98 were in force), 19 of which were with countries in the Asia-Pacific region. India (78 BITs, 65 in force, 15 in the Asian region[11]), Indonesia (63 BITs signed, 45 in force, 16 in the region) and Malaysia (66 BITs signed, 46 in force, 14 in the region) are also enthusiastic supporters of

BITs. Australia (22 BITs, eight in the region) and Japan (15 BITs, nine in the region) are less eager, and New Zealand (four BITs, two in force, two in the region) is probably the least enthusiastic participant in the BIT system. However, New Zealand is party to a number of significant FTAs involving Asia, such as the New Zealand–China FTA (2008) and the Trans-Pacific Strategic Economic Partnership Agreement (TPPA, 2005, currently with Singapore, Brunei and Chile: Kelsey 2010).

Although each BIT is individually negotiated, there are a number of similarities in BITs in terms of both form and substance (Sornarajah 2010b: 172–235; see also Brown and Krishan, eds 2011). BITs generally focus on the obligations of the host state to encourage investment; provide certain treatment and benefits to investors and investments (in both cases as defined in the BIT), including 'fair and equitable treatment' (FET) and protection and security. In some cases they provide for the host state to grant to investors and investments of the other state treatment no less favourable than that accorded to investors from third states ('most-favoured-nation' or MFN treatment). They often grant to investors treatment no less favourable than that accorded to the host state's own national investors ('national treatment' or NT). They also generally require the host state to agree to the entry of expatriates required for the investment, the transfer of funds, and the application of transparent laws. They also almost always deal with the expropriation of assets, providing for a fair process, compensation and a system for the resolution of disputes. Importantly, the BITs generally provide for a form of ISA, although the extent to which a state may be prepared to agree to this can still vary widely. Generally, it may be said that while older generation BITs limited ISA (see Bath, Chapter 4, and Eliasson, Chapter 5, in relation to China), newer generation BITs are more expansive as well as including much more detailed provisions on this topic (Hamamoto and Nottage 2010, in relation to Japan).

Greater detail in BIT provisions also tends to parallel the emergence of FTAs, which usually now contain investment chapters which may promote liberalization as well as provide for protection of foreign investments. Bilateral agreements remain important, but regional treaties are becoming increasingly prominent – especially involving ASEAN as a whole, as well as some individual member states. ASEAN was established for geopolitical reasons in 1967, joining Malaysia, Indonesia, the Philippines, Singapore and Thailand in the context of communist insurgencies in Vietnam, Laos and Cambodia.[12] Economic development became more of a focus over the 1980s, generating the ASEAN Agreement for the Promotion and Protection of Investments (1987) – including some substantive obligations (such as FET) and the right for investors from one ASEAN state to commence ISA proceedings against another. In 1992, ASEAN leaders agreed to establish a free trade and investment area within 15 years, leading first to a Framework Agreement on the ASEAN Investment Area (1998). This was aimed more at liberalizing investment within ASEAN; it did add NT as a further substantive protection, but omitted ISA procedures. In 2003, leaders committed to establishing an ASEAN Community – for political, economic and socio-cultural cooperation – and to strengthen existing initiatives to implement an ASEAN Free Trade Area (for goods and services) as well as an ASEAN Investment Area. The latter is created through the ASEAN Comprehensive Investment Agreement (2009), basically consolidating and strengthening the 1987 and 1998 Agreements (Maxwell and Wegner 2009: 167–73). Pursuant to this agreement, each of the ASEAN states is required to make commitments relating to the liberalization of its investment regime.

This degree of formal treaty-making activity is part of a broader 'formalization' of a regional organization renowned, particularly until the AFC, as a heavily consensus-based and therefore rather cumbersome institution (Murray 2010). The shift over the last decade, particularly in liberalizing regimes for foreign investors from other ASEAN states (but also, following the AFC, by many individual states liberalizing the regime for other investors), has made it easier for ASEAN to commit to FTAs with other major economies in the region. A major development was the Framework Agreement reached with China in 2002, resulting in ASEAN–China FTAs for goods (2004), services (2007) and investment (2009: see also Shen 2010). ASEAN has also included Framework Agreements and some FTAs with Korea (for goods in 2006, except initially for Thailand; for services in 2007; and investment in 2009), Japan (for goods and services in 2008) and India (for goods in 2009).[13] The ASEAN–Japan FTA is due for its first five-yearly review in 2013. Japan also has bilateral FTAs with investment chapters and/ or BITs with most ASEAN states (as outlined in the chapters by Hamamoto and Sitaresmi). The AANZFTA (Agreement establishing the ASEAN–Australia–New Zealand Free Trade Area) has broad coverage, including trade, customs, movement of natural persons and investment.

Another noteworthy development is the likely expansion of the TPPA. Singapore and Brunei were founding members from within ASEAN (along with New Zealand and Chile) in 2005, but by late 2010 negotiations had commenced for accession by Vietnam and Malaysia as well as Australia, Peru and the US – with Japan and several other countries expressing significant interest in joining as well. An investment chapter was not included in the original agreement, and its inclusion in a broader-based treaty has attracted some controversy – for example, in regard to ISA provisions (Kelsey 2010; see also PC 2010). It has also been argued that the original TPPA provisions on inter-state dispute settlement require and encourage much more transparency than the 'closed model' found in the ASEAN and 'ASEAN+' treaties (Lim forthcoming). The expanded TPPA could well also shape up as a somewhat competing model for cross-border investment and economic integration in the wider Asia-Pacific (not just Asian) region.

1.3 Dispute resolution in Asia

Entire books have been written about dispute resolution across Asia (for example, Pryles, ed. 2006), as well as within individual countries in the region. Quite persistently low civil litigation rates compared to Western democracies at comparable stages of economic development have tended to be highlighted as quite uniquely 'Asian', reflecting a widely-shared cultural tradition more prone and open to more harmonious forms of dispute resolution. But other explanations have become more widespread, including the idea that judicial systems – for various reasons – have been comparatively under-resourced, creating 'institutional barriers' to pursuing litigation. Court capacity certainly has been improving in many Asian countries, often thanks to 'legal technical assistance' from developed countries including Japan (Taylor 2005). But more generally it has been suggested that the expansion of investment treaties and ISA may have undermined the process of increasing court capacity and capability in some cases, by reducing incentives on foreign investors to press for more wide-ranging and long-term improvements in the judicial system (Ginsburg 2005; Gillespie 2006). The quite limited regional uptake of international treaties facilitating cross-border litigation has not assisted in this respect either (Spigelman 2007). Nor has the lack of a coherent system for the enforcement of foreign judgments across the region.[14]

Instead, international commercial arbitration remains the preferred means of resolving cross-border commercial disputes in Asia. Asian countries have acceded, extensively and mostly comparatively early on, to the 1958 New York Convention on the Recognition and Enforcement of Foreign Arbitral Awards (NYC) – regulating the first phase of the arbitral process (respecting arbitration agreements to allow the process to begin) and its final phase (enforcement of the arbitrators' award). The region has also witnessed one of the strongest uptakes of the 1985 UNCITRAL Model Law on International Commercial Arbitration – a template for arbitration law particularly for the middle phase, when the arbitration is underway at the seat of arbitration.[15] This uptake has underpinned a remarkable expansion in arbitration caseloads in certain Asian jurisdictions (notably China, Hong Kong, Singapore and even recently Korea), as well as a longer-standing tendency for more and more Asian parties to participate in arbitration cases seated in the traditional Western 'core' venues. Other important factors in Asia have included concerted government support in promoting arbitration centres, and the gradual emergence of a larger new generation of counsel, arbitrators and commentators familiar with the law and practice of international commercial arbitration (Nottage and Garnett 2010).

The growing popularity of international commercial arbitration across the region demands an assessment of simplistic 'culturalist' explanations for dispute resolution practices in Asia. Growing familiarity also probably helps to explain the expansion of ISA provisions within Asian investment treaties,

although there are (and there arguably should continue to be) important differences between this form of arbitration and international commercial arbitration between private parties because of the different public interests
involved (Nottage and Miles 2009). However, the expansion of ISA provisions may also have an impact on implementation of the New York Convention and acknowledgement by domestic legal regimes of the independence
of international commercial arbitration, which is not always consistent
within particular Asian countries (notably in China, Indonesia, India and
Pakistan: Greenberg *et al.* 2011). For example, in *Saipem SpA* v. *Bangladesh*
(ICSID Case No. ARB/05/07) a tribunal interpreting the Italy–Bangladesh
BIT (1990) ruled that Bangladesh had expropriated the Italian investor's
rights because of its local courts' interference with an earlier separate arbitration conducted pursuant to an arbitration agreement (with the seat in
Dhaka, under the Rules of the International Chamber of Commerce) that the
investor had concluded with a state-owned energy company (Petrobangla).
The ICSID's tribunal's decision and reasoning are already proving quite controversial.[16] If similar decisions are developed in other ISA cases, the implications will be far-reaching for dispute resolution in Asia more broadly, by
creating even more incentives for countries to ensure that their law and practices regarding international commercial arbitration meet global standards.

1.4 The book's structure

In Chapter 2, '**Investment arbitration in Asia: five perspectives on law
and practice**', Luke Nottage and Romesh Weeramantry provide a further
overview of developments across the Asian region, but focus more specifically on ISA. They begin by presenting empirical data confirming that,
despite the burgeoning numbers and scope of investments and investment
treaties in Asia, Asian states and especially Asian investors appear to be disproportionately less likely to become involved in formal ISA proceedings.
This 'gap' between treaty law and practice is unlikely to be due mainly to
Asian states abiding by treaty obligations more consistently than others. It
also does not seem to be fully explained by other economic factors (such as
the importance of smaller investors or the importance of maintaining pan-
Asian production networks), or the scope of consent to ISA provided in
investment treaties by Asian countries. If a significant gap does exist and
especially if it persists, there are five major paradigms that can explain such
a phenomenon, paralleling those advanced to explain comparative low litigation filings within the domestic legal systems of Asian countries (such as
Japan). These are 'culturalist', 'institutional barriers', 'elite management',
'predictable processes and outcomes', and 'hybrid' theories. For ISA patterns
in Asia, the best explanation appears to be 'institutional barriers': Asian parties are particularly affected (or conscious) of problems like cost or delay in
investor-arbitration, so they tend to settle disputes more even before filing
formal proceedings.

In Chapter 3, '**A passive player in international investment law: typically Japanese?**', Shotaro Hamamoto points out that Japan remains one of the largest economies and capital exporters in the world, yet Japanese investors and the government appear to have been relatively passive regarding international investment treaties. Japan got off to a slow start for both political and economic reasons, although the government is now negotiating quite ambitious agreements in growing numbers. Japan has also been relatively flexible in the substantive provisions included in its various investment treaties. Partly this reflects changes in arbitral awards, some pro-investor and others pro-host state. But the rationales for some provisions, such as variable definitions of 'FET', are more difficult to comprehend. Finally, the reluctance by Japanese investors to commence arbitral proceedings appears to be driven largely by cost-benefit calculations, but this may not persist given the increasing numbers of treaties now being concluded by Japan.

In Chapter 4, '**The quandary for Chinese regulators: controlling the flow of investment into and out of China**', Vivienne Bath examines the relationship between Chinese regulation of inbound and outbound investment and China's approach at the international level, through bilateral and multilateral treaties, to commitments on investment policy and practice. China, while encouraging inbound investment, maintains tight control over regulation of investment in China. At the same time, Chinese policy is to encourage Chinese companies, both private and state-owned, to invest overseas and China's recent treaty practice reflects the emphasis on outbound investment. The Chinese government's approach to inbound and outbound investment issues highlights the difficulty of striking a balance between the right of states to control the flow of investment into their own territory with the expectation that its investors will be able to make investments in other states and to enjoy appropriate rights and protections in connection with those investments.

Chapter 5 provides a second perspective on developments involving China, but focused on investment treaties and dispute resolution. In '**Chinese investment treaties: a procedural perspective**', Nils Eliasson discusses the scope and adequacy of procedural protections offered under China's BITs. He emphasizes that China has concluded the highest number of BITs in the world, and examines the historical development of ISA clauses and other procedural protections in these treaties. This chapter examines particularly the case of *Mr Tza Yap Shum* v. *The Republic of Peru* (ICSID Case No. ARB/07/6) as an example of the procedural challenges involved in bringing claims under the narrowly worded arbitration clauses of early-generation Chinese BITs. The chapter discusses the arguments made by Mr Tza Yap Shum in order to overcome these limitations, such as extensive interpretation and reliance on MFN clauses to expand the jurisdiction of the arbitral tribunal. This chapter also discusses how such questions are resolved in similar cases in order to determine whether any jurisprudential trends can be detected regarding such procedural issues. Another issue discussed is the territorial scope of protection offered by Chinese BITs – in particular, when such BITs can be invoked by investors from Hong Kong, Macao and Taiwan.

In Chapter 6, Simon Butt provides an overview of '**Foreign investment in Indonesia: the problem of legal uncertainty**'. Since Soeharto's fall in 1998, Indonesia's political and legal systems have undergone radical reform, much of it successful. Indonesia has, by most accounts, transformed from one of Southeast Asia's most repressive and centralized political systems to its most decentralized, free and democratic. Efforts have also been made to improve the legal infrastructure for investment. In particular, Indonesia's parliament enacted Law No. 25 of 2007 on Capital Investment to replace a 1958 Investment Law, aiming to make Indonesia more attractive so as to better compete with other countries in the region. Yet many obstacles to attracting and maintaining foreign investment remain. Legal uncertainty is commonly cited by foreigners as one of the most significant – if not the most serious – problem they encounter when operating in Indonesia. It is also commonly cited as one of the biggest disincentives for attracting new foreign investment in Indonesia. This chapter aims to identify the sources of fundamental uncertainty inherent in the Indonesian legal system: determining the applicable law, contradictory laws, lack of access to laws and unclear laws. It also explains the failure of the courts to provide guidance in resolving these uncertainties.

Chapter 7 indicates the challenges facing the government of a developing country like Indonesia when negotiating and implementing investment treaties. In '**The Japan–Indonesia Economic Partnership Agreement: an energy security perspective**', Sita Sitaresmi draws partly on her experience as former Indonesian Government official involved in treaty negotiations. She points out that the growing trend towards services-based investment has prompted countries such as Indonesia to follow the trend of incorporating investment treaties into FTAs. Her chapter examines the relationship between the Investment Chapter and the Services Chapter in the Japan–Indonesia Economic Partnership Agreement (JIEPA). It shows how such a structure grants the services sector, including energy services, the benefits of substantive standards of treatment and dispute settlement procedures accorded by the Investment Chapter. She suggests that a major goal of the JIEPA (2007) was to promote trade and investment in the energy sector, where there is mutual dependency between both countries. An examination of Indonesia's liberalization commitments in the energy sector shows that the application of a 'ratchet mechanism' on Indonesia's list of reservations may indeed secure Japan's interest in energy security, but prove to be a major testing ground for Indonesia in terms of honouring its treaty obligations, given the immaturity of its domestic policy regime resulting in frequent regulatory changes. Although the likelihood of disputes seems small for now, such regulatory changes create significant potential for future disputes.

In Chapter 8, '**Foreign investment laws and the role of FDI in Malaysia's "new" economic model**', Salim Farrar provides an overview of developments of the laws relating to foreign investment in one of the Asian 'Tiger' economies in the context of the recently announced 'New Economic Model'. The Malaysian economy has continued to grow in the last decade and has been generally successful in attracting high levels of FDI. In the wake of the GFC, however, there was a dramatic drop in investment – suggesting fundamental weaknesses in the economy and forcing the Malaysian government to take proactive steps to woo back investors. In addition to implementing an incentive-based taxation regime, the country liberalized its services sector – removing equity conditions in April 2009. In March 2010, it also modified the 39-year-old affirmative action policy, long thought by foreign investors to be obstacle to doing business in Malaysia. Whether the reforms will rectify structural weaknesses in the Malaysian economy, however, remains an open question.

Chapter 9 adds another perspective on the interpretation of 'investment'. Govert Coppens examines **'Treaty definitions of "investment" and the role of economic development: a critical analysis of the *Malaysian Historical Salvors* cases'**. The chapter scrutinizes two phases of a high-profile ISA dispute in which Malaysia was the respondent state. Both the initial award on Jurisdiction and the Annulment Decision are particularly interesting for their elaborate discussion of the notion of 'investment' under the ICSID Convention, and specifically its relationship with economic development. The initial award (delivered by a leading Singaporean arbitrator) concluded that ICSID jurisdiction was lacking because the contract for salvage of an old shipwreck did not sufficiently contribute to economic development in Malaysia to qualify as an 'investment'. (The practical implication of this finding is that the claimant would have to commence an arbitration against Malaysia outside the ICSID regime, or ask the United Kingdom as home state to commence an inter-state dispute on its behalf, under the BIT.) By contrast, the majority decision of the ad hoc Annulment Committee (with the Guyanese member dissenting) overturned the award, thus opening the way for the claimant to bring new ICSID proceedings. These different views call for a detailed analysis of the reasoning set out by the arbitrators, as well as the use and potential misuse of 'precedent' (arbitral awards in previous ISA cases). The Annulment Decision also raises fundamental questions about the scope and legitimacy of this review procedure provided under the ICSID Convention.

Chapter 10 turns to developments in another emerging economic superpower. India has liberalized its economy and inbound FDI regime since the early 1990s, expanded recently its outbound investment activity, and has a large investment treaty program. In **'The "object and purpose" of Indian international investment agreements: failing to balance investment protection and regulatory power'**, Prabhash Ranjan points out that in many ISA disputes the 'object and purpose' provisions set out in investment treaties have been an important issue. They can play a very important role in interpreting a treaty especially when the terms of a treaty are equivocal and thus subject to different interpretations. The chapter argues that the object and purpose of Indian investment treaties is tilted more towards investment protection than balancing investment protection with the regulatory power of the host state. This is seen to be problematic given the increasing conflicts emerging between investment protection and regulatory power. The chapter first gives an overview of India's treaty programme along with the intentions behind India entering into investment treaties. This is followed by a critical analysis of the object and purpose provisions, studying the preambles and various substantive treaty provisions in over 50 Indian treaties. The chapter concludes by stressing the need for India to develop a new model investment treaty, forming the basis for India's ongoing treaty negotiations, where the expressed object and purpose should be to balance investment protection with regulatory power.

Chapter 11 examines **'The evolution of Korea's modern investment treaties and investor-state dispute settlement provisions'**. Joongi Kim analyses the very wide range of investment treaties that Korea has concluded, with a particular focus on the dispute resolution provisions. He traces the manner in which Korea's investment treaties have evolved over the years, particularly given Korea's rapid economic development and transition from primarily a capital importer to a major capital exporter. Korea's foreign investment laws and rules in practice are also considered. An analysis of the major transformations in Korea's investment laws and treaties can help other countries, particularly in Asia, which hope to gain insight from Korea's development experiences. The chapter critically assesses Korea's investment laws and treaties to suggest how the present legal regimes, especially the dispute resolution provisions, should be further enhanced to provide more effective protection and security for investors.

Chapter 12 outlines **'Legal issues in Vietnam's FDI law: protections under domestic law, bilateral investment treaties and sovereign guarantees'**. Hop Dang first provides an overview of burgeoning inbound FDI and the evolution of the investment law framework in Vietnam over the past 20 years. He then discusses many issues that have been of greatest concern to foreign investors in Vietnam. These include issues related to investment treaties generally, nationalization, changes in law and taxes, foreign exchange risks, investment guarantees, the right to mortgage land, choice of law and dispute resolution. The chapter describes the legal framework from which these issues arose, how they have actually arisen in practice, how investors have tried to deal with these issues and the lessons that can be learnt. Using these issues as examples, this chapter shows more generally how Vietnamese investment law and its background legal system have developed over the past 20 years.

Chapter 13 provides a **'Review of Asian views on foreign investment law'** from M. Sornarajah. It places the specific developments identified in the earlier chapters, as well as other themes and transformations across Asia regarding investment law regimes and dispute resolution, in broader historical context. Sornarajah perceives a traditional unease about FDI in many countries in the region, derived in part from the era of Western colonialism, and cautions that such attitudes may still often play a major role in treaty practice and the application of domestic law in Asia. He also criticizes the liberal underpinnings of international investment law that have intensified over the two decades, and concludes that Asia stands at a crossroads now that the GFC has highlighted problems in the self-regulating properties of free markets.

1.5 Conclusion

Asia is a diverse region, encompassing numerous different countries with different histories, languages, cultures and governmental and legal systems. It includes developed, developing and least developed countries with different political perspectives and objectives. As the introduction above shows, most of them now share a strong interest in economic development through cross-border trade and, increasingly, investment. A considerable part of that trade and investment is conducted with other countries within the region, in many cases under the umbrella of bilateral and multilateral agreements designed to protect and facilitate trade and investment. The rapid growth in economic importance of the Asian region means that the approach of Asian countries to investment and the resolution of investment disputes, both domestically and internationally, are now even more important for other countries in the region and for the world at large. This book sheds light on recent legal developments in Asia in FDI by focusing on domestic and international investment laws and cases involving different Asian jurisdictions, to provide a contemporary overview of international investment and dispute resolution across the region.

Notes

1 Compare also the OECD Benchmark Definition of Foreign Direct Investment (4th edition) and other resources available at www.oecd.org/document/33/ 0,3343,en_2649_33763_33742497_1_1_1_1,00.html (accessed 7 March 2011).
2 Australia and New Zealand are generally treated in this book as part of Asia, due to their close links with Asian countries, not only geographically, but also in terms of trade, investment and international cooperation. However, some authors separate out Australia and New Zealand for particular purposes, as in Chapter 2 (Nottage and Weeramantry) in the context of low involvement by Asian arbitrators as well as parties in treaty-based ISA proceedings. In addition, the terms 'Asia' and the 'Asian region' are used differently by different sources. We have generally not felt it necessary to explain the definition used by each source referred to unless essential to the argument in the main text.
3 See Mohan (2008: 263–5 and 277); Singh (2005: 3–9); and Nabeel Mancheri, 'India's FDI Policies: Paradigm Shift', 24 December 2010, at www.eastasiaforum. org/2010/12/24/indias-fdi-policies-paradigm-shift (accessed 17 March 2011).

4 See also Sauvant and Pradhan (2010) and more generally other publications, including books and FDI Profiles (for example on India and China) available via the Vale Columbia Center on Sustainable International Investment at www.vcc. columbia.edu/content/publications (accessed 17 March 2011).
5 See 'Member States' at www.oic-oci.org/member_states.asp (accessed 28 March 2011).
6 The report includes coverage and comparison of China, India and Japan, as well as Russia, Canada and the United States. Less convincing is the argument (GAO 2008: 9), in a section making the point that 'historical factors affect a country's receptiveness to foreign investment' and attempting to categorize legal systems into common law, civil law and 'mixed' systems, that:

> the laws regulating investment in countries that operate under a common law system tended to be less specific and less detailed than the laws and policies of countries that operate under a civil law system. More specifically, in a common law system, case law determines the scope and intent of a given law.

At least for legislation directly regulating foreign investment, however, even common law systems typically generate no reported case law – in those rare situations nowadays where the government exercises statutory discretion to restrict FDI. Such legislation in Japan (characterized as a 'civil law' system) also is nominally as detailed as the legislation provided in a 'common law' country such as Australia.
7 Compare, for example, APEC Investment Experts Group (2007); and APEC Investment Experts Group (2010).
8 See the WTO website, www.wto.org/english/thewto_e/whatis_e/tif_e/org6_e. htm (accessed 14 February 2011).
9 See the ICSID website, 'List of Contracting States and Other Signatories to the Convention as of 27 December 2010', http://icsid.worldbank.org/ICSID/ (accessed 14 February 2011).
10 Shen (2010: 380–1) points out that the world's first BIT was concluded by Pakistan (with Germany) in 1958. In 1968, Malaysia concluded its first BIT with Germany (and Indonesia, its first with Denmark). In the 1970s came the first BITs for Singapore (1973, with Germany), the Philippines (1976, with France), and Thailand (1979, with the UK). The 1990s saw the first BITs signed by Laos (1993, with China) and Cambodia (1994, with Malaysia), and by 2009 ASEAN member states had concluded a total of 240 BITs.
11 For this purpose, 'Asia' includes Australia and New Zealand, but not the United States.
12 The latter three countries and Myanmar joined ASEAN over the 1990s; Brunei joined in 1984: see www.aseansec.org/64.htm (accessed 18 February 2011).
13 See the ASEAN website, www.aseansec.org/4920.htm (accessed 18 February 2011).
14 Quite exceptionally, for example, see the Australia–Thailand (1998 ATS 18) and Australia–Korea (2000 ATS 5) treaties on judicial cooperation, the Treaty on Trans-Tasman Court Proceedings and Regulatory Enforcement (2008: all available via www.info.dfat.gov.au/treaties/ (accessed 14 February 2011)), and a Memorandum between the Supreme Courts of New South Wales and Singapore to facilitate proof of the substantive law of the other state in its own proceedings (2010: www.

lawlink.nsw.gov.au/practice_notes/nswsc_pc.nsf/6a64691105a54031ca256880000
c25d7/33cfadb586532d46ca25779e00171f9a?OpenDocument (accessed 14 February 2011)).

15 See texts, overviews and adoption status for both instruments, available at www.
uncitral.org/uncitral/en/uncitral_texts/arbitration.html (accessed 14 February
2011). Both New Zealand and Australia, and to a limited extent Singapore, have
also recently amended their international arbitration laws in line with 2006 revi-
sions to the Model Law: see Nottage and Garnett (2010).

16 See, for example, Sattorova (2010); Garnett (2011); Stephenson *et al.* (2011). The
decision is also noteworthy for including, outside the context of earlier Chinese
treaties (discussed especially in Chapter 5 by Eliasson), a narrowly drafted provision allowing for arbitration of disputes 'relating to compensation for expropriation ... including disputes relating to the amount of the relevant payments'.
Following some but not all earlier tribunals interpreting different treaties, the
Saipem tribunal interpreted this clause as permitting it to determine not only the
amount of compensation payable in the event of an established expropriation,
but also whether or not an expropriation had occurred.

Bibliography

APEC (Investment Experts Group) (2007) *Guide to the Investment Regimes of APEC
Member Countries*, 6th Edition. Available at: http://publications.apec.org/
publication-detail.php?pub_id=192 (accessed 28 March 2011).

APEC (Investment Experts Group) (2010) *Guide to the Investment Regimes of APEC
Member Countries*, 7th Edition. Available at: http://publications.apec.org/publication-
detail.php?pub_id=1120 (accessed 28 March 2011).

ATKearney (2010) *Investing in a Rebound: The 2010 ATKearney Investor Confidence Index.*
Available at: www.atkearney.com/images/global/pdf/Investing_in_a_Rebound-
FDICI_2010.pdf (accessed 28 March 2011).

Brown, C. and Krishan, D. (eds) (2011) *Commentaries on Selected Model Investment
Treaties*, Oxford: Oxford University Press.

Chia, S.Y. (2010) 'Regional Trade Policy Cooperation and Architecture in East Asia'.
ADBI Working Paper 191. Tokyo: Asian Development Bank Institute. Available
at: www.adbi.org/working-paper/2010/02/02/3450.regional.trade.policy.east.asia/
(accessed 28 March 2011).

Dixon, C. (2010) 'The 1997 Economic Crisis, Reform and Southeast Asian Growth',
in Rasiah, R. and Schmidt, J.D. (eds) *The New Political Economy of Southeast Asia*,
Cheltenham: Edward Elgar, p. 103.

Dolzer, R. and Schreuer, C. (2008) *Principles of International Investment Law*, Oxford
and New York: Oxford University Press.

Drysdale, P. (2009) 'Australia and Japan: A New Economic Partnership in Asia'.
Available at: www.austrade.gov.au/Japan/default.aspx (accessed 28 March 2011).

GAO (US Government Accountability Office) (2008) 'Foreign Investment: Laws and
Policies Regulating Foreign Investment in 10 Countries'. Report to the Honorable
Richard Shelby, Ranking Member, Committee on Banking, Housing, and Urban
Affairs, US Senate. Available at: www.gao.gov/htext/d08320.html (accessed 28
March 2011).

Garnett, R. (2011) 'National Court Intervention in Arbitration as an Investment
Treaty Claim', *International and Comparative Law Quarterly*, 60: forthcoming.

Gillespie, J. (2006) *Transplanting Commercial Law Reform: Developing a 'Rule of Law' in Vietnam*, Aldershot: Ashgate.

Ginsburg, T. (2005) 'International Substitutes for Domestic Institutions', *International Review of Law and Economics*, 25: 107.

Greenberg, S., Kee, C. and Weeramantry, J.R. (eds) (2011) *International Commercial Arbitration: An Asia-Pacific Perspective*, Melbourne: Cambridge University Press.

G-20 (2011) 'What is the G-20?' Available at: http://publications.apec.org/publication-detail.php?pub_id=192 (accessed 28 March 2011).

Hamamoto, S. and Nottage, L. (2010) 'Foreign Investment in and out of Japan: Economic Backdrop, Domestic Law, and International Treaty-Based Investor-State Dispute Resolution', *Sydney Law School Research Paper*, 10/145. Available at: http://ssrn.com/abstract=1724999 (accessed 28 March 2011).

IMF (International Monetary Fund) (2006) 'Asia's Role in the World Economy' *Finance and Development*, June 2006, Vol. 43, No. 2.

Kelsey, J. (ed.) (2010) *No Ordinary Deal: Unmasking the Trans-Pacific Partnership Free Trade Agreement*, Sydney: Allen and Unwin.

Li, W.K. (2011) 'China's GDP surged 10.3% in 2010', *China Daily*. Available at: www.asianewsnet.net/home/news.php?id=16909 (accessed 28 March 2011).

Lim, C.L. (forthcoming) 'East Asia's Engagement with Cosmopolitan Ideals under Its Trade Treaty Dispute Provisions', *McGill Law Journal*. Available at: http://ssrn.com/abstract=1748146 (accessed 28 March 2011).

Maxwell, I. and Wegner, K.-J. (2009) 'The New ASEAN Comprehensive Investment Agreement', *Asian International Arbitration Journal*, 5(2): 167.

Milhaupt, C. (2008) 'Is the US Ready for FDI from China? Lessons from Japan in the 1980s', *Columbia Law and Economics Working Paper*, 334. Available at: http://ssrn.com/abstract=1135233 (accessed 28 March 2011).

Mohan, R.T.T. (2008) 'Privatisation and Foreign Direct Investment: The Indian Experience', in Rha, J. (ed.) *The Indian Economy Sixty Years after Independence*, New York: Palgrave Macmillan, p. 263.

Murray, P. (2010) 'Regionalism and Community: Australia's Options in the Asia-Pacific', *Australian Strategic Policy Institute – Strategy Paper*. Available at: www.aspi.org.au/ (accessed 28 March 2011).

Nottage, L. and Garnett, R. (2010) 'Introduction', in Nottage, L. and Garnett, R. (eds) *International Arbitration in Australia*, Sydney: Federation Press, p. 1.

Nottage, L. and Miles, K. (2009) ' "Back to the Future" for Investor-State Arbitration: Revising Rules in Australia and Japan for Public Interests', *Journal of International Arbitration*, 26(1): 25.

Oruçu, E. (2007) 'A General View of "Legal Families" and of "Mixing Systems" ', in Oruçu, E. and Nelken, D. (eds) *Comparative Law: A Handbook*, Oxford: Hart, p. 169.

PC (Productivity Commission) (2010) 'Bilateral and Regional Trade Agreements – Research Report'. Available at: www.pc.gov.au/projects/study/trade-agreements (accessed 28 March 2011).

Pryles, M. (ed.) (2006) *Dispute Resolution in Asia*, 3rd edn, Biggleswade: Kluwer Law International.

Sattorova, M. (2010) 'Judicial Expropriation or Denial of Justice? A Note on *Saipem v. Bangladesh*', *International Arbitration Law Review*, 13(2): 35. Manuscript available at: http://ssrn.com/abstract=1632349 (accessed 28 March 2011).

Sauvant, E. and Pradhan, J. (eds) (2010) *The Rise of Indian Multinationals*, New York: Palgrave Macmillan.

Shen, W. (2010) 'Is This a Great Leap Forward? A Comparative Review of the Investor–State Arbitration Clause in the ASEAN–China Investment Treaty – from BIT Jurisprudential and Practical Perspectives', *Journal of International Arbitration*, 27(4): 379.

Singh, K. (2005) 'Foreign Direct Investment in India: A Critical Analysis of FDI from 1991–2005', New Delhi: Centre for Civil Society. Available at: http://papers.ssrn.com/sol3/papers.cfm?abstract_id=822584 (accessed 28 March 2011).

Sornarajah, M. (2010a) 'India, China and Foreign Investment', in Sornarajah, M. and Wang, J. (eds) *China, India and the International Economic Order*, Cambridge, Cambridge University Press, p. 130.

Sornarajah, M. (2010b) *The International Law on Foreign Investment*, Cambridge and New York: Cambridge University Press.

Spigelman, J.J. (2007) 'International Commercial Litigation: An Asian Perspective', *Australian Business Law Review*, 35: 318.

Stephenson, A., Carroll, L. and DeBoos, J. (2011) 'Interference by a Local Court and Failure to Enforce: Actionable under a Bilateral Investment Treaty?', in Brown, C. and Miles, K. (eds) *Evolution in Investment Treaty Law and Arbitration*, Cambridge: Cambridge University Press (forthcoming).

Suriyanarayanan, B. (2010) 'IMF Projects Asia GDP to Exceed G7 by 2030', *International Business Times*. Available at: www.ibtimes.com/articles/28930/20100617/imf-asian-economy-g-7.htm (accessed 28 March 2011).

Taylor, V. (2005) 'New Markets, New Commodity: Japanese Legal Technical Assistance', *Wisconsin International Law Journal*, 23(2): 251.

Taylor, V. and Pryles, M. (2006) 'The Cultures of Dispute Resolution in Asia', in Pryles, M. (ed.) *Dispute Resolution in Asia*, Biggleswade: Kluwer Law International, p. 1.

Trading Economics (2011) 'India GDP Growth Rate', *Trading Economics*. Available at: http://www.tradingeconomics.com/india/gdp-growth (accessed 28 March 2011).

UNCTAD (2009) *UNCTAD Training Manual on Statistics for FDI and the Operations of TNCs*, Vol. I. Available at: www.unctad.org/en/docs/diaeia20091_en.pdf (accessed 28 March 2011).

UNCTAD (2010) *World Investment Report 2010*. Available at: www.unctad.org/templates/WebFlyer.asp?intItemID=5539&lang=1 (accessed 28 March 2011).

UNCTAD (2011) *Statistics*. Available at: http://unctadstat.unctad.org (accessed 28 March 2011).

2 Investment arbitration in Asia

Five perspectives on law and practice[1]

Luke Nottage and J. Romesh Weeramantry

2.1 Introduction

International commercial arbitration (ICA) has become much more important for Asia since the 1990s. New arbitration centres in the region, often
with direct or indirect financial support from the government, attract
growing caseloads (Nottage and Garnett 2010a). This development is supported by widespread accession to the 1958 New York Convention on the
Recognition and Enforcement of Foreign Arbitral Awards (NYC: 330 UNTS
3),[2] and the highest adoption rate for the UNCITRAL Model Law on International Commercial Arbitration (Greenberg, Kee and Weeramantry
2010: 36). Courts throughout Asia, despite some significant exceptions,[3]
have generally come to uphold ICA's core principles – respecting arbitral
proceedings and the awards they generate.

Prominent arbitral institutions based in the traditional Western 'core' of
the arbitration world have also recently established a more permanent presence in the Asian region. Leading European and United States law firms, as
well as Asian 'home grown' firms, have begun providing expert advice for
ICA proceedings in the region. Some Asian practitioners are also now very
active as arbitrators in ICA proceedings, both regionally and world-wide
(Pryles and Moser 2007: 12–13).

Some of these arbitrators, law firms and institutions are also starting to
show interest in the emerging field of investor-state arbitration (ISA). Yet
the incidence of ISA claims against Asian states, compared with states from
other regions, remains relatively low (see Figure 2.3), especially considering
the high numbers of investment treaties concluded by Asian states that
entitle investors to file ISA claims against them. Possible explanations for
this low level of ISA filings will be one of the key issues examined in this
chapter.

This is rather puzzling, first because most Asian countries have now
become parties to the 1965 Convention on the Settlement of Investment
Disputes between States and Nationals of Other States (ICSID Convention:
575 UNTS 159).[4] Article 25 requires a host state to provide 'consent' to
allow an investor from a home state to bring a claim directly against the host

state under the ICSID Convention regime. This consent is now usually found in arbitration provisions contained in investment treaties concluded among ICSID Convention state parties.[5]

Further, as developing countries in Asia became less sceptical of foreign direct investment (FDI) and actively sought to attract it, they began to conclude bilateral investment treaties (BITs) with Western countries, and then major net capital exporters from the region (such as Japan, and now the People's Republic of China, PRC). Chapter 1 outlined the recent growth of BITs particularly in Asia, and their increasingly pro-investor focus – including often extensive ISA provisions. They are also now folding such protections into bilateral and emergent regional Free Trade Agreements (FTAs) or the like (see also Chapter 3 in this volume; Hamamoto and Nottage 2010; Nottage and Miles 2009).

Despite this new international legal framework, however, comparatively few Asian countries appear to be involved in ISA proceedings. A recent UNCTAD report finds 30 ISA claims filed against them, out of 390 known claims under any sets of arbitration rules (8 per cent).[6] This total includes both ICSID claims and all other known investment treaty claims. In Figure 2.1 and Appendix A, we similarly identify 23 (or 7 per cent) out of a total of 324 claims instituted under the ICSID Rules or ICSID Additional Facility Rules, the predominant Rules selected for ISA proceedings, in which foreign investors have brought ISA claims against Asian countries.[7]

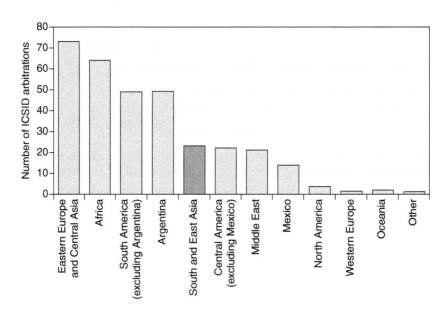

Figure 2.1 Respondent states (by region) in concluded and pending ICSID arbitrations (source: based on ICSID data available at http://icsid.worldbank.org (accessed 9 September 2010)).

This low proportion of ISA proceedings against Asian states may seem less anomalous when we exclude, as in Appendix B, cases involving Mexico (which concluded the North American Free Trade Agreement (NAFTA) with Canada and the US with effect from 1994) and Argentina (subject to 49 ICSID claims mainly instituted as a result of remarkable liberalization followed by a massive economic crisis over 1999–2002). But still the number of claims against Asian states represents a small percentage (9 per cent) of the aggregate number of ICSID claims instituted.

A 'gap' therefore seems to exist in Asia between black-letter law (in particular, treaty-based ISA protections) and actual practice (ICSID and other investment claims). It may also represent a transient 'lag' that will dissipate over time, rather like the upsurge in ICA cases in or involving Asia over the past two decades. However, Figure 2.2 below suggests that the gap is in fact widening as the proportion of ICSID claims against Asian *respondents*, i.e. states, diminishes.

The gap appears even bigger in that, for Asian *claimants*, we have only been able to uncover seven ICSID awards or filings (out of 382 filings in total as of 18 July 2011: 1.7 per cent) as well as five other ISA awards plus one other pre-arbitral BIT filing (all listed in Appendix D).[8] This chapter therefore sketches a roadmap to guide further research aimed at illuminating the reasons for such 'gaps' or persistent 'lags' in ISA 'law in books' (ISA provisions, especially now via treaties) and ISA practice or 'law in action'.

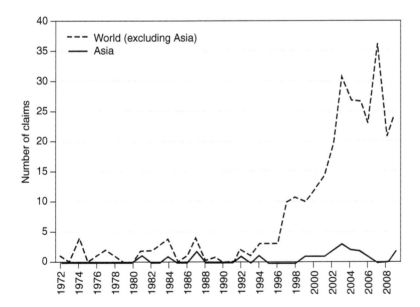

Figure 2.2 ICSID claims filed against State respondents from Asia and the rest of the world (source: based on ICSID data available at http://icsid.worldbank. org (accessed 9 September 2010)).

2.2 Understanding present and future ISA claim trends

Let us begin with the legal sociology literature on dispute resolution. This identifies a 'dispute resolution pyramid' with reported formal claims (let alone reported outcomes) forming only the tip of the iceberg (see, for example, Astor and Chinkin 2002). From one perspective, occurrences of disputes should increase if the number of economic transactions increases simply because that numerical growth gives rise to more situations in which things might go wrong. However, actual filings of civil lawsuits within domestic legal systems, for example, generally decrease during economic booms. This may be because parties face fewer financial constraints in performing their side of the bargain. Even if the other side misperforms, potential claimants in buoyant economies may prefer to limit claims because they are generally better off and can afford to move on without pursuing claims. Conversely, economic downturns generally seem to result in increased formal claims (see generally Ginsburg and Hoetker 2009). But this can sometimes be offset by a reduced propensity to claim, resulting from economic, cultural or other factors. Claims also depend on claimants perceiving a wrong, associating it with a particular defendant, and being aware of credible procedural and substantive law rights – generating significant variation across areas of socio-economic activity (see, for example, Murayama 2007).

Thus, future empirical work into ISA claim patterns should compare more systematically the macro-economic business cycle and other economic trends, including the timing and volume of FDI stocks and flows. For example, as indicated in Figure 2.3 (and Appendix C), inflows increased significantly into Asia only from around 2003 – and the region anyway has demonstrated relatively strong and consistent macro-economic performance. Nonetheless, while Asia has attracted very large stocks of inbound FDI over the past two decades, some countries (such as Pakistan) have recorded lower aggregate economic growth rates than others (see, for example, IMF 2010). In theory, this creates more potential for investment disputes to emerge.

Further analytical studies also would need to take into account claim trends vis-à-vis periods during which economic and governmental structures (as in Argentina) were subjected to major upheaval or change and therefore additional potential stress. At a less macro level, the scope for formal disputes to emerge may depend on the sector or nature of the investment – similarly to the way in which transaction type affects the approach to negotiating and resolving problems with contracts (see, for example, Taylor and Pryles 2006; Nottage 1997). In parallel, it would be instructive to compare the exact timing and extent to which the countries were concluding investment treaties providing for fuller ISA and substantive protections for the potential benefit of investor claimants (see already, briefly, Fink and Molinuevo 2008; see also Hamamoto and Nottage 2011).

More fine-grained analyses may well reveal that burgeoning and possibly more diversified FDI, combined with the number and scope of investment

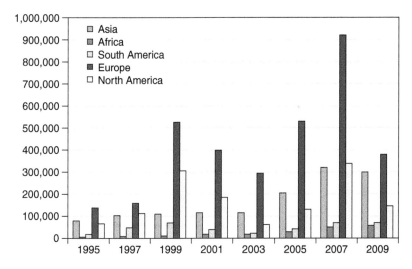

Figure 2.3 Investment inflows (US$ millions, by region) (source: based on UNCTAD data available at http://stats.unctad.org (accessed 23 September 2010)).

treaties concluded more recently by Asian states, tends to give rise to large disputes and ISA claims for particular countries (see generally Alexandrov *et al.* 2009). This would therefore reduce gaps or lags (through an increase in case numbers), even without any change in the propensity of Asian host states to breach investment treaty obligations. At the aggregate level, however, Figure 2.2 indicates that there has not been a significant rise (yet) in formal ISA claims filed against Asian states.

In addition, that propensity itself may rise, for example as states take measures to deal with the global financial crisis (GFC) and its aftermath (see van Aaken and Kurtz 2009). Even without such a change in host state propensity to generate disputes, dissatisfied foreign investors exiting a country may become more tempted to try recouping some of the losses they incurred during the GFC by bringing ISA claims (see Wells and Ahmad 2007). Tracking FDI *divestments* is therefore another important variable for econometricians interested in explaining and predicting ISA claim patterns, although reliable comparative data is often not available.

The case of the PRC should prove particularly interesting. It has been a very large recipient of inbound FDI (as outlined by Bath, in this volume). But investors seem to have been prepared to gamble on generating large short-term profits from one of the world's fastest growing economies, without paying much attention to the legal protections they may have against the host state or in dealings with other firms within the PRC. It was only in 2001 that the PRC joined the World Trade Organization (WTO), which ushered in further significant improvements to the Chinese legal system. And only since the late 1990s has China renegotiated or concluded treaties that included full-scale ISA (Gallagher and Shan 2009). Yet, as those ISA protections potentially apply to more investments *and* profit opportunities diminish for foreign investors, the potential for ISA claims against China may well increase. So far, only one ICSID claim has been brought against China – by a Malaysian investor, registered with ICSID on 24 May 2011, but suspended by agreement on 22 July 2011.[9] But quite a few may follow on now that one foreign investor has decided to take the plunge. This may become more likely (and less dramatic) as Chinese investors themselves begin to invoke the ISA system by claiming abroad (as outlined by Eliasson, in this volume).[10]

Still, the overall paucity so far of ISA claims against Asian states – and especially those brought by Asian investors – seems quite remarkable and likely to persist for some time. Even from the reported ISA cases involving Asian host states, let alone other reports as well as more scholarly analyses (including country-specific chapters in this volume), it seems highly improbable that the low caseload is simply due to those states' exemplary treatment of investors (and hence a lower likelihood of disputes) compared to host states from other parts of the world. Nor is it likely that all Asian countries have simply presented profit opportunities so advantageous that foreign investors have been led to abandon potential claims because they had made enough profit on that investment, and/or have decided that initiating ISA was excessively risky because the investor's future investments in the host state may be the subject to retaliatory measures.[11]

2.3 Five perspectives on 'gaps' or 'lags'

More detailed analysis of investment flows and economic or political circumstances may therefore partially explain why ISA caseloads involving Asian parties appear comparatively low, but a puzzle does seem to remain. Fortunately, there exists a longstanding and sophisticated debate around alleged gaps or lags observed in terms of regular civil proceedings brought before courts, especially in Asia. For example, Japan's per capita civil litigation rate (even including debt collection and court-annexed mediation cases) remains one of the lowest among industrialized democracies (Nottage and Wollschlaeger 1996). Five major perspectives or paradigms, linked to shifting intellectual and economic trends, have emerged to explain this sort of phenomenon (Abe and Nottage 2006):

A   The **culturalist thesis** emerged over the 1960s and 1970s to explain low levels of formal proceedings in terms of a traditional preference for harmony, hierarchy, and diffuse social relationships – in other words, the *Japanese don't like law*, but this aversion might dissipate as values and institutions 'modernize';

B   From the late 1970s, the **institutional barriers** thesis instead emphasized impediments such as delays and costs of bringing suit, related to insufficient judges and lawyers, as well as problems in civil procedure law and in executing judgments – the *Japanese can't like law*;

C   As trade friction escalated between Japan and the US over the 1980s, the **elite management** thesis argued that such barriers were manipulated by conservative politicians, bureaucrats and big business interests, setting up compensation and/or alternative dispute resolution (ADR) schemes to divert disputes away from courts and into more informal but orderly processes of socio-economic change – the *Japanese are made not to like law*; and

D   As deregulation and free-market policy spread from a resurgent US to Japan over the 1990s, the **economic rationalist** thesis instead suggests that substantive law and fact-finding by courts are comparatively predictable, so Japanese claimants can credibly threaten and 'bargain in the shadow of the law' for outcomes that track what they would get in court, thus saving costs for themselves and well as defendants – the *Japanese do like law*; and finally

E   As Japan re-emerged around 2002 from its 'lost decade' of economic stagnation, and the US stumbled after major corporate collapses, **hybrid theories** emerged. These argued, through both quantitative and qualitative analysis, that culture can help explain the persistence of institutional barriers and elites; but that culture is not intractable and that social actors are partly economic rationalists – this perspective tends to conclude that the *Japanese sometimes like law but sometimes don't*.

These diverse paradigms are also useful in explaining developments in ICA in countries like Japan (Nottage 2004). Similarly, this chapter argues that some can help explain any (even residual) gaps or lags that may be observable in ISA claims involving Asian parties. Specifically, we are sceptical about versions of thesis A and especially thesis D; more agnostic about thesis C, given particular difficulties in uncovering convincing evidence either way; and tentatively attracted to theses B and E. We therefore conclude ultimately with some more normative proposals (see Section 2.4), addressing many institutional barriers as well as touching on issues of 'Asian identity', to better integrate Asia into the evolving ISA system world-wide.

First, we believe the **economic rationalist** paradigm D is most implausible, at least in its original formulation. Substantive ISA principles, as well as fact-finding processes (often definitive in ISA cases) and even some procedural issues, are still in a formative and unclear state (Franck 2005). The examples of a lack of uniform interpretation and application of investment treaties are many. One of the most well-known instances, concerning divergent interpretations of BIT 'umbrella clauses', happens to involve Asian respondents: *SGS Société Générale de Surveillance S.A.* v. *Islamic Republic of Pakistan* (ICSID Case No. ARB/01/13, Jurisdiction, 9 August 2003); and

SGS Société Générale de Surveillance S.A. v. *Republic of the Philippines* (ICSID Case No. ARB/02/6, Jurisdiction, 29 January 2004).

A less obvious example of uncertainty in substantive law interpretations, yet very important particularly in the Asian context, arises from a recent case brought by a Chinese investor: *Tza Yap Shum* v. *Peru* (ICSID Case No. ARB/07/6 (Case No. 9 in Appendix D); discussed further by Eliasson in Chapter 5). The arbitral tribunal held that the 1994 China–Peru BIT provision restricting arbitration claims to 'a dispute involving the amount of compensation for expropriation' should be interpreted as implying jurisdiction to determine whether expropriation had occurred, not just to evaluate the quantum of loss that would follow from a prior expropriation finding (as determined for example in a separate dispute resolution process). That decision is in fact consistent with a number of other awards dealing with 'amount of compensation' arbitration provisions in other investment treaties, most notably involving Eastern European states, with outcomes also dependent on the specific wording used in the various treaties invoked.[12] Yet it came as a surprise to many, who had considered that China's 'second-generation' treaties had deliberately chosen such wording to limit investor claims to quantum, as opposed to some 'third-generation' treaties (such as the 2008 China–New Zealand FTA) which contained wording clearly extending jurisdiction to liability issues (see, for example, Gallagher and Shan 2009: 313–18).

A parallel can be drawn with the regime under the General Agreement on Tariffs and Trade (GATT) and especially then in the early era of the subsequent more encompassing WTO system. Significant uncertainty in applying substantive law to the facts resulted in a bulge in case filings, appeals, and delays in having decisions rendered and enforced. ISA's current situation is arguably even worse because, for example, there is no permanent appellate body with powers to review in a consistent manner the interpretations of investment treaties or substantive errors of law (Nottage and Miles 2009: 43–4).

With the law relating to ISA so uncertain, economic rationalist theory generally would predict much higher levels of ISA cases being contested in formal proceedings, unless the costs involved were so vast as to force one party to give up during negotiations. A particular problem for this theory is the lack of evidence that disputes involving Asian parties are significantly simpler or their outcomes easier to predict (and hence less likely to result in contested ISA cases) compared to those involving non-Asian parties.

The **culturalist** thesis A may retain more merit. At the level of the individual, a series of recent studies in experimental social psychology suggests that certain engrained differences do exist between 'Asians' and 'Westerners', despite variations within each group. According to those studies, Asians tend to have more holistic perception, allow for more complex causal attribution, categorize less when organizing knowledge, and favour typicality (plausibility) or normative preferences (rather than logic) when drawing inferences (Nisbett 2003).

Yet, despite for example a broader revival in 'neo-culturalist' approaches to Japanese legal studies (Nottage 2009; Tanase 2010; Puchniak 2010), it remains unclear whether and how any such psychological differences translate into alternative behaviour when filtered through institutions such as firms or entire governments (compare, for example, Kozuka and Nottage 2009). Further, even at the individual level, there may not necessarily exist large culture-driven divergences in attitudes and practices in law-related activities, for example, as has been observed in contract renegotiation following extreme changes in market conditions (Nottage 1997, 2007). Further experimental and attitudinal studies, of individuals and the relevant organizations involved in ISA, are needed to determine the extent and implications of any differences in cultural psychology.

Several challenges already seem to undermine a simple culturalist rationale for the relative paucity of ISA cases involving Asian parties. For example, Asian parties have never been involved in formal mediation proceedings under Articles 28–35 of the ICSID Convention – although there have only been six anyway. In addition, why do Pakistan, the Philippines, Bangladesh and the other Asian respondent states listed in Appendix E still contest ICSID cases vigorously, instead of settling 'harmoniously'? Moreover, Asian state respondents do not seem to settle cases more frequently during ISA proceedings compared to respondents from other parts of the world, as Figure 2.4 indicates.[13]

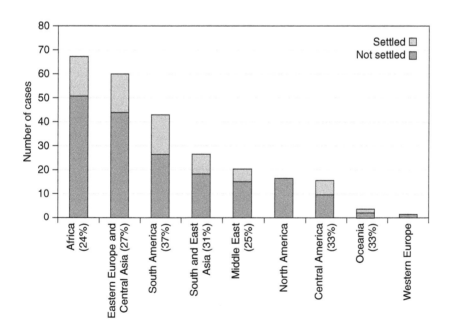

Figure 2.4 ICSID settlement rate of state respondents by region.

In addition, why do China and Japan go to considerable trouble now to include full ISA provisions in their BITs and FTAs? In the case of China, this accords with China's new role as a major capital exporter. For Japan, this approach has been propelled by business federations (notably the *Nippon Keidanren*), and it may also fit with the government's growing 'export' of 'rule of law' based 'legal technical assistance' – especially to South-East Asia (see, respectively, Pekkanen 2008; Taylor 2005; Hamamoto and Nottage 2010). These recent tendencies add to more longstanding and wide-ranging objections to the 'culturalist' hypothesis that the Japanese have some unique and general aversion to the more black-and-white rules prescribed by the law.

Nonetheless, it seems that no Japanese investor has formally initiated ISA procedures under an investment treaty. Japanese firms, especially larger ones with well-established reputations, have long tended to prefer renegotiation and informal solutions to investment and other disputes. This may be due more to commercial considerations. For example, they have been conscious of the short-term costs involved (legal expenses, management time and so on) as well as challenges to internal organizational structures and norms (Kitagawa and Nottage 2007). Particularly regarding cross-border investments, Japanese firms also appear to have been relatively more conscious – rightly or wrongly – about the potential losses that may arise should they opt for a formal dispute resolution procedure, or the possibility that by pursuing a claim they may be foregoing future profits on the investment at issue or other investments they have made in the country concerned (as in the recent Sakhalin Island consortium dispute outlined by Hamamoto in Chapter 3).

Nonetheless, despite this Japanese preference for non-litigious solutions, the Dutch subsidiary of a major Japanese financial institution (Nomura – via its British subsidiary) did bring an investment treaty arbitration claim against the Czech Republic, for example.[14] And a Japanese general trading company (Tomen) was brought into the *Karaha Bodas* power project investment contract arbitration against an Indonesian state-owned enterprise (Pertamina), albeit as a junior equity partner in a consortium led by a US firm (see Wells and Ahmad 2007; Nottage and Miles 2009: Part 3.1.1). Nowadays, Japanese firms may no longer be able to afford to resolve disputes informally. Budgetary pressure has built up from financial crises (1998 in Asia, which exacerbated Japan's 'lost decade' of economic stagnation throughout the 1990s, and especially now the GFC), as well as growing competition among foreign investors seeking to invest directly in Asia.

Elite management theory C also faces problems, just as it does when trying to explain contemporary government–firm relations, for example, purely within Japan (see, for example, Kozuka and Nottage 2009). In the context of Asian countries defending ISA claims, the theory would predict even less willingness to contest such claims. One reason is that, eventually, key facts are likely to come out from the proceedings (at least in a more or less public award[15]) that could drastically undermine the host state's elite – if, as tends to be implied by this theory, the elite relies on maintaining a more opaque system of governance. Moreover, investment treaties – often through 'fair and equitable treatment' provisions – emphasize transparency in governance (Kingsbury and Schill 2009). Deficiencies in the treatment of investors are likely to be exposed in ISA decisions ruling on such obligations. But as we have noted above, Asian states defend claims vigorously and do not appear to settle claims at a rate significantly higher than states from other regions. This is not indicative of strong elite management tendencies at play on the part of Asian states.

As for Asian investors bringing claims, elite management theory implies that they are closely aligned through informal links with their home state, as part of a domestic elite. Specifically, this relationship involves the home state being able then to persuade the investors not to jeopardize its interests, and those of the broader elite they form part of, by bringing direct claims against the host state. Rather, the home state can first credibly emphasize the long-term and more diffuse benefits of investors remaining part of the local elite. Moreover, it may promise the possibility of more short-term benefits through the capacity of the home state (which presumably would have more clout on a governmental level than an investor) to negotiate informally with the host state, so the latter adjusts its business relationships with the investors to some mutual benefit. The home state may also find other ways to make it worthwhile for the investor not to file a claim (for example, by facilitating a new deal for the investor in that state or even abroad).

Such benefits may indeed have been realized in some cases, although that will be difficult to research and prove. But there will always be some temptation for the investors instead to try to extract benefits from the host state directly, by invoking ISA provisions. Whether they will deviate from a home state's wishes in this way should be heavily influenced by whether they form, now or in the foreseen future, part of that state's local elite, by virtue of which longer-term benefits are provided. In Japan, and presumably elsewhere, the companies most likely to invest actively abroad are precisely the more internationalist ones. And generally, directly or through the *Keidanren* industry body, such companies have prompted a gradual reconfiguration of Japan's traditional post-war elite and its policy outlook. They represent a major force behind the government's new 'aggressive legalism' not only in WTO disputes, but also now in FTA and investment treaty practice (see Pekkanen 2008; and more generally Yoshimatsu 2000).

Despite such complications, elite management theory would not expect large and established companies from Asian countries (more likely to be part of a home country elite) to become involved in formal proceedings. Yet, to varying degrees, some large Japanese firms have already had some involvement in quite well-known cases.[16]

Our research has found only 13 ISA cases, as mentioned briefly above and listed in Appendix D, in which a claimant is from Asia. (This is further complicated, for example, by the fact that the *Amco Asia* claim was led by a US parent company.) Some in fact involve seemingly elite firms such as Telekom

Malaysia, which would tend to counter the elite management thesis as applied to ISA proceedings.[17] Yet there are certainly few such claims, so overall it may still be true that most 'elite' firms are indeed not initiating proceedings because of pressure from their home states – or, put more neutrally, due to a mutually beneficial long-term relationship between business elites and their home states. We have also heard anecdotal evidence of home state influence (especially South Korea, but also in one case involving a Japanese investor around 2005) steering an investor away from the path of ISA after disputes had arisen with a host state. There remain serious difficulties in substantiating such a tendency, however, and especially in establishing that it is more common throughout Asia than in other regions of the world. Without cogent support, we cannot yet ascribe an important role to the elite management theory in our attempt to explain the relative paucity of ISA claims by Asian investors.

Meanwhile, **institutional barriers** theory B would already seem to provide one of the best explanatory paradigms for explaining low levels of ISA cases in Asia – especially the limited number of Asian claimants. Turning first to impediments for the host state, these include:

- *Direct costs*, especially lawyers' fees (see Kinnear 2010: 569): bearing in mind Asian respondent governments tend to engage international law firms[18] rather than using their own in-house government lawyers (as they may, at least more so, when now pursuing WTO cases against other states);
- *Indirect costs* (compare Franck 2007): in particular, opportunity costs or loss of time and resources resulting from deployment of government personnel (not limited simply to its lawyers) to marshal evidence and assist in preparation and presentation of the case – especially in English (the main language for ISA proceedings);
- *Long-term costs*: the potential for future investors to perceive that a state's defence of an investment claim (and perhaps also the allegations made by the investor) signals that the state is hostile to foreign investment or possesses some propensity to treat foreign investors badly;[19]
- *Delays* in progressing cases: investment arbitration cases have developed a negative reputation for their long duration (Sinclair *et al.* 2009 concluded that the average duration of ICSID cases is 3.6 years). Longer delays usually result in higher costs (which could lead to a war of financial attrition; see Wälde 2010: 23). This issue is particularly problematic for respondent governments when it comes to awards of interest;
- *Enforcement*: a state does not wish to engage in disputes pursuant to which investors may attempt to enforce against that state's assets located abroad (likely without notice) and it especially does not wish to be dragged into a foreign court should the investor initiate enforcement proceedings; and

• *Problems finding the 'right' arbitrator*, especially from within Asia: although no hard evidence exists that Asian governments seek but cannot locate and appoint suitably experienced, skilled and available Asian arbitrators,[20] there is certainly a disparity in the appointment of European and North American arbitrators as compared with the rest of the world. Figure 2.5 and Appendix F show the disproportionate appointment of such ISA arbitrators within the ICSID regime. Western Europe and North America make up 68 per cent of all arbitrator appointments, compared with Asia (4 per cent), the Middle East (3 per cent), Central America (2 per cent) and Eastern Europe/Central Asia (1 per cent). Furthermore, appointments of Asian arbitrators in ICSID cases are grouped heavily around a few individuals.[21]

For the investor, 'institutional barriers' to ISA would include:

• *Direct costs*, especially lawyers' fees: these may be sizable for investors as well, and it is not uncommon for a successful claimant to bear its own expenses (see, for example, *Saipem S.p.A.* v. *People's Republic of Bangladesh*, ICSID Case No. ARB/05/07, Award, 30 June 2009). Even when the tribunal orders the respondent to pay the claimant's costs, it usually does not cover all of those costs (see, for example, *Siag and Vecchi* v. *Arab Republic of Egypt*, ICSID Case No. ARB/05/15, Award, 1 June 2009);

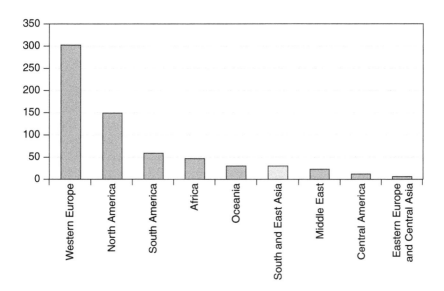

Figure 2.5 Numbers of arbitrators (by nationality) appointed in concluded ICSID arbitrations (source: based on ICSID data available at http://icsid.world-bank.org (accessed 9 September 2010)).

- *Indirect costs*: in particular, time and resources lost from the investor's personnel having to assist the lawyers in gathering evidence and presenting the case; and the uncertainties for the enterprise's future knowing that a great deal could be won or lost on the (unpredictable) outcome of an investment arbitration;
- *Long-term costs*: for example, some practitioners in the region have suggested to us that there could be the possibility of some form of direct or indirect retaliation for proceeding against the PRC, not just for the investor or its subsidiaries but also for law firms representing them that have offices located in the PRC (this suggestion has been made particularly as part of the explanation as to why no claims have so far been pursued against the PRC);
- *Delays* in progressing cases (see the above remarks on delays in relation to host states);
- *Limitation on types of protected investment*: a number of investment treaties signed by Asian states limit treaty protection by restricting covered investments to 'approved projects' or investments 'approved in writing and registered by the host country' (in other words, this is a requirement additional to the usual treaty provisions requiring the investment simply to be lawful under the host state's law) – this type of restriction has led to the dismissal of two ISA claims concerning Asian host states for lack of jurisdiction (see *Gruslin* v. *Malaysia*, ICSID Case No. ARB/99/3, Final Award, 27 November 2000, at para. 25.6; and *Yaung Chi Oo Trading Pte Ltd* v. *Myanmar*, ASEAN ID Case No. ARB/01/1, Final Award, 31 March 2003, at paras 53–63); and
- *Enforcement difficulties*: especially post-award execution against assets under ICSID Convention Articles 54(3) and 55 as well as national legislation on sovereign immunity (Reed 2009).

Yet the **hybrid** theory E also seems feasible in the field of ISA. As relative latecomers to industrialization/modernization and foreign investment/arbitration, Asian states (even developed ones like Japan) may feel that actually invoking its ISA protections runs counter to its 'Asian' identity, culture and values (see also generally Hatakeyama 2008; Taylor 2005; Murray 2008). Though seemingly incongruous, this would be the case despite the intensely competitive and economically driven environment in which most of Asia functions today. In subtle and distinctive ways for many decades to come, this identity therefore may keep 'framing' how Asian governments (and possibly, but less so, Asian private enterprises) weigh up more material interests implicated in the ISA system (highlighted especially by institutional barriers theory) (see also generally Epstein 2008).

2.4 Tentative normative conclusions

This chapter has mainly highlighted a little-discussed but important problem – the gap between ISA law in books and the law in practice involving
Asian parties – and then set out a framework for understanding how and
why such a gap may exist and persist. We have also marshalled some data,
original and derivative, to begin testing various theories or perspectives on
this phenomenon in the international arena, which were developed originally
more for thinking about similar issues involving civil litigation patterns
within national legal systems – notably Japan.

However, our data on ISA, and even some of the questions that we
suggest ought to be asked, are necessarily tentative and heuristic. This is
especially true because the theories we explore require looking below the tip
of the 'dispute resolution pyramid', namely reported arbitral awards. Publicly available quantitative data is also inherently problematic due to the
confidential aspects of many international arbitrations. Future research
should also pursue more qualitative methods, such as structured interviews.
Nonetheless, we conclude by proposing some even more tentative normative
conclusions, as have been attempted in other preliminary empirical work
into ISA recently (see, for example, Franck 2009).

Given that institutional parameters do and should matter, the following
measures should be considered to achieve more active engagement by Asian
nations and their investors in the evolving ISA system. As ISA claims continue
to grow world-wide, these measures will also contribute to a broader normative debate, touched on throughout this article (see, for example, Nottage and
Miles 2009), about the pros and cons of the present system more generally.

- ICSID should make a more concerted effort to maintain a presence in
  Asia and work on ways to actually administer Asian-based ISA claims
  from within the region rather than from the other side of the globe (that
  is, Washington), and to provide targeted training (for example, work-
  shops for government officials or symposia for specific industries such as
  the construction or oil and gas sectors).
- Relatedly, an Asian 'ISA Advisory Centre' could be set up, inspired by
  the Advisory Centre on WTO Law (ACWL) in Geneva and specifically
  the more recent initiative for a Latin American Advisory Facility for
  investor-state disputes (see UNCTAD 2009: 12).
- Strategies to reduce direct costs, particularly legal fees and also arbitrators' fees as well as overheads need examination and implementation (for
  example, whether – in certain cases – legal costs calculated from billable
  hours rather than flat fees are appropriate).[22]
- Asian countries (even or especially developed countries like Japan)
  should become more involved in promoting other reforms to the ISA
  system (such as other procedural/institutional reforms suggested recently
  for the Australia–Japan FTA: Nottage and Miles 2009).

- ICSID should redesign and then promote its conciliation process in the region, considering 'institutional barriers' that may be impeding its acceptance rather than broad-brush 'cultural' factors.
- More universities need to offer courses in international investment law to inform future practitioners who might represent investors or states about the very real rights and obligations under investment treaties, as well as potential problems.
- Their ICA courses and textbooks should also include a significant component that explains the ISA process (see Greenberg, Kee and Weeramantry 2010: chapter 10; Nottage and Garnett 2010b: especially chapters 9 and 10).
- More attempts should be made to educate practitioners in the subject area. They need to realize that ISA is relevant not just for law firm arbitration/litigation departments, but for commercial lawyers who plan and structure international investments.
- Local law societies or other groups should try to demystify the subject area by making available compendiums of their state's BITs and other investment treaties. These should include a commentary that summarizes the core rights contained in them, identifies useful literature, discusses the most pertinent cases, and explains how ISA claims may be instituted and the potential costs and expenses of bringing such a claim (along with some suggestions on how to reduce this cost). At least some of this should be in Asian languages.[23]
- Greater support for more broadly-based conferences, not limited to legal practitioners, and for smaller study groups throughout the region.

Most of these reforms should also help to change not only the more immediate material factors involved in pursuing or defending ISA proceedings as claimant or respondent, but also the broader 'identity' implications (highlighted by some 'hybrid theorists') already involved in doing so. Just as arbitration between corporate entities in the region has witnessed considerable discussion about what might be called 'commercial arbitration Asian-style', such as various degrees and forms of 'Arb-Med' (Nottage and Miles 2009), we might expect and indeed welcome more debate and practices more distinctive to 'investment arbitration Asian-style'. This is particularly important as the ISA system presently faces serious challenges in terms of both legitimacy and efficiency.

These challenges are evident even in the Asia-Pacific region, particularly in the light of Australia's 'Gillard Government Trade Policy Statement' announced in April 2011, which proposes to sharply curtail the inclusion of ISA protections in future investment treaties. In light of Australia's traditional emphasis on concluding treaties with Asia-Pacific states, this new policy stance may well begin to undermine the gradual acceptance of ISA in the region over the past decade or so (Nottage 2011). However, Australia's new policy stance may not endure, and recently there has been a significant rise in the proportion of ICSID case filings against Asia-Pacific states.[24]

Appendix A

Respondent states (by region) in concluded and pending ICSID arbitrations

	Concluded	*Pending*	*Total*	*Percentage*
Eastern Europe and Central Asia	44	29	73	22.53
Africa	51	13	64	19.75
South America (excl. Argentina)	20	29	49	15.12
Argentina	23	26	49	15.12
South and East Asia	18	5	23	7.10
Central America (excl. Mexico)	10	12	22	6.79
Middle East	15	6	21	6.48
Mexico	13	1	14	4.32
North America	3	1	4	1.23
Western Europe	1	1	2	0.62
Oceania	2	0	2	0.62
Other	1	0	1	0.31
	201	123	324	100.00

Source: Figures based on ICSID data available at http://icsid.worldbank.org (accessed 9 September 2010).

Appendix B

Respondent states (by region) in concluded and pending ICSID arbitrations – differentiating Argentina and Mexico

	Concluded	*Pending*	*Total*	*Percentage*
Eastern Europe and Central Asia	44	29	73	27.97
Africa	51	13	64	24.52
South America (excl. Argentina)	20	29	49	18.77
South and East Asia	18	5	23	8.81
Central America (excl. Mexico)	10	12	22	8.43
Middle East	15	6	21	8.05
North America	3	1	4	1.53
Western Europe	1	1	2	0.77
Oceania	2	0	2	0.77
Other	1	0	1	0.38
	165	96	261	100.00

Source: Figures based on ICSID data available at http://icsid.worldbank.org (accessed 9 September 2010).

Appendix C

Investment inflows (US$ million, by region)

	1995	1997	1999	2001	2003	2005	2007	2009
Asia	80,114	105,814	111,537	113,437	115,148	210,026	319,333	301,367
Africa	5655	11,033	12,063	19,905	18,719	29,459	52,982	58,565
South America	18,633	49,310	69,640	38,656	22,938	44,305	71,699	72,398
Europe	139,140	162,321	529,357	401,370	293,552	531,499	925,032	378,388
North America	68,027	114,966	308,481	187,183	60,636	131,820	341,555	148,540

Source: Figures based on UNCTAD data available at http://stats.unctad.org (accessed 23 September 2010).

Appendix D

Selected list of claimants possessing Asian nationality in ISA arbitrations (alphabetical)

1 *Amco Asia Corporation and others* v. *Republic of Indonesia* (ICSID Case No. ARB/81/1) – US company with its Indonesian and Hong Kong affiliates claiming against Indonesia under a hotel development contract

2 *Asian Agricultural Products Limited* v. *Democratic Socialist Republic of Sri Lanka* (ICSID Case No. ARB/87/3) – Hong Kong company's claim under the UK-Sri Lanka BIT

3 *Cemex Asia Holdings Ltd* v. *Republic of Indonesia* (ICSID Case No. ARB/04/3) – Singapore subsidiary of a Mexican firm claiming under the 1987 ASEAN Agreement for the Promotion and Protection of Investments

4 *China Heilongjiang International & Technical Cooperative Corp, Qinhuangdaoshi Qinlong International Industrial, and Beijing Shougang Mining Investment* v. *Republic of Mongolia* – ad hoc arbitration under the UNCITRAL Arbitration Rules and the China–Mongolia BIT, pending as of July 2011

5 *Ekran Berhad* v. *People's Republic of China* (ICSID Case No. ARB/11/15) – Malaysian investor's claim, suspended on 22 July 2011

6 *Malaysian Historical Salvors, Sdn, Bhd* v. *Malaysia* (ICSID Case No. ARB/05/10) – Malaysian company but controlled by UK national and therefore claim brought under the UK–Malaysia BIT

7 *MTD Equity Sdn Bhd and MTD Chile S.A.* v. *Chile* (ICSID Case No. ARB/01/7) – Malaysian investment company and its Chilean subsidiary claimed against Chile under the Chile–Malaysia BIT

8 *Philip Morris Asia* v. *Australia* – Hong Kong subsidiary of international tobacco firm initiating process leading to ad hoc arbitration, reportedly under the UNCITRAL Arbitration Rules and the Australia–Hong Kong BIT

9 *Sancheti* v. *United Kingdom* – Indian citizen's claim in ad hoc arbitration under UNCITRAL Arbitration Rules and the India–UK BIT

10 *Telekom Malaysia Berhad* v. *Republic of Ghana* – Malaysian company's claim in ad hoc arbitration under UNCITRAL Arbitration Rules and the Ghana–Malaysia BIT

11 *Trinh Vin Binh* v. *Vietnam* – ad hoc arbitration under UNCITRAL Arbitration Rules and the Dutch–Vietnam BIT

12 *Tza Yap Shum* v. *Republic of Peru* (ICSID Case No. ARB/07/6) – Chinese citizen's claim under the Chinese–Peru BIT

13 *Yaung Chi Oo Trading Pte Ltd* v. *Government of the Union of Myanmar* (ASEAN I.D. Case No. ARB/01/1) – Singapore company's claim under the ASEAN Agreement for the Promotion and Protection of Investments

Source: Based on ISA data available from http://icsid.worldbank.org (accessed 13 December 2010), the Investment Arbitration Reporter at www.iareporter.com, and the Investment Treaty Arbitration website at http://italaw.com both (accessed 1 August 2011).

Appendix E

Asian respondents in ICSID arbitrations (by year of filing)

Concluded cases:
1 *Amco Asia Corporation and others* v. *Republic of Indonesia* (ICSID Case No. ARB/81/1).
2 *Colt Industries Operating Corporation* v. *Republic of Korea* (ICSID Case No. ARB/84/2).
3 *Asian Agricultural Products Limited* v. *Democratic Socialist Republic of Sri Lanka* (ICSID Case No. ARB/87/3).
4 *Occidental of Pakistan, Inc.* v. *Islamic Republic of Pakistan* (ICSID Case No. ARB/87/4).
5 *Scimitar Exploration Limited* v. *Bangladesh and Bangladesh Oil, Gas and Mineral Corporation* (ICSID Case No. ARB/92/2).
6 *Philippe Gruslin* v. *Malaysia* (ICSID Case No. ARB/94/1).
7 *Philippe Gruslin* v. *Malaysia* (ICSID Case No. ARB/99/3).
8 *Mihaly International Corporation* v. *Democratic Socialist Republic of Sri Lanka* (ICSID Case No. ARB/00/2).
9 *SGS Société Générale de Surveillance S.A.* v. *Islamic Republic of Pakistan* (ICSID Case No. ARB/01/13).
10 *Impregilo S.p.A.* v. *Islamic Republic of Pakistan* (ICSID Case No. ARB/02/2)

11 *SGS Société Générale de Surveillance S.A.* v. *Republic of the Philippines* (ICSID Case No. ARB/02/6).
12 *Impregilo S.p.A.* v. *Islamic Republic of Pakistan* (ICSID Case No. ARB/03/3).
13 *Bayindir Insaat Turizm Ticaret Ve Sanayi A.S.* v. *Islamic Republic of Pakistan* (ICSID Case No. ARB/03/29)
14 *Alstom Power Italia S.p.A. and Alstom S.p.A.* v. *Republic of Mongolia* (ICSID Case No. ARB/04/10)
15 *Cemex Asia Holdings Ltd* v. *Republic of Indonesia* (ICSID Case No. ARB/04/3).
16 *Malaysian Historical Salvors, SDN, BHD* v. *Malaysia* (ICSID Case No. ARB/05/10).
17 *Saipem S.p.A.* v. *People's Republic of Bangladesh* (ICSID Case No. ARB/05/7).
18 *Chevron Bangladesh Block Twelve, Ltd and Chevron Bangladesh Blocks Thirteen and Fourteen, Ltd* v. *People's Republic of Bangladesh* (ICSID Case No. ARB/06/10).
19 *Fraport AG Frankfurt Airport Services Worldwide* v. *Republic of the Philippines* (ICSID Case No. ARB/03/25). (Annulment Proceeding).

Pending cases:
1   *Deutsche Bank AG* v. *Democratic Socialist Republic of Sri Lanka* (ICSID Case No. ARB/09/2).
2   *Cambodia Power Company* v. *Kingdom of Cambodia and Electricité du Cambodge* (ICSID Case No. ARB/09/18).
3   *Niko Resources (Bangladesh) Ltd* v. *People's Republic of Bangladesh, Bangladesh Petroleum Exploration & Production Company Limited ('Bapex') and Bangladesh Oil Gas and Mineral Corporation ('Petrobangla')* (ICSID Case No. ARB/10/11).
4   *Niko Resources (Bangladesh) Ltd* v. *People's Republic of Bangladesh, Bangladesh Petroleum Exploration and Production Company Limited ('Bapex') and Bangladesh Oil Gas and Mineral Corporation ('Petrobangla')* (ICSID Case No. ARB/10/18).
5   *Agility for Public Warehousing Company K.S.C.* v. *Islamic Republic of Pakistan* (ICSID Case No. ARB/11/8).
6   *Fraport AG Frankfurt Airport Services Worldwide* v. *Republic of the Philippines* (ICSID Case No. ARB/11/12).
7   *Rafat Ali Rizvi* v. *Republic of Indonesia* (ICSID Case No. ARB/11/13).
8   *Ekran Berhad* v. *People's Republic of China* (ICSID Case No. ARB/11/15), suspended on 22 July 2011.

Source: Based on ICSID data available at http://icsid.worldbank.org (accessed 1 August 2011.

Note: *The Government of the Province of East Kalimantan* v. *PT Kaltim Prima Coal and others* (ICSID Case No. ARB/07/3) case is not listed here. It concerns a claim made by the Indonesian province of East Kalimantan that it is a third party beneficiary to a contract signed by the respondents and that it has the right to acquire a stake in the respondents' coal project. It is something as an anomaly because it is believed to be the first ICSID case brought by a sovereign state or province, so it is included in our statistics as 'Other'. See www.law.com/jsp/article.jsp?id=900005555709 (accessed 14 December 2010).

Appendix F

Numbers of arbitrators (by nationality) appointed in concluded ICSID arbitrations

	Appointments	*Percentage*
Western Europe	300	45.73
North America	149	22.71
South America	58	8.84
Africa	47	7.16
Oceania	32	4.88
Asia	29	4.42
Middle East	21	3.20
Central America	13	1.98
Eastern Europe and Central Asia	7	1.07
Total	656	100.00

Source: Figures based on ICSID data available at http://icsid.worldbank.org (accessed 9 September 2010).

Note
These figures are based on appointments which have led to that arbitrator issuing an award (whether in proceedings involving original arbitrations, annulments resubmissions or otherwise). Thus, an arbitrator who has been replaced during the course of proceedings was not counted. Finally, where an arbitrator has dual nationality (an infrequent occurrence), for our statistical purposes only the first-mentioned nationality was counted.

Notes

1 We are grateful for research and editorial assistance from Andrew Cong and Wan Sang Lung, and helpful feedback on earlier versions from audiences at various international symposia since 2009 – including participants at the book workshop at the University of Sydney on 29 October 2010 (supported by the Institute of Social Sciences). We also thank Nils Eliasson and Mark Kantor for helpful comments and acknowledge research funding from the Australia–Japan Foundation (for Nottage's broader project 'Fostering A Common Culture in Cross-Border Dispute Resolution: Australia, Japan and the Asia-Pacific'). All cited investment arbitration awards in this paper are available at http://italaw.com and/or www.investmentclaims.com (both accessed 1 August 2011). Figures and corresponding Appendices for ICSID arbitrations are based on data available from http://icsid.worldbank.org as of 9 September 2010, but this chapter does

note a few significant subsequent developments in ICSID (and other) arbitrations. A longer version of this chapter appears in 28(1) *Arbitration International* (2012).

2 See www.uncitral.org/uncitral/en/uncitral_texts/arbitration/NYConvention_status. html (accessed 14 December 2010). From the Asian region, only India, Pakistan, the Philippines and Sri Lanka signed the New York Convention in 1958, when it was first opened for signature. Today, most states in the region have acceded to the Convention. Myanmar, Taiwan and Papua New Guinea are among the few exceptions.

3 See, for example, the setting aside of foreign awards set aside in *Venture Global Engineering* v. *Satyam Computer Services Ltd* (2008) 4 SCC 190; [2008] INSC 40 (Indian Supreme Court) and *Luzon Hydro Corporation* v. *Baybay and Transfield Philippines*, (2007) XXXII *Yearbook of Commercial Arbitration* 456 (Philippines Court of Appeals). See generally Greenberg, Kee and Weeramantry 2010: 418. In a recent survey, corporate counsel from major international companies most often cited the PRC as the state they perceive to be most hostile to the enforcement of foreign arbitral awards: PricewaterhouseCoopers (2008).

4 Much like the signature and accession pattern associated with the NYC, few Asian states signed the ICSID Convention when it was first opened for signature in 1965. Japan, Malaysia, Nepal and Pakistan all signed in that year. Most states in the region are now parties to the Convention; the major exceptions are India, Taiwan, Thailand and Vietnam. See the ICSID homepage at http://icsid.world-bank.org (accessed 13 December 2010).

5 Even if a state is still not party to the ICSID Convention, such treaties may grant rights to investors to bring international arbitration claims. Although the resultant award then cannot be enforced through this Convention's enforcement mechanism, it may, for example, be enforced under the NYC. See, for example, Nakamura (2009).

6 See UNCTAD (2010a: 12–13). Remarkably, nine claims have reportedly been brought against India. These are probably mostly related to the Dabhol Power project dispute, under UNCITRAL Arbitration Rules (or perhaps institutional Rules other than those of ICSID), because India has not yet signed the ICSID Convention (as mentioned above) and has not availed itself of the ICSID Additional Facility Rules (for situations where one party is not from an ICSID Convention state). See Ranjan, Chapter 10 in this volume.

7 ISA proceedings adopting UNCITRAL or other Rules may also be high: see UNCTAD (2010b: 84, Figure III.3), also discussed in Chapter 1.

8 The pending non-ICSID claim was initiated on 27 June 2011 by Philip Morris Asia against Australia, pursuant to its 1993 BIT with Hong Kong. This investor is a subsidiary of the originally American-, now Switzerland-centred tobacco giant, and holds intellectual property rights arguably expropriated by Australia's proposed plain packaging legislation. See L. Nottage, 'Investor–State Arbitration Law and Policy After Philip Morris vs Australia', Japanese Law and the Asia-Pacific Blog, 1 July 2011, at http://blogs.usyd.edu.au/japaneselaw/2011/07/isa_claim.html. Appendix D nonetheless lists this company (and others such as Amco Asia Corporation) as having 'Asian' nationality, if only because it is often difficult to determine whether and to what extent the investor may be owned or controlled by 'non-Asian' interests. This approach therefore may *overstate* the (already small) proportion of claims brought by ('truly') Asian claimants. But nor have we attempted to determine whether claimants in ICSID or other

arbitrations are owned or controlled by 'Asian' interests, even though there do exist such cases. (See, for example, *Opic Karimun Corporation* v. *Venezuela* (ICSID Case No. ARB/10/14), reportedly involving a Panamanian subsidiary of a Chinese state-owned enterprise: L.E. Peterson, 'Effort to Disqualify Arbitrator in Venezuelan Oil Nationalization Case is Unsuccessful', 19 May 2011, *Investment Arbitration Reporter*, at www.iareporter.com/articles/20110520 accessed 18 July 2011.) Not including such cases instead arguably *understates* claims by Asian claimants.

9 *Ekran Berhad* v. *People's Republic of China* (ICSID Case No. ARB/11/15): see http://icsid.worldbank.org/ (accessed 18 July 2011). This may be based on a BIT between Malaysia and China concluded in 1990, but information is still limited and China could have consented to ICSID arbitration under another legal instrument, such as an investment contract. See L.E. Peterson, 'China is Sued for the First Time in an ICSID Arbitration', 26 May 2011, *Investment Arbitration Reporter*, at www.iareporter.com/articles/20110526 (accessed 18 July 2011).

10 It would also be useful to test whether we get such 'case congregation' effects already for other countries, especially a bulge after the first claim being filed against a particular state. Compare generally, in a domestic litigation context, Galanter (1990: 371).

11 Asia now has a particularly high level of intra-regional trade – especially in intermediate goods – combined with extensive investment, underpinning strong pan-Asian production networks for goods (and now services). See Drysdale (2009). Some investors may therefore be particularly cautious about jeopardizing entire production networks by breaking off relations with one state as a result of persisting with an ISA claim. Nonetheless, such networks also tend to be flexible, shifting around multiple countries to exploit evolving comparative advantages. Anyway, this theory – diminishing Asian ISA claim potential – would not apply to large-scale investment in natural resource developments, for example.

12 See, for example, *European Media Ventures S.A.* v. *Czech Republic*, UNCITRAL, Award on Jurisdiction, 15 May 2007 (not public but discussed in *European Media Ventures S.A.* v. *Czech Republic*, Judgment, 5 December 2007, English High Court, (2007) EWHC 2851 (Comm); and *Renta 4 S.V.S.A et al.* v. *Russian Federation*, SCC No. 24/2007, Award on Preliminary Objections, 20 March 2009. But see a relatively recent contrary approach to the interpretation of such 'amount of compensation' arbitration clauses in *Austrian Airlines* v. *Slovak Republic*, UNCITRAL, Final Award, 20 October 2009. See generally Weeramantry and Wilson (2010).

13 In this analysis, 'settlement' includes cases that were discontinued. However, it has been said that the settlement rate for 'Asian IT Arbitrations' (i.e. Asian investment treaty arbitrations generally, which would include both ICSID and non-ICSID arbitrations) is approximately 50 per cent, compared to 30 per cent for all investment treaty arbitrations. See Savage (2011). Further research should review all publicly available filings and results, not just ICSID cases. Given the difficulties of obtaining information particularly in non-ICSID cases, however, qualitative studies should also be undertaken – surveying as many practitioners as possible as to whether or how settlements happen. We suspect that a variety of non-cultural factors play significant roles for Asian and non-Asian parties, such as commercial attitudes held by the investor (for example, the fear of being cut off from one of the world's fastest growing economic regions), the actual impact or nature of the impugned conduct or the transaction type.

14 *Saluka Investments B.V.* v. *The Czech Republic*, UNCITRAL Rules Arbitration, Partial Award, 17 March 2006. This different outcome to the Sakhalin investment dispute reinforces the hypothesis that behaviour as to claims may depend on the industry or transaction type. Another significant difference may be that the Dutch subsidiary was one step further removed from the Japanese 'grandparent' company. It has long been known that Japanese companies adjust their dispute resolution behaviour considerably in light of local circumstances, even at one remove, that is, with local subsidiaries: see, for example, Matsumura (1987).

15 Nottage and Miles (2009: Part 4.1). Elite management theory in the domestic context emphasizes how elites prefer to divert cases from courts to ADR processes, thus predicting more use of arbitration. But if ADR is also quite transparent (as, increasingly, in ISA), and/or cases are not easily brought before courts anyway (as was the case before ISA expanded especially via BITs), then such a prediction will not hold and less use of arbitration would be expected.

16 In addition to those cases involving Tomen and especially Nomura, the large Sakura Bank helped finance the Dieng and Patuha projects in Indonesia, which also resulted in claims (Wells and Ahmed 2007). However, a bank's involvement in ISA proceedings may well be minimal – even less than that of a minority investor – as the bank would typically hold security interests and thus be able to obtain repayments and claim priority even if the investment project went bankrupt.

17 However, that case is complicated because the Malaysian government retains a large shareholding in Telekom Malaysia, so the case is quite similar to an inter-state dispute. More problematic for elite management theory would be a case of a more wholly private investor, yet known to have good connections with its home country, nonetheless initiating a direct ISA claim. Even then, however, the nature of the respondent state might also need to be considered.

18 For example, in *SGS Société Générale de Surveillance S.A.* v. *Islamic Republic of Pakistan* (ICSID Case No. ARB/01/13) and *SGS Société Générale de Surveillance S.A.* v. *Republic of the Philippines* (ICSID Case No. ARB/02/6) the respondents were represented, respectively, by the international law firms Freshfields Bruckhaus Deringer and Allen & Overy. Similarly, in *Gruslin* v. *Malaysia* (ICSID Case No. ARB/99/3) the respondent was represented by Sir Elihu Lauterpacht QC and Freshfields Bruckhaus Deringer, and in *Impregio S.p.A.* v. *Islamic Republic of Pakistan* (ICSID Case No. ARB/03/3) the respondent State party retained, along with a local law firm, the advice of several overseas barristers and international law firm Eversheds.

19 This may be a particularly strong factor in the Asian region, given its very high degree of internal trade in intermediate goods, underpinned by burgeoning cross-border investment. In other words, adverse publicity among existing or potential foreign investors may jeopardize the state's involvement in pan-Asian production networks, to a much greater extent than in other regions.

20 Indeed, it might be argued that respondent states would generally prefer to appoint non-Asian arbitrators who are less likely to present an appearance of bias but with some – but not too obvious or strong – disposition towards host state interests. However, all other things being equal, one would expect Asian states to prefer an Asian arbitrator, as they are generally more likely to understand or be more sympathetic to how business and government are conducted in Asian countries, particularly when it comes to agreeing on a sole arbitrator or tribunal

chair. The (Catch-22) situation of few Asian arbitrators having been appointed to such roles, at least so far, therefore creates for Asian states a barrier to proceeding with a formal arbitration process.

21 Specifically, most appointments went the way of two individuals well-known also for their practice in ICA (Fali Nariman and Michael Hwang: four and five appointments, respectively, in completed ICSID cases), to a former judge of the WTO Appellate Body and the Supreme Court of the Philippines (Florentino Feliciano: seven appointments), and to a former Thai diplomat and professor of international law, Sompong Sucharitkul (seven ICSID case appointments; he was also was an arbitrator in: *Yaung Chi Oo Trading Pte Ltd* v. *Government of the Union of Myanmar*, ASEAN I.D. Case No. ARB/01/1, Final Award, 31 March 2003, 42 ILM 540). Based on ICSID data available at http://icsid.worldbank.org (accessed 9 September 2010).

22 It would also be useful to have a ISA-specific report along the lines of the 'Techniques for Controlling Time and Costs in Arbitration' report from the ICC Commission of Arbitration, ICC Publication No. 843 (2007), available at www.iccwbo.org/uploadedFiles/TimeCost_E.pdf (accessed 14 December 2010).

23 See the case notes on major ISA cases developed by a Study Group in Tokyo and published since October 2010 in the *JCA Jyanaru* (the Japanese-language periodical of the Japan Commercial Arbitration Association).

24 Compare ICSID, *The ICSID Caseload – Statistics* (Issue 2011-2: 22), showing that filings against respondents from Asia and the Pacific comprised 16 per cent of the caseload in the 2011 financial year; *The ICSID Caseload – Statistics* (Issue 2010-2: 21) shows 7 per cent for the 2010 financial year.

Bibliography

Abe, M. and Nottage, L. (2006) 'Japanese Law' in Smits, J. (ed.) *Encyclopedia of Comparative Law*, Cheltenham: Edward Elgar, p. 357.

Alexandrov, S., Moroney, M. and Porges, A. (2009) 'FDI Growth in Asia: The Potential for Treaty-Based Investment Protection', *Global Arbitration Review*, The Asia Pacific Arbitration Review 2009. Available at: www.globalarbitrationreview.com (accessed 13 December 2010).

Astor, H. and Chinkin, C. (2002) *Dispute Resolution in Australia*, Sydney: Butterworths.

Drysdale, P. (2009) 'Australia and Japan: A New Economic Partnership in Asia', consultancy report for Austrade. Available at: www.austrade.gov.au/ArticleDocuments/1358/Australia-and-Japan-Partnership-Report.pdf.aspx (accessed 13 December 2010).

Epstein, C. (2008) *The Power of Words in International Relations: Birth of an Antiwhaling Discourse*, Cambridge, Mass.; London: MIT.

Fink, C. and Molinuevo, M. (2008) 'East Asian Free Trade Agreements in Services: Key Architectural Elements', *Journal of International Economic Law*, 11(2): 263.

Franck, S. (2005) 'The Legitimacy Crisis in Investment Treaty Arbitration: Privatizing Public Law through Inconsistent Decisions', *Fordham Law Review*, 73: 1521.

Franck, S. (2007) 'Empirically Evaluating Claims About Investment Treaty Arbitration', *North Carolina Law Review*, 2007: 861.

Franck, S. (2009) 'Development and Outcomes of Investment Treaty Arbitration', *Harvard International Law Journal*, 50(2): 435.

Galanter, M. (1990) 'Case Congregations and Their Careers', *Law and Society Review*, 24.

Gallagher, N. and Shan, W. (2009) *Chinese Investment Treaties: Policies and Practice*, Oxford: Oxford University Press.

Ginsburg, T. and Hoetker, G. (2009) 'The Effects of Liberalization on Litigation: Notes Toward a Theory in the Context of Japan', *Washington University Global Studies Law Review*, 8: 303.

Greenberg, S., Kee, C. and Weeramantry, J.R. (2010) *International Commercial Arbitration: An Asia-Pacific Perspective*, Melbourne: Cambridge University Press.

Hamamoto, S. and Nottage, L. (2010) 'Foreign Investment In and Out of Japan: Economic Backdrop, Domestic Law, and International Treaty-based Investor-State Dispute Resolution'. Available at: http://ssrn.com/abstract=1724999 (accessed 14 December 2010).

Hamamoto, S. and Nottage, L. (2011) 'Japan' in Brown C. and Krishan D. (eds) *Commentaries on Selected Model Investment Treaties*, Oxford University Press, forthcoming.

Hatakeyama, K. (2008) 'Japan's Aid to Vietnam: Becoming an Intellectual Leader?', *Japanese Studies*, 28(3): 345.

IMF (2010) *World Economic Outlook Database*, available at: www.imf.org/external/ns/cs.aspx?id=28 (accessed 18 July 2011).

Kingsbury, B. and Schill, S. (2009) 'Investor-State Arbitration as Governance: Fair and Equitable Treatment, Proportionality and Global Administrative Law' in Berg, A.J.V.D. (ed.) *50 Years of the New York Convention*, Alphen aan den Rijn: Kluwer Law International, p. 5.

Kinnear, M. (2010) 'Damages in Investment Treaty Arbitration' in Yannaca-Small, K. (ed.) *Arbitration Under International Investment Agreements: A Guide to the Key Issues*, New York; Oxford: Oxford University Press, p. 551.

Kitagawa, T. and Nottage, L. (2007) 'Globalization of Japanese Corporations and the Development of Corporate Legal Departments: Problems and Prospects' in Alford, W. (ed.) *Raising the Bar*, Cambridge, Mass.: Harvard East Asian Legal Studies Program (distributed by Harvard University Press), p. 201.

Kozuka, S. and Nottage, L. (2009) 'The Myth of the Careful Consumer: Law, Culture, Economics and Politics in the Rise and Fall of Unsecured Lending in Japan' in Niemi-Kiesilainen, J., Ramsay, I. and Whitford, W. (eds) *Consumer Credit, Debt and Bankruptcy: Comparative and International Perspectives*, Oxford: Hart, p. 199.

Matsumura, Y. (1987) 'Attitudes of Canadian Firms Towards the Law and the Legal System in Canada', *University of British Columbia Law Review*, 21: 209.

Murayama, M. (2007) 'Experiences of Problems and Disputing Behaviour in Japan', *Meiji Law Journal*, 2007: 141.

Murray, P. (2008) 'Europe and Asia: Two Regions in Flux?' in Murray, P. (ed.) *Europe and Asia Regions in Flux*, Basingstoke; New York: Palgrave Macmillan, p. 1.

Nakamura, T. (2009) 'The Application of the New York Convention to Investment Arbitration', *Mealey's International Arbitration Report*, 24(3): 25.

Nisbett, R.E. (2003) *The Geography of Thought: How Asians and Westerners Think Differently – and Why*, London: Nicholas Brealey.

Nottage, L. (1997) 'Economic Dislocation in New Zealand and Japan: A Preliminary Empirical Study', *Victoria University of Wellington Law Review*, 26: 59.

Nottage, L. (2004) 'Japan's New Arbitration Law: Domestication Reinforcing Inter-nationalisation?', *International Arbitration Law Review*, 7: 54.

Nottage, L. (2007) 'Changing Contract Lenses: Unexpected Supervening Events in English, New Zealand, U.S., Japanese, and International Sales Law and Practice', *Indiana Journal of Global Legal Studies*, 14(2): 385.

Nottage, L. (2009) 'The Cultural (Re)Turn in Japanese Law Studies', *Victoria University of Wellington Law Review*, 39(4): 755.

Nottage, L. (2011) 'The Rise and Possible Fall of Investor–State Arbitration in Asia: A Skeptic's View of Australia's "Gillard Government Trade Policy Statement"', *Transnational Dispute Management*, forthcoming. Available at: http://ssrn.com/abstract=1860505 (accessed 1 August 2011).

Nottage, L. and Garnett, R. (2010a) 'Introduction' in Nottage, L. and Garnett, R. (eds) *International Arbitration in Australia*, Sydney: Federation Press, p. 1.

Nottage, L. and Garnett, R. (eds) (2010b) *International Arbitration in Australia*, Sydney: Federation Press.

Nottage, L. and Miles, K. (2009) '"Back to the Future" for Investor–State Arbitrations: Revising Rules in Australia and Japan for Public Interests', *Journal of International Arbitration*, 26(1): 25.

Nottage, L. and Wollschlaeger, C. (1996) 'What Do Courts Do?', *New Zealand Law Journal*, 1996: 369.

Pekkanen, S.M. (2008) *Japan's Aggressive Legalism: Law and Foreign Trade Politics Beyond the WTO*, Stanford, Calif.: Stanford University Press.

PriceWaterhouseCoopers – Queen Mary College (2008) International Arbitration: Corporate Attitudes and Practices 2008. Online. Available at: www.pwc.co.uk/eng/publications/international_arbitration_2008.html (accessed 13 December 2010).

Pryles, M. and Moser, M. (2007) 'Introduction' in Pryles, M. and Moser, M. (eds) *The Asian Leading Arbitrators' Guide to International Arbitration*, New York: Juris, p. 1.

Puchniak, D. (2010) 'Japan's Love for Derivative Actions: Revisiting Irrationality as a Rational Explanation for Shareholder Litigation', *Paper Presented at the 2nd Annual NUS–Sydney Symposium, Singapore*, 15–16 July 2010.

Reed, L. (2009) 'Scorecard of Investment Treaty Cases against Argentina Since 2001', KluwerArbitrationBlog, 2 March. Available at: http://kluwerarbitrationblog.com/blog/2009/03/02/scorecard-of-investment-treaty-cases-against-argentina-since-2001.

Savage, J. (2011) 'Investment Treaty Disputes in Asia', Paper Presented at CCH International Arbitration, ADR and Mediation Summit, Hong Kong, 13 May.

Sinclair, A., Fisher, L. and Macrory, S. (2009) 'ICSID Arbitration: How Long Does it Take?', *Global Arbitration Review*, 4(5): 18.

Tanase, T. (2010) *Law and the Community: A Critical Assessment of American Liberalism and Japanese Modernity*, Cheltenham: Edward Elgar.

Taylor, V. (2005) 'New Markets, New Commodity: Japanese Legal Technical Assistance', *Wisconsin International Law Journal*, 23: 251.

Taylor, V. and Pryles, M. (2006) 'The Cultures of Dispute Resolution in Asia' in Pryles, M. (ed.) *Dispute resolution in Asia*, 3rd edn, The Hague: Kluwer Law International, p. 1.

UNCTAD (2009) 'Investment Policy Developments in G-20 Countries'. Online. Available HTTP: http://unctad.org/en/docs/webdiaeia20099_en.pdf (accessed 13 December 2010).

UNCTAD (2010a) 'Latest Developments in Investor-State Dispute Settlement: IAA Issues Note No. 1 (2010)'. Online. Available HTTP: www.unctad.org/en/docs//webdiaeia20103_en.pdf (accessed 13 December 2010).

UNCTAD (2010b) 'World Investment Report 2010'. Online. Available HTTP: www.unctad.org/templates/WebFlyer.asp?intItemID=5539&lang=1 (accessed 13 December 2010).

van Aaken, A. and Kurtz, J. (2009) 'The Global Financial Crisis: Will State Emergency Measures Trigger International Investment Disputes?', *Columbia FDI Perspectives*, 3. Available at: http://vcc.columbia.edu/pubs (accessed 13 December 2010).

Wälde, T.W. (2010) 'Procedural Challenges in Investment Arbitration under the Shadow of the Dual Role of the State: Assymetries and Tribunals' Duty to Ensure, Pro-actively, the Equality of Arms', *Arbitration International*, 26(1): 3.

Weeramantry, J.R. and Wilson, C. (2011) 'The Scope of "Amount of Compensation" Dispute Resolution Clauses in Investment Treaties', in Brown, C. and Miles, K. (eds), *Evolution in Investment Treaty Law and Arbitration*, Cambridge: Cambridge University Press, forthcoming.

Wells, L.T. and Ahmad, R. (2007) *Making Foreign Investment Safe: Property Rights and National Sovereignty*, New York; Oxford: Oxford University Press.

Yoshimatsu, H. (2000) *Internationalization, Corporate Preferences and Commercial Policy in Japan*, Houndmills; New York: Macmillan Press; St. Martin's Press.

3 A passive player in international investment law

Typically Japanese?

Shotaro Hamamoto

3.1 Introduction

Considering the size of the Japanese economy and the place that it occupies in world trade, one may wonder why there has been no case brought to arbitration by a Japanese investor or against the Japanese Government on the basis of a bilateral investment treaty (BIT). This chapter[1] succinctly reviews the passive attitude of the Japanese government as well as of Japanese investors towards international investment law and tries to determine its causes. It examines the small number of Japan's BITs and Free Trade Agreement (FTA) investment chapters (Section 3.2), the extreme flexibility in the drafting of their core provisions (Section 3.3), and the absence of cases brought to arbitration by Japanese investors (Section 3.4).

3.2 Few investment treaties

3.2.1 *Japan as a late starter: economic and political explanations*

Japan is the world's third largest economic power in terms of gross domestic product (GDP), after the United States and China, with a very high per capita GDP despite its economic slowdown particularly over the 1990s. In our context, however, it should be noted that the Japanese economy has traditionally depended more on trade than on investment.

Figure 3.1 is revealing. The balance on income – that is, income from investment – has steadily grown and in 2001 it became almost equal to the balance on trade. And it was in 2002 that Japan began to take more initiative in concluding BITs and other investment treaties. While Japan had already concluded several BITs before 2002, it had mainly been the counterparties which had proposed to Japan that such treaties should be concluded. It was also in 2002 that Japan began to conclude 'new generation' BITs and 'economic partnership agreements' (EPAs) – the term favoured by Japan instead of FTAs, as explained in Section 3.3 – including chapters on investment. Both types of treaties were equipped with far more detailed and

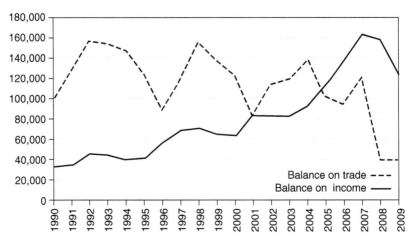

Figure 3.1 Japan's goods and income balances (¥100 million) (source: Ministry of Finance, 'Japan's Balance of Payments', www.mof.go.jp/bpoffice/ebpnet. htm (accessed 17 February 2011)).

pro-investor rules on investment than the pre-2002 'old generation' BITs. (All of Japan's BITs and EPAs are listed in Appendix A.)

In 2006, when the economic shift had become clear, the annual *White Paper on International Economy and Trade* edited by the Ministry of Economy, Industry and Trade (METI) devoted to investment issues a section entitled: 'Towards the Realization of Japan as an 'Investment Powerhouse' (METI 2006: Chapter 3, Section 4). The 2006 White Paper stated that Japan was expected to become a 'mature creditor nation' through a decrease in the balance of goods and services and an increase in income surplus. This tendency is encouraging, according to the White Paper, because the shift to becoming a 'mature creditor nation' implies supplementing Japan's labour force, expected to decrease due to a declining birth rate and ageing population.

This chapter is not an economic study and does not try to examine the accuracy of METI's analysis. What is significant here is that it is only in 2006 that the Japanese government officially placed, for the first time, particular emphasis upon the importance of outward foreign investment for the Japanese economy. However, there are quite a few states, such as Germany, which have concluded a large number of BITs although the surplus in their balance on trade is far more important than that in its balance on income. There must therefore be some reason other than economic ones that explain Japan's late start.

There is also a political explanation, related to Japan's approach towards multilateralism. Japan traditionally relied heavily on multilateral frameworks as regards international economic regulation, for example the General Agreement on Tariffs and Trade (GATT), the World Trade Organization

(WTO), the Organisation for Economic Co-operation and Development (OECD), the World Bank and the International Monetary Fund (IMF). Japan's critical if not hostile attitude towards bilateral and regional frameworks appears, for instance, in its submission on Article XXIV of GATT presented in the Uruguay Round in 1989.[2] It is thus no wonder that Japan was actively involved in negotiations for the OECD's stillborn Multilateral Agreement on Investment (MAI); following the MAI's failure, it also pursued the possibility of concluding a multilateral agreement on investment in the WTO Doha Round.[3] Yet the proposal for a multilateral treaty on investment encountered fierce opposition from the outset, particularly from developing countries, and was formally abandoned in 2004.[4]

The collapse of MAI negotiations and the stalemate in the Doha Round lead the Japanese government to finally abandon, at least partially, its belief in multilateralism. In 2002, Japan's Ministry of Foreign Affairs (MOFA) issued *Japan's Basic Strategy for the WTO New Round Negotiations*, stating that Japan would promote FTAs while emphasizing that they were not alternatives to the WTO (MOFA 2002). *Japan's FTA Strategy*,[5] also issued by MOFA in the same year, explained that the new policy was motivated by the US and the EU, which were already pursuing policies oriented toward the creation of large-scale regional trade frameworks. Japan's intensive negotiations on 'new generation' BITs and EPAs since 2002 should therefore be placed in this broader geopolitical context.

3.2.2 Flying too high? Pre-establishment protections and EPAs

When Japan launched its new policy in 2002, circumstances surrounding BITs and particularly the investor-state dispute settlement (ISDS) system were already changing noticeably. Non-governmental organizations (NGOs) had already set up a campaign against ISDS, which they considered to be anti-democratic (see, for example, Public Citizen 2001). A flood of arbitral cases brought against Argentina following its financial crisis in 2001–02 caused many developing states to realize the magnitude of potential 'dangers' that might be entailed by their BITs. The evolution of arbitral jurisprudence also led some developed states to review their policies regarding BITs, as exemplified by the famous *Notes of Interpretation* issued by the NAFTA Free Trade Commission (2001). It is in this difficult environment that Japan embarked on its new policy of concluding ambitious investment agreements.

One aspects of this program is that Japan's 'new generation' BITs and EPAs provide investors with national treatment (NT) and most-favoured-nation (MFN) treatment not only after the investment has been established, but also with respect to its establishment. As an UNCTAD report indicates:

[t]he use of this approach was traditionally limited to BITs concluded by the United States and, after the mid-1990s when the NAFTA had

entered into force, to agreements concluded by Canada. However, during the last 10 years other nations, such as Japan, have adopted this method.

(UNCTAD 2006: 23, footnotes omitted)

Although some officials involved in BIT/EPA negotiations often manifest anxiety that this approach risks uselessly complicating negotiations (for example, Miyake 2008: 147), all the BITs/EPAs concluded since 2002 but for the Papua New Guinea BIT (2011) follow this line.

A second shift is that, since 2002, Japan has concluded ten EPAs. An EPA is a 'bilateral or multilateral agreement among States to eliminate customs and other domestic import/export regulations, to harmonize economic systems and to facilitate the free movement of persons, goods and capital within a region', while a FTA is 'an agreement, within a region or between States, to reduce or to eliminate tariffs on goods and other barriers to trade in services' (METI 2005). Although the Japanese government laid great emphasis upon the difference between EPAs and FTAs, this distinction is rather obscure – all the more because the notion of FTA is elastic.[6] Although it is highly likely that EPAs will have a far more significant impact in economic relations between the parties than BITs, it is clear that negotiation of EPAs is far more time-consuming.[7] The preference for EPAs over BITs over the past decade, in particular, may be another reason for the limited number of investment agreements concluded by Japan.

3.3 Treaty flexibility in substance

Japan does not have, or at least has not made public, any 'Model BIT' along the lines of many other major economies. Indeed, it is not so easy to reconstitute a sort of de facto Model BIT through an analysis of the existing BITs/ EPAs. One of the particularities of Japan's set of BITs/EPAs is its variety, often subtle but certainly not negligible.

3.3.1 *Adapting to the evolution of arbitral jurisprudence: pro-host and pro-investor shifts*

Given the rapid evolution of arbitral jurisprudence concerning investment law, states have to be flexible enough in their BIT policies to catch up or cope with such an evolution. There are at least three areas in which Japan has altered its policy apparently in consideration of developments in arbitral jurisprudence.

Consider first changes in treaty drafting that tend to favour the host State. The case of *Maffezini* v. *Spain*[8] had raised the complicated problem of the applicability of the MFN provision to the dispute settlement provisions in investment treaties, which still remains unsettled. The Japan-Peru BIT (2008, Article 4(2)) and the Japan-Switzerland EPA (2009, Article 88(2)), the two recent agreements on investment, explicitly exclude clauses on dispute settlement from the scope of MFN treatment, apparently taking into account the much-debated evolution of arbitral jurisprudence on this question (see also the carefully worded Article 86 of the Japan–India EPA (2011)).

In addition, early NAFTA cases[9] aroused apprehensions among developed as well as developing states about the possible restrictions laid down by investment treaties upon the host state's police powers (*lois de police*). In the face of such an evolution of arbitral jurisprudence relating to expropriation, all of Japan's 'new generation' treaties include what may be called 'public interest exceptions'. Thus, the Japan–Uzbekistan BIT (2008) stipulates, in its Article 17(1), that:

> Nothing in this Agreement [...] shall be construed to prevent a Contracting Party from adopting or enforcing measures:
>
> a   Necessary to protect human, animal or plant life or health;
> b   Necessary to protect public morals or to maintain public order
>   Note: The public order exception may be invoked only where a genuine and sufficiently serious threat is posed to one of the fundamental interests of society.

Second, consider some pro-investor shifts in treaty drafting. Many of the BITs/EPAs concluded since 2007 include an obligations observance clause ('umbrella clause').[10] This policy shift was apparently motivated by the evolution of arbitral jurisprudence since *SGS* v. *Philippines*.[11] Although it is difficult to say that the jurisprudence is now well settled,[12] it is clear that the presence of an obligations observance clause in BITs/EPAs will function, if it ever does, only in favour of investors.

The same observation applies to the fair and equitable treatment (FET) clause. While a clear majority of the 'old generation' BITs do not contain a FET clause,[13] all 'new generation' BITs/EPAs do. It is clear that the Japanese government underestimated the practical importance of this abstract clause in the beginning, but that the evolution of arbitral jurisprudence made it aware of its potential.

3.3.2 Incoherent policy or considerate attitude? Examples and causes

However, there are quite a few differences in the BIT/EPA texts that cannot be explained solely by an awareness of evolving arbitral jurisprudence. Two examples are the FET obligation and ISDS procedures.

All the 'new generation' BITs/EPAs and two of the 'old generation' BITs contain an FET clause. This, however, takes on a wide variety of forms. The first group consists of BITs/EPAs that simply stipulate that FET shall be accorded without any particular note or comment.[14] The second consists of BITs/EPAs that provide the FET clause with notes. This second group is divided into three sub-groups. First, the Japan–Brunei EPA (2007) notes that FET:

> do[es] not require treatment in addition to or beyond that which is required by customary international law minimum standard of treatment of aliens.

> (Article 59)

Second, in addition to the first qualification, some BITs/EPAs note that:

> a determination that there has been a breach of another provision of this Agreement, or of a separate international agreement, does not establish that there has been a breach of this Article.[15]

Third, two EPAs add further qualifications. The Japan–Chile EPA (2007) provides that:

> [e]ach Party shall accord to investors of the other Party, non-discriminatory treatment with regard to access to the courts of justice and administrative tribunals and agencies of the former Party in pursuit and in defense of rights of such investors.

> (Article 75, Note 3)

The Japan–Peru BIT (2008) stipulates that:

> '[f]air and equitable treatment' includes the obligation of the Contracting Party not to deny justice in criminal, civil, or administrative adjudicatory proceedings in accordance with the principle of due process of law. Each Contracting Party shall accord to investors of the other Contracting Party, non-discriminatory treatment with regard to access to the courts of justice and administrative tribunals and agencies of the former Contracting Party in pursuit and in defence of rights of such investors.

> (Article 5(2) Note)

A second major example of Japan's flexible approach to treaty drafting comes from ISDS. Almost all Japan's BITs/EPAs, old or new, are equipped with an ISDS procedure. The sole exception is the 2006 Japan–Philippines EPA (2006). Its Article 107(1) provides that:

> The Parties shall enter into negotiations after the date of entry into force of this Agreement to establish a mechanism for the settlement of an investment dispute between a Party and an investor of the other Party.

What lies behind this phenomenon? The above-mentioned variety in FET provisions found in Japan's BITs/EPAs reveals the Japanese government's extreme flexibility – if not unprincipled or compromise-prone attitude. Among 19 BITs/EPAs including an FET clause, 11 have a simple FET clause, while eight provide an FET clause with a note explicitly declaring that the FET does not require treatment in addition to or beyond that which is required by customary international law minimum standard of treatment of aliens.

It is difficult to explain why Japan is so flexible in this matter. One possible explanation is of course that Japan has no clear policy with regard to FET and therefore simply accepts the proposition advanced by the counterparty in the process of the negotiation. This explanation cannot be completely excluded but is not really credible because the importance of the FET clause is today too evident to be ignored, even for a government that has been involved in no investor-state arbitration cases.

Supposing instead that the Japanese policy on the FET clause is coherent, the Japanese government must consider that the FET is no more or no less protective of investors than the 'customary international law minimum standard of treatment of aliens'. This in turn means either that the customary international law standard is as high as the FET standard[16] or that the FET standard is as low as the customary international law standard.[17] Given the generally pro-investor attitude of the Japanese policy, it seems that the first speculation is accurate, although it is impossible to demonstrate it by reference to documentary evidence.

As for the absence of ISDS provisions in the Japan–Philippines EPA, it is reported that the Philippines insisted that the EPA should omit ISDS procedures[18] and that Japan finally accepted the Philippines' position – considering that it would be better to conclude an EPA without ISDS than not to have an EPA at all. The negotiations envisaged under Article 107(1) of this FTA have not started yet, according to MOFA's website (see also Hamamoto and Nottage 2010: 26, n. 65).

3.4 Hesitance in litigation

3.4.1 *No treaty arbitration*

All Japanese BITs/EPAs, except for the EPA with the Philippines – and the EPA with ASEAN (2008), which lacks an investment chapter altogether – provide for an ISDS procedure. Yet no Japanese investor has ever instituted arbitral proceedings on the basis of a BIT/EPA. Suzuki, the automobile company, is reported to have brought a claim to the Court of Arbitration of the International Chamber of Commerce against India in 1997,[19] but it was on the basis of an investment contract and the proceedings were terminated by agreement between the parties in 1998 (Takezawa 1998). Saluka[20] may be considered as a Japanese company in an economic sense, but it was legally a

Dutch corporation established by an English company – itself 100 per cent owned, admittedly, by a Japanese holding company (Nomura). It is also noteworthy that no arbitration proceedings have ever been instituted against Japan under Japan's BITs/EPAs.

3.4.2 *Possible explanations*

The absence of cases brought *against Japan* by foreign investors may be ascribed to the scarcity of foreign investment in Japan (see Appendix B; Hamamoto and Nottage 2010), as well as the generally satisfactory governance standards in Japan. As for the absence of arbitral cases brought *by Japanese investors*, several reasons have been suggested.[21]

It is interesting that the cultural thesis[22] is advanced even today by Shuji Yanase, an experienced practising lawyer and expert in international trade law, who considers that:

> Disputes in relation to foreign direct investment by Japanese companies have been avoided or resolved by such companies' own efforts, rather than through the reliance on dispute resolution clauses in BITs with Japan. Such efforts are the natural outcome of the business mentality of Japanese companies which reflects the conventional and very traditional tendency in Japanese culture which respects the amicable settlement of conflicts.
>
> (Yanase 2003: 441)

This cultural thesis does not seem to correspond to reality.[23] Nippon Keidanren, the Japan Business Foundation, composed of major Japanese business corporations, has repeatedly issued policy proposals strongly urging the Japanese government to conclude more BITs/EPAs equipped with an ISDS procedure (Nippon Keidanren 2008). In 2002 it even proposed a Model BIT – albeit in summary form – including an ISDS procedure.[24] To that extent, therefore, the Japanese business community has clearly been in favour of dispute settlement by arbitration.

Why no cases, then? Judging from my very limited personal experience, it is because Japanese companies, while they understand the utility of arbitration in general terms, are not sure about the cost-effectiveness of arbitration in given cases. Japanese companies are said – though this observation is based on no quantitative empirical evidence – to stick and stay, and not to easily leave a country where they have made investments.[25] If they wish to continue to operate in a state, they will consider dispute settlement by arbitration not to be economically justified, as it is highly likely that litigation with governmental authorities will destroy a cordial relationship with the government and possibly also with the local people.[26]

One clear example is the problems relating to the so-called 'Sakhalin II project', an oil and gas development project offshore from Sakhalin Island

(Russia) in the Sea of Okhotsk. In September 2006, the Russian government rescinded its approval for the project, then executed by Sakhalin Energy Investment Company (SEIC), held by Royal Dutch Shell (55 per cent), a Dutch subsidiary company of Mitsui & Co. (25 per cent) and another Dutch subsidiary company of Mitsubishi Corporation (20 per cent).[27] The Russian government alleged that its order was handed down due to inadequate environmental safeguards taken by SEIC, but it is reported that environmental concerns were only part of the whole story.[28] Negotiations between the Russian government and foreign developers ended in December 2006 with an agreement according to which Gazprom, the Russian energy monopoly, would acquire 50 per cent plus one share of SEIC for US$7.45 billion – 'a price that analysts said was below market'.[29] Neither Mitsui nor Mitsubishi dared institute arbitration, although the Japan–Russia BIT is equipped with a full-fledged ISDS procedure (Article 11).[30] Although this is a matter of pure speculation, it would not seem entirely wrong to say that if either of the Japanese companies had launched arbitration proceedings, the claimant party would have been totally excluded from the project by the Russian government. Interestingly, it is reported that SEIC is economically quite successful in 2010, four years after the affair (Shiryaevskaya 2010).

3.5 Conclusion

According to MOFA (see Appendix A), Japan is currently negotiating (or has agreed to enter into negotiations of) EPAs with Australia and the Gulf Cooperation Council; and BITs with Saudi Arabia, Kuwait, Colombia, Kazakhstan, Qatar, Algeria and Ukraine (MOFA 2011; 2010). In addition, negotiations for a trilateral investment agreement are underway with the ROK and China (MOFA 2010). This geographical distribution corresponds quite closely to that of Japanese investments abroad (see Appendix C).

While the number of BITs/EPAs is likely to continue to grow slowly but steadily, it is not certain that the number of arbitral cases will grow accordingly, though it seems to be only a matter of time before the first case is brought by a Japanese investor (or against the Japanese government) on the basis of a BIT/EPA.

Appendix A

Japan's BITs and EPAs

BITs

Party	Signature	Entry into force
Egypt	28 Jan. 1977	14 Jan. 1978
Sri Lanka	1 Mar. 1982	7 Aug. 1982
China	27 Aug. 1988	14 May 1989
Turkey	12 Feb. 1992	18 June 1997
Hong Kong	15 May 1997	18 June 1997
Pakistan	10 Mar. 1998	29 May 2002
Bangladesh	10 Nov. 1998	25 Aug. 1999
Russia	13 Nov. 1998	27 May 2000
Mongolia	15 Feb. 2001	24 Mar. 2002
Korea (ROK)*	22 Mar. 2002	1 Jan. 2003
Vietnam*	14 Nov. 2003	19 Dec. 2004
Cambodia*	14 June 2007	31 July 2008
Laos*	16 Jan. 2008	3 Aug. 2008
Uzbekistan*	15 Aug. 2008	24 Sept. 2009
Peru*	22 Nov. 2008	10 Dec. 2009
PNG	1 Aug. 2011	not yet in force
Saudi Arabia	agreement in principle reached on 2 May 2008	
Kuwait	agreement in principle reached on 26 November 2010	
Colombia	agreement in principle reached on 17 December 2010	
China/ROK	under negotiation	
Kazakhstan	under negotiation	
Angola	under negotiation	
Qatar	preparing for negotiations	
Algeria	preparing for negotiations	
Ukraine	negotiations being considered (some steps taken)	
Nigeria	negotiations being considered (some steps taken)	

EPAs

Party	Signature	Entry into force
Singapore*	13 Jan. 2002	30 Nov. 2002
Mexico*	17 Sept. 2004	1 April 2005
Malaysia*	13 Dec. 2005	13 July 2006
Philippines*	9 Sept. 2006	11 Dec. 2008
Chile*	27 Mar. 2007	3 Sept. 2007
Thailand*	3 April 2007	1 Nov. 2007
Brunei*	18 June 2007	31 July 2008
Indonesia*	20 Aug. 2007	1 July 2008
Switzerland*	19 Feb. 2009	1 Sept. 2009
India*	16 Feb. 2011	1 Aug. 2011
Australia	under negotiation	
GCC	under negotiation	
ASEAN	preparing for negotiations regarding the addition of an investment chapter	

Note
* 'New generation' treaty.

Appendix B

Japan's inward FDI (stock) (US$ million)

	End of 1997	*End of 2002*	*End of 2009*
Asia	3309	3705	17,336
North America	14,372	38,389	76,184
Central and South America	175	2408	20,990
Oceania	109	540	1095
Western Europe	9018	33,350	83,883
Eastern Europe and Russia	15	46	63
Middle East	84	46	51
Africa	2	1	342
World	27,084	78,490	199,991

Appendix C

Japan's outward FDI (stock) (US$ million)

	End of 1997	*End of 2002*	*End of 2009*
Asia	77,258	58,421	175,645
North America	107,060	140,982	240,246
Central and South America	14,519	18,167	99,056
Oceania	13,268	11,852	36,175
Western Europe	55,632	72,404	174,939
Eastern Europe and Russia	1180	732	4112
Middle East	1246	893	4453
Africa	671	1232	5734
World	271,967	305,585	740,364

Notes

1 For an overview of the Japanese legal framework regarding foreign investment and Japan's BITs/EPAs, see Hamamoto (2011). For a closer analysis of Japan's domestic law and commentaries on Japan's BITs/EPAs, see Hamamoto and Nottage (2010), focusing on dispute settlement provisions; Hamamoto and Nottage (2011), adding more analysis of substantive provisions.
2 'Today, the regional arrangements have covered a significant proportion of world trade. In other words, a large part of world trade today is not being transacted upon the principle of most-favoured-nation treatment.' Submission by Japan, 'Article XXIV', 22 December 1989, MTN.GNG/NG7/W/66, p. 1.
3 Communication from Japan, 'Consideration of the Necessity of Multilateral Investment Rules from Diversified Viewpoints', 11 April 2003, WT/WGTI/W/158.
4 Decision Adopted by the General Council, 1 August 2004, WT/L/579.

5 For the English summary, see www.mofa.go.jp/policy/economy/fta/strategy0210. html (accessed 17 February 2011). For the full text in Japanese, see www.mofa. go.jp/mofaj/gaiko/fta/policy.html (accessed 17 February 2011).

6 The Japanese Government often uses the terms EPAs and FTAs interchangeably. See *Diplomatic Bluebook 2008*, English version, Chapter 3(3)(b), available at www. mofa.go.jp/policy/other/bluebook/2008/html/index.html (accessed 17 February 2011).

7 It is often the case that Japan first concludes a BIT and later an EPA that incorporates the already-concluded BIT as an integral part. See Appendix A for EPAs with Vietnam (2008) and Peru (2010).

8 *Maffezini y España*, CIADI Caso No. ARB/97/7, Decisión del Tribunal sobre excepciones a la jurisdicción, 25 de enero de 2000, available at http://icsid. worldbank.org/ (accessed 17 February 2011).

9 See, for example, *Ethyl* v. *Canada*, Award on Jurisdiction, 24 June 1998, available at www.international.gc.ca/ (accessed 17 February 2011).

10 Japan–Cambodia BIT (2007, Article 4(2)), Japan–Laos BIT (2008, Article 5(2)), Japan–Uzbekistan BIT (2008, Article 3(3)) and Japan–Switzerland EPA (2009, Article 86(3)). Two of the 'old generation' BITs also include the clause: Japan–Hong Kong BIT (1997, Article 2(3)), Japan–Russia BIT (1998, Article 3(3)).

11 *SGS* v. *Philippines*, ARB/02/6, Decision on Objections to Jurisdiction, 29 January 2004. http://icsid.worldbank.org/ (accessed 17 February 2011).

12 See particularly *El Paso Energy* v. *Argentina*, ICSID Case no. ARB/03/15, Decision on Jurisdiction, 27 April 2006, available at http://icsid.worldbank.org/ (accessed 17 February 2011).

13 BITs with Egypt (1977), Sri Lanka (1982), China (1988), Turkey (1992), Bangladesh (1998), Pakistan (1988) and Mongolia (2001). Those concluded with Hong Kong (1997) and Russia (1998) include the FET clause.

14 Japan–Hong Kong BIT (1997, Article 2(3)), Japan–Russia BIT (1998, Article 3(3)), Japan–ROK BIT (2002, Article 10(1)), Japan–Singapore EPA (2002, Article 77(1)), Japan–Vietnam BIT (2003, Article 9(1)), Japan–Malaysia EPA (2005, Article 77), Japan–Cambodia BIT (2007, Article 4(1)), Japan–Indonesia EPA (2007, Article 61), Japan–Uzbekistan BIT (2008, Article 3(1)) and Japan–Switzerland EPA (2009, Article 86(1)) and Japan–PNG BIT (2011, Article 4(1)).

15 With slight differences in the terms used: see the Japan–Mexico EPA (2004, Article 60 Note), Japan–Philippines EPA (2006, Article 91 Note), Japan–Thailand EPA (2007, Article 95 Note), Japan–Laos BIT (2008, Article 5(1) Note 1) and Japan–India EPA (2011, Article 87(1) Note).

16 '[W]hat customary international law projects is not a static photograph of the minimum standard of treatment of aliens as it stood in 1927 when the Award in the *Neer* case was rendered. For both customary international law and the minimum standard of treatment of aliens it incorporates are constantly in a process of development.' *ADF* v. *Canada*, ICSID Case No. ARB(AF)/00/1, Award, 9 January 2003, *ICSID Rev.-FILJ*, 2003, Vol. 18, p. 195, p. 277, para. 179.

17 '[A]lthough situations may be more varied and complicated today than in the 1920s, the level of scrutiny is the same. The fundamentals of the Neer standard thus still apply today'. *Glamis Gold* v. *USA*, Award, 8 June 2009, para. 616. The tribunal however added that 'it is entirely possible, however that, as an international community, we may be shocked by State actions now that did not offend us previously' (para. 616).

18 According to the list of BITs available on the UNCTAD website, available at www.unctad.org/ (accessed 17 February 2011), the Philippines has not concluded a BIT since 2002. The last two of its BITs, concluded respectively with Austria (2002) and Portugal (2002), did include a fully-fledged ISDS provision (Article 9 of both BITs). When Japan was negotiating the EPA with the Philippines, the latter was respondent in *SGS* v. *Philippines* (ICSID Case No. ARB/02/06) and *Fraport* v. *Philippines* (ICSID Case No. ARB/03/25).
19 'Suzuki Approaches International Court', *The Statesman* (India), 19 September 1997.
20 *Saluka* v. *Czech Republic*, Partial Award, 17 March 2006, http://ita.law.uvic.ca/ (accessed 17 February 2011).
21 Luke Nottage and Romesh Weeramantry (Chapter 2 in this volume) present five major perspectives or paradigms that try to explain the paucity of arbitral cases brought by Asian investors: culturalist thesis, institutional barriers thesis, elite management thesis, economic rationalist thesis and hybrid theories.
22 'On n'aime pas le droit au Japon' ('The Japanese don't like law'): this is the famous thesis advanced by Noda (1966: 175).
23 To be fair to Yanase, his paper (2003) was presented in 2002, when the Japanese government had only just started concluding 'new generation' BITs/EPAs.
24 'Annex 2: Model Bilateral Investment Treaty', in Nippon Keidanren (2002).
25 This may be considered as one of the cultural particularities of Japanese companies, but if they choose to stay, it is because they consider that it is *economically* more reasonable to stay than to leave with an arbitral award.
26 'If payment of damages can be avoided, business relationships are more likely to survive.' See Wells and Ahmed (2007: 291).
27 'Russia Cancels Approval for Sakhalin II Energy Project', *Jiji Press Ticker Service*, 19 September 2006.
28 See Mathiason (2008). '[A]nalysts say the green attack on Sakhalin-2 might be designed to ease entry for Gazprom into Russia's first LNG project. Sakhalin-2 is the only foreign PSA under way in Russia without a domestic partner and government policy is to increase the state's role in the oil and gas industry while limiting foreign influence in the strategic sector.' *Petroleum Economist*, October 2006.
29 Kramer (2006). Today, Shell has 27.5 per cent minus 1 share, Mitsui 12.5 per cent and Mitsubishi 10 per cent.
30 Article 9 of the Dutch–Russia BIT provides an ISDS procedure limited to the amount of compensation in case of expropriations. For a discussion of the controversial and evolving arbitral jurisprudence on what the state parties intended by such a provision, see Eliasson, Chapter 5 in this volume.

Bibliography

Hamamoto, S. (2011) 'Japan', in Shan, W. (ed.) *The Legal Protection of Foreign Investment*, Oxford: Hart Publishing, forthcoming.
Hamamoto, S. and Nottage, L.R. (2010) 'Foreign Investment in and out of Japan: Economic Backdrop, Domestic Law, and International Treaty-Based Investor-State Dispute Resolution', Sydney Law School Legal Studies Research Paper, No. 10/145. Available at: http://ssrn.com/abstract=1724999 (accessed 17 February 2011).

Hamamoto, S. and Nottage, L. (2011) 'Japan', in Brown, C. and Krishan, D. (eds) *Commentaries on Selected Model Investment Treaties*, Oxford: Oxford University Press, forthcoming.

Kramer, A.E. (2006) 'Gas Investors Bow to Pressure on Recovering Expenses', *The New York Times*, 29 December 2006, p. 7.

Mathiason, N. 'Shell Comes under Fire for Role in Sakhalin Audit', *Observer*, 31 August 2008, www.guardian.co.uk/business/2008/aug/31/royaldutchshell.sakhalin (accessed 17 February 2011).

METI (2005) 'Japan's Policy on FTAs/EPAs'. Available at: www.meti.go.jp/english/information/downloadfiles/FTAprogress200503.pdf (accessed 17 February 2011).

METI (2006) 'White Paper on International Economy and Trade 2006'. Available at: www.meti.go.jp/english/report/data/gWT2006fe.html (accessed 17 February 2011).

Miyake, Y. (2008) *'Toshi Kyotei/Keizai Renkei Kyotei ni okeru Wagakuni no Torikumi* [Dispute Settlement under International Investment Agreements: Practice of Japan and a Way Forward]', *Kokusai Keizai Ho Gakkai Nenpo [International Economic Law* (Japan Association of International Economic Law)], 17: 135.

MOFA (2002) 'Japan's Basic Strategy for the WTO New Round Negotiations'. Available at: www.mofa.go.jp/policy/economy/wto/round0210.html (accessed 17 February 2011).

MOFA (2010) *'Toshi* [Investment]'. Available at: www.mofa.go.jp/mofaj/gaiko/investment/index.html (accessed 18 February 2011).

MOFA (2011) *'Keizai Renkei Kyotei* (EPA)/*Jiyu Boeki Kyotei* (FTA)'. Available at: www.mofa.go.jp/mofaj/gaiko/fta/index.html (accessed 18 February 2011).

NAFTA Free Trade Commission (2001), *Notes of Interpretation of Certain Chapter 11 Provisions*, 31 July 2001. Available at: www.international.gc.ca/trade-agreements-accords-commerciaux/disp-diff/NAFTA-Interpr.aspx?lang=en (accessed 17 February 2011).

Nippon Keidanren (2002), 'Toward [sic] the Creation of International Investment Rules and Improvement of the Japanese Investment Environment', 16 July 2002. Available at: www.keidanren.or.jp/english/policy/2002/042/index.html (accessed 17 February 2011).

Nippon Keidanren (2008) 'On the Improvement of Japan's Global Investment Environment: Toward the Creation of a Legal Framework for Japanese Foreign Investment', 15 April 2008. Available at: www.keidanren.or.jp/english/policy/2008/017/proposal.html (accessed 17 February 2011).

Noda, Y. (1966) *Introduction au droit japonais {Introduction to Japanese Law}*, Paris: Dalloz.

Public Citizen (2001) 'NAFTA Chapter 1 Investor-to-State Cases: Bankrupting Democracy'. Available at: www.citizen.org/trade/ (accessed 17 February 2011).

Shiryaevskaya, A. (2010) 'Gazprom, Shell Sakhalin Gas Venture Reports Unexpected Profit on Shipments', Bloomberg, 16 July 2010, www.bloomberg.com/news/2010–07–16/gazprom-shell-sakhalin-gas-venture-reports-unexpected-profit-on-shipments.html (accessed 18 February 2011).

Takezawa, M. (1998) 'Indian Government End Dispute Partners in Auto Venture Reach Compromise, Agree to Replace Top Executive', *The Nikkei Weekly*, 15 June 1998, p. 18.

UNCTAD (2006) 'Bilateral Investment Treaties 1995–2006: Trends in Investment Rulemaking', UN Doc. UNCTAD/ITE/IIT/2006/5.

Wells, L.T. and Ahmed, R. (2007) *Making Foreign Investment Safe: Property Rights and National Sovereignty*, Oxford: Oxford University Press.

Yanase, S. (2003) 'Bilateral Investment Treaties of Japan and Resolution of Disputes with Respect to Foreign Direct Investment', in Albert Jan van den Berg (ed.), *International Commercial Arbitration: Important Contemporary Issues*, The Hague: Kluwer, p. 426.

4 The quandary for Chinese regulators

Controlling the flow of investment into and out of China

Vivienne Bath

4.1 Introduction

This chapter examines the relationship between Chinese regulation of inbound and outbound investment and China's approach at the international level, through bilateral and multilateral treaties, to commitments on investment policy and practice. China, while encouraging inbound investment, maintains tight control over regulation of investment in China. At the same time, Chinese policy is also to encourage Chinese companies, both private and state-owned, to invest overseas. The Chinese government's approach to the issues of inbound and outbound investment highlights the difficulty of striking a balance between the right of states to control the flow of investment into their own territory with the expectation that their investors will be able to make investments in other states and enjoy appropriate rights and protections in connection with those investments.

China is a major recipient of foreign direct investment, reaching a new record of US$105.74 billion in 2010. Major investors in China in 2009 were Hong Kong, Taiwan, Japan, Singapore, the United States, South Korea, the United Kingdom, Germany, Macau and Canada (Fletcher 2011; US–China Business Council 2011). In addition, China is the source of substantial amounts of outbound investment, with Chinese private companies, state-owned enterprises, government agencies and the Chinese sovereign wealth fund, the China Investment Corporation, all actively engaging in investment with the encouragement and support of the Chinese government (OECD 2008: 65–142). According to Chinese statistics, total FDI in 2009 was US$56.5 billion, of which non-financial foreign direct investment was US$47.8 billion (Davies, K. 2010; Xinhuanet 2010b). Much of this investment has been directed to the Asia-Pacific region, with Australia (total stocks of US$5.9 billion at the end of 2009) and Singapore (US$4.9 billion) the largest recipients after Hong Kong (US$164.5 billion). It should be noted that the immense amount of funds which flow in and out of Hong Kong and other tax havens such as the Cayman Islands and the British Virgin Islands make it difficult accurately to access the sources and locations of Chinese outbound FDI (Gugler and Boie 2008: 3–4; Davies, K. 2010).

4.2 Investment policy

China regulates inbound investment closely, balancing controls over investment structure, investment capital and the areas in which investments may be made with encouragement of particular types of investment, largely by means of incentives provided through taxation policy, reductions in land grant prices and other benefits (see, for example, State Council 2010a). China has also developed a comprehensive system for the regulation and monitoring of investment outside China by Chinese companies, again balancing approval requirements for individual investments with policies encouraging and supporting particular types of investment.

At the international level, China is a party to the 1965 Convention on the Settlement of Investment Disputes between States and Nationals of Other States (ICSID Convention),[1] the New York Convention on the Recognition and Enforcement of International Arbitral Awards,[2] and the World Trade Organization treaties[3] and has entered into an extensive network of more than 120 bilateral investment treaties, of which 98 are in force, including 19 with countries in the Asia-Pacific region (UNCTAD 2010), double tax treaties, and, increasingly, free trade agreements (FTAs; see Gallagher and Shan 2009, Appendix I for a comprehensive list of China's agreements up to July 2008). China has signed seven FTAs and two closer economic partnerships (with Hong Kong and Macau) (MOFCOM 2011). China signed an Economic Cooperation Framework Agreement with Taiwan on 29 June 2010 (Harris 2010).

4.3 Domestic policy relating to inbound investment

Chinese policy towards investment has been amended and modified on numerous occasions since 1979, when the Sino-Foreign Equity Joint Venture Law of the People's Republic of China (Equity Joint Venture Law) was passed. The basic objectives and fundamental parameters have, however, been very consistent. On the one hand, the Chinese government has encouraged foreign companies to invest in China, bringing with them capital and advanced technology and creating jobs, export revenue (foreign exchange) and government revenue. Incentives (many of which are no longer available) were provided at the government level in the form of tax holidays and reductions, a special tax rate for foreign companies and foreign investment entities and customs exemptions for the import of equipment to be used for productive activities. For example, Article 7 of the original version of the Equity Joint Venture Law granted income tax holidays and reductions to newly established joint ventures, and Article 71 of the Implementing Regulations for the Sino-Foreign Equity Joint Venture Law of the People's Republic of China (State Council 1987) (Equity JV Regulations) provided for a waiver of customs duties on certain imported equipment. The Law of the People's Republic of China on Foreign-Capital Enterprises (1986 Article 3) originally required that wholly foreign owned enterprises focus on exports or introduce advanced technology to the Chinese economy.

On the other hand, in order to achieve these objectives, the Chinese government has consistently maintained a policy of exercising a high level of regulatory control over both the admission of foreign investment and the scope of operations of foreign investors within China. This is achieved in the following four ways.

First, the establishment of any form of foreign investment enterprise or any form of entity in China, whether established by a green fields investment, or through the acquisition of an existing business, is subject to government control through an approval (or verification and approval) process which requires that the project and its documentation be reviewed by the relevant level of government and that the documentation be subject to review and approval (or ratification) by the relevant government department. This process involves a variety of government agencies, particularly the National Development and Reform Commission (NDRC) and the Ministry of Commerce (MOFCOM) or one of its provincial or municipal level entities. The basic framework is outlined in documents issued by the State Council (2004) and the NDRC (2004b). Approval requirements for acquisitions of domestic enterprises by foreign investors are spelt out in Chapter 3 of the Provisions on Foreign Investors' Merger with and Acquisition of Domestic Enterprises (M&A Provisions) issued in 2006 (amended 2009). The level of government at which a foreign investment project must be reviewed and approved is determined based on its status – encouraged, permitted or restricted (State Council 2002), its size, its type and the manner of establishment – joint venture, wholly owned enterprise, investment company, joint stock company and so on (see, for example, MOFCOM 2004). The level of government and the particular agency which is authorized to approve an investment project varies depending on the method by which the company is established or acquired. The intensity of the review, the time taken and, on occasion, the amendments or modifications requested, will vary depending on the location, the approval level, the size of the project and the sensitivity of the investment. In addition, regulations issued in 2011 require a heightened level of review for investments which may have an effect on national security, the national economy, basic order or research and development in areas of key technology which may have an impact on national security (General Office of the State Council 2011 Article 2). In contrast, the establishment of private Chinese companies is not subject to an approval requirement except in specified areas – registration can be effected by satisfaction of the capital and other criteria set out in the Company Law and its associated regulations (Company Law 1993 Article 7; State Council 2005 Article 21).

Second, the admission of investments and in some cases the amount of equity in a Chinese company which can be held by a foreign investor is regulated by government policies, which may be adjusted from time to time.

The primary source of control over the industries in which foreigners may invest is the 'Catalogue of Industries for Guiding Foreign Investment', the most recent version of which was issued in 2007 (NDRC and MOFCOM 2007), which lists activities in which foreign investment is encouraged, restricted or prohibited. Investment in other activities should be permitted (State Council 2002). In addition, the Catalogue may specify restrictions on the form of entity (for example, investment in coal-bed mining may be made only through a joint venture) or limit the percentage interest which a foreigner may own in a particular sector, such as securities companies.[4] Chinese policies have changed from time to time to open up new sectors to foreign investment or to impose additional restrictions (OECD 2008: 33–8 on changes made by the 2007 version of the Catalogue). Notably, as part of the preliminary negotiations between China and other countries prior to China's accession to the World Trade Organization in 2001 (mainly with the United States and the European Union), China opened up a considerable number of sectors to foreign investment and removed its traditional requirements for export orientation or technology import for many industries (Ji 2003; Qin 2007). Other policies, such as the automotive policy (NDRC 2004a) or the tyre industry policy (Ministry of Industry and Information 2010) may set out national criteria relating to the ownership and growth of particular industry sectors, which will have an impact on foreign investment in those sectors. In addition, the so-called 'key pillars' or 'national champions' policy essentially reserves sectors of the economy for state control and promotes a small number of state-owned enterprises to dominate those sectors (State Council 2006b).

Third, the Chinese government maintains a system of structural separation for foreign investment (Bath 2007). Thus, foreigners can invest directly only in 'foreign investment enterprises', which are distinct types of corporate (or other) entities, generally created pursuant to separate laws or regulations, and subject to their own approval and establishment procedures. Although these are generally limited liability companies (with some exceptions), which are incorporated in China and are therefore considered to be Chinese domestic entities, and come under the general corporate structure and governance rules set out in the Company Law (Article 218), they are established through a separate process and the business licence for the entity (the equivalent of a certificate of incorporation) clearly indicates that it is a form of foreign investment enterprise (State Administration for Industry and Commerce *et al.* 2006 Article 6). Because such an entity is a foreign investment enterprise, its stated 'scope of business' (which controls and restricts the businesses and activities in which it can engage) is reviewed and approved before the business licence is issued and penalties may be applied if the company engages in business beyond its scope of authorization (Article 27). The scope of business of Chinese-owned companies, in contrast, is not subject to approval unless laws or regulations specifically so provide (State Council 2005 Article 17).

Fourth, foreign investment companies are subject to a regulatory regime specifically directed at foreign investments and applicable throughout their operating life. Amendment or modification of a foreign investment project, transfer of an equity interest in a foreign investment enterprise or termination or liquidation of a foreign investment company requires the approval of the relevant government agency (Equity JV Implementing Regulations Articles 20, 21, 90) and is handled as part of a separate legal regime (recently confirmed in Supreme People's Court 2010). Although, from 2008, Chinese companies and foreign companies have been subject to the same system of income taxation (Enterprise Income Tax Law of the People's Republic of China 2007), foreign investment companies are subject to an annual compliance review by a number of Chinese government departments (Ministry of Foreign Economic Relations and Trade 1988; MOFCOM *et al.* 2010).

Chinese domestic foreign investment law does not distinguish between investments from different countries, with the exception of benefits granted to 'compatriots' from the Special Administrative Regions of Hong Kong and Macau through such instruments as the Mainland–Hong Kong Closer Economic Partnership (Development Bureau, Government of Hong Kong 2010) and the Economic Cooperation Framework Agreement between Taiwan and China (*China Post* 2010).

A final point relates to dispute resolution, another area in which matters which are considered to be 'foreign-related' are dealt as a separate legal regime. Although generally tolerant of the right of participants in business transactions involving Chinese and foreign parties to choose the law governing their contractual relations, China has been consistent in its view that the law governing joint ventures and natural resources projects in China must be Chinese (Contract Law of the People's Republic of China 1999 Article 126; confirmed in the Law of the People's Republic of China on Application of Laws to Foreign-Related Civil Relations 2010 Article 4). In 2007, the People's Supreme Court expanded these categories to include performance in China of shareholders agreements, acquisition agreements and so on relating to Chinese companies and assets (Supreme People's Court 2007 Article 8).[5] If a dispute involving a Chinese–foreign joint venture or exploitation of Chinese natural resources is taken to court, Chinese courts have exclusive jurisdiction over the dispute (Civil Procedure Law of the People's Republic of China 1987 Article 244). Failure to comply with this provision would obviously have an effect on enforcement of any judgment in China. China does, however, allow use of international arbitration inside and outside China as an appropriate method of dispute resolution for investment disputes (Civil Procedure Law Article 255) and, as noted above, China is a party to the New York Convention, which deals with enforcement of international awards. Consequently, international arbitration is often adopted as a method of resolving dispute involving investment in China and the number of disputes involving Chinese parties which are submitted to arbitration have shown a constant increase. For example, in 1985, 37 disputes were submitted to the China International Economic and Trade Arbitration Commission (CIETAC) and nine were submitted to the Hong Kong International Arbitration Centre (HKIAC). In 2009, 1482 disputes were submitted to CIETAC (of which 559 were considered to be 'foreign-related') and 429 were submitted to HKIAC, of which 309 were international (HKIAC 2011; CIETAC 2011).

4.4 Regulation of outbound investment

China has also become a major source of outbound investment. In addition to negotiating the international treaties which may be relevant to Chinese companies investing overseas, Chinese regulators play an active role in controlling and monitoring overseas investment activities.

The system for outbound investment by Chinese companies is of more recent origin to the system for inbound investment, but shares a number of features with the system for regulating foreign investment in China. In particular, it extends a number of the regulatory features of the internal investment system to Chinese companies planning to invest outside China. The NDRC, which plays a significant role in relation to major foreign and domestic investments within China and investment in certain significant industries, plays a prominent role in verifying and approving outbound investments by Chinese companies. MOFCOM is responsible for the approval process for outbound investment. Other government departments involved include the State-owned Assets Supervision and Administration Commission of the State Council (SASAC), which is responsible for overall supervision of centrally administered state owned enterprises, and the State Administration of Foreign Exchange (SAFE). The involvement of SAFE in the process is required in order to facilitate the remittance of foreign exchange capital and to expedite foreign currency loans and other payments.

The current form of the outbound investment system dates from 2004. Changes made to the system in 2009 resulted in MOFCOM delegating more power in relation to investment projects to lower level authorities (MOFCOM 2009b). The NDRC, however, initially responded to the massive increase in investment overseas by Chinese companies over this period by tightening regulatory controls (Gugler and Boie 2008) and has only recently delegated power to lower levels of government (NDRC 2011).

Pursuant to the NDRC provisions (NDRC 2004c, 2011), projects involving investment by a Chinese investor of US$300 million or more in a natural resources project or of US$100 million or more in a non-resources project require verification and approval by the NDRC. Smaller projects may be verified and approved by provincial level authorities, although sensitive projects involving countries which do not have diplomatic relations with China or where there is a war, or investments in telecommunications, water resources, large-scale land development, media or other sensitive areas must be reported to the NDRC or the State Council for verification or approval after preliminary review (NDRC 2011 Article 2). Projects where a Chinese investor proposes to invest more than US$100 million must also go through a process of preliminary review before any substantive work, including signing legally effective agreements, submitting binding bid documents or applying to foreign governments for an approval, can be undertaken (NDRC 2009 Article 2; NDRC 2011 Article 6). In deciding whether to approve an investment, the NDRC will consider such matters as whether the project endangers national sovereignty or security, the public interest or breaches international law; the requirements of sustainable economic and social development and compliance with state requirements on such matters as promoting the export of domestic technology, products, equipment and labour and attracting foreign technology and whether the investment entity has the relevant investment strength for the investment. Enterprises must, however, make investment decisions and take risks on their own (NDRC 2011 Article 3).

The approval of central MOFCOM is required only for large or sensitive projects, such as investment in a country that has no diplomatic relations with China or establishing special purpose vehicles overseas (MOFCOM 2009a Article 6). MOFCOM focuses on international relations in determining whether to approve investments. It does not review feasibility (Article 9). Each enterprise also has ongoing reporting requirements to MOFCOM, and MOFCOM and SAFE conduct a joint inspection each year to check whether the required information has been properly reported, the overseas enterprise has complied with Chinese laws and regulations, and whether the enterprise is involved in any disputes relating to its compliance with local laws and regulations (MOFCOM and SAFE 2009).

This system of verification and review is supported by SAFE rules, which were amended in 2009 to strengthen the ability of enterprises to provide loans to overseas investment enterprises (SAFE 2009), and a system of funding and supporting loans from Chinese banks such as China Eximbank to investments overseas in encouraged areas and other incentives (OECD 2008: 90; Bosshard 2008: 3–4; Davies, M. 2010).

An interesting aspect of this comprehensive system is that, with the exception of projects for which loans can be obtained, this system deals with foreign exchange and funds which belong to the enterprises themselves. It applies to all enterprises established in China, not just state-owned enterprises, although state-owned enterprises are prominent participants in overseas investment (see Eliasson, Chapter 5 in this volume). Central state-owned enterprises are also subject to the overall system of supervision and regulation conducted by SASAC, including review of their overseas merger and acquisition activities (SASAC 2010).

This system of regulatory control does not deal with dispute resolution or governing law questions, which are left to the enterprises themselves to negotiate. Despite the system of inspections and reporting, the ongoing ability of Chinese regulators effectively to monitor and control the operations of

Chinese enterprises overseas is clearly questionable (Liou 2009; Gill and Reilly 2007). In addition, the interest of Chinese authorities in the monitoring process is limited in scope. In 2006, the State Council issued *The Opinion on Encouraging and Normalizing Our Enterprises' Investment Cooperation*, which contains nine fairly generic principles relating to outbound investment and the operations of Chinese companies operating abroad. The fifth principle emphasizes the importance of compliance with local laws and regulations, exercising social responsibility to protect local employees and awareness of environmental protection, while the ninth principle refers to the importance of maintaining China's good image and corporate reputation. In 2010, MOFCOM issued the *Guiding Opinion of the Ministry of Commerce on the Work Regarding the Nationwide Work in Overseas Investment and Cooperation in 2010*. The Opinion emphasizes the strengthening of external publicity and creating a good image through respecting local laws and religious practices and implementing social responsibilities.

4.5 China's approach to investment through BITs and FTAs

China is an active participant in the international investment treaty community. As noted above, as of 1 June 2010, it had signed over 120 BITs (UNCTAD 2010), and it continues actively to pursue negotiations for new bilateral investment treaties and free trade agreements. For example, after a 20-year gap, China and the United States have recommenced negotiations on a bilateral investment treaty (White House 2009; Cai 2009; Economist Intelligence Unit 2010). In the Asia-Pacific region, China has bilateral investment treaties with 20 states[6] (including two which are not in force), as well as its free FTAs and economic partnerships. An investment agreement was signed with ASEAN in 2009 (ASEAN–China Investment Agreement),[7] and China has been negotiating an FTA with Australia since 2005 (Department of Foreign Affairs and Trade 2011).

China's bilateral investment treaties are by no means uniform. They are based on the three different models which it has used between 1982 to the present as the basis for negotiation of its bilateral investment treaties (Gallagher and Shan 2009: 35–49; see also Appendices II, III and IV for English versions). The Australia–China BIT[8] is used in this chapter as an example of the first model; the investment provisions of the NZ–China FTA are used to show the approach taken by China in recent negotiations. Provisions of the ASEAN–China Investment Agreement are also referred to as an example of China's current international approach to investment. Due to considerations of space, this discussion focuses on a limited number of issues relating to China's approach to bilateral investment agreements – admission of investments and most-favoured-nation (MFN) and national treatment, and a brief note on dispute resolution (which is covered in more detail by Eliasson in Chapter 5).

As described above, China maintains a very prescriptive approach to the admission and establishment of investments in its territory.[9] The question then arises how this domestic regime relates to or is reflected in China's international commitments. China, along with many other countries, generally subscribes to what the United Nations Conference on Trade and Development (UNCTAD) describes as the 'investment control model', pursuant to which the state admitting investment maintains control over what investments it allows in its territory (UNCTAD 1999: 17–20; Pollan 2006: 138–55). This is consistent with China's domestic approach to investment and to the approach taken by many other countries, which are equally reluctant to give up the right to regulate the admission of investments (Salacuse 2010: 195–204). Thus the Australia–China BIT of 1988 deals with admission very simply by stating that '[E]ach Contracting Party ... shall, in accordance with its law and investment policies from time to time, admit investments' (Article II(1)). Potentially, however, the treatment granted to investors or investments from one state that is a party to a BIT can be improved by the grant by the host country of national treatment (that is, treatment which is no less favourable than that accorded to its own investors) or by MFN provisions pursuant to which investors or investments are to be accorded treatment no less favourable than that accorded to investors or investments of a third country.

The Australia–China BIT provides that each state will extend MFN treatment to 'investments and activities associated with investments in its own territory' (Article III(c)), but does not extend either national or MFN treatment to admission or establishment. The NZ–China FTA, which was signed 20 years after the Australia–China BIT, goes considerably further by according to investors of each party 'treatment no less favourable than that accorded, in like circumstances, to the investments and associated activities by the investors of any third country with respect to admission, expansion, management, conduct, operation, maintenance, use, enjoyment and disposal' (Article 139). The commitment in relation to establishment is heavily qualified, however. Footnote 9 to the FTA makes clear that elements of the definition of a Party relating to establishment apply only to Articles 139 and 142 (transfers of funds), and footnote 11 states that 'the reference to amounts necessary for establishing or expanding the investment only applies following the successful completion of the approval procedures for inward investment'. Admission of investments, or establishment, therefore, is subject to the laws and regulations, and approval requirements of each state. Article 138, which refers to national treatment, is limited to 'management, conduct, operations, maintenance, use, enjoyment or disposal' of investment and the responsibility of the host state is qualified by being limited to 'treatment no less favourable than that accorded, in like circumstances, to its own investors'.

A provision granting MFN treatment to the admission and establishment of investments is also included in the ASEAN–China Investment Agreement (Article 5(1)). Article 5(2), however, provides that if a Party subsequently agrees to accord more favourable treatment to investors of another Party or third country by virtue of a future agreement, it is not obliged to extend that treatment to the other Parties, although it should offer them an opportunity to seek to negotiate it. Article 4, which provides for national treatment for investors and investments, is restricted to 'management, conduct, operation, maintenance, use, sale, liquidation, or other forms of disposal of such investments' and is again qualified by the expression 'in like circumstances'. This is further limited by Article 6, which allows parties to retain or implement non-conforming measures. The substance of these provisions contrasts with the aim of the 2002 Framework Agreement, referred to in the Preamble to the ASEAN–China Investment Agreement 2009, which was 'to negotiate and conclude as expeditiously as possible an investment agreement in order to progressively liberalize the investment regime, strengthen co-operation in investment, facilitate investment'.[10] Overall, China's commitments in relation to the liberalization of its regime relating to the admission of investments are very limited. So long as China maintains its strict domestic restrictions in relation to foreign investment, the few concessions it has granted in its international treaties are unlikely to be particularly useful to investors.

China has also been reluctant to agree to the grant of national treatment, even for post-establishment operations and investments (Gallagher and Shan 2009: 167–73; see also Cai 2009: 469–74). As the provisions outlined above suggest, however, China's policy on national treatment has changed over time and its application in China's investment treaties is by no means uniform. China's reluctance on this point may be explained as due to the fact that China has not yet created a market economy and therefore is not in a position to grant national treatment to foreign investors (Gallagher and Shan 2009: 165–6). It is clear that the grant of national treatment at a pre-establishment level would be inconsistent with Chinese policies which aim to reserve certain areas of the economy for the state sector (State Council 2006b) and limit and control foreign investment in certain sectors through the Foreign Investment Industries Catalogue and other policies. As a practical matter, the grant of national treatment to foreign investors at the post-establishment level is also problematic if the Chinese government wishes to continue to implement the regulatory system which administers foreign-invested companies separately and in some ways more stringently, and to grant differential treatment to certain state-owned companies. For example, Article 7 of the Anti-Monopoly Law 2007 suggests that major state-owned companies with monopoly powers will be supervised by the government rather than regulated by the law, as all other companies are.

As noted above, however, China's position in its BITs is far from uniform on this question. For example, Gallagher and Shan (2009: 170) note that Article 5 of the 2007 Seychelles–China Bilateral Investment Treaty grants an unrestricted right of post-establishment national treatment with respect to investments and activities related to investments, which is therefore

presumably available to investors from all countries which have BITs including MFN clauses (see also Economist Intelligence Unit 2010: 14 and Salacuse 2010: 252). How such a clause would or could be applied in the
Chinese context has yet to be determined, although Gallagher and Shan
(2009: 170) question whether, in view of the possible implications of this
provision, the acceptance of such a clause by China was a prudent decision.
The national treatment clause in the NZ–China FTA, for example, which
was signed in 2008, is more qualified in nature.

4.6 Challenges arising from Chinese policies and regulation

It is, of course, an unanswered question whether and to what extent China's
BITs and FTAs are likely to be of use to foreign or Chinese investors. China's
initial approach to dispute resolution in the form of investor-state arbitration was very restricted. For example, the Australia–China BIT provides for
arbitration where the parties agree or 'where the dispute relates to the
amount of compensation payable' (Article XII(2)(b)). In the first arbitration
brought under a Chinese BIT, *Tza Yap Shum* v. *The Republic of Peru*,[11] the
investor was obliged to satisfy the tribunal that the terms of the China–Peru
BIT[12] (which is very similar to the Australia–China BIT) allowed the tribunal to consider not only the amount of compensation due for expropriation
but the question whether expropriation took place (Decision on Jurisdiction
and Competence; see Reinisch 2011: 13–17; Eliasson, Chapter 5 in this
volume). The NZ–China FTA, by contrast, represents China's most recent
position and allows for submission to ICSID arbitration or arbitration under
UNCITRAL rules (Article 153(1)) of 'any legal dispute arising under this
[Investment] Chapter' (Article 152), subject to certain requirements relating
to conciliation and administrative review. China's more relaxed approach to
dispute resolution has been hailed by commentators as providing additional
remedies to investors (Heymann 2008).

According to the website of the International Centre for Settlement of
Investment Disputes, there has been only one case brought against China: a
case brought by a Malaysian investor which was registered in May 2011 and
suspended by agreement on 22 July 2011 (*Ekran Berhad* v. *People's Republic of
China* ICSID Case No. ARB/11/15). There are a variety of possible explanations for this: the limited scope of the dispute resolution clauses in China's
earlier BITs; the availability of international arbitration as a method of
dispute resolution for investments in China; or the reluctance of foreign
businesses to alienate the Chinese government (Economist Intelligence Unit
2010). Similarly, Chinese investors have not so far availed themselves of the
right to bring an investor-state arbitration, with the exception of the *Tza
Wah Yip* case against Peru referred to above, which involves a Hong Kong
investor taking advantage of the Peru–China BIT and the recent case of *Heilongjiang International and Technical Cooperative Corp, Qinhuangdaoshi Qinlong*

International Industrial and Beijing Shougang Mining Investment v. *Republic of Mongolia*.[13]

Of China's top ten investors in 2009, excluding Hong Kong, Taiwan and Macau, the United States and Canada do not have bilateral investment treaties with China and the BITs with Japan, Singapore and the United Kingdom date from the mid-1980s (the earliest model). Similarly, China has major investments in a number of countries with which it does not have BITs (notably Canada, the United States, the Cayman Islands and the British Virgin Islands) and its BITs with Australia, Japan, Singapore and the United Kingdom – also countries in which Chinese companies have made substantial investments – all date from the 1980s. At a minimum this suggests that the existence of BITs may have only a peripheral relationship with Chinese inbound and outbound investment.

The more liberal approach being taken by China in relation to BITs, as exemplified in the NZ–China FTA, suggests however that China has become more sensitive to the possible advantages of BITs. Indeed, a number of writers have assumed that China's more relaxed policies, particularly in relation to dispute resolution, have been driven by the objective of improving the protection of China's outbound investment (Heymann 2008; Schill 2007). Item 3(1) of the 2010 **MOFCOM** *Guiding Opinions* provides that Chinese enterprises should utilize fully preferential policies and measures in existing bilateral FTAs. A recent study also suggests that there has been an increased understanding and utilization by Chinese companies of the benefits provided by FTAs (Zhang 2010). At the same time, China is becoming more forthright in commenting on the policies that other countries have adopted which may affect Chinese investments. The Chairman of the China Investment Corporation was recently quoted as urging the United States government to relax scrutiny of Chinese investments in the United States on the basis that Chinese companies should be treated in the same way as anyone else (Ng 2010).

China's approach internationally to investment is, however, closely related to and affected by domestic regulatory policies. Internally, China's investment system, relating to both inbound and outbound investment, presents a number of issues. The system is cumbersome, bureaucratic and time-consuming. It is expensive for inbound investors who are obliged to go through the approval process and time-consuming for outbound investors who must also go through various levels of approval in order to make investments abroad. From the administrative point of view, it presents a number of major issues. First, many of the changes which have been made to the system over time are essentially cosmetic. The Foreign Investment Industry Catalogue has been modified on a number of occasions in order to change the categories in which foreign investment is permitted. However, these changes do not invariably result in liberalization of investment categories or criteria or the treatment of foreign companies (OECD 2008: 35–8). For example, rules relating to the establishment of foreign representative offices were tightened in 2010 (State Council 2010b). Similarly, changes made to the approval process by, for example, allowing lower levels of government to approve projects (State Council 2010b; NDRC 2010) may have facilitated the process of approving investments, but do not change the basic require-ments.[14] Although the system pursuant to which all contracts for the import or export of technology required government approval was replaced in 2001 by a system in which only contracts involving restricted or prohibited types of technology were subjected to government control (State Council 2001), no such change has been made for foreign investment. Where registration of a Chinese-owned company has been made relatively straight-forward by the Company Law 1993 (particularly pursuant to the amendments made in 2005), foreign investors are still obliged to go through a different, more time-consuming and expensive process.

The same criticism can be made of the outbound investment system. Although MOFCOM made changes in 2009 to delegate approvals to lower level authorities (MOFCOM 2009a), it was not until 2011 that the NDRC also acted to delegate approval powers over smaller or less-sensitive projects to lower level government authorities (NDRC 2011). Sensitive projects must still be reviewed at the central government level. The effect of these rules means that it is necessary for the Chinese government to maintain a large bureaucracy, incorporating a number of different government departments (which do not necessarily cooperate with each other) to review, approve and monitor the activities of foreign investment companies and Chinese com-panies investing outside China. This raises issues of cost, expense, the pos-sibility of corruption (which the policy of abolishing and simplifying licensing and approval requirements in the Administrative Licensing Law 2003 was intended to reduce: Bath 2008) and the sheer difficulty of main-taining a functioning system as the amount of investment increases.

As a practical matter, it is not clear how much control can be or is exer-cised over Chinese entities with strong overseas structures and financial reserves held outside China. The substantial amount of outbound investment which goes to Hong Kong, for example, when combined with the amounts of inbound investment from similar jurisdictions, strongly suggests large amount of 'round robin' or circulating investments by Chinese firms and casts some doubt on the general efficiency of the regulatory system (Gugler and Boie 2008). The ever-increasing amount of investment overseas must also place considerable strains on the resources of the bureaucracy required to regulate it. In addition, the involvement of multiple parts of the Chinese bureaucracy in overseas operations – as investors, supporters and regulators – adds additional complexity to the practical implementation of the regulatory system for Chinese enterprises operating overseas (Gill and Reilly 2007).

Second, the system presents issues for both foreign investors and Chinese companies in terms of cost, expense and complexity. A system which requires the review of all incoming foreign investment projects, as well as annual reviews and supervision of changes to the project and its documents, involves considerable ongoing expense for investors. Chinese companies investing outside China must comply both with internal requirements and with the rules of the countries where they propose to invest. In the case of both inbound and outbound investment, the Chinese approval process is not transparent, and review of government decisions whether or not to approve a particular investment project is limited. Parties are required to submit a comprehensive list of documents when seeking approval, but there is no assurance that approval will be granted even if all documents are submitted in the appropriate form. The Equity JV Implementing Regulations, for example, provide that approval will not be granted to a project on grounds such as damage to Chinese sovereignty, breach of the law, environmental pollution, obvious unfairness or non-compliance with the needs of development of the national economy, but does not provide that approval will be granted otherwise (Article 4). The lack of transparency in the approval system makes it difficult to rebut claims that the application of the system is subject to government influence and protectionism. A survey by the US–China Business Council (2010) suggests that US businesses are indeed concerned by a number of factors that relate to equality of treatment, including competition with state-owned enterprises and growing protectionism (see also Areddy 2011).

Third, this system has potential costs in terms of China's BITs and FTAs, which are based on principles of reciprocity. China's strict control system relating to inbound and outbound investment and the bifurcated foreign-domestic regulatory system may have advantages for China, but the restrictions in its international agreements which are necessary to maintain that system have obvious costs for China as it becomes a major source of outbound investment. The rights of its companies in relation to investment access under the BITs in particular are very limited. It is also strongly arguable that China's rigid system of control over outbound investment is counter-productive because it can easily be used as a justification for further restrictions being imposed by other countries which affect Chinese investors. This can arise first because of the role of state-owned corporations and entities in overseas investment, and second because China's adoption of an active role as regulator suggests that it should also accept responsibility for the conduct of Chinese corporations abroad. Despite its provisions and controls over overseas investment, as noted above, Chinese regulators have not been proactive in controlling the activities of its companies abroad in terms of social responsibility. The State Council opinion in 2006 and MOFCOM *Guiding Opinion* of 2010 referred to above deal with social responsibility and related issues in the vaguest of terms. In particular, there is no reference in these documents to the important issue of corruption by Chinese companies or their officers abroad. The point system presented in the 2009 Notice of the MOFCOM and the State Administration of Foreign Exchange on Joint Annual Inspection of Overseas Investments gives a clear indication of priorities. The system awards 60 points for regulatory compliance and registrations under Chinese rules, including a maximum of 20 points for not being in default under host country rules and regulations or not having any environmental or labour-management disputes and 40 points for compliance with foreign exchange controls. Interestingly, an amendment to the *Criminal Law of the People's Republic of China 1997*, effective 1 May 2011, which for the first time specifically criminalizes the payment of bribes to foreign officials or officers of international public organizations (Covington and Burling 2011), may indicate a change in this approach.

Some of these issues can be illustrated by reference to China's investment relationship with Australia. Although China and Australia are engaging in negotiations on an FTA, the Australia–China BIT (1988) does not deal with the admission of investment. Thus, although Australia, unlike China, appears to be becoming more flexible in making agreements with particular countries relating to the liberalization of investment admission, China is unable to benefit from them. As a result of priorities included in the Australia–US FTA,[15] for example, US investors may make larger investments in Australia than investors from other countries (other than in sensitive areas) before the requirement for notification and review by the Foreign Investment Review Board is triggered (see Treasurer 2011). Similarly, the AANZFTA provides the potential for concessions by Australia, New Zealand and the ASEAN countries in relation to the admission of investment.[16] Although the promise in this agreement has yet to be realized through the work of an Investment Committee which is entrusted with the duty of negotiating the list of reservations to the investment chapter and the scope of MFN treatment (Articles 16 and 17), it may mean that opportunities for the admission of new investments among these countries will ultimately be more advantageous than those afforded to China. The effect of Article 139 of the China–NZ FTA (2008),[17] which extends MFN treatment to admission of investments, may be that Chinese investors in New Zealand would be able to utilize any agreements by New Zealand to grant favoured treatment to investments from ASEAN, but the same does not apply under the Australia–China BIT or, indeed, under most of China's BITs.

Australia (and other countries with which China has BITs) is able to change its rules in relation to the admission and establishment of investments in order to restrict or control certain types of investments in a way which may be particularly disadvantageous to China and Chinese companies. An example of this is Australian policy on the interpretation of the Australian 'national interest' in connection with investment by foreign governments and 'their related entities', which includes companies in which 'foreign governments, their agencies or related entities have more than a 15 per cent interest' or which they otherwise control (Treasurer 2011). Such investments require notification and prior approval by the Australian government in all cases, in contrast to the relatively relaxed treatment accorded by the Australian government to many other investments. The reason for this is that 'the Australian Government also considers if the investment is commercial in nature or if the investor may be pursuing broader political or strategic objectives that may be contrary to Australia's national interest' (Treasurer 2011). The implementation of the current policy followed a thorough review by the Senate Economics References Committee (2009), which looked at investment by sovereign wealth funds and state-owned enterprises, with particular reference to the role of Chinese investment.

While it is true that the relationship between the Chinese government and state-owned enterprises is complex, the strong and consistent involvement of the Chinese government and bureaucracy in outbound investment is not likely to be helpful in persuading other countries that its state-owned enterprises are acting on a purely commercial basis (Gugler and Boie 2008 on the relationship between the state and state-owned enterprises; Liou 2009 on the commercial conflicts between state-owned enterprises). Chinese companies and officials are certainly aware of this issue. A spokesman for the MOFCOM, Yao Jian, recently expressed concern about US policies towards Chinese investment, particularly criticizing the lack of transparency relating to the 'so-called security reasons' (cited in Ding 2011). Similarly, an article in August 2010 describes the blocking of investment in the United States on national security grounds as a 'protectionist move that will only harm its own interests' (Xinhuanet 2010a). The decision by the State Council, however, to conduct security reviews of foreign acquisitions of Chinese companies which could have an impact on national security – broadly defined to include the influence of an acquisition on national security (including capacity), the stable operation of the national economy, the basic order of society and key technology related to national security – is unlikely to assist China's position in relation to the policies of other countries on Chinese outbound investment (State Council 2011 Article 2; see also UNCTAD 2009).

4.7 Conclusion

The extent of China's network of BITs and FTAs suggests active involvement by China in the international investment community and the law of international obligations in investment, corresponding to China's status as a major host country for investment and an important source of outgoing investment. It is argued, however, that China's rigid system of control over both inbound and outbound investment presents difficulties for China as it seeks more opportunities for investment outside its borders. Although the development of China's Model BITs shows some relaxation of policies in relation to investment, particularly in relation to its willingness to submit disputes to investor-state arbitration, the corresponding development of China's domestic regulatory policies indicates a determination to maintain an investment system which is complex, intensely regulated and arguably counterproductive in some respects. China's success as an investment destination and the rapid growth in its overseas investment notwithstanding, this

suggests that, despite some recent changes to its negotiating position in relation to BITs and FTAs, it is highly questionable whether China will utilize
BITs and FTAs to open up markets for its investors if this requires that
major changes be made within its own regulatory system.

Notes

1 575 UNTS 159. China's accession entered into force on 6 February 1993. See
   ICSID homepage, http://icsid.worldbank.org (accessed 5 January 2011).
2 330 UNTS 3. See UNCITRAL, 'Status' www.uncitral.org/uncitral/en/uncitral_
   texts/arbitration/NYConvention_status.html (accessed 5 January 2011).
3 Accession effective 11 December 2001; see Report of the Working Party on the
   Accession of China, WT/ACC/CHN/49/Add.1; WT/MIN(01)/3/Add.1, available
   at www.wto.org/english/thewto_e/acc_e/completeacc_e.htm (accessed 18 January 2011).
4 State Council (2002), Encouraged list, Item II(1); Restricted list, Item VII(3),
   limits foreign investment to 'underwriting of A Shares, underwriting and transaction of B Shares, H Shares, and government and corporate bonds, with the proportion of foreign investment of not exceeding one third'.
5 See, however, Article 2 of the Law of the PRC on Application of Laws to
   Foreign-Related Civil Relations, which provides that only a law can prescribe
   provisions relating to the mandatory application of a particular system of law.
6 Australia (1988), Bangladesh (1996), Brunei (2000 – not yet in force), Cambodia
   (1996), Indonesia (1994), Japan (1988), Korea, DPR (2005 – not yet in force),
   Republic of Korea (2007), Laos (1993), Malaysia (1988), Mongolia (1991), New
   Zealand (1988 – see the China–New Zealand Free Trade Agreement signed in
   2008), Pakistan (1989), Papua New Guinea (1991), Philippines (1992), Singapore (1985), Sri Lanka (1986), Thailand (1985), Vietnam (1992).
7 Agreement on Investment of the Framework Agreement on Comprehensive Economic Co-operation between the Association of Southeast Asian Nations and the
   People's Republic of China, signed at Bangkok, 15 August 2009, effective 1
   January 2010.
8 Agreement between the Government of Australia and the Government of the
   People's Republic of China on the Reciprocal Encouragement and Protection of
   Investments [1988] ATS 14.
9 The United Nations Conference on Trade and Development (UNCTAD 1999)
   distinguishes between admission (the right to enter or be present in a jurisdiction) and establishment (the right to set up a particular type of entity). For the
   purposes of this chapter, the terms are used primarily to refer to the question of
   admission of investments.
10 Framework Agreement on Comprehensive Economic Co-Operation Between
   ASEAN and the People's Republic of China, signed at Phnom Penh, 4 November 2002, available at www.asean.org/13196.htm (accessed 10 January 2011).
11 *Tza Yap Shum* v. *The Republic of Peru, Decision on Jurisdiction and Competence*,
   (ICSID Case No. ARB/07/6) – Decision on Jurisdiction and Competence, 19
   June 2009. ICSID Case No. ARB/07/6.
12 Agreement between the Government of Peru and the Government of the
   People's Republic of China Concerning the Encouragement and Reciprocal

Protection of Investments completed in Beijing on 9 June 1994, entered into force 1 February 1995, 1901 U.N.T.S. 257.

13 Investment Arbitration Reporter, Vol. 3, No. 10 (2010). Discussed in Eliasson, Chapter 5 in this volume.

14 An exception to this general rule was the issue of rules allowing for the establishment of foreign-invested partnerships without a prior approval from MOFCOM being obtained (State Council 2009).

15 Australia–US Free Trade Agreement [2005] ATS 1.

16 Agreement establishing the ASEAN–Australia–New Zealand Free Trade Area [2010] ATS 1.

17 Free Trade Agreement Between the Government of New Zealand and the Government of the People's Republic of China [2008] NZTS 19 (NZ–China FTA).

Bibliography

Areddy, J. (2011) 'US Firms Decry China's Heavy Hand: Alleged Bias by Regulators Is Likely to Be Contentious Issue Between Two Countries'. Available at: http://online.wsj.com/article/SB10001424052748704678004576089872396298 438.html#printMode (accessed 21 January 2011).

Bath, V. (2007) 'The Company Law and Foreign Investment Enterprises in the People's Republic of China: Parallel Systems of Chinese-Foreign Regulation', *UNSW Law Journal*, 30(3): 774.

Bath, V. (2008) 'Reducing the Role of Government: the Chinese Experiment', *Asian Journal of Comparative Law*, 3(1): Article 9.

Bosshard, P. (2008) 'China's Environmental Footprint in Africa. SAIC Working Papers in African Studies'. Available at www.sais-jhu.edu/bin/i/f/BosshardWorkingPaper.pdf (accessed 19 January 2011).

Cai, C. (2009) 'China–US BIT Negotiations and the Future of Investment Treaty Regime: A Grand Bilateral Bargain with Multilateral Implications', *Journal of International Economic Law*, 12(2): 457–506.

China Post (2010) 'ECFA Signed'. Available at: www.chinapost.com.tw/taiwan/china-taiwan-relations/2010/06/30/262692/p2/ECFA-signed.htm.

CIETAC (2011) 'CIETAC 2010 Work Report and 2011 plan'. Available at: http://cn.cietac.org/ (accessed 15 February 2011).

Covington and Burling (2011) 'China Amends Criminal law to Cover Foreign Bribery: Bribery of Non-PRC Government Officials Criminalized'. Available at www.cov.com/files/Publication (accessed 2 March 2011).

Davies, K. (2010) 'Outward FDI from China and its Policy Context', Vale Columbia Center on Sustainable International Development, Columbia FDI Profiles.

Davies, M. (2010) 'How China is Influencing Africa's Development', Background Paper for the Perspectives on Global Development 2010, OECD Development Centre.

Department of Foreign Affairs and Trade (2011) 'Australia–China Free Trade Agreement Negotiations' www.dfat.gov.au/fta/acfta/index.html (accessed 31 January 2011).

Development Bureau, Government of Hong Kong (2010) 'About Mainland–Hong Kong Closer Economic Partnership'. Available at: www.devb.gov.hk/en/construction_sector_matters/service_promotion/about_mainland_hong_kong_closer/index.html (accessed 19 January 2011).

Ding, Q. (2011) 'China's investment in US to surge', *China Daily*. Available at: www.asianewsnet.net/home/new.php?id=16856 (accessed 20 January 2011).

Economist Intelligence Unit (2010) 'Evaluating a potential US–China bilateral investment treaty: Background, context and implications', prepared for the US–China Economic and Security Review Commission. Available at: www.uscc.gov/researchpapers/2010/EIU_Report_on_US-China_BIT–FINAL_14_April_2010.pdf (accessed 19 January 2011).

Fletcher, O. 'Foreign Direct Investment in China Rises 17%', *Wall Street Journal*, 19 January 2011. Available at: http://online.wsj.com/article/SB10001424052748703396604576088903930134910.html (accessed 20 January 2011).

Gallagher, N. and Shan, W. (2009) *Chinese Investment Treaties: Policies and Practice*, Oxford: Oxford University Press.

Gill, B. and Reilly, J. (2007) 'The Tenuous Hold of China Inc. in Africa', *The Washington Quarterly* 30(3): 37–52.

Gugler, P. and Boie, B. (2008) 'The Chinese International Investments: Corporate and Government Strategies', *NCCR trade regulation*, Working Paper No. 2008/25. Available at: http://ssrn.com/abstract=1372013 (accessed 16 February 2011).

Harris, S. (2010) 'Taiwan and its new economic agreement with China', East Asia Forum, 9 July 2010. Available at: www.eastasiaforum.org/2010/07/09/taiwan-and-its-new-economic-agreement-with-china/ (accessed 14 February 2011).

Heymann, M.C.E. (2008) 'International Law and the Settlement of Investment Disputes Relating to China', *Journal of International Economic Law*, 11(3):–507–26.

HKIAC (2011) 'About the HKIAC: Statistics'. Available at: www.hkiac.org/show_content.php?article_id=9 (accessed 14 February 2011).

Ji, W. (2003) 'Legal Changes in China's Trade and Investment System to Enhance WTO Compliance: 2000–2002'. Available at: http://ssrn.com/abstract=985987 (accessed 10 August 2011).

Liou, C.S. (2009) 'Bureaucratic Politics and Overseas Investment by Chinese State-owned Oil Companies', *Asian Survey*, XLIV(4): 670–90.

Ng, E. (2010) 'State fund urges Washington to ease curbs', *South China Morning Post*, 21 January 2010.

OECD (2008) 'OECD Investment Policy Reviews: China 2008'. Available at: www.oecd.org/document/40/0,3343,en_2649_34893_41735656_1_1_1_34529562,00.html (accessed 16 February 2011).

Pollan, T. (2006) *Legal Framework for the Admission of FDI*, The Netherlands: Eleven International Publishing.

Qin, J.Y. (2007) 'The Impact of WTO Accession on China's Legal System: Trade, Investment and Beyond', *Wayne State University Law School Research Paper*, No. 07–15. Available at: http://ssrn.com/abstract=985321 (accessed 18 January 2011).

Reinisch, A. (2011) 'How Narrow are Narrow Dispute Resolution Clauses in Investment Treaties?', *Journal of International Dispute Settlement*, 1–60.

Salacuse, J.W. (2010) *The Law of Investment Treaties*, Oxford: Oxford University Press.

Schill, S.W. (2007) 'Tearing Down the Great Wall: The New Generation Investment Treaties of the People's Republic of China', *Cardozo Journal of International and Comparative Law*, 15: 73–118.

Senate Economics References Committee (2009) 'Foreign Investment by State-owned Entities'. Available at: www.aph.gov.au/Senate/committee/economics_ctte/firb_09/report/report.pdf (accessed 24 January 2011).

Treasurer (2011) 'Foreign Investment Policy'. Available at: www.firb.gov.au/content/_downloads/Australia's_Foreign_Investment_Policy_Jan_2011.pdf (accessed 24 January 2011).

United Nations Conference on Trade and Development (UNCTAD) (1999) 'Admission and Establishment', UNCTAD Series on Issues in International Investment Agreements, UNCTAD/ITE/IIT/10 (Vol. II).

UNCTAD (2009) 'The Protection of National Security in IIAs', UNCTAD Series on International Investment Policies for Development. Available at: www.unctad.org (accessed 25 January 2011).

UNCTAD (2010) 'Country-specific lists of BITs. China, list of treaties concluded as of 1 June 2010'. Available at: www.unctad.org/Templates/Page.asp?intItemID=2344&lang=1.

US–China Business Council (2010) 'Member Priorities Survey Results'. Available at: www.uschina.org/public/documents/2010/membership_survey.pdf (accessed 20 January 2011).

US–China Business Council (2011) 'Foreign Direct Investment in China', citing *China Statistical Yearbook 2009*, issued by the PRC MOFCOM and the PRC National Bureau of Statistics. Available at: www.uschina.org/statistics/fdi_cumulative.html (accessed 31 January 2011).

White House: Office of the Press Secretary (2009) 'US–China Joint Statement', Beijing, China. Available at: www.whitehouse.gov/the-press-office/us-china-joint-statement (accessed 16 February 2011).

Xinhuanet (2010a) 'Chinese investment, a real threat to US national security?'. Available at: http://news.xinhuanet.com/english202/indepth/2010–08/27/c_13466369.htm (accessed 24 January 2011).

Xinhuanet (2010b) 'China's outbound investment hits $56.5 bln in 2009'. Available at: http://news.xinhuanet.com/english2010/china/2010–09/05/c_13479616.htm (accessed 31 January 2011).

Zhang Y. (2010) 'The Impact of Free Trade Agreements on Business Activity: A Survey of Firms in the People's Republic of China', ADBI Working Paper Series. Available at: http://ssrn.com/abstract=1707784 (accessed 31 January 2011).

List of Chinese laws

Administrative Licensing Law of the People's Republic of China 2003; National People's Congress.

Anti-Monopoly Law of the People's Republic of China 2007; Standing Committee of the National People's Congress.

Civil Procedure Law of the People's Republic of China 1987, amended 2007; Standing Committee of the National People's Congress.

Company Law of the People's Republic of China 1993, amended 1999, 2004 and 2005; Standing Committee of the National People's Congress.

Contract Law of the People's Republic of China 1999; National People's Congress.

Criminal Law of the People's Republic of China 1997, amended 1999, 2001 (twice), 2002, 2005, 2006, 2009 and 2011; National People's Congress.

Enterprise Income Tax Law of the People's Republic of China 2007; National People's Congress.

Law of the People's Republic of China on Application of Laws to Foreign-Related Civil Relations 2010; Standing Committee of the National People's Congress.

Law of the People's Republic of China on Foreign-Capital Enterprises 1986, amended 2000; National People's Congress.

Sino-Foreign Equity Joint Venture Enterprise Law of the People's Republic of China (1979), amended 1990 and 2001; National People's Congress (Equity Joint Venture Law).

List of Chinese subordinate legislation

General Office of the State Council (2011) *Notice on Launching the Security Review System for Mergers and Acquisitions of Domestic Enterprises by Foreign Investors*, Guo Ban Fa [2011] No. 6.

MOFCOM (2004) *Provisions on the Establishment of Investment Companies by Foreign Investors*, as amended 2006, effective 17 December 2004.

MOFCOM (2009a) *Measures for the Administration of Overseas Investment*, Shang Zi Han [2009] No. 5.

MOFCOM (2009b) *Notice Delegating the Authority Limit for Examination and Approval of the Establishment of Investment Companies by Foreign Investment* Shang Zi Han [2009] No. 8, effective 6 March 2009.

MOFCOM (2010) *Guiding Opinions of the Ministry of Commerce on the Work Regarding the Nationwide Work in Overseas Investment and Cooperation in 2010*, February 2010.

MOFCOM (2011) 'China FTA Network'. Available at: http://fta.mofcom.gov.cn/english/index.shtml (accessed 15 January 2011).

MOFCOM, State Administration of Foreign Exchange (2009) *Notice of the Ministry of Commerce and the State Administration of Foreign Exchange on Joint Annual Inspection of Overseas Investments*, Shang He Han [2009] No. 60.

MOFCOM; State-owned Assets Supervision and Administration Commission of the State Council; State Administration of Taxation; State Administration of Industry and Commerce; China Securities Regulatory Commission; State Administration of Foreign Exchange (2006) *Provisions on Foreign Investors' Merger with and Acquisition of Domestic Enterprises*, promulgated 8 August 2006, amended 22 June 2009 (M&A Provisions).

MOFCOM; Ministry of Finance; State Administration of Taxation; State Administration for Industry and Commerce; National Bureau of Statistics; State Administration of Foreign Exchange (2010) *Notice on the Commencement of 2010 Joint Annual Inspection of Foreign-invested Enterprises*, Shang Zi Han [2010] No. 101.

Ministry of Foreign Economic Relations and Trade (1988) *Notice on the Implementation Plan Concerning the Joint Annual Inspection of Foreign-invested Enterprises* [1988] Wai Jing Mao Zi Fa No. 938.

Ministry of Industry and Information (2010) *Tire Industry Policy*, Gong Chan Ye Zheng Ce [2010] No. 2.

NDRC (2004a) *Policies on the Development of the Automotive Industry*, [2004] No. 8, amended 2009.

NDRC (2004b) *Interim Administrative Measures for the Verification and Approval of Foreign Investment Projects*, NDRC [2004] No. 22.

NDRC (2004c) *Verification and Approval of Overseas Investment Projects Tentative Administrative Procedures*, 9 October 2004.

NDRC (2009) *Notice on Several Questions Relating to Improvement of Management of Overseas Investment Projects*, Fagai Waizi [2009] No. 1479.

NDRC (2010) *Notice on Delegating Powers on Approval of Foreign Investment Projects to Authorities at Lower Levels*, Fa Gai Wai Zi [2010] No. 914.

NDRC (2011) *Notice on Delegating Powers on Approval of Overseas Investment Projects to Authorities at Lower Levels*, Fa Gai Wai Zi [2011] No. 235.

NDRC; MOFCOM (2007) *Catalogue of Industries for Guiding Foreign Investment*, Order No. 57 of National Development and Reform Commission and Ministry of Commerce.

State Administration for Industry and Commerce; MOFCOM; General Administration of Customs; State Administration of Foreign Exchange (2006) *Implementation Opinions on Certain Issues Concerning the Application of Laws on the Approval and Registration Administration for Foreign-Invested Companies*, Gong Shang Wai Qi Zi [2006] No. 81 (FIE Registration Opinions 2006).

State Administration of Foreign Exchange (SAFE) (2009) *Provisions on Foreign Exchange Administration for Overseas Direct Investment of Domestic Institutions*, Hui Fa [2009] No. 30.

State Council (1987) *Implementing Regulations for the Sino-Foreign Equity Joint Venture Enterprise Law of the People's Republic of China*, amended 2001 (Equity JV Implementing Regulations).

State Council (2001) *Regulations of the People's Republic of China on Administration of Technology Import and Export*, Order No. 331.

State Council (2002), *Provisions Guiding Foreign Investment Direction*, Order No. 346 of the State Council, effective 1 April 2002.

State Council (2004) *Decision on Investment System Reform*, Guo Fa [2004] No. 20.

State Council (2005) *Regulations of the People's Republic of China on Registration Administration of Companies*, Order No. 451.

State Council (2006a) *The Opinion on Encouraging and Normalizing Our Enterprises' Investment Cooperation.* Summary available at: www.chinanews.com/other/news/2006/10–25/809947.shtml (accessed 21 January 2011).

State Council (2006b) *Circular of the General Office of the State Council concerning Transmitting the Opinions of SASAC on Guidance for Promotion of Adjustment of State-owned Assets and Restructuring of State-owned Enterprises*, Guobanfa [2006] No. 97, issued 5 December 2006.

State Council (2009) *Measures for the Administration of the Establishment of Partnership Enterprises in the Territory of China by Foreign Enterprises or Individuals*, Decree No. 567, effective 1 March 2010.

State Council (2010a) *Certain Opinions of the State Council on Further Facilitating the Utilization of Foreign Capital*, Guo Fa [2010] No. 9, 6 April 2010.

State Council (2010b) *Administrative Regulations on the Registration of Permanent Representative Organizations of Foreign Enterprises*, Decree No. 584.

State-owned Assets Supervision and Administration Commission of the State Council (SASAC) (2010) *Notice on Conducting Special Inspection of Foreign Merger and Acquisition Matters of Central Enterprises*, Guo Zi Ting Fa Jian Du [2010] No. 48.

Supreme People's Court (2007) *Provisions of the Supreme People's Court on Certain Issues Concerning the Application of Law in the Trial of Cases Involving Disputes over Civil or Commercial Contracts Involving Foreign Elements*, Fa shi [2007] No. 14.

Supreme People's Court (2010) Provisions of the Supreme People's Court on Various Issues Concerning the Trial of Cases involving Disputes Relating to Foreign-invested Enterprises (1), Fa Shi [2010] No. 9.

5 Chinese investment treaties

A procedural perspective

Nils Eliasson

5.1 Introduction

Although empirical studies on the effects of bilateral investment treaties (BITs) largely remain inconclusive as to whether the conclusion of these treaties in fact leads to any increase in the flow of foreign investments (Muchlinski 2008: 4–44; Berger 2010), the international investment treaty regime must, at least based on the large number of BITs that have been concluded, be considered successful. Since the first BIT was concluded between Germany and Pakistan in 1959, more than 2700 BITs have been signed.[1]

The People's Republic of China (China) has contributed to this development by concluding 127 BITs as of 1 June 2010, which is among the highest number concluded by any individual state. China's foreign investment regime and BIT programme is a huge topic. This chapter does not purport to address all or even most aspects of it. Rather, it will focus on certain *procedural aspects* of Chinese BITs, in particular the adequacy of the procedural protection offered to investors under such BITs. Arguably, the investor's right to settle investment disputes against the host state through international arbitration is one of the most important provisions of such treaties. In most cases, the absence of an effective investor-state arbitration clause in BITs renders the substantive protection of such treaties meaningless. Procedural aspects will, therefore, be at the centre of any discussion regarding the effectiveness of the Chinese BIT programme. The decision on jurisdiction in *Mr Tza Yap Shum* v. *The Republic of Peru*,[2] the first ever case brought under a Chinese BIT, will serve to illustrate some of these procedural aspects, including the scope of the investor's right to arbitration, the protection of indirect investments, most favoured nation (MFN) clauses and the importing of procedural provisions. The decision will also illustrate the territorial application of Chinese BITs.

5.2 Foreign investments in China and Chinese outbound investments

Since the beginning of the 1980s, when China concluded its first bilateral investment treaty with the Kingdom of Sweden,[3] China has demonstrated a significant shift from a relatively protectionist policy on foreign investment to a gradually more liberal view. Such development is reflected, *inter alia*, in the great number of investment treaties concluded by China in recent years. As mentioned above, by 1 June 2010, China had concluded 127 BITs.[4] China has also modernized a number of its older BITs. This development of the Chinese policy on investment protection is frequently described as the shift from the *first* to the *second generation* of Chinese BITs.[5]

Discussions regarding Chinese BITs have generally adopted the perspective of foreign investments into China (see, for example, Hobér and Eliasson 2009; Eliasson 2009; Schill 2007). This is understandable. Looking at the statistics, during the past decades, foreign investment in China has by far exceeded Chinese outbound investments (Eliasson 2009). Due to the rapid economic growth in China during recent years,[6] however, China has also become an increasingly important source of outbound foreign investment, with the Chinese government taking important steps to encourage this (Berger 2008: 17). In 2009, China's outbound investments (including financial investments) totalled over US$56.5 billion (MOFCOM 2009: 78–83). This is an almost 100 per cent increase since 2003, when Chinese outbound investments amounted to US$28.5 billion (Eliasson 2009). The Chinese outbound investments are to a large extent made by state-owned enterprises, which in 2009, according to official governmental statistics, accounted for more than 90 per cent of the total value of all registered Chinese outbound investments.[7]

The rapid economic growth in China has also created a demand for a stable and secure supply of natural resources. Securing this supply has therefore become an important strategic objective for Chinese outbound investments,[8] something which is also reflected by the increasing number of Chinese oil and gas and mining investments (Eliasson 2010).

So far, however, the rapid growth of Chinese inbound and outbound investments has not caused any surge in investment treaty claims under Chinese BITs. To date, there has only been one reported case brought by a foreign investor against China, *Ekran Berhad* v. *People's Republic of China*.[9] This case, registered by ICSID on 24 May 2011, was at the time of publication of this book suspended pursuant to the parties' agreement.[10] Claims by Chinese investors are similarly scarce: there have, so far, only been two reported cases brought by Chinese investors against other states. The first, *Tza Yap Shum*, is a case brought by a Hong Kong investor against the Republic of Peru. The second, *Heilongjiang International and Technical Cooperative Corp, Qinhuangdaoshi Qinlong International Industrial and Beijing Shougang Mining Investment* v. *Republic of Mongolia*,[11] is a case brought by three Chinese companies concerning their investment in the Tumurtei iron ore mine in Mongolia.[12]

What is particularly interesting in relation to the claim against Mongolia is that, unlike Mr Shum who was a private investor with a relatively small investment in the fishing industry, the Mongolia case concerns a strategic Chinese investment in the mining industry, and two of the claimants (China Heilongjiang International and Technical Cooperative Corp and Beijing Shougang Mining Investment) are state-owned enterprises. We have so far seen relatively few investment claims brought by state-owned enterprises generally.[13] The Mongolia case could be the starting point for further investment claims by state-owned companies. With a substantial proportion of Chinese outbound investments originating from state-owned enterprises, there is a clear potential for such cases.

5.3 The different generations of Chinese BITs

Chinese BITs are frequently referred to as *first* and *second generation* BITs. First generation Chinese BITs are characterized by their rather limited *substantive* and *procedural* protection. China started to enter into these first generation BITs in the early 1980s, following the 'open-door policy', which was announced in 1978 in an effort to attract foreign investment.[14] However, China's first BITs, which it concluded with Sweden in 1982[15] and with Romania in 1984,[16] did not fully correspond to this new approach to foreign investments. Instead, China opted for limited investment protection and narrowly defined investor-state arbitration clauses.

A characteristic of these early Chinese BITs was that they either did not provide for any investor-state arbitration, or contained an investor-state arbitration clause, which only covered disputes relating to the *amount of compensation payable following an expropriation.*[17]

Arguably, one of the most important provisions in investment treaties is the investor's right to settle disputes against the host state under such treaty, by international arbitration (see, for example, Malintoppi and Reinisch 2008). In most cases, the absence of an effective investor-state arbitration clause in BITs renders the substantive protection of such treaties meaningless. To submit the claims to a judicial or administrative body of the host state, as provided by many early Chinese BITs,[18] is normally not a viable option. Nor can the investor, in most cases, rely on its home state to extend diplomatic protection and to bring the claims on its behalf. The investor's home state may, for instance, decline to extend diplomatic protection because it does not wish to disturb its relationship with the other state. Nor is there any guarantee that a claim by the home state on the investor's behalf would produce any results or binding resolution. Therefore, in most cases, in the absence of an efficient arbitration clause in the BIT, the investor will have no effective and/or realistic means of enforcing its substantive rights under the BIT.

Similarly, a narrowly defined arbitration clause, which only covers the quantification of the amount of compensation in case of expropriation, may prove equally redundant for the investor. Cases of direct expropriation, where the only dispute between the host state and the investor is the amount of compensation, are becoming increasingly rare. Instead, other forms of host state misconduct, for example, indirect or creeping expropriation or violation of the 'fair and equitable treatment' standard constitute more common risks (see, for example, Hobér 2010). Arbitration clauses limited to the quantification of compensation in case of expropriation may therefore (depending on the precise wording of such clauses) seriously limit the value of the first generation of Chinese BITs for Chinese investors and foreign investors alike.

China's unwillingness to accept international arbitration as a means of resolving investor-state disputes has been explained with reference to China's traditional scepticism vis-à-vis international law, as well as a political call for the primacy of state sovereignty (Schill 2007: 8). Today, however, with the ever-increasing amount of Chinese overseas investments, these narrowly defined arbitration clauses may work to the detriment of Chinese investors whose overseas investments have been negatively affected by governmental action in the investment country.

Some first generation BITs also lacked a clear definition of 'investor' (for example, the Norway–China BIT 1984) or 'investment' (for example, the Denmark–China BIT 1985), or, in some cases, both (for example, the Norway–China BIT 1984). Lack of clear definitions obviously causes uncertainty for prospective investors.

Early Chinese BITs were often also unsatisfactory from a substantive perspective. Some BITs, for instance, lacked clauses guaranteeing national treatment.[19] Such clauses, assuring a foreign investor the same treatment vis-à-vis the host state as a domestic entity and prohibiting discrimination on grounds of nationality, are standard guarantees in investment treaties (Dolzer and Schreuer 2008: 178). Instead, early Chinese BITs provided for national treatment only 'to the extent possible', thus weakening the level of protection.[20]

However, beginning in 1998 with the conclusion of the China–Barbados BIT, one can detect a new trend with respect to Chinese BITs. With this first BIT of the *second generation*, China started to develop a more liberal view on investment protection. In stark contrast to the first generation BITs, the second generation BITs have remedied most of the fore-mentioned deficiencies. In particular, the new BITs provide for arbitration of *all investor–state disputes* under the treaty without any restrictions as to the subject matter of the dispute. For example, in the BIT with Botswana, concluded in 2000, China consented to international arbitration of 'any dispute between an investor of a Contracting Party and the other Contracting Party in connection with an investment'.[21] In addition to covering 'all disputes in connection with an investment', the arbitration clause in this BIT also offers the investor the choice between the International Centre for Settlement of Investment Disputes (ICSID) and UNCITRAL arbitration.

Another significant step in the gradual development of Chinese BITs was taken by the Netherlands–China BIT of 2001 and the Germany–China BIT of 2003. These BITs include substantive and procedural provisions that meet the standard of modern investment treaties. The Germany–China BIT, for instance, provides for a broad definition of 'investment', which ensures that all essential rights and interests necessary for engaging in economic activities, including indirect investments, are covered by the treaty (Article 1(1)). The Germany–China BIT also offers all the protection standards normally found in modern investment protection treaties, such as fair and equitable treatment, full protection and security, national and MFN treatment, no expropriation without prompt, adequate and effective compensation and so on. In addition to the substantive protection, the Germany–China BIT includes a comprehensive investor-state arbitration clause. Article 9 of the Germany–China BIT provides that:

1   Any dispute concerning investments between a Contracting Party and an investor of the other Contracting Party should as far as possible be settled amicably between the parties in dispute. If the dispute cannot be settled within six months of the date when it has been raised by one of the parties in dispute, it shall, at the request of the investor of the other Contracting State, be submitted for arbitration.
2   The dispute shall be submitted for arbitration under the Convention of 18 March 1965 on the Settlement of Investment Disputes between States and Nationals of Other States (ICSID), unless the parties in dispute agree on an ad hoc arbitral tribunal to be established under the Arbitration Rules of the United Nations Commission on the International Trade Law (UNCITRAL) or other arbitration rules.

However, the birth of the second generation of Chinese BITs does not mean that all investments in China and Chinese overseas investments always enjoy the comprehensive protection afforded by modern investment treaties. Although China has renegotiated several of its first generation BITs, many investments in China and Chinese overseas investments still remain covered by them.[22] The Peru–China BIT is only one example of a first generation BIT still is in force, and the *Tza Yap Shum* case is therefore a good illustration of the problems such BITs may cause for investors.

5.4 The decision on jurisdiction in *Tza Yap Shum*

5.4.1 Background

Tza Yap Shum is the first ever case brought under a Chinese BIT. This case raises many questions that are of interest for the evaluation of the strengths and weaknesses of Chinese BITs. The case concerned alleged breaches by the Republic of Peru of the Peru–China BIT (1994) that affected the investment made by Mr Tza Yap Shum in TSG Peru S.A.C. (TSG), a Peruvian Company in the business of producing fish-based food products and their subsequent exports to Asian markets.

In 2004, the Peruvian Tax Administration started a number of actions, which – according to Mr Shum – ended up destroying TSG's business operations and economic viability. Mr Shum alleged that the immediate cause of this impact on the company was an unlawful and arbitrary tax lien on the company's bank accounts, which precluded the company from operating without disruption.

5.4.2 Mr Shum's claim in the arbitration

On 29 September 2006, Mr Shum initiated arbitration proceedings under the BIT against the Republic of Peru before the ICSID.[23] In the arbitration, Mr Shum claimed that the Republic of Peru had violated the following articles of the Peru–China BIT:

1   Duty to accord fair and equitable treatment to investments (Article 3.1);
2   Duty to protect investments (Article 3.1);
3   No expropriation without compensation (Article 4); and
4   Duty to allow the transfer of capital and earnings (Article 6).

The Republic of Peru denied the Claimant's allegations, and also objected to the jurisdiction of the Tribunal on the grounds that:

1   Claimant was not an investor under the Peru–China BIT;
2   Claimant had not made an investment before the dispute arose;
3   Claimant had not asserted a *prima facie* case of expropriation; and
4   The claims brought by Mr Shum did not fall within the scope of the arbitration clause in the Peru–China BIT.

5.4.3 The decision on jurisdiction

On 19 June 2009, the Tribunal ruled on Peru's jurisdictional objections.[24] The Tribunal denied objections 1–3 above. Regarding the fourth objection, however, the Tribunal found that only one of the breaches of the Peru–China BIT alleged by Mr Shum, the expropriation claim, came within the jurisdiction of the Tribunal. The other three claims were dismissed for lack of jurisdiction (para. 221). The determination of the merits of the expropriation case is still pending.

In order to make its ruling on jurisdiction, the Tribunal was called upon to deal with certain procedural issues which are of general interest for the evaluation of Chinese BITs:

i The *scope of the investor's right to arbitration* under narrowly-worded arbitration clauses in 'first generation' Chinese BITs;

ii *MFN clauses* and the importing of more favourable procedural provisions in other BITs;

iii Protection of *indirect investments* through companies incorporated in a third country which is not a party to the applicable BIT; and

iv The *territorial application* of Chinese BITs.

These issues will be discussed in Sections 5.5–5.8. Since this chapter only deals with the jurisdictional issues raised in *Tza Yap Shum*, the merits of Mr Shum's expropriation case will not be further discussed. It should be noted, however, that in the award, which was rendered on 7 July 2011, the Tribunal found that Peru had expropriated Mr Shum's investment.[25]

5.5 The scope of the investor's right to arbitration under narrowly-worded arbitration clauses in 'first generation' Chinese BITs

As mentioned above, the arbitration clause in Article 8 of the Peru–China BIT is a good example of a narrowly-worded arbitration clause referring to the quantification of damages. It reads (emphasis added):

1 Any dispute between an investor of one Contracting Party and the other Contracting Party in connection with an investment in the territory of the other Contracting Party shall, as far as possible, be settled amicably through negotiations between the parties to the dispute.

2 If a dispute *involving the amount of compensation for expropriation* cannot be settled within six months after resort to negotiations as specified in Paragraph 1 of this Article, it may be submitted at the request of either party to the international arbitration of the International Centre for Settlement of Investment Disputes (ICSID), established by the Convention on the Settlement of Investment Disputes between States and Nationals of Other Sates, signed in Washington, DC on March 18, 1965. *Any disputes concerning other matters between an investor of either Contracting Party and the other Contracting Party may be submitted to the Centre if the parties to the disputes so agree.* The provisions of this Paragraph shall not apply if the investor concerned has resorted to the procedure specified in Paragraph 2 of this Article.

Thus, according to Article 8(3) of the Peru–China BIT, *disputes involving the amount of compensation for expropriation* may be referred to arbitration under the ICSID Convention. Other disputes may only be referred to arbitration following a separate agreement between the investor and the state accepting the investment.

As mentioned above , Mr Shum claimed that the actions of Peru violated four separate obligations of Peru under the Peru–China BIT. Peru argued that none of these claims were within the jurisdiction of the Tribunal, since the arbitration clause only covered 'disputes involving the amount of compensation for expropriation'. In the view of Peru, not even Mr Shum's expropriation claim was covered, since the determination of the claim necessarily involved the question whether an expropriation had taken place, not only the amount of compensation following a confirmed expropriation. According to Peru, the only correct interpretation of the arbitration clause was that an expropriation claim only is covered by the arbitration clause if domestic courts first have decided that the investment in fact was expropriated, with the only remaining issue was the amount of compensation for such expropriation.

Whereas the Tribunal accepted Peru's arguments that Mr Shum's claims for violation of the fair and equitable treatment standard, the duty to protect investments and the obligation to allow the free transfer of capital and earnings were outside the scope of its jurisdiction, it did not accept Peru's argument that the expropriation claim was outside its jurisdiction. In arriving at this conclusion, the Tribunal referred to the specific wording used by Article 8(3) of the Peru–China BIT:

> if a dispute *involving the amount of compensation* for expropriation cannot be settled within six months after resort to negotiations as specified in Paragraph 1 of this Article, it may be submitted at the request of either party to the international arbitration of the International Centre for Settlement of Investment Disputes (ICSID) [. . .].

The Tribunal held that:

> The BIT uses the word 'involving' which, according to the Oxford Dictionary means 'to enfold, envelope, entangle, include.' A bona fide interpretation of these words indicate that *the only requirement established in the BIT is that the dispute must 'include' the determination of the amount of a compensation, and not that the dispute must be restricted thereto*. Obviously, other wording was available, such as 'limited to' or 'exclusively', but the wording used in this provision reads 'involving'.
>
> (para. 151; emphasis added)

The Tribunal concluded that to give meaning to all the elements of the article, it must be interpreted that the words:

> involving the amount of compensation for expropriation *includes not only the mere determination of the amount but also any other issues normally inherent to an expropriation*, including whether the property was actually expropriated in accordance with the BIT provisions and requirements, as well as the determination of the amount of compensation due, if any. In the opinion of the Tribunal, a contrary conclusion would invalidate the

provision related to ICSID arbitration since according to the final sentence of Article 8(3), turning to the courts of the State accepting the investment would preclude definitely the possibility choosing arbitration under the ICSID Convention. Consequently, since the Claimant has filed a prima facie claim of expropriation, the Tribunal, pursuant to Articles 25 and 41 of the ICSID Convention and Rule 41 of the Arbitration Rules, *considers that it is competent to decide on the merits of the expropriation claim filed by Claimant.*

(para. 188; emphasis added)

Thus, in finding that it had jurisdiction to hear Mr Shum's expropriation claim, the Tribunal put great emphasis on the wording of the treaty. A similar approach has been taken by other tribunals that have been called upon to rule on narrowly-worded arbitration clauses in BITs concluded by the Soviet Union or Eastern European states during the communist era.[26] However, there are also tribunals that have reached the opposite conclusion, that is, that the tribunal's jurisdiction is limited to the quantification of damages.[27] Generally, such seemingly conflicting outcomes can be attributed to variations in the precise wording of the arbitration clauses in different BITs. Although such clauses share common features, the precise wording often differs. It would therefore not be advisable to rely on the ruling in *Tza Yap Shum* as a precedent for the conclusion that investors will *always* be able to bring expropriation claims under Chinese BITs providing for arbitration of disputes *concerning* or *involving* the amount of compensation for expropriation. Each treaty must be interpreted separately.

5.6 MFN clauses and the importing of more favourable procedural provisions in other BITs

In *Tza Yap Shum*, Mr Shum argued for two sources establishing the jurisdiction of the tribunal. The first, which concerned his expropriation claim, has already been discussed. The second, which concerned the other alleged treaty breaches by Peru, was the MFN provision in Article 3(2) of the Peru–China BIT. The essence of such a MFN clause is that it allows the investor to rely on more favourable protection standards afforded to investors of other states by the state which has accepted the investment. Article 3(1) and 3(2) in the Peru–China BIT provides (emphasis added):

Investments and activities associated with investments of investors of either Contracting Party shall be accorded fair and equitable treatment and shall enjoy protection in the territory of the other Contracting Party.

The treatment and protection referred to in Paragraph 1 of this Article *shall not be less favourable than that accorded to investments and activities associated with such investments of investors of a third State.*

Mr Shum argued that since Peru had signed BITs with other countries, which allowed the submission of *any disputes* between the investor and the host state to ICSID arbitration, the same treatment had to be extended also to him in accordance with Article 3(2) in the Peru–China BIT. For instance, the Colombia–Peru BIT gives investors protected by that treaty, the right to bring a claim for any form of alleged breach by Peru of the Colombia–Peru BIT to ICSID arbitration. Mr Shum argued that he (and other Chinese investors protected by the Peru–China BIT) on the basis of the MFN clause in Article 3(2) in the Peru–China BIT in connection with the broader arbitration clause of the Colombia–Peru BIT is entitled to submit to ICSID arbitration not only disputes related to expropriation, but also disputes related to fair and equitable treatment and other breaches of the Peru–China BIT. Thus, Mr Shum argued that the MFN clause in the Peru–China BIT gave him the right to rely on the more favourable procedural standards of other BITs entered into by Peru.

The Tribunal found that Article 3(2) of the Peru–China BIT was open to a broad interpretation, which could include access to more favourable procedural protection than that afforded by the Peru–China BIT, such as ICSID arbitration for alleged violations of fair and equitable treatment (para. 213). Yet, the Tribunal did not accept Mr Shum's argument. The Tribunal found that the specific wording of the arbitration clause in Article 8(3) in the Peru–China BIT excluded the possibility of broadening the jurisdiction of the Tribunal by importing more favourable procedural provisions in other BITs. In the words of the Tribunal:

> The Tribunal considers that the literal wording of Article 8 reflects that the Contracting Parties reached an agreement on two fundamental issues. First, as indicated above, they agreed to submit expropriation disputes to ICSID arbitration. *Secondly, they specifically considered the possibility of submitting other types of disputes to ICSID arbitration and specifically reserved the right to do it only 'if the parties to the dispute so agree.'* Since the Contracting Parties specifically established the possibility of submitting "other matters" to ICSID arbitration and since they have established specifically such occurrence in the wording of the BIT, we, the Tribunal, conclude that it is our duty to give the BIT wording the meaning it was really intended. *As a result, the Tribunal hereby determines that the specific wording of Article 8(3) should prevail over the general wording of the MFN clause in Article 3 and Claimant's arguments on the contrary must be dismissed.*
> (para. 216; emphasis added)

Thus, the Tribunal in *Tza Yap Shum* found that it did not have jurisdiction to hear Mr Shum's case on the basis of the MFN clause in the Peru–China BIT.

The possibility of relying on MFN clauses to broaden a Tribunal's jurisdiction by importing a more favourable arbitration clause in another BIT has been a frequent topic for academic and other discussions during recent years (see, for example, UNCTAD 2010; Markert 2010: 270–308). Tribunals have reached different conclusions on the interpretation of such clauses. For instance, the tribunal in *RosInvest UK Ltd* v. *The Russian Federation*[28] found that it was possible to extend its jurisdiction under the UK-Soviet BIT by applying the MFN clause in the treaty, whereas the tribunal in *Plama Consortium Ltd (Cyprus)* v. *Bulgaria*[29] reached the opposite conclusion based on the Cyprus–Bulgaria BIT.

However, as clearly evidenced by the reasoning of the respective tribunals in these two cases, as well as by the reasoning of the tribunal in the decision on jurisdiction in *Tza Yap Shum*, each MFN clause and each arbitration clause must be interpreted based on its own wording in accordance with the rules on interpretation of international treaties codified by the Vienna Convention on the Law of Treaties. Seemingly conflicting conclusions may often be explained by differences in the precise wording of the respective treaties. Thus, tribunals called upon to interpret MFN clauses in other Chinese BITs might reach a different conclusion than that of the Tribunal in *Tza Yap Shum*. It all depends on the precise wording of the applicable treaty.

5.7 Indirect investments, investment planning and treaty shopping

5.7.1 *Do Chinese BITs protect indirect investments made through companies incorporated in third states?*

For various reasons (for example, tax, corporate governance, and so on) cross-border investments are often channelled through one or several interposed holding companies or Special Purpose Vehicles (SPVs).[30] It is of great importance for the evaluation of the protection offered by Chinese BITs whether the fact that one or several corporate entities are interposed between the ultimate beneficiary and the final 'investment' would cut-off the investment protection which the ultimate beneficiary otherwise would enjoy.

In *Tza Yap Shum*, Mr Shum had structured his investment in his Peruvian fishing project in the following manner: (i) a local Peruvian company, TSG, was set up in Peru for the fishing project; and (ii) Linkvest International Ltd, incorporated in the British Virgin Islands, whose sole shareholder and beneficiary was Mr Shum, acquired 90 per cent of the shares in TSG. In the dispute, Peru argued that Mr Shum had not made an 'investment' in Peru that was protected by the Peru–China BIT. In the view of Peru, Mr Shum had only invested in Linkvest, which was not a Peruvian company, and therefore did not hold an investment in the territory of Peru. Peru argued that the only entity which had made a direct investment in Peru was Linkvest, and Linkvest, being a British Virgin Island entity, was not protected by the Peru–China BIT.

The Peru–China BIT defines 'investment' in the following manner (emphasis added):

The term 'investment' means *every kind of asset invested by investors of one Contracting Party in accordance with the laws and regulations of the Other Contracting Party in the territory of the latter*, and in particular, though not exclusively, includes:

a   movable, immovable property and other property rights such as mortgages and pledges,
b   *shares, stock and any other kind of participation in companies,*
c   claims to money or to any other performance having an economic value,
d   concessions conferred by law or under contract, including concessions to search for or exploit natural resources.

Thus, unlike some investment treaties which expressly protects 'every kind of asset *invested directly or indirectly* by Investors of one Contracting Party in the territory of the other Contracting party' (e.g. Article 1(1) of the Germany–China BIT 2003, emphasis added), the definition of 'investments' in the Peru–China BIT does not include any reference to *indirect investments*. Yet, the Tribunal in *Tza Yap Shum* found that, interpreted in good faith in accordance with the ordinary meaning of the terms of the treaty, in their context, and in light of its object and purpose as stipulated by Article 31 of the Vienna Convention, the definition of 'investment' in the Peru–China BIT did not exclude from the protection of the treaty the indirect investment made by Mr Shum in the present case:

> [. . .] the Tribunal interprets that the Contracting Parties in its intention to promote and protect investments, decided to define them through an ample formulation which, by general rule, will protect all kind of investments. Additionally, in consideration of the Tribunal no evidence has been produced that indirect investments are not 'in accordance with the laws and regulations' of the Republic of Peru. *Consequently, the Tribunal does not find any indications in the BIT leading them to exclude indirect investments of Chinese nationals in Peruvian territory from the scope of application of the Treaty, particularly when it is proven that they exert the property and control over such investments.*
>
> The Tribunal would expect such a limitation would have been included explicitly in the BIT. For example, *the Contracting Parties to the BIT could have agreed on an article excluding from the benefits of the Treaty any investors with investments channelled through third-party countries* who otherwise would be eligible thereunder.
>
> (paras 106–7; emphasis added)

Similar conclusions have been reached by other tribunals that have been called upon to interpret definitions of 'investments' in other treaties, which do not include any express reference to indirect investments. For instance, the Tribunal in *Siemens A.G.* v. *República Argentina*[31] held that:

One of the categories consists of 'shares, rights of participation in companies and other types of participation in companies' The plain meaning
of this provision is that shares held by a German shareholder are protected under the Treaty. *The Treaty does not require that there be no interposed companies between the investment and the ultimate owner of the company.*
Therefore, a literal reading of the Treaty does not support the allegation
that the definition of investment excludes indirect investments.

(para. 137; emphasis added)

However – caveat investor! – the decision by the Tribunal in *Tza Yap Shum*
(and other similar rulings) does not mean that investors can safely assume
that indirect investments channelled through companies incorporated in
third states are *always* protected under Chinese BITs. No BIT, and no case,
is identical. The precise wording of the individual provisions of each BIT
must always be interpreted on their own in light of all relevant circumstances of the case. For instance, the New Zealand–China Free Trade Agreement provides:

> Investments includes investments of legal persons of a third country
> which are owned or controlled by investors of one Party and which have
> been made in the territory of the other Party. The relevant provisions of
> this Agreement shall apply to such investments only when such third
> country has no right or abandons the right to claim compensation after
> the investments have been expropriated by the other Party.

Thus, this provision seems to exclude claims by the ultimate beneficiary of
the investment unless the company directly involved in the investment lacks
protection of its own or abandon its right to compensation.

5.7.2 *The possibility of establishing protection by 'investment planning' or 'treaty shopping'*

There is also another aspect to the question of indirect investments, that is,
'investment planning' or 'treaty shopping'.[32] Foreign investors in China and
Chinese investors investing overseas, just like investors in the rest of the
world, may use interposed companies to strengthen their investment protection. For instance, if a Chinese investor is planning to invest in a country
with which China has not entered into any BIT, or with which China only
has a first generation BIT, which offers unsatisfactory procedural and/or substantive protection, one option might be to structure the investment so that
it is channelled through a company incorporated in a jurisdiction with which
the state, in which the investment is made, has entered into a satisfactory
investment treaty. Similarly, an investor from a country with which China
has entered into an unsatisfactory BIT might make its investment in China
through a company incorporated in a jurisdiction with which China has

entered into a satisfactory BIT. If this is done, the investor does not need to rely only on the unsatisfactory protection, but can benefit from the protection offered by the investment treaty covering the interposed holding company. The only difference is that a potential claim will be brought by the holding company, in its own name, and not by the ultimate beneficiary of the investment. This type of 'investment planning' or 'treaty shopping' might be a fairly inexpensive way of strengthening the protection of a particular investment, and is frequently done today – in particular, in the energy sector and the natural resources sector – as part of the overall investment structuring by companies investing in high risk countries.

Such arrangements have been upheld by arbitral tribunals ruling on objections by the host state that such holding companies should not be permitted to bring a claim, since they are not the *real party in interest*, but a mere *vehicle* for the final beneficiary through which the investment has been carried out. So far, tribunals presented with this type of objections have ruled that as long as the holding company fulfils the definition of 'investor' in the applicable investment treaty, and such investment treaty does not exclude from its applicability entities controlled by nationals of a third state or entities without substantial business activities in the state of incorporation, such holding companies enjoy the same protection as other corporate investors.

For instance, in *Tokios Tokelés* v. *Ukraine*,[33] the Tribunal held that the only relevant consideration to decide whether the Claimant qualified as an 'investor' under the Ukraine–Lithuania BIT 'is whether the Claimant is established under the laws of Lithuania' (para. 38). The Tribunal thereby rejected the Respondent's request to restrict the scope of covered investors under the BIT, and to deny jurisdiction on the ground that the Claimant did not maintain a substantial business activity in Lithuania. In so doing, the Tribunal also rejected Respondent's argument that the relevant persons for the purpose of establishing the nationality of the 'investor' were the controlling shareholders. While acknowledging the fact that a number of investment treaties do allow a party to deny the benefits of the treaty to entities of the other party that are controlled by foreign nationals, the Tribunal pointed out that the Ukraine–Lithuania BIT contained no such 'denial-of-benefits' provision. The Tribunal continued:

> We regard the absence of such provision as a deliberate choice of the Contracting Parties. In our view, *it is not for the tribunals to impose limits on the scope of the BITs not found in the text*, much less limits nowhere evident from the negotiating history. An international tribunal of defined jurisdiction should not reach out to exercise a jurisdiction beyond the borders of the definition. But equally an international tribunal should exercise, and indeed is bound to exercise, the measure of jurisdiction with which it is endowed.
>
> (para. 36; emphasis added)

Another example where the Tribunal refused to 'import' restrictions, not following from the wording of the treaty, is *Saluka* v. *Czech Republic*.[34] In this case, the Czech Republic argued that the Claimant was a Dutch shell company, controlled by a Japanese group of companies, and as such lacked standing under the Netherlands–Czech Republic BIT. The Tribunal interpreted the definition of 'investor' according to Article 1 of the Czech–Netherlands BIT, stating that

> Even if it were possible to know an investor's true motivation in making its investment, nothing in Article 1 makes the investor's motivation part of the definition of an 'investment'.
>
> (para. 209)

> [T]he Tribunal must always bear in mind the terms of the Treaty under which it operates. Those terms expressly give a legal person constituted under the laws of the Netherlands – such as, [the Claimant] – the right to invoke the protection under the Treaty. To depart from that conclusion *requires clear language in the Treaty*, but there is none. [...] [I]t is beyond the powers of this Tribunal to import into the definition of 'investor' some requirement [...] having the effect of excluding from the Treaty's protection a company which the language agreed by the parties included within it.
>
> (para. 229; emphasis added)

Thus, tribunals have been reluctant to exclude investors from the protection of an otherwise applicable treaty by the mere fact that such investors are holding companies or vehicles for the ultimate beneficiary of the investment. However, as mentioned previously, the prudent investor shall *not* rely on past arbitration cases as precedents. The precise wording of the applicable treaty must be carefully scrutinized in each individual case.

5.8 Territorial application of Chinese BITs

In most BITs, the definition of protected 'investments' or covered companies requires them to be in the *territory* of one of the contracting state parties to the BIT. Similarly, covered natural parties are required to have the *nationality* of one of the contracting states. With some exceptions,[35] Chinese BITs do not include a separate definition of 'territory'. In accordance with the law of China, Hong Kong, Macau and Taiwan are all part of Chinese territory. The question might therefore arise to what extent investors from Hong Kong, Macau or Taiwan may have recourse to BITs concluded by China. Conversely, the question may arise to what extent the government of China may incur liability under Chinese BITs for loss suffered by foreign investors in the territories of Hong Kong, Macau or Taiwan. With the exception of the Russia–China BIT (2006), no Chinese BIT has expressly excluded from its scope of application Hong Kong, Macau or Taiwan.

In *Tza Yap Shum*, Peru argued (i) that Mr Shum had not demonstrated that he was a Chinese national; and (ii) that even if he was a Chinese national, he was not entitled to recourse under the Peru–China BIT because he was a resident of Hong Kong. The definition of 'investor' in Article 1(2) of the Peru–China BIT provides that 'the term 'investors' means: [...] in respect of the People's Republic of China: (a) natural persons who have the *nationality* of the People's Republic of China *in accordance with its laws*' (emphasis added). In this case, the Tribunal found that, although a resident of Hong Kong, Mr Shum was a Chinese national born in the province of Fujian in Mainland China. He therefore fulfilled the definition of 'investor'. The Tribunal also found that since the BIT did not exclude Chinese nationals with residence in Hong Kong (or elsewhere in the world) from its scope of application, the Tribunal did not have to determine the applicability of the Peru–China BIT to individuals of Chinese descent who are born in Hong Kong (para. 70).

However, based on the definition of 'investor' in the Peru–China BIT, the outcome of the case would probably have been the same even if Mr Shum had been born in Hong Kong or Macau. Hong Kong and Macau residents of Chinese descent who were born in Chinese territories (including Hong Kong and Macau) are, in accordance with the Nationality Law of the People's Republic of China, considered to be Chinese nationals.[36] As mentioned above, the definition of 'investor' in Article 1(2) of the Peru–China BIT provides that 'the term 'investors' means: [...] in respect of the People's Republic of China: (a) natural persons who have the *nationality* of the People's Republic of China *in accordance with its laws*' (emphasis added).

The discussion so far has only concerned 'investors' who are natural persons. The position of corporate investors from Hong Kong and Macau is similar, but raises additional questions. Whether or not such corporate investors are protected ultimately turns on the precise wording of the applicable treaty.

The Peru–China BIT, for instance, provides that 'the term 'investors' means: [...] in respect of the People's Republic of China: (b) economic entities *established in accordance with the laws of the People's Republic of China* and domiciled in the *territory* of the People's Republic of China' (emphasis added). Thus, the argument could be made that companies incorporated in Hong Kong or Macau would not be covered by this definition, since they are established in accordance with Hong Kong law or Macau law, and not the law of the People's Republic of China. However, it could also be argued that such argument fails to recognize that there may exist different jurisdictions within the People's Republic of China. The Hong Kong SAR is after all a special administrative region of the People's Republic of China. The laws of Hong Kong are therefore, arguably, also laws of China. It remains to be seen, however, how arbitral tribunals applying Chinese BITs will resolve this question.

The situation with respect to Taiwan and Taiwanese nationals is even more complex. However, the argument could be made that Taiwanese nationals may also invoke the protection of Chinese BITs containing similar definitions of 'investor' as the definition in the Peru–China BIT since, under the law of China, persons of Chinese descent born in Taiwan are also considered to be nationals of China.[37] The possibility for Taiwanese nationals of having recourse to China's 127 BITs would of course greatly increase the availability of protection under BITs for Taiwanese overseas investments. Due to the limited number of states that are maintaining official diplomatic relations with Taiwan, Taiwan has so far only concluded a limited number of BITs.[38]

Another issue, which was briefly touched upon in *Tza Yap Shum* was whether the fact that Hong Kong (and Macau) has the power to enter into their own international agreements in a number of areas, including investment and trade, could affect the applicability of Chinese BITs to Hong Kong (or Macau) residents. In accordance with such power,[39] Hong Kong has to date entered into 15 BITs – with Australia, Austria, Belgium, Denmark, France, Germany, Japan, Italy, Korea, Netherlands, New Zealand, Sweden, Switzerland, Thailand and United Kingdom. Macau has entered into one BIT – with Portugal.

The argument made by Peru in *Tza Yap Shum* was that the fact that Hong Kong has entered into its own BITs containing their own definitions of covered investors must mean that Hong Kong residents (even though considered to be Chinese citizens) must be excluded from the application of Chinese BITs. As already indicated above, the Tribunal did not accept such an argument by Peru, since the Tribunal concluded that the Peru–China BIT covers Chinese nationals no matter where they are domiciled (para. 70). On the issue of Hong Kong's power to enter into BITs of its own the Tribunal added:

> Hong Kong's power to conclude its own investment promotion and protection treaties with countries wherewith China also has entered into a BIT is not necessarily redundant. Historically, Hong Kong has hosted people from multiple nationalities. It may be for that reason that the government of this region has deployed a policy that seeks the promotion and protection of investments in other countries for the benefit of all of its residents, regardless of their nationalities. In conclusion, as it has been explained before, the Tribunal has determined that Claimant has proven his Chinese nationality in accordance with legal provisions relevant to nationality that govern the acquisition and loss thereof, including people residing in Hong Kong.
>
> (para. 76)

As observed by the Tribunal, Hong Kong BITs extend protection to *all* natural persons irrespective of nationality 'who have the right to abode in its area' and to 'corporations, partnerships and associations incorporated or constituted and registered where applicable under the law in force in its area'.[40]

However, the question nevertheless arises what would happen if a Hong Kong Chinese individual or Hong Kong company invests in the Republic of Korea (Korea), and the investment is affected by arbitrary actions taken by the Korean authorities. Korea is one of the countries that has entered into BITs both with China and with the Hong Kong Special Administrative Region (SAR). However, as long as neither of the treaties provides otherwise, such Hong Kong Chinese investors are likely to enjoy protection of both treaties.

5.9 Conclusion

With the birth of the second generation of Chinese BITs in 1998, China has brought its new investment treaties in line with modern practice. Such BITs contain all substantive and procedural provisions expected to be found in modern investment treaties. Such second generation BITs therefore generally offer a satisfactory level of protection for Chinese overseas investments.

However, many first generation BITs, which have not yet been renegotiated, still remain the only recourse for investors who are only covered by such treaties. For instance, 83 per cent of the BITs that China has concluded with countries specifically targeted for Chinese natural resources investments are first generation BITs.[41] If disputes arise under the narrowly-worded arbitration clauses of these BITs, we can anticipate the same type of jurisdictional disputes as we have experienced with regard to the old Soviet Union and Eastern Europe BITs.[42] *Mr Tza Yap Shum* v. *The Republic of Peru* can therefore be expected to be the first of many further cases raising similar issues. For example, the China–Mongolia BIT also contains a narrowly-worded arbitration clause. These types of jurisdictional issues are therefore likely to be raised in the ad hoc arbitration against Mongolia that was recently commenced by China Heilongjiang International and Technical Cooperative Corp, Qinhuangdaoshi Qinlong International Industrial and Beijing Shougang Mining Investment. The fact that this is an ad hoc arbitration might mean that less information will be made publicly available in relation to this case than in relation to *Mr Tza Yap Shum* v. *The Republic of Peru*, which is conducted under the ICSID Convention.

To avoid such protracted battles over jurisdiction, it might therefore be of interest for Chinese investors investing overseas as well as for foreign investors in China to try to strengthen their protection from the outset by structuring their investments so that they are channelled through companies incorporated in a country which has concluded a more satisfactory investment treaty with the country in which the final investment is made. However, investors should then ensure, of course, that such a treaty does not include any Denial of Benefit provisions.

Notes

1 The UNCTAD *World Investment Report* (2010) reported 2750 BITs at the end of 2009.

2 *Mr Tza Yap Shum* v. *The Republic of Peru*, ICSID Case No. ARB/07/6 Decision on Jurisdiction and Competence, 19 June 2009 (*Tza Yap Shum*), available at: http:// icsid.worldbank.org/ICSID/FrontServlet?requestType=CasesRH&actionVal=show Doc&docId=DC1831_En&caseId=C420 (accessed 28 February 2011) and Award, 7 July 2011, available at: http://italaw.com/documents/TzaYapShm Award.pdf (accessed 8 August 2011).

3 The Kingdom of Sweden was also the first Western state to recognize the People's Republic of China on 9 May 1950, and in the 1980s and early 1990s, arbitration in Stockholm was in practice the only politically acceptable alternative to arbitration in China for Chinese entities engaged in foreign trade: see, for example, Moser (2010).

4 China's list of BITs concluded by 1 June 2010 is available on the UNCTAD website, www.unctad.org (accessed 19 February 2011). For the purposes of this chapter, BITs entered into by the People's Republic of China will be referred to as 'Chinese BITs'.

5 See, for example, Schill (2007). Compare also Gallagher and Shan (2008), who distinguish between three generations of Chinese BITs: no immediate consent to arbitration, consent limited to quantum arising from expropriation, and full consent to arbitration.

6 In 2010, China's gross domestic product (GDP) was 39.8 trillion Yuan, compared with 21.6 trillion Yuan in 2006. See, for example, National Bureau of Statistics of China, 2006–2010 GDP statistics available at: www.stats.gov.cn/ english/newsandcomingevents/t20110228_402705764.htm (accessed 10 March 2011).

7 MOFCOM (2009). Moreover, 48 of the 50 largest Chinese capital exporters are state-owned enterprises.

8 This is reflected in the so-called 'Tentative Administrative Measures for Verifying and Approving Outbound Investment', promulgated by the National Development and Reform Commission (NDRC), which lists as a criteria for the approval of Chinese outbound investments that the investment 'is beneficial to the development of strategic resources required for national economic development'.

9 *Ekran Berhad* v. *People's Republic of China*, ICSID Case No. ARB/11/15.

10 The suspension took effect on 22 July 2011 before the tribunal had been constituted.

11 (2010) Investment Arbitration Reporter, Vol. 3, No. 10.

12 See, for example, Li (2011) for a broader reading on Chinese investments in Mongolia.

13 *Vattenfall AB, Vattenfall Europe AG, Vattenfall Europe Generation AG & Co. KG* v. *Federal Republic of Germany*, ICSID Case No. ARB/09/6 is one notable exception.

14 See, for example, http://news.bbc.co.uk/2/shared/spl/hi/in_depth/china_politics/ key_people_events/html/8.stm (accessed 28 March 2011).

15 The China–Sweden BIT was later amended by the adoption of an Amendment Protocol, which entered into force in 2004. (The Amendment Protocol provides for an investor-state dispute resolution mechanism and allows investors to bring

'any legal disputes' between investor and the host state before an ICSID tribunal or an ad hoc tribunal'.) See, for example, the Investment Claims website, www. investmentclaims.com/ (accessed 28 March 2011).

16 China and Romania have signed several BITs that have replaced each other; one in 1994, and the latest which entered into force in 2009. See the UNCTAD website UNCTAD, www.unctadxi.org/templates/docsearch_____779.aspx (accessed 28 March 2011).

17 See, for example, the Denmark–China BIT (1985), the China–Croatia BIT (1993), and the Indonesia–China BIT (1994).

18 See, for example, Article 8 of the China–Kuwait BIT (1985), and Article 13 of the China–Singapore BIT (1985).

19 See, for example, Article R.3(3) of the UK–China BIT (1986).

20 See, for example, Article 3(3) of the China–Iceland BIT (1994).

21 Similar arbitration clauses were subsequently included in many other second generation BITs.

22 Eighty-three per cent of BITs between China and countries that have been specifically targeted by the Chinese government for natural resources investments by Chinese companies are first generation BITs. See, for example, Eliasson (2010: 17–20) for a further discussion on the Chinese foreign investment regime in the natural resources sector.

23 China signed the 1965 Convention on the Settlement of Investment Disputes between States and Nationals of Other Sates (the ICSID Convention) in 1990, and it entered into force with respect to China on 6 February 1993.

24 The Tribunal comprised Mr Judd Kessler (USA) as President, with Professor Juan Fernandez Armesto (Spain) and Mr Hernando Otero (Columbia) as Arbitrators.

25 *Mr Tza Yap Shum* v. *The Republic of Peru*, ICSID Case No. ARB/07/6, Award, 7 July 2011, available at: http://italaw.com/documents/TzaYapShumAward.pdf (accessed 8 August 2011).

26 See, for example, *European Media Ventures S.A.* v. *Czech Republic* (ICSID Case No. ARB/03/20); *Saipem S.p.A* v. *The Republic of Bangladesh* (ICSID Case No. ARB/05/07); *Telenor Mobile Communications A.S.* v. *Republic of Hungary* (ICSID Case No. ARB/04/15); and *Sedelmayer* v. *The Russian Federation*, IIC 106 (1998); *Renta 4 S.V.S.A et al.* v. *Russian Federation* (SCC No. 024/2007).

27 See for example, *Berschader* v. *The Russian Federation*, Award dated 21 April 2006 (SCC Case No. 080/2004) and *RosInvest UK Ltd* v. *The Russian Federation*, Award dated 5 October 2007 (SCC Case No. V(079/2005).

28 *RosInvest UK Ltd* v. *The Russian Federation* (SCC Case No. V(079/2005)).

29 *Plama Consortium Ltd (Cyprus)* v. *Republic of Bulgaria* (ICSID Case No. ARB/ 03/24).

30 For instance, according to official governmental statistics, a substantial proportion of all registered Chinese outbound investments are channelled through Hong Kong subsidiaries of Chinese companies before reaching their final destination. Chinese investments are also frequently channelled through entities incorporated in the British Virgin Islands: MOFCOM (2009).

31 *Siemens A.G.* v. *República Argentina*, ICSID case No. ARB/02/8, Decision on Jurisdiction, 3 August 2004.

32 See also generally Skinner, Miles and Luttrell (2010).

33 *Tokios Tokelés* v. *Ukraine*, ICSID Case No. ARB/02/18, Decision on Jurisdiction, 29 April 2004.

34 *Saluka Investments B.V.* v. *The Czech Republic*, Partial Award, 17 March 2006 (UNCITRAL rules). See further briefly Hamamoto, Chapter 3 in this volume.

35 See, for example, the Finland–China BIT (2004), and the China–Bosnia-Herzegovina BIT (2002).

36 Nationality Law of the People's Republic of China (PRC), Adopted at the Third Session of the Fifth National People's Congress, promulgated by Order No. 8 of the Chairman of the Standing Committee of the National People's Congress and effective as of 10 September 1980, Article 2. See also Article 18 of the Basic Law of the Hong Kong Special Administrative Region of the PRC, which gives effect to the Nationality Law of the PRC through Annex III, 'Interpretation by the Standing Committee of the National People's Congress on Some Questions Concerning Implementation of the Nationality Law of the People's Republic of China in the Hong Kong Special Administrative Region', Adopted at the 19th Meeting of the Standing Committee of the Eighth National People's Congress on 15 May 1996; and Article 18 of the Basic Law of the Macao Special Administrative Region of the People's Republic of China, which gives effect to the Nationality Law of the PRC through Annex III.

37 Since many states recognize the People's Republic of China to be the sole legitimate representative of all China, such states might find it difficult to take the position that nationals of Taiwan should not be treated as nationals of the People's Republic of China for the purpose of investment protection.

38 See, for example, the UNCTAD website, www.unctadxi.org/templates/Doc Search.aspx?id=779 (accessed 19 February 2011).

39 Article 151 of the Basic Law of the Hong Kong SAR reads: 'The Hong Kong Special Administrative Region may on its own, using the name "Hong Kong, China", maintain and develop relations and conclude and implement agreements with foreign states and regions and relevant international organizations in the appropriate fields, including the economic, trade, financial and monetary, shipping, communications, tourism, cultural and sports fields.'

40 See, for example, the Germany–Hong Kong BIT (1996).

41 See, for example, Eliasson (2010: 17–20) for a further discussion on the Chinese foreign investment regime in the natural resources sector.

42 These jurisdictional battles often continue before national courts or ICSID ad hoc Annulment Committees. For a discussion of challenge proceedings in investment treaty cases, see Hobér and Eliasson (2010); and Coppens, Chapter 9 in this volume.

Bibliography

Berger, A. (2008) 'China and the Global Governance of Foreign Direct Investment: The Emerging Liberal Bilateral Investment Treaty Approach', Discussion Paper 10/2008, German Development Institute.

Dolzer, R. and Schreuer, C. (2008) 'Principles of International Investment Law', Oxford: Oxford University Press.

Eliasson, N. (2009) 'Investor-State Arbitration and Chinese Investors', *Contemporary Asia Arbitration Journal*, 2(2): 347.

Eliasson, N. (2010) 'Investment Treaty Protection of Chinese Natural Resources Investments', *Transnational Dispute Management*, 7(4). Available at: http: www. transantional-dispute-management.com (accessed 19 February 2011).

Gallagher, N. and Shan, W. (2008) *Chinese Investment Treaties: Policies and Practice*, Oxford: Oxford University Press.

Hobér, K. (2010) 'Compensation: A Closer Look at Cases Awarding Compensation for Violation of the Fair and Equitable Treatment Standard', in Small, K. (ed.) *Arbitration Under International Investment Agreements*, Oxford: Oxford University Press, p. 573.

Hobér, K. and Eliasson, N. (2009) 'Investor-State Arbitration and China: An Overview', in Moser, M. (ed.) *Resolving Business Disputes in China*, 2nd edn, Huntington: Juris Publishing, p. 209.

Hobér, K. and Eliasson, N. (2010) 'Review of Investment Treaty Awards by Municipal Courts', in Small, K. (ed.) *Arbitration under International Investment Agreements*, Oxford: Oxford University Press, p. 635.

Li, J. (2011) 'Chinese Investment in Mongolia: An Uneasy Courtship between Goliath and David', *East Asia Forum*. Online. Available at: www.eastasiaforum. org/2011/02/02/chinese-investment-in-mongolia-an-uneasy-courtship-between-goliath-and-david/ (accessed 19 February 2011).

Malintoppi, L. and Reinisch, A. (2008) 'Methods of Dispute Resolution', in Muchlinski, P., Ortino, F. and Schreuer, C. (eds) *The Oxford Handbook of International Investment Law*, Oxford: Oxford University Press, p. 694.

Markert, L. (2010) *Streitschlichtungsklauseln' in Investitionsschutzabkommen {Arbitration Provisions in Investment Protection Treaties}*, Cologne: Nomos.

MOFCOM (2009) '2009 Statistical Bulletin of China's Outward Foreign Investment'.

Moser, M. (2010) 'Ulf Franke, Stockholm Arbitration, and the Bridge to China', in Hobér, K., Magnusson, A., Öhrström, M. (eds) *Between East and West: Essays in Honour of Ulf Franke*, New York: Juris Publishing, pp. 343–50.

Muchlinski, P. (2008) 'Policy Issues', in Muchlinski, P., Ortino, F. and Schreuer, C. (eds), *The Oxford Handbook of International Investment Law*, Oxford: Oxford University Press, p. 4.

Schill, S.W. (2007) 'Tearing Down the Great Wall: the New Generation Investment Treaties of the People's Republic of China', *The Berkeley Electronic Press Legal Series*, 1928. Available at: http://law.bepress.com/expresso/eps/1928 (accessed 28 March 2011).

Skinner, M., Miles, C. and Luttrell, S. (2010) 'Access and advantage in investor-state arbitration: The law and practice of treaty shopping', *Journal of World Energy Law and Business*, forthcoming.

UNCTAD (2010) 'Most-Favoured-National Treatment', UNCTAD Series on Issues in International Investment Agreements II, New York, Geneva. Available at: www.unctad.org/en/docs/diaeia20101_en.pdf (accessed 19 February 2011).

6 Foreign investment in Indonesia

The problem of legal uncertainty

Simon Butt

6.1 Introduction

For most of Soeharto's 32-year reign, Indonesia's economic development was outstanding. Within a few years of Soeharto taking power from Indonesia's first president, Soekarno, the Indonesian economy was growing at an average of around 7 per cent per annum – a rate that continued until 1996. Soeharto's self-titled New Order (*Orde Baru*) significantly reduced poverty (World Bank 1990) and markedly improved living and educational standards (Thee 2008). Progress was so good that in 1994 the World Bank proclaimed Indonesia one of the eight 'High Performing Asian Economies', alongside Japan, South Korea, Taiwan, Hong Kong and Singapore (World Bank 1994).

By 1997, however, many Soeharto-era economic and developmental gains had unravelled. Commencing in that year, and for several years thereafter, Indonesia suffered one of the world's biggest economic and monetary crises in the post-Second World War era (Levinson 1998). The so-called Asian Financial Crisis, a flow-on from the collapse of the Thai baht in July 1997 that had caused many foreign investors to re-examine their portfolios, hit Indonesia harder than any other country (McLeod 2004: 95). Indonesia lost 13 per cent of its GDP in 1997 alone, and its currency plummeted from Rp2,000 per US dollar to almost Rp20,000 by February 1998. Hundreds of companies could not service their US dollar loans and went bankrupt as Indonesia's foreign debt ballooned to US$80 billion (Hosen 2010: 50). Around half of Indonesia's approximately 200 million people faced poverty and one-quarter faced unemployment (Levinson 1998).

The legitimacy of the Soeharto regime had been tied to Indonesia's economic performance, and the resulting improvement to the lot of ordinary Indonesians. While the economy was booming, the New Order had been able to justify its authoritarianism and repression as necessary for economic development. It could do so no longer. Pressure for wide-ranging political, social and economic reform intensified as riots broke out across Indonesia. Soeharto was forced to resign on 21 May 1998 and the era of *reformasi* began.

Indonesia's subsequent recovery – economic, political and legal – has been remarkable. Indonesia has, by most accounts, transformed itself from being one of Southeast Asia's most repressive and centralized political systems to its most decentralized, free and democratic. Indonesia's economic growth has steadily increased since 2000 to almost pre-crisis levels (Thee 2008). Though FDI did not begin to flow readily again until 2004, it too has recovered to pre-1997 levels (OECD 2010: 19). Significantly, post-1997 reforms, particularly to the banking sector, appeared to largely insulate Indonesia from the Global Financial Crisis, which interrupted, but has not significantly reduced, Indonesia's economic growth and FDI flows. FDI was US$8 billion in 2005, US$4.5 billion in 2006, US$7 billion in 2007 and almost US$10 billion in 2008 (OECD 2010: 46), as shown in Figure 6.A.

The Indonesian government and many international financial institutions consider, however, that these FDI rates are inadequate. More FDI, they claim, will enable Indonesia to meet its infrastructure needs, and will increase employment and export-led growth (OECD 2010: 19).

To improve Indonesia's investment climate for both foreign and domestic investors, the Indonesian government has enacted a number of laws in recent years. This chapter will discuss some of them, such as the 2007 Investment Law. Yet, despite improvements, many obstacles to attracting and maintaining foreign investment remain. Indonesia may have abundant natural resources and a large internal market (OECD 2010: 24), but international business perception indicators do not portray Indonesia's investment climate in a positive light. The World Bank's *Doing Business* 2011 indicators rank Indonesia 121st out of 183 countries for overall ease of doing business.[1]

In particular, complaints abound about the legal system and the uncertainty that seems inherent in it. Business surveys reveal that, for investors, Indonesian law is generally unclear and mechanisms for its enforcement rarely lead to predictable outcomes. For example, for enforcing contracts Indonesia ranked 154th on the *Doing Business* scale. Asian Development

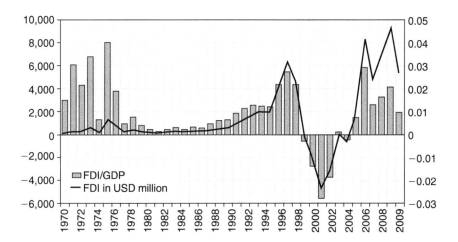

Figure 6.A FDI inflows in Indonesia (US$ millions) (source: OECD 2010: 46).

Bank (ADB) investor surveys reveal similar concerns about legal uncertainty, including in enforcing contracts (ADB 2005). In this context, legal uncertainty is often portrayed as a barrier to those considering investing, or adding to their investments, in Indonesia.[2]

This chapter identifies and describes some of the primary contributors to legal uncertainty within the Indonesian legal system, particularly its vast mass of law and lack of an effective mechanism to order it. It also discusses the failure of the courts to provide guidance in resolving legal uncertainty and shows how regional autonomy makes it worse. Some of the very reforms demanded and granted in the post-Soeharto *reformasi* era – decentralization and judicial independence – have compounded the uncertainty. An overarching issue is corruption – particularly within the bureaucracy and law enforcement – for which legal uncertainty provides fertile ground. If payee and payer are willing, particular laws can be enforced, bent or ignored. This problem has been well-documented elsewhere,[3] however, and will not therefore be considered here in detail.

6.2 Post-Suharto law reform

Within two years of Soeharto's resignation, a flurry of legislative activity was undertaken in an attempt to reconfigure Indonesia's political and economic environment. Under Soeharto's successor, former Vice-President Bacharuddin Jusuf Habibie, almost 70 statutes, 300 government regulations and 100 presidential decrees were issued. Many of these laws seemed likely to affect the investment climate, for better or worse. For example, various international labour conventions were ratified,[4] and a new labour law was passed in an attempt to improve employment conditions and permit unions (Arnold 2008).[5] Some investors complained about onerous compliance costs for employers and increased strikes (ADB 2005: 20). Several laws – including on freedom of speech,[6] the press,[7] human rights,[8] political parties,[9] and general elections[10] – appeared geared towards reviving Indonesian democracy, but raised the spectre of political instability and stagnation, due largely to a highly factionalized parliament.

Some laws appeared to be directed at improving the Indonesian economy and business climate. An Anti-Monopoly and Unfair Competition Law purports to improve business competitiveness.[11] Several statutes sought to encourage private sector involvement in infrastructure and natural resource extraction and management, including in telecommunications,[12] oil and gas,[13] water resources,[14] and electricity.[15] A 1998 Bankruptcy Law,[16] enacted under IMF direction, was intended to facilitate debt recovery in newly-established commercial courts but, despite replacement in 2004,[17] it is widely considered to have been a failure. In particular, decisions of the commercial courts appear to have been tainted by judicial corruption, incompetence or both. Of particular concern was the declaration of bankruptcy of the Canadian Insurance Company, Manulife, for failing to pay a disputed debt (Linnan 2008).

6.2.1 *The Investment Law*

In 2007, the parliament enacted an Investment Law[18] that explicitly seeks to attract foreign and domestic investment. The 2007 Law replaced a 1967 Foreign Investment Law and 1968 Domestic Investment Law, passed soon after Soeharto took power from Soekarno. The statute describes the need for investment to increase economic growth, employment, sustainable economic development, national competitiveness, technological capacity and public welfare (Article 3(2)). It was intended to make Indonesia more competitive compared to other countries in the region, such as Cambodia, Malaysia, Vietnam, India and China.

Some of its key features are as follows. Foreign investors must get a permit from the Investment Coordinating Board (*Badan Koordinasi Penanaman Modal*, BKPM) and must incorporate under Indonesian law. The Law promises equal treatment to domestic and foreign investors, having regard to the national interest (Articles 4 and 6), and the free repatriation of capital, profit, income, and funds to buy raw or other types of materials (Article 8).

The Law provides investment 'facilities' or inducements for investors whose enterprises:

- absorb many employees;
- operate in high-priority fields or so-called 'pioneer' industries;
- involve infrastructure development, technology transfer or partnerships with small or medium enterprises, or cooperatives;
- conduct research, development or innovation;
- are located in isolated, remote, border regions;
- protect the environment; or
- use capital goods or machines or equipment produced in Indonesia (Article 18).

The facilities include time-limited reduced income tax; exemption from or reduction of some import duties and land taxes; and help obtaining rights to land, immigration services and import permits (Articles 18, 21, 23).

The Law also imposes obligations upon foreign investors. For example, foreign investors must prioritize the employment of Indonesians (Article 10). Although they are permitted to employ foreign experts, they must train and transfer technology to their Indonesian employees.

Article 15 requires foreign investors to

- employ principles of good governance;
- fulfil corporate social responsibilities;
- report their investment activities to the BKPM;
- respect cultural traditions of the community at the site of investment; and
- comply with all laws.

These are perhaps the most controversial obligations, particularly in respect of corporate social responsibility (CSR), discussed below. Non-compliance with Article 15 can lead to administrative sanctions, which include warnings or even the limitation, freezing or cancelling of investment activities (Article 34(1)). These sanctions can be 'imposed by the institution with authority as declared by law' (Article 34(2)).

Article 16 requires investors to also:

- ensure the availability of capital from a legal source;
- honour all debts if it ceases operating or leaves Indonesia;
- engage in fair competition;
- protect the environment; and
- ensure the safety, health and welfare of employees.

Investors involved in exploitation of non-renewable natural resources must also allocate money to restore the location according to environmental principles (Article 17).

The Law also closes some industries to foreign investment and requires the President to stipulate, in a Presidential Regulation, other fields that are closed or subject to limitations (Article 12). The so-called 'negative list' was, as of March 2011, contained in Presidential Regulation No. 36 of 2010.[19] Some fields are closed altogether to foreign investment; some require government permission; some are reserved for micro, small and medium enterprises; and others require partnership with local small to medium enterprises. For specified industries, foreign capital is capped at between 25 and 99 per cent.

The Indonesian government, through the BKPM, is to provide a one-stop service to coordinate the investment, including with regional governments, and to help investors overcome impediments they face when investing (Articles 25–28).

The Law also sought to allow foreigners to obtain and hold various land rights for longer than previously permitted, though foreigners are still unable to obtain freehold title. These rights include land cultivation (*hak guna usaha*), the right to build (*hak guna bangunan*) and the right to use (*hak pakai*). Under the pre-2007 system, after the initial grant of between 25 and 35 years (depending on the right) had expired, these land rights could be extended for 20–30 years (depending on the right). The 2007 Law sought to allow the upfront extension of those rights, if the investment met particular requirements, presumably to give certainty to investors.[20] The upfront extensions have been disallowed by the Constitutional Court, however. In a 2008 case, the Court found that allowing up-front extensions breached Article 33(3) of the Constitution, which requires state ownership and control over natural resources, even though the Investment Law does allow the government to revoke the grant (Hukumonline 2008).[21]

The Law purports to grant investors several other rights, many of which appear vague and uncertain in scope. These include to certainty of rights, of law and of protection (*kepastian hak, hukum, dan perlindungan*), information about the sector in which they operate, services and the investment facilities provided by law (Article 14). To this end, the Law requires Indonesia's central and local governments to guarantee certainty and security (*kepastian dan keamanan*) to investors (Article 30(1)).

Legal certainty is defined in the Elucidation[22] to Article 14 as:

> the government guarantee that law will be the primary foundation of its every action and policy for investors.

This 'right' to legal certainty is, however, largely a legal mirage because Indonesia's legal system is dysfunctional to the point that it is often difficult – sometimes impossible – to determine what the 'law' is on any given matter. The legal uncertainty inherent in the Indonesian system is the focus of this chapter.

As for dispute settlement between government and investors, the Law provides the following in Article 32:

1   Investment disputes between the Government and investors are to be first settled through deliberation and consensus.
2   If a settlement cannot be reached by deliberation and consensus, the dispute can be settled through arbitration, alternative dispute resolution or the courts, under prevailing laws.
3   Investment disputes between the Government and domestic investors are to be settled through arbitration, if the parties have agreed to do so, and if resolution is not achieved through arbitration, then the dispute is to be resolved in court.
4   Investment disputes between the Government and foreign investors are to be resolved through international arbitration upon which the parties must agree.

It is important to note that the 2007 Law exists alongside the Bilateral Investment Treaties (BITs) that Indonesia has signed with many countries, as shown in the Appendix. Most of these BITs contain provisions familiar to most investors (see Dolzer and Schreuer 2008: Chapter VII). They seek to encourage and promote investments in its territory by investors of the other Party, ensure fair and equitable treatment, and provide within their territories protection and security to investments. They provide MFN provisions, guarantees against nationalization or expropriation, and require that laws pertaining to investments be public and readily accessible. As for settlement of disputes between a government and an investor, most BITs provide that the parties must first attempt to resolve the dispute by consultations and negotiations. If this fails, then the dispute can be settled by the courts in the country where the investment is admitted, or sent to the International Centre for the Settlement of Investment Disputes (ISCID) for conciliation or arbitration, using the procedures of the 1965 Convention on the Settlement of Investment Disputes between States and Nationals of Other States (the ICSID Convention). If the parties cannot agree whether conciliation or arbitration is the more appropriate procedure, the investor affected has the right to choose. If both state parties are not parties to the ICSID Convention, then the dispute can be resolved using procedures agreed between the parties. If these are not agreed within three months, generally the host state must submit to arbitration under the Arbitration Rules of the United Nations Commission on International Trade Law (UNCITRAL).

Indonesia is also party to several regional instruments that seek to protect investments, including the ASEAN Comprehensive Investment Agreement, the ASEAN–Korea Investment Agreement, the ASEAN–China Investment Agreement, and the ASEAN Free Trade Agreement with Australia and New Zealand. It is pursuing several other FTAs and has concluded the Economic Partnership Agreement with Japan (OECD 2010: 81).

Of course in arbitration proceedings these BITs and FTAs would be primary reference points for dispute resolution. It is unclear, however, whether, domestically, these BITs add much to the 2007 Investment Law. Formally, it appears that, under Indonesian law, treaties automatically become part of Indonesian domestic law when they are ratified (Supriatna 2008: 157). Yet, in practice, ratified treaties are rarely treated as such until their terms have been adopted within Indonesian laws. Perhaps, though, they might be used as an aid to interpretation of Article 32(4). That is, if the parties have not agreed or cannot agree upon the forum and procedures for arbitration, then the forum and procedure, if mentioned in a relevant BIT, might prevail.

Critically, however, Article 32(4) does not clearly stipulate how disputes between investors and the Indonesian government should be resolved if the parties cannot agree upon the seat of the arbitration and procedures, and no BIT, FTA or contract otherwise governs the investment. Could one of the parties stall arbitration by refusing to agree on the particulars, thereby thwarting Article 32(4)'s apparent right to arbitration? Or would failure to agree force recourse to Article 32(2) which, as mentioned, allows disputes to be settled through the courts? If this were the accepted interpretation, the Indonesian government could stonewall agreement, thereby exposing the investor to the Indonesian judicial process and its associated problems, discussed in Section 6.4.2.

6.3 Legal uncertainty: what is 'the law'?

Put simply, there are just too many laws on the books in Indonesia. Too many lawmakers have power to produce too many types of laws. By itself, this huge mass of law adds great complexity to the system. Uncertainty then compounds this complexity in several ways. Some laws contradict others, but no reliable mechanisms exist to settle inconsistencies. Statutes are usually drafted broadly, with specifics left to be incorporated in executive regulations, some of which take years to issue, and can be difficult to obtain, if they are issued at all. Some laws are out of date, leading to confusion about how they should be applied, if at all, to modern circumstances. The Courts are, however, reluctant to fill in any gaps, despite being authorized to do so. It can also be difficult to identify the law governing a particular situation and to keep track of whether particular laws have been amended or replaced. These uncertainties are accentuated by decentralization, and the multitude of lawmakers it has spawned, discussed below.

6.3.1 *The mass of law*

Of Indonesia's sources of laws, 'state law' is of most relevance to investors. State law can be broadly defined as (i) codes and statutes enacted by the national parliament or which remain in force since Dutch colonization ended in 1945; (ii) the many thousands of executive regulations and decisions; and (iii) laws issued by sub-national parliaments and executives.

Today, Indonesia's legal backbone is still Dutch law. Though now heavily supplemented with hundreds of statutes enacted by successive Indonesian governments since independence in 1945, large portions of Dutch Codes remain on the books in the form in which they were first transplanted into Indonesia during the colonial period. While there are official Indonesian translations of these Codes, the authoritative versions are in the Dutch language. This is problematic, given that most Indonesian lawyers now do not speak Dutch.

These Dutch codes are well over 100 years old and have themselves been overhauled or repealed in Holland (Subekti 1978: 23; Lev 1965). For example, the Civil Code was passed in 1838 in Holland and brought into force in Indonesia largely unamended in 1848 (Ahmad 1986: 5). The Code still governs principal areas of commercial law, including the law of contracts and torts. Indonesia has two Codes of Civil Procedure: the *Herziene Indonesisch Reglement* 1941 (which applies in Java and Madura) and the *Reglement Buitengewesten* 1927 (which is valid in the rest of Indonesia). Parts of these Codes have, too, been supplanted by more modern legislation. Many provisions remain untouched, however. Some are so outdated, unclear and incomplete that they create significant problems for judges, lawyers and litigants in even the most basic areas of procedural law.

Formally, other sources of law exist, but prevail only in the absence of state law. These include customary or traditional law (*adat*), which though largely supplanted by the Agrarian Law of 1960,[23] is still widely used to determine entitlements to land, particularly in regional areas (Daryono 2010). Elements of *Syariah* (Islamic law) apply to Muslims. Until recently, Syariah's applicability was limited to aspects of family law, such as marriage and divorce (Butt 2008a, 2010a). The role of Islamic law appears to have been expanded, however. In 2006, jurisdiction was granted to Islamic courts to adjudicate matters of Islamic finance,[24] and laws were passed in 2008 to support Indonesia's growing Islamic banking sector.[25]

Indonesia's so-called 'hierarchy of laws' (*tata urutan peraturan perundang-undangan*) aims to bring some order to this mass of law. It contains a list of various types of formally-recognized state laws and ranks their authority vis-à-vis each other as follows:[26]

1   The 1945 Constitution (*Undang-undang Dasar 1945*);
2   Statutes (*Undang-undang*)/Interim Emergency Laws (*PERPU*);[27]
3   Government Regulations (*Peraturan Pemerintah*);
4   Presidential Regulations (*Peraturan Presiden*);
5   Regional Regulations (*Peraturan Daerah*).

A law must not conflict with any law higher than its own type in the hierarchy; and a law can amend or revoke any law that is lower than its own type in the hierarchy. Theoretically, a lower-level law is supposed to 'implement' a law higher than it, usually by providing further details about an issue the higher law raises. For example, as discussed above, the 2007 Investment Law – a statute – declares that some fields are closed for foreign investment and mentions some of them, but leaves it to a Presidential Regulation to set out the full negative list.

The hierarchy, however, is highly problematic. Many commonly-used types of laws are not on the list, including Presidential Decisions (*Keputusan Presiden*), Ministerial Regulations (*Peraturan Menteri*) and Ministerial Decisions (*Keputusan Menteri*). There are many thousands of these documents. Their status relative to other laws on the list is therefore unclear. This is a live issue in decentralized Indonesia, where, as discussed below (Section 4.1), the Ministry of Home Affairs reviews, for compliance with national laws, some types of sub-national laws. Could the Minister, by issuing a Ministerial Decision, invalidate a regional regulation? Instinctively one might answer yes, arguing that central government laws should trump those of local government. Yet there is no basis in law for this argument. Indeed, given that local parliaments and executives are freely and fairly elected and that national ministers need not be, this argument is not supported by democratic principles. Notably, treaties are not included in the list. Their relative legal status in Indonesian domestic law is, therefore, unclear, as mentioned above in Section 4.2.1.

Worse, most mechanisms for resolving inconsistencies are deeply flawed and largely ineffective. For the most part, the hierarchy is unenforceable. The Supreme Court can invalidate types of laws on the hierarchy below statutes, but has simply declined to do so on many occasions, as discussed below. The President can invalidate local laws on several grounds, including that they contradict higher-level laws, but this power has been exercised, controversially, by the Minister for Home Affairs, to invalidate only a narrow range of laws. Only the Constitutional Court has been effective in enforcing the hierarchy, but its jurisdiction is narrow: to review statutes as against the Constitution (Butt 2007). The great mass of Indonesian laws – contained in laws below statutes on the hierarchy – is, therefore, not in practice, restrained by it.

6.3.2 Broadly cast legislation

Some provisions of Indonesian statutes are clear and 'self-sufficient'. Like the so-called 'basic laws' of many civil law systems (David and Brierley 1985: 114), most Indonesian statutes aim to provide a general framework for regulation, leaving the detail to lower-level laws, such as government and presidential regulations.[28] According to Damian and Hornick (1972: 511):

> [A]s is customary with the so-called "basic" laws of Indonesia, these laws function more as policy declarations than as statutory schemes. Implementation usually depends on the enactment of subsequent legislation and the promulgation of special implementing regulations. Until such implementing rules are established, the "basic" law operates mostly as a statement of national intention.

The need for further implementing regulations is problematic for legal certainty in Indonesia. Often, years pass before they are issued, if they are issued at all. Current practice is that most legislative provisions which anticipate further regulations lie dormant until the regulations are passed – the courts will very rarely, if ever, 'fill in the gaps' left by statutes.

Laws that are broadly cast and require implementation present real problems for investors. Laws making Corporate Social Responsibility (CSR) mandatory in some sectors provide good examples. As mentioned above (Section 6.2.1), Article 15(b) of the 2007 Investment Law requires investors (domestic and foreign) to 'fulfil social corporate responsibilities and to respect cultural traditions of the community at the site of investment'. CSR is defined as 'the responsibility attaching to all investment companies to create harmonious, balanced and appropriate relationships/connections with the environment, values, norms or culture of the local society'. The Law provides no definitions of 'cultural traditions' or 'social responsibilities', however. With little guidance about what is necessary for compliance, many companies feel exposed to the whim of government interpretation of these requirements and fear that the uncertain requirements will be used to leverage bribes. After all, compliance is critical. As mentioned, under Article 34(1) of the 2007 Investment Law, failure to comply can lead to investment activities being limited, frozen or even cancelled.

The Company Law (Law No. 40 of 2007), too, requires companies affecting natural resources to implement 'social and environmental corporate responsibility' (Article 74(1)), defined as the company's 'commitment' to participate in sustainable economic development so as to increase the quality of life and environment, for the company itself, the local community and the community in general (Article 1(3)). This, the Law requires, is to be calculated as a company cost, calculated by reference to 'decency and fairness' (*kepatutan dan kewajaran*) (Article 74(2)). The Law requires a government regulation to provide further details on CSR requirements, but at time of writing this regulation had not been issued.

Finally, some regulations contradict the statute they purport to implement, as discussed below (Section 6.4). Because for most types of laws the hierarchy of laws is unenforceable, confusion often emerges over which law to follow.

6.3.4 *Accessing laws*

Though obtaining statues and regulations was difficult during the pre-*reformasi* period, internet databases, initially hosted by non-government organizations such as Hukumonline[29] but now also by government,[30] have alleviated many of the problems. Yet many of these databases host only higher-order laws, such as statutes, government regulations and presidential decisions. Other lower-level laws are more difficult to find and obtaining them may require a visit to the government institution from which it was issued. Often the lower the level of the law, the more important it is to establishing 'the law' on a particular point: the lower in the hierarchy, the more specific the laws tend to be. Access to them is, therefore, critical.

6.4 Factors compounding uncertainty

6.4.1 *Regional autonomy*

One of the strongest demands of the *reformasi* period was decentralization, or regional autonomy (*otonomi daerah*) as it is called in Indonesia. Resentment of the concentration of political power within the central government – itself tightly controlled by Soeharto – had become deeply unpopular well before Soeharto resigned. After he stepped aside, however, regional aspirations for a greater role in local government, which he had strongly repressed, became so strong and, in some parts of Indonesia, so violent, that they could not be ignored. Many feared, quite reasonably, that Indonesia would disintegrate if power was not dispersed (Vickers 2005: 220).

Laws establishing the political, legal and economic frameworks for regional autonomy were enacted in 1999 and replaced in 2004.[31] Of most significance for the purposes of this chapter was the delegation or devolution of wide-ranging lawmaking powers from the national government to regional governments at the provincial and the city/municipality levels. There are now 33 provinces in Indonesia and almost 500 cities/municipalities, each with their own legislatures and executive governments. With regional autonomy, then, came around 1000 new lawmakers with broad powers to pass laws on a very wide range of subject matters.

Of course, this proliferation of lawmakers has significantly expanded the mass of law described above. It is difficult to estimate by how much as there is no central repository of local government laws. If each new lawmaker passed only one law per annum in the dozen or so years since regional autonomy, then more than 12,000 new laws have been added to Indonesia's statute books. It is likely that lawmakers have issued more than one law each per year, however. The number is probably twice or three times this estimate.

Many local governments were quick to use their new lawmaking powers to raise revenue by imposing local taxes, user charges and licence fees. Early studies suggested that around 1000 new taxes and charges were created by local governments in the first year of decentralization (Lewis and Sjahir 2009: 231). The focus of these imposts was trade, as local government lacked the power to tax incomes or assets (Ray 2003: 10). More recent studies indicate that local governments may have established as many as 6000 new taxes and charges during the period 2000 to mid-2005 (Lewis and Sjahir 2009: 231). If this trend has continued, then more than 10,000 new local taxes may have been created.

The concern is that local, provincial and central governments issuing their own licence and tax laws creates duplication and complexity which, in turn, significantly complicates and hampers investment (Antara 2007; OECD 2010: 21). A common complaint is that these revenue raising laws are creating a 'high cost economy', injuring internal trade and providing a disincentive for investment, both foreign and domestic.[32] However, the precise extent of the disincentive is unclear and debated (Brodjonegoro 2004). It is also of real concern that officials without legal or drafting experience are often given the task of conceiving and wording local laws. The result has been local laws that are so unclear as to be unworkable, unnecessary or oppressive.

The national government has, with a 2009 Law on Local Taxes and User Charges, attempted to restrict the types of local imposts to those enumerated on positive lists (Lewis and Sjahir 2009: 233). Yet, the Law still authorizes cities and municipalities to levy three general categories of user charges including for public services, including those associated with public health clinics, public markets, and waste removal; licensing fees of various kinds, including construction permits, land utilization permits; and business operating licences (Lewis and Sjahir 2009: 225–6).

The proliferation of irksome and potentially harmful sub-national taxes is only part of the problem decentralization presents, however. These new laws, of course, must operate within the dysfunctional system mentioned above. The result is nothing short of legal chaos. Many sub-national legislatures and executives do not provide easy access to the laws they produce. As mentioned, no central repository of all sub-national laws exists, and attempts to collect them, such as the World Bank's Perda (local law) Online project,[33] are no longer running, apparently due to funding constraints.

The most significant contributor of regional laws to Indonesia's legal disorder, however, appears to be contradictory laws. The central government and local government have overlapping jurisdiction. Under the 2004

Decentralization Law, the central government retained exclusive jurisdiction over foreign affairs, defence, security, religion and national monetary, fiscal and justice-sector matters (Article 10(3)). Local governments have power to legislate in all other areas. Yet, the 2004 Law also gives power to the central government to regulate in areas not mentioned in Article 10(3), meaning that, legally speaking, the central government can continue to regulate any matter over which regional governments also have jurisdiction.

Jurisdiction over investment matters is a case in point. The 2007 Investment Law gives the central government power to regulate investments: involving non-renewable resources, national security and high-priority industries; carrying a high risk of environmental damage; crossing provincial borders; or financed by foreign governments (Article 30). These categories of investments are vague, but any uncertainty is probably academic: the 2007 Law also reaffirms that the central government has jurisdiction to regulate investments falling within the fields over which it has jurisdiction. Presumably, this is a reference to the fields mentioned in Article 10(3) of the 2004 Autonomy Law. It could, however, also reinforce the central government's overarching jurisdiction over all matters, as Article 10(5), discussed above, seems to intend. As for the powers of regional governments, the Investment Law reaffirms that they maintain power to administer investments in fields over which they have authority, but not over which the central government has authority (Article 30).

There are two primary mechanisms designed to prevent and resolve inconsistencies between national and regional laws, but they do not work well. The first mechanism is judicial and involves the Supreme Court enforcing the hierarchy of laws by inconsistent regional laws. As discussed above (Section 6.3.1), statutes, government regulations and presidential regulations legally trump regional laws. The Supreme Court has been reluctant to issue such declarations and when it has done so, it has only been in a narrow category of cases.

The second mechanism is 'bureaucratic review', under which local laws are sent for review to a higher level of government. The 2004 Law requires provincial lawmakers to send many types of their laws to the Ministry of Home Affairs within seven days of enactment. The Ministry then has 60 working days to review the local laws as against 'higher laws' (*peraturan perundang-undangan yang lebih tinggi*) and the 'public interest' (*kepentingan umum*).[34] After this 60-day period expires, the law automatically comes into force, whether the Ministry has, in fact, reviewed it or not. City and municipality governments must send their laws to provincial governments for review using similar processes. Several thousand local laws have so far been reviewed through these processes, and several hundred revoked (Rosdianasari, Anggriani and Mulyani 2009: ix). However, many local laws, it seems, bypass the review mechanism altogether, either because the local government does not send its laws for review, or because the reviewing agency is unable to review the law within 60 days (Lewis 2003: 178; Ray 2003: 18).

Virtually all of the laws that have been revoked using this process seek to impose user charges (*retribusi*) or taxes (Butt 2010b).

The net result of this is that if two laws – one central, one local – are on the books and contradict each other, they are both likely to stay there. This, of course, leaves investors in a quandary over which law to follow and which to ignore. A common scenario is as follows. The central government passes a law requiring a mining company to pay licence fees and royalties to the central government. The local government at the site of the investment passes a law requiring payments to be made to it (Oktaviani and Irawan 2009). The investor is left in a quandary – does it need to comply with both laws, only one of them, or even none of them? What is certain is that, on a practical level, both central and local governments can make life difficult for the investor in an attempt to ensure compliance with their laws. So in practice, to be safe, investors often feel compelled to comply with both, which, in most cases, substantially increases their costs.

6.4.2 Uncertainty and the courts

The Indonesian judicial system has long been viewed as dysfunctional, by Indonesians and foreigners alike. A widely-held perception is that most Indonesian judges are unprofessional – that is, largely incompetent, inefficient and corrupt – and cannot be trusted to hand down impartial, predictable and well-reasoned decisions (Assegaf 2002).

A key reform sought in the post-Soeharto era was judicial independence. The New Order had tightly controlled the courts and was able to, in essence, dictate the decisions it wanted. The government obtained this control by using its powers, held primarily by the Ministry of Justice but also by the Religions Affairs Ministry and Defence and Security Ministry, to administer the courts and judges – particularly their pay, promotions, transfers and dismissals. Butt and Lindsey (2010b) explain:

> A system ... developed by which judicial promotions were very rarely based on merit; rather, they mostly were based on seniority, 'dedication to service', and 'demonstrated loyalty' (Supreme Court of Indonesia 2003: 132). The Department's power to transfer was also a powerful weapon (KHRN & LeIP 1999: 50). Indonesia has a broad range of living conditions – from major centres, particularly in Java and Bali, with world-class facilities and luxuries, to more remote, underdeveloped and, at times, even dangerous, locales. The prospect of five years in a major centre for 'toeing the line', instead of in a backwater as punishment for recalcitrance, was strong incentive indeed. (Supreme Court of Indonesia 2003: 131)

The so-called one-roof (*satu atap*) reforms, set in motion in 1999 and commencing from 2004,[35] sought to break down this government influence and control. Under these reforms, the organizational, administrative and financial affairs of Indonesia's lower courts were transferred from the Ministries to the Supreme Court.

The main objective of the reform – improving judicial independence – appears, on the whole, to have been successfully met. One now rarely hears complaints of government interference, and there have, in fact, been significant cases in which the government or state actors have been defeated (Butt 2008b). It appears, therefore, that foreign investors can, for the most part, expect a level playing field against the government in disputes heard before Indonesian courts.

6.4.3 Unpredictable decisions

However, many of the dysfunctional features of Indonesia's judicial system remain untouched by this reform. For reasons of space, this chapter will not discuss them all. Instead it offers a brief explanation of the courts' failure to hand down decisions that are predictable and consistent with previous decisions – something for which the courts, including the Supreme Court, are notorious.

It is often presumed that Indonesian judicial decisions are inconsistent largely because Indonesia follows the civil law tradition and does not therefore have a system of precedent. While formally it is true that Indonesia does not have this system, as a practical matter, first-instance and appeal courts will, like courts in other civil law countries, generally consider previous decisions from the highest court to be persuasive and will usually try to follow them (Lotulung 2000). In Indonesia, however, it is rarely possible to do this. Supreme Court decisions have, historically, been rarely published and are therefore difficult to obtain, even for courts. This has been changing over the past several years, with Supreme Court decisions now being published on the Supreme Court's website.[36] At time of writing, almost 20,000 decisions had been uploaded.

This is an impressive advance, but significant impediments remain. For example, the Supreme Court usually hears, on average, more than 10,000 cases per year. In 2010 alone, the Supreme Court decided almost 14,000 cases (Hukumonline 2011). Decisions on the website range from 2001 to 2010. It hosts therefore less than one-fifth of all cases the Supreme Court has heard during that period. Furthermore, many of the published decisions do not disclose all relevant facts and do not discuss previous similar decisions and competing legal arguments (Butt 2007). Most decisions therefore provide very little guidance on how Supreme Court cases should be applied in subsequent cases.

Lack of predictability and certainty in judicial decisions, combined with other court deficiencies, significantly contributes to legal uncertainty in Indonesia and, therefore, to the general reluctance of foreign investors and Indonesians alike to use the courts (ADB 2005). Well-advised investors tend to arbitrate their disputes with both state and non-state parties. Under the Law on Arbitration and Conciliation (Law No. 12 of 1999), parties can choose the law that will apply to any disputes which may arise between them (Article 56(2)). Awards, domestic or foreign, are enforceable by Indonesian courts in the same way as a civil decision of a court (Article 64). The Law sets out default procedures used in arbitration proceedings (Articles 27–51). These might be employed, for example, if the parties do not agree to follow the UNCITRAL Arbitration Rules (see Mills 2000).

For the most part, arbitration helps improve legal certainty. Indonesian courts usually respect arbitration agreements and enforce arbitral awards, both domestic and foreign (Hukumonline 2007). Arbitration is not, however, failsafe. Many Indonesian judges are said to remain uneasy about recognizing and enforcing agreements and some have been refused enforcement on grounds that they breach public order (*ketertiban umum*) (Hukumonline 2010a, 2010b), such as in the notorious Karaha Bodas case (Wells and Ahmed 2007). This involved a contract for the production and distribution of thermal energy between KBC, a largely foreign-owned company, and Indonesia's state-owned oil and electricity companies. Soeharto had suspended the project by decree when the 1997 economic crisis hit. Arbitration was conducted in Switzerland. The state-owned enterprises were found to bear government related risks and KBC was awarded US$260 million. Though the award was successfully enforced against their assets overseas, a Jakarta district court held that to enforce the award would be against public policy. The Supreme Court overturned this decision on appeal, however.

6.4.4 *Judicial review*

The judiciary – in particular, the Supreme Court – is contributing to legal uncertainty in another important way: as an arbiter of the legal order in decentralized Indonesia. The Supreme Court can review regional regulations using its judicial review jurisdiction. This enables the court to invalidate executive legal instruments – including local government laws – that contradict higher-order laws, including government regulations, presidential regulations or statutes enacted by Indonesia's national parliament.[37] Review applications can be brought by local legislatures whose local laws have been revoked or by citizens who believe that a particular local law breaches statutory rights.[38]

This is a critical task and the Court has not been performing it adequately. Recent studies have made two important findings. The first is that the Supreme Court has been reluctant to invalidate non-revenue-raising local laws.[39] In review cases where it has been asked to do so, it has simply decided that the subject matter of the local law falls within the power of the local government, without attempting to categorize that subject matter (Butt 2010b).

The second finding is that the Supreme Court strictly follows a 180-day limitation period set by internal regulations the Court issued to govern lodgment procedures in review cases. A significant proportion of reviews lodged with the Supreme Court fell foul of this limitation and were, therefore, thrown out.

6.5 Conclusion

On paper, the 2007 Investment Law provides to investors minimum protections and incentives, including legal certainty. The BITs and FTAs Indonesia has signed restate many of these protections and incentives and add to them. The primary significance of the BITs and FTAs seems to be for arbitration proceedings, given their questionable status under domestic Indonesian law. Yet while arbitration helps investors avoid Indonesia's largely corrupt and incompetent judiciary, it does not bypass the need for identifying the body of Indonesian law – whether national, provincial, municipal, legislative or executive – governing a particular investment.

Attempting to identify any given body of applicable Indonesian law often exposes the right to legal certainty as a nullity. This endeavour is difficult and unlikely to yield clear results due to several fundamental systemic problems with the legal system. These include almost total lack of effective mechanisms, bureaucratic or judicial, to resolve legal uncertainties. In particular, the inability to resolve inconsistent laws, despite the dramatic increase in lawmaking in recent years, has created a seemingly impenetrable mass of law from which extracting relevant legal principles is exceedingly difficult. Judicial intervention, itself often unpredictable and inconsistent, only seems to compound this uncertainty. Also cited as barriers to investment are illicit payments required to commence and run investments and to resolves disputes arising from them, said to be more common in decentralized Indonesia.

Except for the consequences of regional autonomy, these are problems of long standing in Indonesia. Yet, aside from the 1997 Asian Financial Crisis and the following decade-long economic catastrophe, Indonesia has enjoyed impressive and sustained economic growth since the early Soeharto years. It has achieved this economic success, much of it sustained by foreign investment, 'without the benefit of functional legal rules for commerce, and without reliable [legal] institutions' (Lindsey and Taylor 2000: 6). Despite the legal uncertainty and the corruption, investors have kept 'coming back', apparently attracted by Indonesia's large domestic market, natural resources, low-cost labour-force and reduced tariff and taxation incentives. Investors seem to have traditionally factored in the legal uncertainties described above when considering whether to invest in Indonesia and running their investment there and, it seems, they will continue needing to do so.

Appendix A

Indonesia's BITs

Partner	Date of Signature	Date of entry into force
Algeria	2000	
Argentina	1995	2001
Australia	1992	1993
Bangladesh	1998	1999
Belgium-Luxembourg	1970	1972
Bulgaria	2003	2005
Cambodia	1999	
Chile	1999	
China	1994	1995
Croatia	2002	
Cuba	1997	1999
Czech Republic	1998	1999
Denmark	2007	
Egypt	1994	1994
Finland	2006	2008
France	1973	1975
Germany	1968	1975
	2003	2007
Guyana	2008	
Hungary	1992	1996
India	1999	2004
Iran	2005	
Italy	1991	1995
Jamaica	1999	
Jordan	1996	1999
Korea, North	2000	
Korea, South	1991	1994
Kyrgyzstan	1995	1997
Laos	1994	1995
Libya	2009	
Malaysia	1994	1999
Mauritius	1997	200
Mongolia	1997	1999
Morocco	1997	2002
Mozambique	1999	2000
Netherlands	1994	1995
Norway	1991	1994
Pakistan	1996	1996
Philippines	2001	
Poland	1992	1993
Qatar	2000	
Romania	1997	1999
Russia	2007	

continued

Partner	Date of Signature	Date of entry into force
Saudi Arabia	2003	
Singapore	2005	
Slovakia	1994	1995
Spain	1995	1997
Sri Lanka	1996	1997
Sudan	1998	
Suriname	1995	
Sweden	1992	1993
Switzerland	1974	1976
Syria	1997	2000
Tajikistan	1994	
Thailand	1998	1998
Tunisia	1992	1992
Turkey	1997	1998
Turkmenistan	1994	
Ukraine	1996	1997
UK	1976	1977
Uzbekistan	1996	1997
Venezuela	2000	2003
Vietnam	1991	1994
Yemen	1998	
Zimbabwe	1999	

Source: Adapted from OECD (2010: 238–9).

Notes

1 See www.doingbusiness.org/data/exploreeconomies/indonesia/ (accessed 2 March 2011). However, these indicators have attracted some methodological criticism: see Michaels (2009).

2 This chapter does not seek to show that legal uncertainty actually hinders invest- ment. To prove that it does would be a very difficult exercise. It seems reasonable to presume, however, that if legal uncertainty is a common complaint of inves- tors operating in Indonesia, then it may also operate as a disincentive to FDI.

3 See, for example, Kuncoro (2006); Rinaldi, Purnomo and Damayanti (2007); Hosen (2010); Chene (2009); Goodpaster (2002); World Bank (2004).

4 ILO Convention No. 105 Concerning The Abolition Of Forced Labour, ILO Convention No. 138 Concerning Minimum Age For Admission To Employ- ment, ILO Convention No. 111 Concerning Discrimination In Respect Of Employment And Occupation (ratified by Laws No. 19–21 of 1999).

5 Law No. 13 of 2003 on Manpower.

6 Law No. 9 of 1998.

7 Law No. 40 of 1999.

8 Law No. 39 of 1999.

9 Law No. 2 of 1999.

10 Law No. 3 of 1999.

11 Law No. 5 of 1999.

12 Law No. 36 of 1999.

13 Law No. 22 of 2001.

14 Law No. 7 of 2004.

15 Law No. 20 of 2002. This statute was, however, struck down by the Constitutional Court for allowing excessive private sector involvement in an industry that Article 33 of the Constitution required the state to control (Butt and Lindsey 2010a). In 2009 Indonesia's parliament passed a new electricity law (Law No. 30 of 2009).

16 Law No. 4 of 1998.

17 Law No. 37 of 2004.

18 Law No. 25 of 2007 on Capital Investment, replacing Investment Laws of 1967 and 1968.

19 Progressively, more sectors opened up to more foreign ownership, beginning from the mid-1980s. In 1989, Indonesia switched from a positive to a negative list, opening hundreds of sectors to foreign investment, though subject to conditions: (OECD 2010: 45). The list is too long to set out in full here: an English translation is available on the Indonesia Investment Coordination Board website: at://www5.bkpm.go.id/ (accessed 2 March 2011).

20 To obtain an upfront extension the investment must meet particular requirements. These include improving the competitiveness of Indonesia's economy, being high risk, not offending society's sense of justice and not damaging the public interest (Article 22).

21 The government could suspend or revoke the grant or extension of those land rights if the investor abandons the land, damages the public interest, uses or exploits the land contrary to the purpose for which it was granted, or breaches land laws (Article 22(4)).

22 The Elucidation (*Penjelasan*) is the explanatory memorandum that accompanies most Indonesian statutes and government regulations. It is often determinative in the interpretation of the law, though not formally part of the law itself.

23 Law No. 5 of 1960.

24 Law No. 3 of 2006.

25 Law No. 21 of 2008 on Syariah Banking and Law No. 19 of 2008 on Syariah Securities.

26 Contained in Article 7(1) of Law on Making Laws (Law No. 10 of 2004).

27 Article 22 of Indonesia's Constitution permits the President to issue Government Regulations in lieu of a Statute (*Peraturan Pemerintah sebagai Pengganti Undang-undang*, PERPU) which have authority equivalent to ordinary statutes. These laws must be ratified by the DPR in its following sitting to remain valid.

28 In pre-*reformasi* Indonesia some were called 'basic laws' (*undang-undang pokok*), though in post-Soeharto Indonesia the term is rarely used.

29 See www.hukumonline.com.

30 See the State Secretariat's website (www.setneg.go.id) and the Legalitas website (www.legalitas.org) hosted by the Department of Law and Human Rights.

31 Law No. 32 of 2004 on Regional Government.

32 See, for example, Pratikno (2005: 21), Saad (2003), Brodjonegoro (2004: 8), UNDP (2008: 7), Maryono (2009).

33 See www.perdaonline.org (accessed 2 March 2011).

34 Article 145(2) of the 2004 Autonomy Law.

35 Law No. 4 of 2004 on Judicial Power; Law No. 5 of 2004 amending Law No. 14

of 1985 on the Supreme Court; Law No. 8 of 2004, amending the General Courts Law (Law No. 2 of 1986); and Law No. 9 of 2004, amending Law No. 5 of 1986 on the Administrative Courts.

36 See putusan.mahkamahagung.go.id (accessed 2 March 2011).

37 Article 24A(1) of the Constitution; Article 11(2)(b) of the Judicial Power Law (Law No. 4 of 2004); Article 31(2) of the Supreme Court Law (Law No. 5 of 2004).

38 Article 145(5) of the 2004 Autonomy Law.

39 See, for example, Supreme Court Decision Nos 14 P/HUM/2004; 20 P/HUM/2007; 03 P/HUM/2009.

Bibliography

ADB (2005) *Improving the Investment Climate in Indonesia*, Joint Asian Development Bank–World Bank Report.

Ahmad, Z.A. (1986) *Sejarah dan kedudukan BW di Indonesia*, Jakarta: Rajawali.

Antara (2007) 'Indonesia Failing to Cash in on Mineral Surge: Analysts', 12 November.

Arnold, L. (2008) 'Labour Law and Practice in Post-Soeharto Indonesia' in Lindsey, T. (ed.) *Indonesia: Law and Society*, Annandale, N.S.W.: Federation Press, p. 532.

Assegaf, I. (2002) 'Legends of the Fall: An Institutional Analysis of Indonesian Law Enforcement Agencies Combating Corruption' in Lindsey, T. and Dick, H.W. (eds) *Corruption in Asia: Rethinking the Governance Paradigm*, Annandale, N.S.W.: Federation Press, p. 127.

Brodjonegoro, B. (2004) *Three Years of Fiscal Decentralization in Indonesia: Its Impacts on Regional Economic Development and Fiscal Sustainability*, Tokyo: Hitotsubashi University. Available at: www.econ.hit-u.ac.jp/~kokyo/APPPsympo04/Indonesia (Bambang).pdf (accessed 17 March 2011).

Butt, S. (2007) *Judicial Review in Indonesia: Between Civil Law and Accountability? A Study of Constitutional Court Decisions 2003–2005*, PhD thesis, Law Faculty, Melbourne University.

Butt, S. (2008a) 'Polygamy and Mixed Marriage in Indonesia: Islam and the Marriage Law in the Courts' in Lindsey, T. (ed.) *Indonesia: Law and Society*, Annandale, N.S.W.: Federation Press, p. 266.

Butt, S. (2008b) 'Surat Sakti: The Decline of the Authority of Judicial Decisions in Indonesia' in Lindsey, T. (ed.) *Indonesia: Law and Society*, Annandale, N.S.W.: Federation Press, p. 346.

Butt, S. (2010a) 'Islam, the State and the Constitutional Court in Indonesia', *Pacific Rim Law & Policy Journal*, 19(2): 279.

Butt, S. (2010b) 'Regional Autonomy and the Proliferation of Perda in Indonesia: An Assessment of Bureaucratic and Judicial Review Mechanisms', *Sydney Law Review*, 32(2): 177.

Butt, S. and Lindsey, T. (2010a) 'Judicial Mafia: The Courts and State Illegality in Indonesia' in Van Klinken, G. and Aspinall, E. (eds) *The State and Illegality in Indonesia*, Jakarta: KITLV Press, p. 189.

Butt, S. and Lindsey, T. (2010b) 'Who Owns the Economy? Privatisation, property rights and the Indonesian Constitution' in McHarg, A., Barton, B., Godden, L. and Bradbrook, A. (eds) *Property and the Law in Energy and Natural Resources*, Oxford: Oxford University Press, p. 236.

Chene, M. (2009) *Corruption Challenges at the Sub-National Level in Indonesia*, Bergen, Norway: Anti-Corruption Resource Centre.

Damian, E. and Hornick, R. (1972) 'Indonesia's Formal Legal System: an Introduction', *American Journal of Comparative Law*, 20: 492.

Daryono (2010) 'The Transformation of Land Law in Indonesia: The Persistence of Pluralism', *Asian Journal of Comparative Law*, 5(1): 1.

David, R. and Brierley, J.E.C. (1985) *Major Legal Systems in the World Today: An Introduction to the Comparative Study of Law*, 3rd ed, London: Stevens.

Dolzer, R. and Schreuer, C. (2008) *Principles of International Investment Law*, Oxford: Oxford University Press.

Goodpaster, G. (2002) 'Reflections on Corruption in Indonesia' in Lindsey, T. and Dick, H.W. (eds) *Corruption in Asia: Rethinking the Governance Paradigm*, Annandale, N.S.W.: Federation Press, p. 87.

Hosen, N. (2010) *Human Rights, Politics and Corruption in Indonesia: a Critical Reflection on the Post Soeharto Era*: Republic Of Letters Publishers, Dordrecht.

Hukumonline (2007) 'Mustahil membatalkan putusan arbitrase?', 18 September.

Hukumonline (2008) 'MK Hapus Frase Di Muka Sekaligus', 25 March.

Hukumonline (2010a) 'Problematika eksekusi putusan arbitrase asing di Indonesia', 24 March.

Hukumonline (2010b) 'Putusan Arbitrase seharusnya dipatuhi', 31 March.

Hukumonline (2011) 'MA Prioritaskan Lima Agenda Pembaruan', 24 February.

KHRN and LeIP, I. (1999) *Menuju independensi kekuasaan kehakiman: position paper*, Jakarta: Indonesian Center for Environmental Law; Lembaga Kajian dan Advokasi untuk Independensi Peradilan.

Thee, K.W. (2008) *Indonesia's Economic Development During and after the Soeharto Era: Achievements and Failings*, Tokyo. Available at: www.devone.biz/development.pdf (accessed 17 March 2011).

Kuncoro, A. (2006) 'Corruption and Business Uncertainty in Indonesia', *ASEAN Economic Bulletin*, 23(1): 11.

Lev, D. (1965) 'The Lady and the Banyan Tree: Civil-Law Change in Indonesia', *The American Journal of Comparative Law*, 14(2): 282.

Levinson, J. (1998) ' "Living Dangerously": Indonesia and the Reality of the Global Economic System', *Detroit Journal of International Law & Practice*, 7(3): 425.

Lewis, B.D. (2003) 'Tax and Charge Creation by Regional Governments under Fiscal Decentralization: Estimates and Explanations', *Bulletin of Indonesian Economic Studies*, 39(2): 177.

Lewis, B.D. and Sjahir, B.S. (2009) 'Local Tax Effects on the Business Climate' in McCullough, N. (ed.) *Rural Investment Climate in Indonesia*, Singapore: ISEAS, p. 224.

Lindsey, T. and Taylor, V. (2000) 'Rethinking Indonesian Insolvency Reform: Contexts and Frameworks' in Lindsey, T. (ed.) *Indonesia: Bankruptcy, Law Reform and the Commercial Court*, Sydney: Desert Pea Press, p. 2.

Linnan, D. (2008) 'Commercial Law Enforcement in Indonesia: The Manulife Case' in Lindsey, T. (ed.) *Indonesia: Law and Society*, 2nd edn, Annandale, N.S.W.: Federation Press, p. 596.

Lotulung, P. (2000) *Peranan Yurisprudensi Sebagai Sumber Hukum*, Jakarta: Badan Pembinaan Hukum Nasional, Departemen Kehakiman.

McLeod, R. (2004) 'Dealing with Bank System Failure: Indonesia 1997–2003', *Bulletin of Indonesian Economic Studies*, 40(1): 95.

Maryono, A. (2009). *Thousands of Bylaws Halt Investment: BKPM*, Jakarta: Jakarta Post, 26 October. Available at: www.thejakartapost.com/news/2009/10/26/thousands-bylaws-halt-investment-bkpm.html (accessed 17 March 2011).

Michaels, R. (2009) 'Comparative Law by Numbers? Legal Origins Thesis, Doing Business Reports, and the Silence of Traditional Comparative Law', *American Journal of Comparative Law*, 57: 765–95.

Mills, K. (2000) 'Enforcement of Arbitral Awards in Indonesia', *International Arbitration Law Review*, 3(5): 192.

OECD (2010) *OECD Investment Policy Reviews: Indonesia*, Paris: Organisation for Economic Co-operation and Development.

Oktaviani, R. and Irawan, T. (2009) 'Does Decentralisation Foster a Good Trade and Investment Climate? Early Lessons from Indonesian Decentralisation', *ARTNeT Policy Brief*, 20: 1.

Pratikno (2005) 'Exercising Freedom: Local Autonomy and Democracy in Indonesia, 1999–2001' in Sulistiyanto, P., Erb, M. and Faucher, C. (eds) *Regionalism in Post-Suharto Indonesia*, USA: RoutledgeCurzon, p. 21.

Ray, D. (2003) 'Decentralization, Regulatory Reform, and the Business Climate' in *Decentralization, Regulatory Reform, and the Business Climate*, Jakarta, Indonesia: Partnership for Economic Growth, p. 1.

Rinaldi, T., Purnomo, M. and Damayanti, D. (2007) *Fighting Corruption in Decentralized Indonesia: Case Studies on Handling Local Government Corruption*, Jakarta: Justice for the Poor Project, World Bank.

Rosdianasari, E.S., Anggriani, N. and Mulyani, B. (2009) *Dinamika Penyusunan, Substansi dan Implementasi Perda Pelayanan Publik*, Jakarta: Justice for the Poor Project, World Bank.

Saad, I. (2003) 'Implementasi Otonomi Daerah Sudah Mengarah pada Penciptaan Distorsi dan High Cost Economy' in *Decentralization, Regulatory Reform, and the Business Climate*, Jakarta, Indonesia: Partnership for Economic Growth, p. 115.

Subekti (1978) *Yurisprudensi Hukum Tidak Tertulis dan Hukum Adat Dalam Pola Perencanaan Hukum dan Perundang-Undangan Nasional*, Denpasar: Biro Dokumentasi dan Publikasi Hukum Fakultas Hukum & Pengetahuan Masyarakat Universitas Udayana.

Supreme Court of Indonesia (2003) *Policy Paper on Judicial Personnel Management Reform*, Jakarta: Supreme Court of Indonesia.

Supriatna, L. (2008) *The Implementation of International Human Rights Law in the Indonesian Legal System*, Germany: Herrmann.

UNDP (2008) *Enhancing Communications, Advocacy and Public Participation Capacity for Legal Reforms (CAPPLER) PHASE II*, United Nations Development Programme.

Vickers, A. (2005) *A History of Modern Indonesia*, Cambridge: Cambridge University Press.

Wells, L.T. and Ahmed, R. (2007) *Making Foreign Investment Safe: Property Rights and National Sovereignty*, New York: Oxford University Press.

World Bank (1990) *World Development Report*, New York: Oxford University Press.

World Bank (1994) *The East Asian Miracle Economic: Growth and Public Policy*, New York: Oxford University Press.

World Bank (2004) *Combating Corruption in Indonesia: Enhancing Accountability for Development*, Jakarta: World Bank.

7 The Japan–Indonesia economic partnership agreement

An energy security perspective

Sita Sitaresmi

7.1 Introduction

In the absence of a multilateral investment agreement,[1] more states are inclined to negotiate an investment agreement under a bilateral or a free trade agreement (FTA) framework. Inclusion of an investment agreement in a FTA will arguably support the creation of a larger market (Hoekman and Newfarmer 2005: 949), which will offer an incentive for investment as it ensures greater demand for the investor's goods and services. Furthermore, the relaxation of trade barriers lowers the cost of importing capital resources eventually making the cost of investment more economical. Therefore, it is not surprising to find that states are increasingly including an Investment Chapter in their FTAs. In 2008, the OECD observed that 20 FTAs at the bilateral and regional levels incorporated an investment discipline in one of their FTA chapters (OECD 2008: 242).

Under the FTA framework, it is common to find dual coverage of services in both the Services and the Investment Chapters. Incorporation of a services discipline into an Investment Chapter is largely a result of the shift in the composition of foreign direct investment (FDI) from manufacturing to services (UNCTAD 2005: 5–8). With the exception of the Japan–Philippines Economic Partnership Agreement (EPA), most of Japan's EPAs (the banner for Japan's FTAs: see generally Hamamoto, Chapter 3 of this volume) allow dual coverage of services in both the Services and the Investment Chapters.

This chapter examines the roles of and relationship between the Investment Chapter and the Services Chapter in the Japan–Indonesia Economic Partnership Agreement (JIEPA),[2] and inquires whether such the JIEPA structure grants services with the benefits of the treatment and procedures accorded by the Investment Chapter of the JIEPA. This chapter argues that it is likely that this dual coverage allows standards of protections accorded by the Investment Chapter to be extended to services.

This study also suggests that JIEPA was intended to secure trade and investment particularly in the energy sectors. There are a number of underlying reasons for this hypothesis. First, JIEPA is one among only a few EPAs that dedicate a specific chapter to energy. Second, Indonesia is one of the key energy suppliers to Japan, which in turn is a major source of FDI in Indonesia. Third, the energy sectors (which involve activities such as consultation, advice, construction, transportation and distribution) consist fundamentally of services despite the UN International Standard Industrial Classification categorizing energy sectors as primary industry.[3]

This chapter first offers a brief overview of Indonesia's bilateral investment treaty (BIT) practice and domestic law reform that may affect foreign investment.[4] It then focuses on the reasons for negotiation of the JIEPA. Section 7.3 explains the structure of the JIEPA, with emphasis on the Services and Investment Chapters, and, to a lesser extent, the Energy and Mineral Resources (EMR) Chapter. Section 7.4 examines the implications that arise from dual coverage on services, particularly key provisions such as the definition of 'investment'[5] and the approaches to liberalization commitments. Section 7.5 examines the implications of Indonesia's investment liberalization commitments in the energy sectors on its regulatory autonomy. Section 7.6 discusses potential causes of investment disputes in the energy sectors, and Section 7.7 concludes.

7.2 Indonesia: BIT practice and domestic law reform

JIEPA adds to numerous BITs concluded by Indonesia over the past few decades. The first BIT was signed with Denmark in 1968. To date, Indonesia has signed and implemented 53 BITs with countries across five continents,[6] albeit only one-fifth of these are with countries that are consistently or potentially major FDI sources to Indonesia (Bank Indonesia 2010: 148–9).[7] Indonesia has concluded or is negotiating BITs with all major capital exporter countries except Canada and the United States. The high standard of protection demanded by these capital exporting countries contributes to lengthy negotiations. Negotiations with Canada have been ongoing for more than three years while the investment agreement with the United States was eventually confined to an agreement on the subrogation rights of the Overseas Private Investment Corporation (OPIC, the US government's insurer against political risks).[8] Negotiations on JIEPA commenced in early 2005 and the agreement was signed on 20 August 2007, before entering into force on 1 July 2008.

JIEPA reflects Indonesia's current investment policy approach as it was concluded shortly after the government amended its investment law and the negative lists of investment. JIEPA's Investment Chapter was the first investment treaty entered into by Indonesia that required parties to set up detailed lists of reservations and exceptions using a 'negative list' approach (that is, by listing sectors or industries in which foreign investment is prohibited or restricted). The Foreign Investment Law (No. 1/1967) was replaced by the new Foreign Investment Law (No. 25/2007) after 40 years in operation and negative lists of investment were updated.[9] Several provisions in the new Foreign Investment Law mirror provisions in BITs or the

Investment Chapter of the JIEPA. The Law guarantees 'most favoured nation' (MFN) treatment as well as recognizing MFN exemptions granted by virtue of preferential agreements (Article 6). The Law also ensures compensation at market value in the event of nationalization or expropriation (Article 8).

With regard to arbitration practice, Indonesia is a member of the International Centre for Settlement of Investment Disputes (ICSID), having ratified the 1965 ICSID Convention in 1968. Indonesia is also a signatory to the 1958 New York Convention on the Recognition and Enforcement of Foreign Arbitral Awards, which it ratified in 1981.[10] Indonesia has also promulgated the Arbitration and Mediation Law (No. 30/1999) and Regulations on the Procedure for the Implementation of Foreign Arbitral Awards.[11] The Arbitration Law confirms that Indonesia adopts the territoriality approach to the characterization of arbitrations whereby awards rendered outside Indonesia are regarded as a foreign award regardless of the nationality of the parties. Article 1(9) of the Arbitration Law defines international arbitration as a 'decision of an arbitration institution or individual arbitrator outside the jurisdiction of the Republic of Indonesia'; Article 3 prevents parties from launching parallel proceedings by prohibiting courts from adjudicating a dispute between parties which have agreed to and are bound by an arbitration agreement. An additional legal basis for recourse to international arbitration is also provided by the new Investment Law in Article 32(4).[12] Such a stipulation of recourse to international arbitration as a default forum for foreign investor-state dispute settlement mechanism in the new Investment Law may be read as a response to the customary practice of international investment dispute settlement.

7.2.1 Reasons for the JIEPA negotiation

A senior Japanese government official stated that an underlying factor for a negotiation strategy based on BITs and FTA investment chapters was that the Japanese economy is now supported by investment as well as exports (METI, undated). Changes in global economic production chains have forced Japan to diversify its investment destinations from Asia to other regions and hence to expand the geographical scope of its BIT negotiations. According to a senior government official, the criteria used by Japan in selecting a counterpart country is that it shall (i) have 'a certain level of investment risk' (such as frequent changes of regulation and lack of transparency); (ii) have a substantial existing stock of Japanese investment; (iii) be a producer of natural resources such as oil, gas or rare metals; and/or (iv) be able to serve as a gateway to the region. Discussion later in this chapter will show that Indonesia meets the first three criteria.

Another factor in the Japanese negotiation strategy is the intense international competition for natural resources and energy. An early indication of Japan's interest in energy security can be found in the pre-negotiation *Joint Study Group Report* (MOFA 2005). Japan stressed the importance of mineral resources and energy security in the negotiation of JIEPA particularly in issues related to foreign equity participation, improvement of investment climate and the steady supply of mineral resources and energy.

This focus on energy security is due to the fact that Japan is only self-sufficient for 16 per cent of its energy needs (US EIA 2010a). Its limited domestic resources rank it as the world's largest importer of liquefied natural gas (LNG) and coal, and the second largest net importer of oil. On a global scale, Japan's oil consumption ranks third after the US and China. It relies on oil imports to meet 45 per cent of its energy needs and on LNG imports for virtually all of its natural gas needs (US EIA 2009). It is also the third largest coal importer in the world after the China and the US and accounts for 3.3 per cent of total world coal consumption. Japan is also the third largest importer of LNG with Indonesia as its largest supplier meeting 20.1 per cent of Japan's total LNG imports (BP 2010: 31–5).

JIEPA was expected to be an instrument to maintain the historic presence of Japan as one of the major sources of FDI in Indonesia. Japanese energy companies have actively pursued participation in upstream oil and natural gas projects in Indonesia (US EIA 2010b). From 2004 to the first quarter of 2010, Japan ranked first as the source of FDI in Indonesia in energy related sectors (such as electricity, gas and infrastructure) and, it ranked second after the US as a source of investment in the mining sector (Bank Indonesia 2010: 158–9).

Japan's dependence on the supply of natural gas from Indonesia and the constant flow of Japanese investment to Indonesia argue for the need to have a stronger framework for cooperation at a treaty level. A treaty-based framework is considered to be an effective instrument to strengthen economic cooperation. The inclusion of an Investment Chapter in an EPA is intended to improve standards of protection, ensure compensation in the event of expropriation and provide greater stability regarding domestic investment policy (UNCTAD 2005: 16).

7.3 Structure of the agreement

The JIEPA is composed of 15 Chapters and 12 related Annexes. The main focus of this article is the Chapters on Investment (Chapter Five) and Services (Chapter Six) and, to a lesser extent, the EMR Chapter (Chapter Eight). The Investment Chapter has two Annexes: Annex 4 on the reservation of existing non-conforming measures and Annex 5 on the reservation of future measures. The Services Chapter has two Annexes: Annex 8 as a schedule of liberalization commitments and Annex 9 on MFN exemptions. The EMR Chapter also has two Annexes: Annex 11 on the list of traded energy and mineral goods and Annex 12 on the promotion and facilitation of energy investment, import and export restrictions, export licensing procedures and energy regulations. General and security exceptions for goods and services are maintained by incorporating Articles XX and XXI of GATT (1994) for goods and Articles XIV and XIV *bis* of GATS for services-related issues (WTO 2009). Transparency of laws and regulations applies to all Chapters and is governed by Article 3 of the JIEPA's General Provisions Chapter.

7.3.1 Services Chapter

The Services Chapter requires parties to accord to services and services suppliers standard treatment such as National Treatment (NT, Article 79) and MFN (Article 82). Services liberalization commitments take a 'positive list' approach and are contained in Annex 8. Each schedule specifies terms, limitations and conditions on market access, national treatment and, if any, additional commitments and the timeframe for implementation of such commitments (Article 81(1)). The liberalization of trade in services follows a 'positive list' approach with a ratchet mechanism (generally, a mechanism by which a state agrees that it will not replace existing measures with more restrictive measures – see below). Article 81(4) states that the ratchet mechanism for specific commitment undertaken by a party in Annex 8 is indicated by 'S'. Thus, for sectors or sub-sectors indicated by 'S' in Annex 8 and its terms, the level of liberalization concerning market access or national treatment cannot be reduced after the date of entry into force of the agreement as parties have agreed to lock in the existing level of liberalization as a status quo policy.

7.3.2 Investment Chapter

The Investment Chapter specifies treatment and procedures commonly found in investment treaties. Parties are required to apply NT, MFN, and performance requirement rules to all sectors including services (Articles 59, 60 and 63 respectively). Parties must provide fair and equitable treatment (FET) and full protection and security (Article 61) as well as the minimum standard of treatment (Article 62). Protections apply in relation to expropriation (Article 65) including expropriation arising out of taxation measures (Article 73). Parties must recognize the subrogation rights of a designated agency (Article 68). The Chapter also provides an investor-state dispute settlement mechanism (Article 69). This distinguishes this Chapter from the other Chapters, which are only subject to state-state dispute settlement provisions.[13]

The parties agreed to exempt certain sectors from the application of NT, MFN and performance requirements as stated in Article 64(1):

Articles 59 [NT], 60 [MFN] and 63 [prohibition of performance requirement] shall not apply to:

a   any non-conforming measure that is maintained by the following on the date of entry into force of this Agreement, with respect to the sectors or matters specified in Annex 4;..., d   an amendment or modification to any non-conforming measure referred to in subparagraphs (a) and (b), provided that the amendment or modification does not decrease the conformity of the measure, as it existed immediately before the amendment or modification, with Articles 59, 60 and 63.

Article 64(1) thus addresses two different issues: first, it sets out the rights of parties to exempt certain sectors from the application of the measures; and second, it recognizes the rights of the host state to balance its international commitment with flexibility and regulatory autonomy (UNCTAD 2006). However, the rights are subject to a condition that such a reservation should not 'decrease the conformity of the measure' or, in other words, be more restrictive than what was notified on the date of entry of JIEPA into force. This clause is the basis for including Annexes on reservations and exceptions (also known as the schedules of liberalization commitments under an Investment Chapter). The schedule is structured using a 'negative list' approach, whereby each party must provide details of the non-conforming measures and the legal basis for such measures (Article 64(2)(e)).

7.3.3 *Energy and Mineral Resources Chapter*

Not all Japanese EPAs contain a chapter dedicated to EMR. This feature is only found in the JIEPA (Chapter 8) and the Japan–Brunei EPA (2007, Chapter 7). Their presence in these agreements is not surprising as Indonesia and Brunei are among the key energy suppliers to Japan. The JIEPA's EMR Chapter addresses the promotion and facilitation of investment particularly in the areas of energy infrastructure construction and upstream activities (Articles 82(1) and (3)). Article 82(4) emphasizes the importance of 'creating a stable, equitable, favourable and transparent conditions' for foreign investors. On the issues of import restrictions and export licensing procedures, the Chapter stresses the importance of state parties ensuring FET treatment on the application of such measures (Articles 83 and 84(1)). More importantly, the Chapter addresses the importance of contract stability by requiring any regulatory measures in energy sectors to be applied in a manner that will 'avoid disruption of the contractual relationship that exists at the time of application' (Article 85(1)). The emphasis placed by the EMR Chapter on investment facilitation, reduction of import or export restrictions and contract stability indicates that the objective of the EMR Chapter is to provide an additional layer of protection for Japanese investors in energy sectors.

7.4 Implications of dual coverage of services investment

The structure of JIEPA as a comprehensive FTA allows each subject to be governed by a separate agreement. It is therefore not surprising to find dual coverage of services investment in both the Services and the Investment

Chapters. This is not to say that a clean distinction cannot be made and, for example, in the Japan–Philippines EPA (2006), services are clearly excluded from the Investment Chapter. However, dual coverage on services seems to be intended in the JIEPA. The risk of overlaps and discrepancies are dealt with in Article 57(2) which clarifies the relationship between the Services and the Investment Chapters as follows:

> In the event of any inconsistency between this Chapter [Investment] and Chapter 6 [Services]:
>
> a   with respect to matters covered by Articles 59, 60 and 63, Chapter 6 shall prevail to the extent of inconsistency; and,
> b   with respect to matters not falling under subparagraph (a), this Chapter shall prevail to the extent of inconsistency.

7.4.1 Standards of treatment and dispute settlement procedure

For agreements with dual coverage on services investment, the reach of the standard of treatment and investor-state dispute settlement provisions depends critically on the linkage clause that defines the relationship between the Investment and Services Chapters (Fink and Molinuevo 2008: 301). In this context, the wording of Article 57(2)(b) is sufficiently clear – the Services Chapter governs matters related to national treatment, MFN and prohibition on performance requirements while other matters are governed by the Investment Chapter. Paragraph (b) implies that matters related to other standards of treatment and dispute settlement procedures will be governed by the Investment Chapter. The paragraph extends the standard of treatment and procedure conferred by the Investment Chapter to services that qualify as investment.

Services investors can enjoy all treatment accorded by the Investment Chapter such as FET, full protection and security, minimum standard of treatment, and protection against expropriation. They also benefit from the investor-state dispute settlement mechanism, whereby they can directly bring the claim without pleading that their home state do so on their behalf as in the case of state-state dispute settlement. This legal power granted to services investors is likely to be distinctive and a 'strong term of protection' (Hoekman and Newfarmer 2005: 951). Furthermore, the investor-state dispute settlement mechanism grants investors the potential of an award of monetary damages. Such a remedy is not available under the state-state dispute settlement mechanism where the decision usually results in an obligation of the losing state to remove the disputed measure. The inclusion of services in the coverage of the Investment Chapter is likely to provide services and services investors with more favourable treatment and a stronger dispute settlement procedure than where services investment is only governed by a Services Chapter.

7.4.2 *Definition of investment*

With regard to the definition of 'investment', it is the definition in the Investment Chapter that applies to all sectors. Both the Services and Investment Chapters are quite similar in defining what should be considered as 'covered investment' (OECD 2008: 246). Each Chapter uses a different term to define a business entity but the notion of investors is basically the same. The Services Chapter uses the term 'juridical person' to describe a recognized business entity while the Investment Chapter uses the term 'enterprise' to describe a legal person. 'Juridical person' and 'enterprise' are each defined as a legal person constituted or organized under the applicable law of the state parties (Article 77(e)(1); compare Article 58(a)). As a result, there is not much difference in substance.

In addition, the Investment Chapter defines 'investment activities' similarly to 'commercial presence' to include activities such as 'establishment, acquisition, expansion, management, conduct, operation [and] maintenance' (Article 58(g); compare Article 77(b)(1)). This definition implies that both Chapters only recognize legal persons that are commercially present in the jurisdiction of the host state. To further narrow the definition of legal persons, both Chapters impose a minimum of 50 per cent ownership in that entity by foreign investors as a minimum threshold for it to enjoy the benefit of the Chapters (Article 58(b)(1); compare Article 77(e)(1)). The owner also needs to have 'the power to name the majority of the directors or otherwise to legally direct its actions' (Article 58 (b)(2); compare Article 77(f)(2)).

Similar to Article 57(2), the Article on the definition of 'investment' in the Investment Chapter may have a far-reaching effect of the scope of the Chapter (UNCTAD 2005: 28). Since natural resource exploration and energy generation are largely performed under contracts, qualification of such contracts as 'investment' provides a stronger ground for establishing jurisdiction *ratione materiae* of an international arbitral tribunal to adjudicate investment disputes in energy services. The ground is likely to be provided by Article 58(f) which qualifies contracts and rights under contract as investment, as follows:

> (4) rights under contracts, including turnkey, construction, management, production or revenue-sharing contracts;...,
> (7) rights conferred pursuant to laws and regulations or contracts such as concessions, licenses, authorizations and permits.

Based on this Article, energy contracts such as production-sharing contracts, concessionary contracts, exploration licences and other rights to exploit natural resources conferred by legislation fulfil the definition of 'investment' (Duval *et al.* 2009: 58–84).[14]

7.4.3 *Liberalization commitments*

As discussed above, Services and Investment Chapters take a different approach with regard to liberalization commitments. The 'negative list' approach is considered to provide greater predictability in investment liberalization policy. Businesses are better informed about the actual level of openness of the host state and may be directed to the laws and regulations having a discriminatory effect on their ability to compete against domestic investors (Fink and Molinuevo 2008: 275). A well-formulated negative list is capable of specifying the exempted sector as well as providing a succinct description on the reserved non-conforming measures, as well as on their legal source. Similarly, a ratchet mechanism is deemed to enhance the credibility of the regulatory regime. Such a commitment creates an incentive for further liberalization as the host state is bound not to decrease the level of openness.

However, the value of regulatory certainty is likely to be less if the negative list is extensive. The clarity of the approach will be undermined by the difficulties of scrutinizing the sectors and measures (Fink and Molinuevo 2008: 275). The listing of a relatively large number of sub-sectors or groups of sectors under a negative list also implies a low degree of openness. In comparison, a 'positive list' approach can offer more certainty and clarity, provided that the list specifies the sector-based exemption and clearly describes non-conforming measures.

It is well understood that dual coverage may create complementarities as well as inconsistencies (Fink and Molinuevo 2008: 283). Complementarity occurs when measures affecting services in commercial presence mode are excluded from a Services Chapter and become part of an Investment Chapter (Fink and Molinuevo 2008: 283), as is done, for example, in the Japan–Philippines EPA. Inconsistency occurs when an identical sector appears under both schedules of commitment with a different level of openness. In light of this, it is interesting to see whether the JIEPA retains inconsistencies as a result of differences in approach to the schedules. A comparison of the schedules of commitment to the Services and Investment Chapters of the JIEPA (Annexes 4 and 8) shows that a number of sectors (specialized hospital services, leasing, insurance and reinsurance, insurance and reinsurance brokerage) differ with respect to the level of liberalization. On the Services Schedule, their level of liberalization appears as a horizontal commitment of 49 per cent; but on the Investment's reservation list, their level of liberalization ranges between 49 and 85 per cent. Any such inconsistency is resolved by Article 57(2), quoted above. Since this matter relates to national treatment, Article 57(2) states that it will be the schedule of commitments of the Services Chapter that applies (Annex 8). The insertion of a linkage clause has helped to deal with the problem of potential inconsistency, albeit in a rather complex and round-about fashion.

7.5 Liberalization commitments and regulatory autonomy

What matters in an investment treaty negotiation is likely to be the reservation of an existing non-conforming measures list. Application of an upward ratchet mechanism to the list implies that all sectors listed under this type of reservation are bound at ever more liberal levels (Fink and Molinuevo 2008: 273). Therefore, it is unsurprising to find that the annex on reservations of existing non-conforming measures often becomes the centrepiece of the negotiation. Capital exporting states would certainly prefer to include as many strategic sectors as possible on this list, to minimize regulatory changes that may affect their investment. From the perspective of capital importing states, this annex may also enhance their investment credibility. A clearly described and succinct annex of existing non-conforming measures will send a signal about regulatory certainty. Conversely, application of a ratchet mechanism to this list may also turn the reservation list into a restraint on the host state's regulatory autonomy. The annex therefore becomes a balancing point for the host state between *ex ante* strong commitment devices and the need for greater regulatory flexibility *ex post* (Aaken 2009: 509). The *ex ante* strong commitment is aimed at accomplishing the 'object and purpose' of the agreement of increasing investment inflow. But *ex post* flexibility is a mechanism to deal with unforeseen circumstances that create future uncertainties, a problem that may well arise under investment agreements due to their long duration.

Non-conforming measures in general are adopted from, or are developed with reference to, the host state's domestic investment policy. Indonesia, for instance, developed the reservation lists based entirely upon a domestic negative investment list.[15] Hence, the locking-in of sectors under such reservations can imply a strategy to freeze domestic investment policy, particularly when a ratchet mechanism applies. Where the list is developed entirely based on domestic regulations, there is a greater chance that changes in domestic laws and regulations after the date of entry into force of the agreement that reduce the level of liberalization of an already listed sector may amount to violation of reservation commitments. Under an investment treaty framework, domestic investment policies are no longer an exercise of the state's regulatory autonomy; instead, they are now being transformed or elevated, by way of the reservation list, to the level of treaty obligations. Consequently, any unilateral amendment and modification may amount to a breach of a treaty obligation. If such a breach is established, the state cannot use its domestic law to justify its inability to comply with the treaty obligation.[16] One may argue that treaty commitments apparently restrict the regulatory autonomy of the host state (Manger 2008: 2457).

It is interesting to examine this issue in relation to Indonesia's reservations on energy sectors. There are 12 energy services reserved by Indonesia under Annex 4 on reservation of existing non-conforming measures. The listing confirms that energy services are opened to foreign investment subject to certain limits on foreign equity participation, as presented in Table 7.A. (Since energy services are only listed under the Investment Chapter, there is no issue of inconsistency.) The type of reservation is national treatment concerning foreign equity restrictions.

By placing the 12 energy services under Annex 4, Indonesia binds itself to a ratchet commitment pursuant to which the government cannot decrease the maximum level of foreign equity participation in the specified sectors. Notification of such levels of openness on the date of entry into force implies that the investment policy, which was originally a domestic decision, has now been transformed into a treaty obligation with Japan which is binding at international law. Any changes in domestic policy that result in a lower level of foreign equity participation affecting Japanese investors would amount to a breach of an international obligation. Viewed from an investor's

Table 7.A Indonesia's list of reservations of existing non-conforming measures on energy sectors

Sectors/subsectors/activities	Type of reservation
Off-shore oil and gas drilling services outside eastern area of Indonesia	Maximum foreign equity participation of 95%
On-shore oil and gas drilling services	Maximum foreign equity participation of 95%
Operation and maintenance services for oil and gas facilities	Maximum foreign equity participation of 95%
Engineering procurement construction (EPC) services	Maximum foreign equity participation of 95%
Power plant	Maximum foreign equity participation of 95%
Transmission of electric power	Maximum foreign equity participation of 95%
Electric power consultant	Maximum foreign equity participation of 95%
Construction and installation of electric power instrument	Maximum foreign equity participation of 95%
Maintenance and operation of electric power instrument	Maximum foreign equity participation of 95%
Development of technology power plant equipment supplies	Maximum foreign equity participation of 95%
Distribution of electric power	Maximum foreign equity participation of 95%
Nuclear power plant	Maximum foreign equity participation of 95%

Source: List of Reservation of Existing Measures of Indonesia, available at www.mofa.go.jp/ policy/economy/fta/indonesia.html;http://ditjenkpi.depdag.go.id/index.php?module-ijepa.

perspective, the listing of Indonesia's energy sectors, which are services in nature, under investment chapters is therefore likely to offer more favourable protection to foreign investors. Regarding Indonesia, this is the point where reservations and exceptions clauses can be of a matter of balancing domestic regulatory autonomy against international obligations (UNCTAD 2006). The effectiveness of attempts to reach and maintain this balance often depends on the maturity of the domestic policy regime.

A mature policy regime would produce policies that are not frequently changed. Under such a regime, a host state has more readiness to elevate its domestic investment policy to a level of treaty obligation and at the same time allow itself to be bound by the international obligation. With such a high level of commitment and policy certainty, reservations and exceptions provisions can be a device to enhance credibility and attract a greater flow of foreign investment. In contrast, under an immature policy regime, it is difficult to expect the same level of commitment and policy certainty. This immaturity tends to produce domestic investment policy and approaches to investments that are subject to frequent changes. A common factor that contributes to the frequent changes in an immature policy regime is poor policy planning, which creates disconnection and disintegration between investment policy and industrial policy and put policy makers in a position where there seems to be no clear comprehensive objective to be accomplished and no clear policy direction to be followed. The frequent changes of domestic policies are a consequence of such policy failures.

An immature investment policy regime is reflected by the fact that the reservations on energy services (listed in Table 7.1) are subject to a review within three years after the date of entry into force of the agreement. On the one hand, this condition provides more flexibility for Indonesia to make policy adjustments in coping with changes in economic circumstances, which may arise from domestic demand as well as from external shocks such as a global or regional financial crisis.[17] On the other hand, insertion of such a condition may undermine the host state's credibility and indicate a lack of readiness to be bound by treaty obligations. For long-term investments and highly politicized sectors such as the energy sector, the three-year review period may create uncertainty and insecurity on the investors' side. The periodic review can be read as a sign of possibly frequent policy changes in the future.[18] This does not seem to be a positive indication of the host state commitment to preserve regulatory certainty. This situation therefore represents a delicate balance between policy flexibility and international credibility that a host state with an immature policy regime needs to deal with.

Another feasible technique to retain policy flexibility is by utilizing an annex on reservations of future measures (such as JIEPA, Annex 5). Future measures do not necessarily relate to, nor are they necessarily based, on existing law and regulations; they allow states to introduce new measures in the relevant sectors at any point after the agreement enters into effect, provided that the sectors are listed in the annex (Fink and Molinuevo 2008: 273).

However, it is important to note that a broad reservation on future measures does not provide regulatory certainty either. In the end, only future measure reservations that are based on strategic and long-term domestic investment policy will work effectively.

7.6 Potential causes of investment disputes

Will the growing number of concluded BITs expose Indonesia to a greater number of investment disputes in the future? There is no definite answer to this question. Some recent studies have argued that East Asian investors tend to follow less aggressive legalism (Nakagawa 2007: 837–67), due to commercial considerations such as legal costs and delays as well as preserving long-term business relationships. Apparently, no Japanese investors, particularly the larger ones, have formally initiated investor to state dispute settlement under an investment treaty; they have also been long known for preference to renegotiation and informal solutions to investment and other disputes.[19] It is understood that the pursuit of investment arbitration may rupture the business relationship between investor and government, which may be difficult to reconcile with continued business operations (Fink and Molinuevo 2008: 301).

Indonesia's legal reforms have led to greater autonomy of regional governments regarding the management of economic resources. This may create more tension between regional governments and foreign investors. For example, the Regional Autonomy Law confers the right on regional governments to raise revenue by tax and to determine the percentage of revenue sharing out of natural resources exploitation.[20] The autonomy of regional governments to collect tax can often result in excessive and arbitrary taxation, which may have effects tantamount to expropriation. In the context of the JIEPA, where tax measures may amount to expropriation (Article 73), such measures can be a trigger for a dispute if the measures are conducted contrary to the general exceptions to expropriation (Article 65(1)).[21] The Regional Autonomy Law also includes provisions on revenue sharing, joint licensing and issuance of permits between regional governments regarding the exploitation of natural resources and power generation in border areas (Articles 17(1) and (2)). Autonomy to determine the percentage of revenue sharing on a coal mining investment may create another trigger for a dispute.

A dispute on revenue sharing over an oil field situated in the border of Central and East Java has already occurred between Exxon Mobil and two regional governments in Java Island. The dispute did not lead to arbitration as it was resolved through diplomatic channels. Another dispute that did lead to ICSID arbitration is *East Kalimantan* v. *Kaltim Prima Coal and others.*[22] The provincial government of East Kalimantan took up a claim on behalf of the Indonesian government against a group of foreign coal mining companies on the grounds of a breach of the revenue sharing arrangement. The case was declined on the basis of *jurisdiction personae* as the Tribunal held that the Province of East Kalimantan is not and cannot be a Contracting State to the ICSID Convention.

It is interesting to find that the increasing number of concluded and negotiated investment treaties does not correspond to an increasing number in investment disputes. In addition to *East Kalimantan*, Indonesia has been so far a respondent in ICSID arbitration only in the *Amco Asia* dispute.[23] Other two high-profile arbitrations involved investment contracts in energy sectors, *Karaha Bodas* and *Himpurna Energy*,[24] and regarded claims against the government in respect of issuance of a 'letter of comfort' aimed at encouraging foreign investment. However, Indonesia did not appear as a respondent in any of those cases: first, the cases were brought as commercial arbitration proceedings based on breach of commercial contracts to which the government of Indonesia was not a party; and second, there was no BIT concluded between Indonesia and the US that may have provided the American investors with treaty rights to arbitrate against Indonesia.

The small number of disputes against Indonesia is perhaps due to the reluctance of foreign investors to be involved in such lengthy arbitrations with little assurance of enforceability or execution of an award. The three arbitrations involving Indonesian parties were known for their lengthy and muddled proceedings. There were even uncertainties regarding the enforceability or execution of awards in the case of *Karaha Bodas* and *Himpurna Energy*. From a sceptical point of view, the arbitration experience hardly provides much assurance that the handling and outcome of future arbitration practice would be more efficient and predictable if Indonesia itself were a respondent. Interference by the domestic courts and even reference to Dutch law have been considered as the impediments to finality and enforceability of foreign arbitral awards in Indonesia (Junita 2008: 369–92). It seems premature to expect reform in domestic laws in the form of the recognition of recourse to international arbitration in the new Investment Law or the prohibition in the Arbitration Law on domestic courts ruling on a dispute between parties bound by an arbitration agreement. These reforms would effectively ease access to justice for foreign investors.

Nevertheless, the past arbitrations to some extent help to predict potential causes of future investment disputes. In *Amco Indonesia*, conflict between parties led to arbitrary termination of licences and the unlawful taking of the hotel. In *Karaha Bodas* and *Himpurna Energy*, the disputes were triggered by the issuance of three Presidential Decrees postponing all expensive energy projects in the face of the Asian Financial Crisis, which impeded Pertamina and PT PLN from performing their contractual obligations. The most recent arbitration, *East Kalimantan*, involved a breach of contract in a revenue sharing arrangement in coal mining. These cases indicate that future disputes may arise from a mere breach of contracts or as a result of government measures, such as the issuance of letters of comfort and the issuance or termination of licences – all of which might amount to a breach of FET, for example, under some investment treaty provisions.

7.7   Conclusion

The intense bilateral energy relationship between Japan and Indonesia has reinforced the need for a stronger framework for cooperation at the treaty level. There is mutual dependency between both states as Japan is dependent on Indonesia for energy supplies whereas Indonesia is dependent on Japan for FDI and JIEPA serves these mutual interests. The strategic objective to secure energy security is evident in the EMR Chapter, aimed at securing the supply of – and contract stability in – energy, as well as the dual coverage of services, including energy services, in both the Investment and Services Chapters.

The dual coverage on services does not necessarily create overlaps or discrepancy. The insertion of Article 57(2) clarifies the interaction between both Chapters and provides a clean distinction about the governing domain of each Chapter. The role of Article 57(2) is not limited to this point. The language of the clause has further implications for extending the standards of treatment and procedure accorded by Investment Chapter to services that qualify as investments. As a result, such services enjoy the stronger level of protection accorded by the Investment Chapter's provisions, including access to the investor-state dispute settlement mechanism. In addition, qualification of energy and natural resources contracts as 'investment' by definition provides a ground for the establishment of arbitral jurisdiction in the event of a dispute. Such arrangements offer more benefit for investors in energy services than a case where energy services are only governed by a Services Chapter.

Indonesia's list of reservations on energy sectors indicates that the placement of the 12 energy sectors under the Investment Chapter's Annex of reservations of existing non-conforming measure binds Indonesia to a ratchet mechanism. The mechanism prohibits the government from reducing the level of openness in those energy sectors. From the perspective of Japan and its investors, these commitments provide a greater assurance of regulatory stability in energy sectors. For Indonesia, this step may be seen as an elevation of domestic investment policies to the level of treaty obligations. The placement of energy sectors on the list where the ratchet mechanism applies is likely to be a testing ground for the ability of the government to maintain its international obligation in the face of greater domestic demand for regulatory flexibility. An imposed conditionality that subjects the reservation list to a short-term review, however, indicates that the intention of Indonesia is to maintain greater regulatory discretion. This intention may in turn come at the expense of Indonesia's credibility, as investors may read it as a sign of regulatory uncertainty.

It is impossible to predict the likelihood of future disputes involving Indonesia, as a result of the growing number of concluded BITs and now the JIEPA. Yet, given the possibility of frequent regulatory changes and arbitrary measures against foreign investors, there is certainly potential for disputes to arise particularly on the grounds of expropriation and breach of the FET obligation.

Notes

1 Despite being proposed in the 1996 WTO Rounds as part of the 'Singapore issues', investment was dropped from the Doha Agenda in August 2004 as a result of the member states' failure to reach consensus on negotiating the mandate after the Cancun Ministerial Meeting.

2 The full text of the Japan–Indonesia Economic Partnership Agreement (2008) is available at www.mofa.go.jp/policy/economy/fta/indonesia.html (accessed 22 March 2011).

3 See http://unstats.un.org/unsd/cr/registry/regcst.asp?Cl=27 (accessed 22 March 2011).

4 For a more general discussion on domestic law issues and reform, see Butt, Chapter 6 in this volume.

5 See generally Coppens, Chapter 9 in this volume.

6 The number excludes investment treaties or economic cooperation agreements entered by Indonesia as a member of ASEAN, accessible at www.unctadxi.org/templates/DocSearch_____779.aspx?PageIndex=0&TextWord='Indonesia',%20" %20,1&CategoryBrowsing=False&syear=. See also the Appendix of BITs in the chapter by Butt, Chapter 6 in this volume.

7 Major sources of FDI in Indonesia are Japan, the US, Canada, France, the UK, other EU countries, China, Hong Kong SAR, South Korea, Malaysia, Singapore and Australia.

8 Indonesia–United States Investment Support Agreement, entered into force August 2010, ratified by Indonesia by Government Regulation No. 48/2010, on the recognition of the subrogation rights of OPIC and its consortium.

9 Presidential Decree Number 76/2007; Presidential Decree 77/2007 as amended by 111/2007 and 36/2010.

10 Presidential Decree No. 34 of 1981.

11 Regulation Number 1/1990.

12 See, however, a difficulty in interpreting Article 32 set out by Butt, Chapter 6.

13 On investor–state arbitration patterns generally in Asia, see Nottage and Weeramantry (Chapter 2) as well as Sornarajah (Chapter 13), in this volume.

14 Such a definition is also in line with provisions in domestic legislation. Indonesia's Oil and Gas Law (No. 22/2001) and Mining Law (No. 4/2009) recognize the contractual forms of energy investment.

15 Presidential Decree Number 111/2007.

16 *Vienna Convention on the Law of Treaties (1969)*, Article 27; *International Law Commission's Article on the Responsibility of the State for International Wrongful Act, 2001*, Article 3.

17 See also the *Karaha Bodas Company LLC* and *Himpurna California Energy Ltd* disputes, discussed in the next Part and mentioned also in the chapters by Butt and Sornarajah, in this volume.

18 The potential for frequent policy changes in Indonesia is one of the underlying reasons for Japan in negotiating the EPA, see earlier discussion on Part I.

19 See Hamamoto, Chapter 3 in this volume; see also Nottage and Weeramantry, Chapter 2.

20 Law No. 32/2004, Article 21(e), (f). See also generally Butt, Chapter 6.

21 This provides that expropriation must occur for a public purpose on a

non-discriminatory basis in accordance with due process of law and FET, and upon payment of prompt, adequate and effective compensation.

22 *Government of the Province of East Kalimantan* v. *PT. Kaltim Prima Coal and others ('East Kalimantan')*, ICSID case No. ARB/07/03, 28 December 2009.

23 *Amco Asia Corp* v. *Republic of Indonesia*, (Decision on Annulment) (1986) 1 ICSID Rep 509; (Resubmitted Case: Award) (1990) 1 ICSID Rep 569.

24 *Karaha Bodas Company LLC* v. *Perusahaan Pertambangan Minyak dan Gas Bumi Negara and PT PLN*, ad hoc arbitration under UNCITRAL rules, Final Award of December 2000; *Himpurna California Energy Ltd* v. *PT PLN Persero*, ad hoc arbitration under UNCITRAL rules, Final Award of May 1999.

Bibliography

Aaken, Anne van (2009) 'International Investment Law Between Commitment and Flexibility: A Contract Theory Analysis', *Journal of International Economic Law*, 12(2): 507–38.

Bank Indonesia (2010) 'Foreign Direct Investment Flows in Indonesia by Economic Sectors and Country of Origin', *Indonesian Financial Statistic*, 12(7): 158–9.

BP (2010) *Statistical Review of World Energy*. Available at: www.bp.com/liveassets/ bp_internet/globalbp/globalbp_uk_english/reports_and_publications/statistical_ energy_review_2008/STAGING/local_assets/2010_downloads/statistical_ review_of_world_energy_full_report_2010.pdf (accessed 24 January 2011).

Duval, C., H. Le Leuch, A. Pertuzio and J.L. Weaver (2009) *International Petroleum Exploration and Exploitation Agreements: Legal, Economic and Policy Aspect*, 2nd edn, New York: Barrows.

Fink, C. and M. Molinuevo (2008) 'East Asian Free Trade Agreements in Services: Key Architectural Elements', *Journal of International Economic Law*, 11(2): 263–311.

Hoekman, B. and R. Newfarmer (2005) 'Preferential Trade Agreements, Investment Disciplines and Investment Flows', *Journal of World Trade*, 39(5): 949–73.

Junita, F. (2008) 'Experience of Practical Problems of Foreign Arbitral Awards enforcement in Indonesia', *Macquarie Journal of Business Law*, 5: 369–92.

Manger, M. (2008) 'International Investment Agreements and Services Markets: Locking in Market Failure?', *World Development*, 36(110): 2456–67.

METI (Ministry of Economy Trade and Industry) (undated), *Japan's Policies and Strategies on Bilateral Investment Treaties*. Available at: www.rieti.go.jp/jp/ events/08072501/pdf/3–1_E_Mita_t.pdf (accessed 14 February 2011).

MOFA (Ministry of Foreign Affairs of Japan) (2005) *Joint Study Group Report*. Available at: www.mofa.go.jp/region/asia-paci/indonesia/summit0506/joint-3–2.txt (accessed 14 February 2011).

Nakagawa, J. (2007) 'No More Negotiated Deals?: Settlement of trade and Investment Disputes in East Asia', *Journal of International Economic Law*, 10(4): 837–67.

OECD (2008) 'The Interaction Between Investment and Services Chapters in Selected Regional Trade Agreements' in *International Investment Law: Understanding Concepts and Tracking Innovations*, Paris: OECD.

UNCTAD (2005), *International Investment Agreements in Services*, New York, Geneva: United Nations.

UNCTAD (2006) *Preserving Flexibility in International Investment Agreements: The Use of Reservation*, New York, Geneva: United Nations.

US EIA (US Energy Information and Administration) (2009) based on 2009 data. Available at: http://tonto.eia.doe.gov/country/country_energy_data.cfm?fips=JA (accessed 24 January 2011).

US EIA (US Energy Information and Administration) (2010a) *Country Analysis Brief.* Available at: www.eia.doe.gov/emeu/cabs/Japan/Background.html (accessed 24 January 2011).

US EIA (US Energy Information and Administration) (2010b) *Country Analysis Briefs: Japan.* Available at: www.eia.doe.gov/emeu/cabs/Japan/pdf.pdf (accessed 24 January 2011).

WTO (2009) *Factual Presentation, Economic Partnership Agreement between Japan and Indonesia: Report by Secretariat*, WT/REG241/1, Geneva: WTO.

8 Foreign investment laws and the role of FDI in Malaysia's 'new' economic model

Salim Farrar

8.1 Introduction

On 30 March 2010, in the wake of a close general election and the aftermath of the Global Financial Crisis, Malaysian Prime Minister Najib Abdul Razak announced a New Economic Model (NEM) for the country. A country that had once boasted average annual economic growth rates of 8 per cent between 1990 and 1997, had been listed as one of the few countries to post an average 7 per cent growth rate over a 25-year period, and confidently announced aspirations of achieving high-income status by 2020, was slowing down and grinding to a halt. Post-1997, annual economic growth had halved, investment as a proportion of GDP dropped precipitously and the country was leaking foreign direct investment (FDI) to its regional competitors. Although absolute poverty had been practically eradicated, Malaysia was now stuck in a 'middle income trap,' with most Malaysians still occupying low-skilled jobs, 40 per cent earning less than US$15 per day and 350,000 of Malaysia's most educated preferring to work and live overseas.

The NEM was forged with the intent to jumpstart the Malaysian economy and restore (domestic and foreign) investor confidence. Although the government has termed this plan, the *'New* Economic Model,' I will argue there is nothing fundamentally 'new' about it in terms of economic and trade policy nor the investment legal regime in which it will be given effect. There has been (and will be) new legislation passed giving effect to the government's agenda, but there appear to be no fundamental departures from government policy when looked at in a historical continuum.

This chapter will survey and discuss the most important laws, policies and regulations which impact directly upon foreign investment. This will include a discussion of the Industrial Coordination Act 1975, which originally gave legal effect to the Malaysian Government's affirmative action policies in the pivotal manufacturing sector, as well as an historical overview of the deregulation and liberalization process which have taken centre-stage in more recent times and figure prominently in the NEM. Before I explain the laws underpinning Malaysia's foreign investment regime, it is necessary to examine the historical role of FDI and the part it has played in Malaysia's economic and social development.

8.2 The historical role of FDI in Malaysia's pre-NEM socio-economic development

Malaysia has a culturally heterogeneous population of approximately 28.3 million, comprising 65.1 per cent *Bumiputera*, 26 per cent Chinese, 7.7 per cent Indian and 1.2 per cent others. Literally, the term *Bumiputera* means 'sons of the soil' and is a term understood as referring to both the Malays and Indigenous populations, though Article 153 of the Malaysian Federal Constitution, which acknowledges their 'special position,' merely refers to them as 'Malays and Natives.' Since Independence from the British in 1957, the challenge has always been to tap this rich cultural mix for the economic and social betterment of the country whilst at the same time containing inter-ethnic tensions.[1]

Although its use and application is not without controversy in the developing world, as inflows of FDI can cause social problems through exacerbation of existing inequalities (Salz 1992; Reuveny and Quan 2003; Feenstra and Hanson 1997) and East Asia achieved fully developed status without it, FDI and its regulation has been among the tools historically employed by successive Malaysian governments to achieve a socially equitable and economically sustainable balance.[2]

In pre-independent Malaya, (mainly British)[3] FDI was present in the primary sectors, invested primarily in the rubber and tin plantations with the purpose of fuelling the colonial economy. FDI moved into manufacturing during the 1950s and post-Independence Malaysia was used to develop import-substitution in order to promote economic diversification, reduce the reliance on tin and rubber (Jomo and Tan 2008: 25) and start the process of industrialization that had been stifled during colonial rule. For the most part, the post-colonial government resisted interfering with business interests, defended British interests in the economy and allowed Chinese local businesses to consolidate their already strong position in the economy (Jomo and Tan 2008: 24). Applying a laissez-faire approach, it was assumed that the economic benefits would 'trickle down' to the majority *Bumiputera* who then predominated in the rural sector but, with the exception of a few well-connected individuals, were virtually absent in the private business sector. An unintended consequence of this policy was worsening income distribution, a widening of the income gap between town and country and, most importantly, greater inter-ethnic inequality (Jomo and Tan 2008: 26; Snodgrass 1995: 6–7; Shome and Hamidon 2009: 41).

Political mobilization along ethnic lines, Malay resentment of capital domination and its association with the Chinese, coupled with the loss of key political seats in the May 1969 general elections, provoked race riots on 13 May and the most serious ethnic disturbances the country had (and has) ever seen (Jomo and Tan 2008: 26). The country was locked into a state of emergency and began to formulate an economic and political trajectory, termed the 'New Economic Policy' (NEP), which has dictated its development and influenced foreign investors (actual and potential) ever since.

The NEP was short on specifics but had two overriding goals the attainment of which would address the perceived root causes of the 1969 riots: first, the eradication of poverty; and second, the restructuring of Malaysian society 'to correct economic imbalance, so as to reduce and eventually eliminate the identification of race with economic function' (Government of Malaysia 1971: 1, cited in Snodgrass 1995: 5). Technically, the NEP was race neutral but as Malays experienced massive economic disparity, ethnic quotas for employment were imposed including a requirement that all companies submit plans to the Ministry for their recruitment, training and promotion policies with a view to securing 40 per cent Malay representation of the total workforce. The problem of enforcing and monitoring ethnic quotas, however, soon became apparent enabling local Chinese companies to work their way around the restrictions. Foreign investors, however, were not as fortunate for they could not obtain a licence or any tax concessions without complying with the ethnic quotas (Shome and Hamidon 2009: 42).

In addition to employment quotas, foreign investors suffered the brunt of the NEP's targeting of 30 per cent *Bumiputera* ownership of listed corporate wealth. When the NEP was first announced, it was intended for *Bumiputera* to receive 30 per cent (from a low of 2.5 per cent in 1970), non-*Bumiputera* 40 per cent and foreigners the remaining 30 per cent of corporate wealth. In 1971, foreign ownership of corporate wealth stood at 63.2 per cent which meant foreign investors had the most to lose from the affirmative action policies.

Laissez-faire, then, was abandoned in favour of greater state intervention and bureaucratic interference in private enterprise. The state took on the role of the Malay capitalist, establishing public enterprises and statutory bodies, re-distributing capital and economic benefits to the *Bumiputera* and overseeing its enforcement. Adverse consequences on the Chinese local business community (loss of contracts and equity restrictions) triggered capital flight (Jomo and Tan 2008: 28), but government officials were able to minimize overall damage to the economy and 'bypass' the Chinese through new agreements binding the Malay-dominated government with multinational corporations (MNCs). Chinese domination of the economy, therefore, was reduced through a strategic embrace and directing of FDI (Woo-Cummings 1999: 142), further facilitated by the shift in economic policy from import substitution to export-orientated industrialization that had started in the late 1960s. Government advisers had been urging such a shift prior to the NEP owing to falls in real output, the realization that high profits were being remitted to overseas companies rather than re-invested in Malaysia and the failure of MNCs to deliver sufficient local employment (Jomo 2008b: 178–80).

After a sluggish start in the early 1970s and evidence of capital flight up to 1985 caused by the NEP,[4] FDI inflows gradually returned as the export manufacturing sector picked up (Athukorala and Menon 1995: 14). A protected domestic economy lacking linkages with a thriving foreign-led export sector, however, showed clear signs of a dual economy. With his accession to the leadership in mid-1981, Mahathir Mohamed staked his claim on making Malaysia a newly industrialized country and embarked on an ambitious programme of industrialization and modernization (Jomo and Tan 2008: 30) which sought to emulate South Korean industrialization between 1972 and 1979. Known as the 'Look East' policy, this included collaboration with mostly Japanese, South Korean and Taiwanese firms in the development of heavy industry (largely automobiles, steel and cement). The idea was that through these joint ventures, Malaysia would develop its capital goods sector and provide deeper linkages with the domestic economy, and especially with *Bumiputra*-owned enterprises (Jomo 2007: 13).

These forays into heavy industrialization ended up very costly failures (Jomo 2008b: 183–4, 2007: xix–xx) and, in combination with the collapse in commodity prices, could have seriously damaged the Malaysian economy. But damage was minimized by the relocation of North Asian firms in 1985–6 to Malaysia following the removal of their General System of Preference privileges under the GATT and also the Plaza Accord in 1985 on exchange rates, both of which had made manufacturing in North Asia uneconomic. De-regulation, good infrastructure, the low cost of labour as well as a number of incentives for FDI (see further below) offered by the Malaysian government for high-tech industries (especially in the electric and electronics, E/E, sector), enticed Japanese, South Korean and Taiwanese companies to the Malaysian Export Processing Zones.

In spite of successive high growth (post 1985, Malaysia recorded annual growths rates of more than 8 per cent), successes in eradicating absolute poverty and the emergence of a prominent Malay middle class, gaps widened between the rich and the poor and also between the ethnic groups. Although *Bumiputera* corporate ownership reached 19.1 per cent in 1985 (up from 2.4 per cent in 1970), and 20.3 per cent in 1990 (the official ending date of the NEP), most of that ownership was in the hands of Government-Linked Companies (GLCs), such as state-led banks and trust agencies and not private individuals. Indeed, according to the Economic Planning Unit in 1991, individual ownership comprised only 8.2 per cent. Foreign ownership of corporate wealth had fallen to 25.1 per cent, but the non-*Bumiputera* share (predominantly Chinese) had actually increased to 46.2 per cent (Snodgrass 1995: 11–12; Jomo and Tan 2008: 27–8), representing a partial policy failure when viewed in the light of the NEP's original objectives.

During this period and up to the onset of the Asian Currency Crisis (ACC), Malaysia remained open to FDI. When the ACC struck in 1997, that policy continued but it was combined with capital exchange controls to stop the exodus of foreign money. Most of the capital flight had already taken place by mid-1998 when the controls were imposed, but as a result of a re-capitalization of the economy and government purchase and re-structuring of non-performing loans through the establishment of special purpose vehicles, Malaysia's economy was one of the first to bounce back from the ACC (Wong and Jomo 2008: 203–19).

Yet in the period post ACC, and especially in the aftermath of 9/11, the economy failed to recapture the dynamism it had previously projected.[5] While the country had listed regularly in the top 25 best FDI destinations (Kearney 2011), between 2000 and 2008 Malaysia seemed to lose its competitive edge with economic growth slowing to an average of 5.5 per cent and, as indicated by the figure below, Thailand becoming the most attractive FDI destination in South-East Asia.

Decline in Malaysia's comparative attractiveness as a destination for FDI was matched by large rises in outflows of FDI. The Malaysian government had never restricted Malaysian companies from investing overseas and following the slowdown in 2001, the Mahathir government positively encouraged overseas investment hoping Malaysian companies would access the global supply chain and benefit from economies of scale, perhaps presuming funds would be remitted and re-invested in Malaysia. Malaysian companies took him at his word investing in countries in Africa, China and other parts of South-East Asia so that by 2007 FDI outflows were already exceeding inflows.

In the aftermath of the Global Financial Crisis in 2008–9, FDI inflows to Malaysia dropped a massive 81.3 per cent which, while not surprising in light of the financial woes of its principal investors in the US and Japan, was a worry for the Malaysian government as the falls in Indonesia, Thailand and Vietnam were all substantially lower, and Singapore went on to record a 54.04 per cent increase.[6] Malaysia had also suffered a similar steep decline in 2001 (UNCTAD 2002: 3, 57 and 305), but concerns were increasingly focused on more fundamental problems and possibly structural faults in the Malaysian economy. Collapse in FDI inflow were now coupled with large FDI outflows in 2009[7] which, though not necessarily signs of structural weaknesses in the Malaysian economy, were sufficient to provoke a defensive response.[8]

The following section, therefore, takes a look at the legal structure and framework of Malaysia's investment laws to ascertain potential weaknesses.

8.3 Malaysian investment laws

Unlike Thailand or Indonesia,[9] Malaysia does not have a general foreign investment law: a set of legal rules and general principles to regulate foreign participation in local businesses and the domestic economy. Rather, for the past three decades, all foreign investment has required approvals from the Malaysian Industrial Development Authority (MIDA), the Foreign Investment Committee (FIC) in case of substantial investments, and also permissions from local licensing bodies. This has provided maximum flexibility to the Malaysian government to direct FDI to relevant sectors of the Malaysian economy in furtherance of its ethnic redistribution policies set out earlier. To counter the negative influence of state control and admission conditions on inbound FDI and to positively encourage FDI in the relevant sectors, the Malaysian government has adopted a generous system of incentives. With the exception of the exchange controls imposed immediately after the ACC, outbound FDI has been left unregulated.

To foster a positive climate for foreign investment, Malaysia is a party to the 1965 Convention on the Settlement of Investment Disputes between States and Nationals of States (ICSID Convention, since 1966), the New York Convention on the Recognition and Enforcement of International Arbitral Awards (the NYC, since 1985), and the WTO treaties (since 1 January 1995). It also has entered into 68 Bilateral Investment Treaties (BITs) and 65 Double-Taxation Agreements,[10] as well as four FTAs (all with investment chapters[11]), and another four in the process of negotiation.

8.3.1 Domestic policy relating to FDI

Inbound foreign investment is encouraged by a number of incentives provided by the federal government for companies who demonstrate long-term commitment to the country by being legally incorporated in Malaysia (under the Malaysian Companies Act 1965). This enables such companies to apply for a number of incentives in manufacturing, agriculture, tourism, certain approved services, research and development, training and environmental protection activities (see further, the MIDA website). Incentives comprise direct and indirect tax concessions and applications are granted subject to conditions under the Promotion of Investments Act 1986 (PIA), Income Tax Act 1967, Customs Act 1967 and Free Zones Act 1990. Breach of conditions is subject to withdrawal of the concession. Direct concessions take the form of income tax holidays and indirect concessions include exemptions from import duty, sales tax and excise duty.

In the manufacturing sector, the main incentives are for companies granted 'Pioneer Status,' (Promotion of Investments Act 1986 [PIA], sections 5–25) or an 'Investment Tax Allowance' (PIA, sections 26–30). The former confers partial or total income tax relief for a five-year period (depending on the location of the investment in Malaysia) for companies certified by MIDA as working in 'promoted activities' or manufacturing 'promoted products'. The definition of a 'promoted activity' or 'promoted product' is left to the discretion of the Minister, but potential investors are guided by the list of existing promoted activities and products accessible on the MIDA website and published in the *Gazette* by statutory order. If the suggested activity or product is not stated on the list, investors can still apply for 'Pioneer Status' for their companies but only vague guidance is given in the statute as to the factors the minister may take into account in the exercise of that discretion.[12] Where a company has not been certified with 'pioneer status' or has been issued with a certificate relating to another activity or product, but is participating or intends to participate in a 'promoted activity' or 'promoted product,' the investor can apply for an Investment Tax Allowance. This grants successful applicants a tax allowance of between 60 per cent and 100 per cent on its qualifying capital expenditure over a five-year period (again, with the rate depending on the location of the investment).[13]

Apart from the 'pioneer status' and the 'investment tax allowance', other additional allowances, tax relief and exemptions are available to the foreign investor in areas outside the manufacturing sector,[14] but are still directed to the export sector because of the NEP. Of particular note are the tariff-related incentives. These are subject to the discretion of the Minister and can be granted in whole or in part (Excise Act 1976, s. 11(1)). As a general rule, applications for full exemption for imported raw materials where the finished products are intended for the export market are granted. However, much closer scrutiny is afforded where finished products are intended for the domestic market. Where investor companies export at least 80 per cent of their products and are located in one of the export-oriented Free Industrial Zones (Free Zones[15] Act 1990, section 3(1)), they are subject to minimal customs formalities and are also exempt import duties, sales and service taxes (section 4). Similarly, companies located outside the FIZs, but who also export 80 per cent of their production, can apply for the same concessions by being set up as Licensed Manufacturing Warehouses (LMWs). They are only subject to import duties if the goods are intended to be sold to the domestic market.[16]

Although inbound foreign investment is clearly encouraged, it has been closely regulated in order to meet with the objectives of Malaysia's socio-economic policies (NEP post-1972, NDP post-1990, and now the NEM). Foreign investment has been subject to an approval process and the imposition of equity conditions. Their precise details, level of scrutiny and degree of enforcement has depended upon the nature of the investment and the particular sector. These equity conditions, strictly speaking, are no more than administrative guidance and do not have the force of law (*Ho Kok Cheong Sdn Bhd & Anor* v. *Lim Kat Hong* [1979] 2 MLJ 224; *Thong Foo Ching & Ors* v. *Shigenori* [1998] 4 MLJ 595). But previous experience of Malaysian courts voiding contracts of foreign investors for non-compliance on grounds of 'public policy' (*David Hey* v. *New Kok Ann Realty Sdn Bhd* [1985] 1 MLJ 167), along with the statutory-based licensing system conferring an absolute discretion on civil servants to refuse and revoke licences, as well as to add whatever conditions 'they think fit',[17] gives them quasi-legal status.

In the commercial sector, foreign acquisitions of interests in a high-value Malaysian corporation were subject to the approval of the Foreign Investments Committee (FIC),[18] and in the case of any activities relating to the national interest (such as water, telecommunications, broadcasting, ports and energy), they were capped at 30 per cent. All companies had to maintain and achieve a certain proportion of *Bumiputera* participation, and strive for a minimum of 30 per cent. Once they reached 51 per cent, they were not permitted to go below that level of share ownership and would lose their licences (Australian Department of Foreign Affairs and Trade 2005: 19; Foreign Investment Committee 1999).

None of these measures relating to service sectors or corporate wealth were particularly conducive to the promotion of investment nor was the uncertainty to which the approval process gave rise. But the Malaysian government extended the scope of foreign ownership after 1998 (through the Securities Commission – which had taken over some of the responsibilities of the FIC). From 2002, it also allowed unlisted foreign companies to take over the assets of listed firms without requiring compliance with the minimum *Bumiputera* ownership (Jomo 2008b: 19).

De-regulation has continued under the New Economic Model. As of 30 June 2009, unless the merger relates to 'strategic' industries (mentioned above), approval from the Foreign Investment Committee or the Economic Planning Unit is no longer required and the 30 per cent *Bumiputera* equity requirement is abolished along with all other equity conditions.[19] Nevertheless, restrictions still remain upon flotation, with the Malaysian Security Commission requiring 50 per cent of the 25 per cent public spread to be allocated to *Bumiputera* private investors. This policy is clearly directed at the concerns of the NEP.

In the manufacturing sector, foreign investment has been regulated under the Industrial Coordination Act 1975. All firms (local and foreign) engaged in manufacturing with a shareholder equity in excess of RM2.5 million, or who employ more than 75 employees, are obliged to apply for a manufacturing licence from the Secretary General of the Ministry for International Trade and Industry (MITI), though in practice they apply to MIDA.[20] Already licensed operations also need to re-apply for a licence if they wish to expand their production or diversify their product range (MIDA 2010b; Jomo 2008b: 185).

Since the NEP, manufacturing licences have been subject to the equity guidelines. But history demonstrates the Malaysian government has been very flexible and pragmatic in this regard (Snodgrass 1995). Since the 1970s, companies located in the Free Zones have been exempt from equity-sharing requirements and subject to only low level screening (Jomo 2008b: 182). From 1986, the government embarked on deregulation measures, extending these exemptions to companies who supplied Free Zone firms (Jomo 2008b: 188). In 1990, equity requirements were completed lifted for small- and medium-sized enterprises (Wah 2010: 4), and in 1992 Industrial Coordination Act guidelines were amended allowing firms exporting 80 per cent of their produce to own all of the equity. Following the 1997–8 Asian Financial Crisis, under the National Economic Recovery Plan, all companies undertaking manufacturing projects were allowed to hold 100 per cent of equity irrespective of the volume of their exports (Jomo 2008b: 201). This exemption continued to remain in place after the ending of the crisis, with the exception of those industries where Malaysia was deemed to have expertise. In June 2003, even these exceptions were removed, completing full liberalization of the manufacturing sector. Furthermore, companies who had had equity and export conditions imposed before 17 June 2003 were also given the opportunity of applying to have them removed based on the merit of their particular application (MIDA 2009b: 8).

As far as services have been concerned, the regulations and guidelines, though varying considerably between the different sectors, were applied much more restrictively. In relation to banking, there had been a large foreign presence before the NEP, with 16 fully fledged foreign banks, including HSBC, Standard Chartered, Citibank and the United Overseas Bank, operating more than 100 branches throughout the country. In 1966, Bank Negara Malaysia (the Malaysian Central Bank) prohibited the expansion of existing foreign bank branches in order to protect and help develop the domestic banking industry (Marashdeh 1990: 113). In 1974, after the NEP, it was announced that no more foreign banks would be allowed to establish branches (that is, to accept deposits) in Malaysia. However, they were free to set up representative offices so long as they only booked transactions offshore between Malaysia and their home countries (Marashdeh 1990: 113). In 1985, because of the proliferation of domestic and foreign banks, Bank Negara prohibited the development of *any* new banks. Even when the Malaysian Government decided to endorse Islamic banking and begin a dual banking sector, with the passing of the Islamic Banking Act 1983, it was intended for the industry to be led by domestic Islamic financial providers (e.g. Bank Islam and Bank Muamalat) and not those from overseas.

The potential benefits of liberalizing the sector were not fully articulated until 2001, with the government's launching of its Financial Sector Master Plan. This laid out a ten-year strategy for the financial sector, which included gradual liberalization and restructuring of the banking sector to enhance its competitiveness and effectiveness in the face of stiff regional competition (Ngan and Kandiah, 2008: 88). By 2006, this succeeded in diversifying financial services with more investment banks, *Takaful* (Islamic insurance) operators and Islamic banks (including one foreign bank) entering the market (Ngan and Kandiah 2008: 88). By 2009, the domestic banks were deemed resilient (in terms of capital ratios and assets) and sufficiently competitive to allow a further wave of liberalization and issuing of nine new banking and insurance licences both in the conventional and Islamic sectors.[21] New increased foreign equity limits of up to 70 per cent were also passed to facilitate strategic tie-ups between foreign and domestic players in the conventional and Islamic banking and insurance sectors (Bank Negara Malaysia 2009). As of June 2010, Bank Negara had issued 19 commercial banking licences and six Islamic banking licences to foreign players (Agence France-Presse 2010).

As for foreign participation in the distributive trade service sector,[22] access was formerly restricted and subject to strict equity conditions. Foreign companies or companies with foreign equity were not prohibited from operating, but they had to obtain all the necessary licences and permits which would not be granted without compliance with the dictates of the NEP. Fears of stifling Malaysian small businesses also had a restrictive impact on the sector, so much so that it was not until 1993 that the government felt able to issue a local licence for the first foreign-owned hypermarket (Macro). Later in the decade, some of the bigger international chains (Carrefour, Tesco and Giant) set up in the Klang Valley, but on 20 April 2004 a five-year freeze was imposed on future hyper-market applications in the Klang Valley, Penang and Johor Bahru due to fears for local Malaysian businesses. More stringent pre-conditions, including requirements for a local population of at least 350,000, local product displays and for impact studies on local businesses were imposed.[23]

Even this sector, however, has been liberalized following the NEM and new guidelines issued (Ministry of Domestic Trade Cooperatives and Consumerism 2010: 3–5). From 6 January 2010, all distributive trade formats (departmental store, superstore and speciality store), with the exception of hypermarkets, can be 100 per cent owned by foreign interests; hypermarkets remain subject to the 30 per cent *Bumiputera* equity requirement (Ministry of Domestic Trade Cooperatives and Consumerism 2010: 5). However, proposals for foreign involvement (including acquisitions of interests, mergers and take-overs) in all distributive trade formats must apply for approval from the Ministry of Domestic Trade and Consumer Affairs (MDTCA) and are required to:

- appoint *Bumiputera* director/directors;
- hire personnel at all levels including management to reflect the racial composition of the Malaysian population;
- formulate clear policies and plans to assist *Bumiputera* participation in the distributive trade sector;
- hire at least 1 per cent of the total hypermarket workforce from persons with disabilities;
- to increase the utilization of local airports and ports in the export and import of the goods;
- to utilize local companies for legal and other professional services which are available in Malaysia;
- submit annual financial reports to the Ministry of Domestic Trade Cooperatives and Consumerism; and
- comply with all by-laws and regulations of Local Authorities
  (Ministry of Domestic Trade Cooperatives and Consumerism 2010: 3)

The extent to which these requirements will be enforced and reflected in the conditions attached to approvals from the MDTCA, however, remains to be seen.

Other than banking and distributive trade services, the rules governing accounting, taxation, engineering and legal services have also been restrictive. Foreign lawyers, for example, have not been able to operate in Malaysia unless they are Malaysian citizens or Permanent Residents and passed a Malay language exam, or giving opinions on foreign law or in relation to offshore corporation law. Foreign law firms cannot be established anywhere in Malaysia apart from in the Federal Territory of Labuan; even there it is limited to other offshore corporations established in Labuan. Foreign accounting firms can only provide accounting and taxation services through affiliates, and the same residential requirements applied to individual accountants as to lawyers. As for engineering services, foreign engineers could only work on specific projects under licence from the Board of Engineers and be sponsored by the Malaysian company undertaking the project. In turn, the latter has to demonstrate it is unable to find a Malaysian engineer (Australian Department of Foreign Affairs and Trade 2005: 34–5).

Notwithstanding requests from Australia, the Republic of Korea, Japan, the EEC and Poland for unrestricted access to the services market, and the Malaysian government's commitment to liberalize services under GATS, the ASEAN Framework on Services (AFAS, 1995)[24] and various BITs or FTAs – the above sectors remain restricted. On 22 April 2009, the Malaysian government agreed to liberalize 27 sub-sectors,[25] but accounting, taxation, engineering and general legal services were not included in this particular wave. In line with the New Economic Model and Malaysia's aspiration to become an international Islamic financial hub, the Government has agreed to allow five top international law firms with expertise in Islamic financial services to practice in Malaysia. However, any application will be carefully screened based on credentials and business plans. Licences will also be restricted to providing *international* Islamic financial services, thereby preserving the niche for domestic law firms specializing in Islamic banking and finance.[26]

Though foreign investors are free to litigate in Malaysian courts like domestic investors, because of the limited access given to foreign lawyers in Malaysia, they tend to prefer arbitration in Malaysia for resolution of their investment disputes. The Legal Profession Act 1976, which denies representation in Malaysian courts to foreign lawyers, does not apply to arbitral proceedings as arbitrators are appointed by the parties pursuant to their arbitration agreement and thus not a 'court of justice' (*Zublin Muhibbah Joint Venture v Government of Malaysia* [1990] 3 MLJ 125). Foreign investors also prefer arbitration because counsel can choose to make their legal submissions in whatever language they wish, being exempt from the statutory requirement to speak in Bahasa Malaysia under section 8 of the National Language Act 1963–1967. They also can resolve their disputes more quickly by skipping the increasingly long queues in the domestic courts (Pradhan and Doi 2006: 242–4).

As a rule, the legal environment in Malaysia is supportive of arbitration and alternative dispute resolution (ADR) more generally (Pradhan and Doi 2006: 240–6). Malaysia is a party to the NYC, and will enforce arbitration awards of other states so long as they are also signatories to the Convention and the arbitration award is deemed 'commercial' under national law. It will also enforce awards by foreign parties against a domestic party (Arbitration Act 2005, section 38). The law governing arbitration in Malaysia is the Arbitration Act 2005 (Act 646 of 2005), which is based on the original (1985) UNCITRAL Model Law on International Commercial Arbitration. Under section 8 of the Act, unless the parties agree otherwise, the courts may not intervene in an international arbitration apart from in the terms set out in the Model Law (as enacted). If the parties choose Malaysia as the seat of arbitration, they can apply to the Malaysian courts for interim or conservatory measures, including applications to stay proceedings in breach of an agreement to arbitrate. As a result of recent Malaysian case law, however, those rights do not apply if the parties choose to arbitrate outside Malaysia (*Aras Jalinan Sdn Bhd* v. *Tipco Asphalt Public Company Ltd & Ors* [2008] 5 CLJ 654).

8.3.2 Malaysia's approach to investment through BITs and FTAs

Malaysia is committed to a multilateral trading system through its membership of the GATT and the WTO,[27] but is also an enthusiastic participator in BITs and FTAs. As noted earlier, Malaysia has signed 68 BITs, largely because it does not have a comprehensive investment law. These BITs routinely provide:

- protection against nationalization and expropriation;
- promises of prompt and adequate compensation in the event of nationalization or expropriation;
- free transfers of profits, capital and other fees; and
- promises to settle investment disputes in accordance with ICSID.

These agreements have been signed with developed and developing countries, but by far the majority with the developing world representing groupings within ASEAN and the Organisation of the Islamic Conference (OIC). Having signed more than 40 BITs with other developing countries, Malaysia is one of the most enthusiastic exponents of South-South cooperation (UNCTAD 2006: 4). However, 34 of the 68 BITs are not yet in force, with many of them involving developing countries whose political instability may have precluded ratification.

Like many other countries, but also because of its pro-*Bumiputera* policies enacted through the NEP, Malaysia has elected to adopt the 'investment control model' BIT (UNCTAD 1999: 17–20), reserving absolute sovereign control over the type and extent of foreign investments it allows into the country. It offers most favoured nation (MFN) treatment only after establishment and admission.[28] Typically, the wording of the BITs with the developing countries with whom Malaysia does not already have a close working relationship (like Indonesia), is more general and so may not have been expected to be as strictly enforced. So in the treaties with Kazakhstan (1996) and Jordan (1994), for example, Article 3(1) of both treaties states simply:

> Investments made by investors of either Contracting Party in the territory of the other Contracting Party shall receive treatment which is fair and equitable, and not less favourable than that accorded to investments made by investors of any third State.

This contrasts with the standard MFN clause with developed countries. Article 3(2) of the treaty with the Republic of Korea (1988), for example, states both countries will

> accord to nationals or companies of the other Contracting Party as regards *the management, use, enjoyment or disposal of their investments*, treatment which is fair and equitable and *not less favourable than that which it accords to its own nationals* and companies or to the nationals and companies of any third State. (emphases added)[29]

The additional detail and protection probably reflects the ongoing and substantial financial investments of those countries in Malaysia. By contrast, many of the BITs with least developed countries from the OIC and Africa, for example, seem more symbolic. Their wording suggests a spirit of cooperation and a willingness to open doors to Malaysian outward investment should opportunities arrive and local circumstances permit.

In more recent times, Malaysia has also begun to jump on the FTA bandwagon. Four FTAs have already been signed: with Japan (2006), Chile (2006), Pakistan (2007) and New Zealand (2009). Four more FTAs are under negotiation: with the United States, Australia, Turkey and India. In addition, Malaysia has signed a number of regional FTAs as part of its membership in ASEAN with China (2002), Japan (2003), Australia/New Zealand (2009), Korea (2005) and India (2009). It is also in the process of negotiating a Preferential Trading System (PTS) Agreement with the OIC, a Preferential Tariff Agreement (PTA) with seven other developing Islamic countries (Bangladesh, Indonesia, Iran, Egypt, Nigeria, Pakistan and Turkey) and a Trans-Pacific Partnership Agreement (TPPA) with New Zealand, Chile, Singapore, Brunei, Australia, the US, Peru and Vietnam.[30]

In terms of coverage, the signed and implemented FTAs are not comprehensive. They have not given away Malaysia's rights to screen foreign investment, nor removed its protections of the steel and automobile industries,

GLCs and services sector (Das and Chongvilaivan 2010: 266). The PTS and PTA agreements with countries from the OIC focus on trade and reductions in tariff and non-tariff barriers; they do not include services. The most wide-ranging of these potential agreements is the TPPA which, in addition to inclusion of services, focuses on 'horizontal issues', such as regional integration, regulatory coherence, competitiveness, development and transparency. Negotiations, however, are still at the initial stages and unlikely to be completed any time soon.[31]

According to MITI,[32] Malaysia has taken these initiatives to secure: better market access by addressing tariffs and non-tariff measures; facilitation and promotion of trade, investment and economic development; enhancement of the competitiveness of Malaysian exporters, and strengthening of capacity in specific targeted areas through technical cooperation and collaboration. But in addition to these economic justifications, there may be strategic advantages to Malaysia entering these relationships (Das and Chongvilaivan 2010: 266). Its involvement in the proposed TPPA and FTA with the US can be seen as both an attempt to avoid exclusion from preferential trade agreements involving the EU and US, and to run at the same diplomatic pace as its main ASEAN competitors, Singapore and Thailand (Das and Chongvilaivan 2010: 267). Concern had been expressed by the NEAC in their report detailing the NEM that Malaysia was falling behind its fellow Asian 'tigers,' a fact borne out by Table 8.A.

Similarly, its increasing involvement in the OIC reflects Malaysia' status and aspiration to be an economic and political role model in the Islamic world. This is evidenced in its promotion and increasing control of the global Halal products industry and its acknowledged role as a regional hub in the world of Islamic banking and finance. It is also one of the few Muslim countries to have a relatively successful and stable democracy, notwithstanding the continuing controversies with former Deputy Prime Minister Anwar Ibrahim and certain concerns over civil liberties (Lopez 2010).

8.4 Conclusion

Reviewing the history of Malaysia's policy in relation to FDI and its legal framework, its litany of BITs and current love affair with FTAs, one cannot help thinking the government has wanted to have its cake and eat it. The country has remained open to foreign investment on a continuous basis since Independence and has generally pursued a liberal trade policy, offering plenty of incentives to foreign investors. Yet it has also maintained a strong central government and directed economy in order to give effect to its ethnic re-distribution policies, a characteristic more reminiscent of a socialist state.[33] This has produced imbalances and a distorted economy (Gomez and Jomo 1999), with a private sector left out in the cold (NEAC 2010: 45).

So to what extent has the NEM given effect to radical reform? The NEM proclaims re-distribution and affirmative action will no longer be based on

Table 8.A Global rankings for ease of doing business

	Ease of doing business	Starting a business	Dealing with construction permits	Registering Property	Trading across borders	Enforcing contracts	Protecting Investors
Singapore	1	4	2	15	1	13	2
Hong Kong	2	6	1	56	2	2	3
New Zealand	3	1	5	3	28	9	1
UK	4	17	16	22	15	23	10
US	5	9	27	12	20	8	5
Thailand	19	95	12	19	12	25	12
Japan	18	98	44	59	24	19	16
South Korea	16	60	22	74	8	5	74
Malaysia	21	113	108	60	37	59	4

Source: World Bank and International Finance Corporation, *Doing Business Report 2011: Making a Difference for Entrepreneurs*.

ethnicity but on need.[34] The 30 per cent *Bumiputera* equity target, however, remains. The impression that little has changed is reinforced by the 10th Malaysian Plan which continues to emphasize *Bumiputera* interests. Even the current government's rhetoric surrounding the NEM sounds remarkably familiar. Prime Minister Najib's 'One Malaysia' concept, for example, echoes Tun Abdul Razak's 'Masyarakat Adil' (Just Society) announced in 1971 immediately before launching the NEP in the 2nd Malaysian Plan.

The NEM has led to some important legal reforms, such as the Competition Act 2010. That is intended to stimulate the private sector by reducing the influence of government parastatals (GOCs) and high net-worth individuals with close ties to members of the government, domination of the market by MNCs and family conglomerates as well as anti-competitive practices more generally. This may well be enough, along with other reforms increasing the transparency and efficiency in the processing of investment applications,[35] and further waves of liberalization in the services sector, to arrest Malaysia's slide into developmental mediocrity. The 10th Malaysian Plan, however, has also announced there will be 'smart partnerships' between public and private based on shared equity which, without independent and careful monitoring, is likely to lead to the same 'cronyism' that characterized the Mahathir and Badawi eras. Government pumping of 230 billion ringgit into the Development Budget via the 10th Malaysian Plan also smacks of extensive government involvement in the economy and not simply facilitation of the private sector.

Given the highly complex demographics Malaysia has had to contend with following Independence, its governments have been remarkably successful. But in order to break free of the 'middle income trap,' perhaps the country needs to break free from its past. Businesses remain wrapped up in red tape, the process for construction permits are still slow and laborious, and the resolution of commercial disputes prolonged because of log-jams in the courts (NEAC 2010: 47–8). Business entrepreneurs are also being frustrated by inconsistent government policies, unfavourable taxation regimes and corruption (NEAC 2010: 48). Perhaps the time has come for a true market economy.

Notes

1 For discussions of the particular challenges facing ethnically 'tripolar' states, see Horowitz (1985).
2 It should be noted that empirical studies conducted in Malaysia demonstrated a positive correlation between poverty alleviation and inflows of FDI; see Rasiah (2008).
3 On Independence, British companies owned 90 per cent of the stock of FDI in Malaysia; see Athukorala and Menon (1995: 14).
4 Between 1976 and 1985, capital flight was estimated at US$12 billion (Jomo 2008b: 185).
5 Growth rates hit 10 per cent on four occasions: 1973, 1977, 1989 and 1997 (NEAC 2010: 42).

6 Indonesia dropped 47.66 per cent, Thailand 30.37 per cent and Vietnam 44.09 per cent (UNCTAD 2010: 170).

7 According to UNCTAD's *World Investment Report 2010* FDI outflows were 5.82 times the level of inflows.

8 See further Abidin (2010), strongly defending the government's record. It should also be noted that Chinese 'disinvestment' from the country and the movement of their capital overseas has been a known phenomenon since the establishment of the NEP in 1971; see further, Gomez and Jomo (1999: 44).

9 See Butt, Chapter 6 in this volume.

10 See MIDA 2010a.

11 See MITI 2010.

12 Section 4(3) states: 'In exercising his powers under subsection (1), the Minister may take into consideration the following: *(a)* whether or not any activity is being carried out or any product is being produced in Malaysia on a commercial scale suitable to the economic requirements or development of Malaysia or at all; or *(b)* whether there are — (i) favourable prospects for further development of the activity or product; or (ii) insufficient facilities in Malaysia to enable the activity to be carried out or a product to be produced on a commercial scale suitable to the economic requirements.

13 For other allowances, see further PIA 1986, ss 31A–41B.

14 See MIDA (2011a). More precise details on the allowances can be obtained from the same website.

15 Free Zones are divided into Free Commercial Zones (FCZs) and Free Industrial Zones (FIZs). The former (of which there are currently 13) allows trading, re-packing, transit, bulk-breaking, etc with minimum customs interference. The latter (currently numbering 16) are reserved for manufacturers who export. MIDA (2009b: 145).

16 See MIDA 2011a.

17 See, for example, the Industrial Coordination Act 1975, sections 3 and 4.

18 See Jomo (2008: 199). This was a watchdog administrative committee, staffed with representatives from 13 government departments, and charged with implementation of the NEP.

19 See Public Private Partnership Unit 2011.

20 The current level was set in 1986 as part of government liberalization measures (Jomo 2008b: 185).

21 In April 2009, Bank Negara announced it would be issuing in 2009 two licences for overseas Islamic banks with paid-up capital of at least US$1 billion to enhance global inter-linkages, two commercial banking licences for foreign players (with a further three in 2011), and two family Islamic insurance (takaful) licences in 2009 (Bank Negara Malaysia 2009).

22 This is defined as trade relating to 'all linkage activities that channel goods and services down the supply chain to intermediaries for resale or to final buyers'. It specifically excludes manufacturing. See Ministry of Domestic Trade Cooperatives and Consumerism (2010: 2).

23 See Lee (2004: 18). The more hostile environment for foreign involvement in the distributive trade services sector was clearly evident in the re-issuing of the guidelines in 2004. See further Ministry of Domestic Trade and Consumer Affairs (2004).

24 See the ASEAN website, www.aseansec.org/6628.htm (accessed 23 March 2011).

25 For further details, see MIDA (2009a).
26 Ibid.
27 See MITI 2010.
28 This is also true of the investment chapters of Malaysia's FTAs, although without the same level of scrutiny, nor discretionary power as given by the BITs. For example, the Malaysia–Japan FTA (2006), Article 75(3) on National Treatment provides: 'Notwithstanding the provisions of paragraph 1 of this Article, each Country may prescribe special formalities in connection with the establishment of investments by investors of the other Country in the former Country such as the compliance with registration requirements, provided that such special formalities do not impair the substance of the rights under this Chapter' (see Japanese Ministry of Economy, Trade and Industry 2011).
29 For a similar example, see the 1981 BIT between Malaysia and the United Kingdom, www.unctad.org/sections/dite/iia/docs/bits/uk_malaysia.pdf).
30 See MITI (2010).
31 Ibid.
32 Ibid.
33 Compare also more generally Sornarajah, Chapter 13 in this volume.
34 Ethnic Indians, in particular, have lost out in the shift from agriculture to manufacturing and high-tech industries, and not gained from educational quotas under the NEP aimed exclusively at the *Bumiputeras*. Ethnic Indians now control only 1.2 per cent of the economy, down from 1.5 per cent since the 8th Malaysian Plan. This has generated such resentment that, in 2008, it led to the formation of civil rights organizations, such as HINDRAF, street demonstrations and political unrest (Shome and Hamidon 2009). The NEP had even failed to deliver to the majority of the *Bumiputeras*. Only 5 per cent benefited directly; affirmative action privileges were being 'creamed' by Malay elites and by those politically well-connected (Crouch 1992; Gomez and Jomo 1999; Yusuf 2001; Shome and Hamidon 2009).
35 The inherent uncertainty and bureaucracy in applying for and securing a licence has now vastly diminished, with MIDA acting as a one-stop shop for investment applications and with a facility for making applications online. Licence application guidelines and forms are also freely available on the MIDA website in English, Bahasa Malaysia, Arabic, Chinese and Japanese through an e-Services Portal (2011b). Further, as a result of changes implemented at the beginning of December 2008, licences in non-sensitive industries have been granted automatically. Approvals and detailed evaluations are required only if the manufacturing activity or industry relates to security, safety, health, environment and religious considerations, projects proposed to be located in Sabah and Sarawak, and to projects requiring approval under the Petroleum Development Act 1974 (MIDA 2010b).

Bibliography

Abidin, M.Z. (2010) 'The Great FDI Debate: Substance or Subterfuge', *New Straits Times*, 31 July.
Agence France-Presse (2010) 'Malaysia issues licences to five foreign banks', 17 June. Available at: www.news-insurances.com/malaysia-issues-licences-to-five-foreign-banks/0167145728 (accessed 23 March 2011).

Association of Southeast Asian Nations (1995) 'ASEAN Framework Agreement on Services'. Available at: www.aseansec.org/6628.htm (accessed 23 March 2011).

Athukorala, P. and Menon, J. (1995) 'Developing with Foreign Investment: Malaysia', *The Australian Economic Review*, 28(1): 9–22.

Australian Department of Foreign Affairs and Trade (2005), 'An Australia-Malaysia Free Trade Agreement: An Australian Scoping Study'. Available at: www.dfat. gov.au/fta/amfta/index.html (accessed 24 February 2011).

Bank Negara Malaysia (2009) 'Liberalisation of the Financial Sector'. Available at: www.bnm.gov.my/index.php?ch=8&pg=14&ac=1817 (accessed 23 March 2011).

Crouch, H. (1992) 'Authoritarian Trends, the UMNO Split and the Limits to State Power' in Kahn, J.S. and Wah, F.L.K. (eds) *Fragmented Vision: Culture and Politics in Contemporary Malaysia*, North Sydney, Australia: Allen and Unwin.

Das, S.B. and Chongvilaivan, A. (2010) 'Rationale for free trade agreements (FTAs) in South East Asia' in Rasiah, R. and Schmidt, J.D. (eds) *The New Political Economy of South East Asia*, Cheltenham: Edward Elgar Publishing, 257–77.

Feenstra, R.C. and Hanson, G.H. (1997), 'Foreign Direct Investment and Relative Wages: Evidence from Mexico's Maquiladoras', *Journal of International Economics*, 42, 371–93.

Gomez, E.T. and Jomo, K.S. (1999) *Malaysia's Political Economy: Politics, Patronage and Profits*, Cambridge: Cambridge University Press.

Government of Malaysia (1971) *Second Malaysian Plan, 1971–1975*, Kuala Lumpur.

Horowitz, D. (1985) *Ethnic Groups in Conflict*, Berkeley: UCLA Press.

Japanese Ministry of Economy, Trade and Industry (2011) *Agreement between the Government of Japan and the Government of Malaysia for an Economic Partnership*. Available at: www.meti.go.jp/english/policy/external_economy/trade/FTA_EPA/malaysia. html (accessed 23 March 2011).

Jomo, K.S. (2007) *Malaysian Industrial Policy*, Singapore: National University of Singapore Press.

Jomo K.S. (2008b) 'Investment and Technology Policy: Government Intervention, Regulation and Incentives' in Jomo K.S. and Ngan. W.S. (eds) *Law, Institutions and Malaysian Economic Development*, Singapore: National University of Singapore Press.

Jomo, K.S. and Tan, Chang Yii (2008) 'The Political Economy of Post-colonial Transformation' in Jomo K.S. and Ngan. W.S. (eds) *Law, Institutions and Malaysian Economic Development*, Singapore: National University of Singapore Press.

Kearney, A.T. (2011) *Foreign Direct Investment Confidence Index.*). Available at: www. atkearney.com/index.php/Publications/foreign-direct-investment-confidence-index.html.

Lee, C. (2004) *Competition Policy in Malaysia*, Centre on Regulation and Competition, Working Paper Series No 68, Institute for Development Policy and Management, University of Manchester.

Lopez, G. (2010) 'Mahathir's regional legacy', *East Asia Forum*. Available at: www. eastasiaforum.org/2010/06/17/mahathirs-regional-legacy (accessed 23 March 2011).

Malaysian Industrial Development Authority (MIDA) (2009a) *Invest in Malaysia: Liberalisation of the Services Sector*. Available at: www.mida.gov.my/en_v2/index. php?page=liberalisation-of-the-services-sector (accessed 23 March 2011).

Malaysian Industrial Development Authority (2009b) *Malaysia: Investment in the Manufacturing Sector – Policies, Incentives and Facilities*, Kuala Lumpur.

Malaysian Industrial Development Authority (2010a) *Invest in Malaysia: Taxation.* Available at: www.mida.gov.my/en_v2/index.php?page=double-taxation-agreement (accessed 23 March 2011).

Malaysian Industrial Development Authority (2010b) ML (08) (17-02-2010).

Malaysian Industrial Development Authority (2011a) *Invest in Malaysia: Incentives for Investment.* Available at: www.mida.gov.my/en_v2/index.php?page=manufacturing-sector-2 (accessed 23 March 2011).

Malaysian Industrial Development Authority (2011b) *MIDA e-Services Portal.* Available at: www.mida.gov.my/en_v2/index.php?page=forms-guidelines (accessed 5 February 2011).

Malaysian Ministry of Domestic Trade Cooperatives and Consumerism (2010) Guidelines on Foreign Participation in the Distributive Trade Services Malaysia. Available at: www.kpdnkk.gov.my/kpdnkk_theme/images/pdf/WRT_Guideline.pdf (accessed 18 August 2011).

Malaysian Ministry of Domestic Trade and Consumer Affairs (2004) *Guidelines on Foreign Participation in the Distributive Trade Services Malaysia*, Kuala Lumpur.

Malaysian Ministry of International Trade and Industry (MITI) (2010) *Free Trade Agreement.* Available at: http://www.miti.gov.my/cms/content.jsp?id=com.tms.cms.section.Section_8ab55693-7f000010-72f772f7-46d4f042&curpage=tt (accessed 4 August 2011).

Marashdeh, O. (1990) 'Foreign Banks Activities and Factors Affecting their Presence in Malaysia', *Asia-Pacific Journal of Management*, 11(1): 113–23.

NEAC (2010) *New Economic Model for Malaysia: Part 1 Strategic Policy Directions*, Putrajaya.

Ngan, W.S. (2008) 'Postcolonial Legal Developments' in Jomo K.S. and Ngan, W.S. (eds) *Law, Institutions and Malaysian Economic Development*, Singapore: National University of Singapore Press.

Ngan, W.S. and Kandiah, S. (2008) 'Financial Sector Legal Developments' in Jomo, K.S. and Ngan, W.S. (eds) *Law, Institutions and Malaysian Economic Development*, Singapore: National University of Singapore Press.

Pradhan, V.P. and Doi, V. (2006) 'Dispute Resolution and Arbitration in Malaysia' in McConnaughay, P.J. and Ginsburg, T.B., *International Commercial Arbitration in Asia*.

Public Private Partnership Unit (2011) *Liberalisation of FIC Guidelines.* Available at: www.ukas.gov.my/web/guest/fic_guidelines2;jsessionid=C7D59D1788E6C87AFCA974FDF430BF00 (accessed 23 March 2011).

Qin, J.Y. (2005) 'Defining Non-discrimination under the law of the World Trade Organisation', *Boston University International Law Journal*, 23(2): 215–97.

Rasiah, R. (2008) 'Drivers of growth and poverty reduction in Malaysia: government policy, export manufacturing and foreign direct investment', *Malaysian Journal of Economic Studies*, 45(1): 21–44.

Reuveny, R. and Quan, L. (2003) 'Economic Openness, Democracy, and Income Inequality: An Empirical Analysis', *Comparative Political Studies*, 36(5): 575–602.

Salz, I.S. (1992) 'Foreign Direct Investment and the Distribution of Income' *Atlantic Economic Journal*, 20(1): 106.

Shome, A. and Hamidon, S. (2009) 'The Contradiction of Entrepreneurship through Affirmative Action: The Case of Malaysia', *The Copenhagen Journal of Asian Studies* 27(1): 38–66.

Snodgrass, D.R. (1995) 'Successful Economic Development in a Multi-ethnic

Society: The Malaysian Case'. Available at: www.earthinstitute.columbia.edu/site-files/file/about/director/pubs/503.pdf (accessed 5 February 2011).

UNCTAD (1999) 'Admission and Establishment', UNCTAD, Series on Issues in International Investment Agreements, UNCTAD/ITE/IIT/10 (Vol. II).

UNCTAD (2002) *World Investment Report: Transnational Corporations and Export Competitiveness.*

UNCTAD (2006) *Recent Developments in International Investment Agreements*, IIA Monitor, No 2 of 2005.

UNCTAD (2010) *World Investment Report 2010.*

Wah, C.Y. (2010) 'Towards Inter-Ethnic Business Development and National Unity in Malaysia', CRISE Working Paper No 73.

Woo-Cummings, M. (1999) 'Reforming Corporate Governance in East Asia', Macalester International, 7: 133–85.

Wong S.C. and Jomo K.S. (2008) 'Institutional Initiatives for Crisis Management, 1998' in Jomo K.S. and Ngan. W.S. (eds) *Law, Institutions and Malaysian Economic Development*, Singapore: National University of Singapore Press: 203–19.

Yusuf, S. (2001) 'The East Asian Miracle at the Millennium' in Stiglitz, J.E. and Yusuf, S. (eds) *Rethinking the East Asia Miracle*, Oxford: Oxford University Press.

9 Treaty definitions of 'investment' and the role of economic development

A critical analysis of the *Malaysian Historical Salvors* cases

Govert Coppens

9.1 Introduction

The definition of an 'investment' is a highly contentious topic in investment arbitration. A range of indicative 'characteristics' or binding 'requirements' – depending on one's interpretation – have been identified: a contribution of resources, sufficient duration, incurring a certain risk, acquiring a regular profit and return, and a contribution to the economic development of the host state. Remarkably, there is still no consensus in the case law on whether any criteria should be applied at all, or what criteria those would be, or how such criteria should be interpreted. The characteristic that has been interpreted most diversely is probably the 'contribution to the economic development of the host state'. Some tribunals have deemed it a fundamental pillar of investment arbitration; others have not even considered it important enough to mention it. In this contribution, two of those divergent decisions will be considered more closely: the Award on Jurisdiction, a case brought based on the United Kingdom–Malaysia Bilateral Investment Treaty (BIT, 1981),[1] and the Annulment Decision in *Malaysian Historical Salvors, SDN, BHD* v. *Malaysia*.[2]

Arguably, both decisions can be seen as a form of 'judicial activism', in the sense of judicial decision-making whereby arbitrators allow their personal views about public policy, among other factors, to guide their decisions.[3] This makes them all the more interesting to analyse since one can at times hear the creaking of the law while it is being bent.

The relevant facts for the discussion below can be briefly summarized. In 1991, Malaysian Historical Salvors Sdn Bhd (MHS), a company incorporated in Malaysia, was contracted by the Malaysian government to find, salvage and auction the historically and financially significant cargo of the *Diana*, an early nineteenth-century British trade ship. The revenue of the auction would be split between MHS and the government. After a successful salvage operation in 1995, the cargo was auctioned for approximately US$2.98 million. The dispute arose when MHS allegedly did not receive its agreed share of the proceeds. The company then started the first of numerous legal proceedings, which were all unsuccessful. Eventually, in September 2004, MHS filed a Request for Arbitration at ICSID under the UK–Malaysia BIT, which came into force on 21 October 1988.

9.2 The MHS Award on Jurisdiction

The Tribunal saw the notion of an 'investment', particularly under the ICSID Convention, as the crux of the dispute. While the Arbitrator (Michael Hwang SC from Singapore) recognized that there were multiple jurisdictional objections, the question whether there was an investment under the BIT and the ICSID Convention was the first that was raised by Claimant. Subsequently, the Arbitrator spent around 70 per cent of the Award exploring the case law on this point — likely the most extensive overview any tribunal has given on this topic. The seven cases he considered to be of particular importance on this issue were analysed in detail: *Salini, Joy Mining, Jan De Nul, L.E.S.I.-DIPENTA, Bayindir, CSOB* and *Patrick Mitchell*.[4]

While the Arbitrator identified a 'typical characteristics approach' and a 'jurisdictional approach' in the arbitral case law, he dismissed this distinction as 'academic' (*MHS*, Award on Jurisdiction, para. 105). He continued by setting out and illustrating the different and often rather piecemeal approaches of preceding tribunals that had ruled on whether the considered transaction was an investment. Despite this emphasis on the differences in tribunals' approaches and despite the fact that there are very few cases that have considered the '*Salini* criteria' as cumulative requirements, the Tribunal eventually concluded in general terms that 'if any of these [*Salini*] hallmarks are absent, the tribunal will hesitate (and probably decline) to make a finding of "investment"' (para. 106(e)).

In the author's view, even the *Salini* Decision itself cannot be seen as precedent for a 'test' of four cumulative criteria. However, this Decision is often cited as if it represents the formalistic extreme on the spectrum of opinions on 'investment'. The Tribunal in *Salini* admitted that the criteria are necessarily 'derived from cases in which the transaction giving rise to the dispute was considered to be an investment without there ever being a real discussion of the issue in almost all the cases' (*Salini*, Decision on Jurisdiction, para. 52). Moreover, the Tribunal went on to say explicitly that '[i]n reality, these various elements may be *interdependent*' and '[a]s a result, these various criteria should be *assessed globally* even if, for the sake of reasoning, the Tribunal considers them individually here' (para. 52; emphasis added). Consequently, it seems highly unlikely the *Salini* Tribunal meant to expound a set of hard and fast criteria and it does not seem justified that *Salini* has become the epitome for a strict approach of cumulative requirements to defining an 'investment' under ICSID.

More than most other tribunals that have looked into this question, the *MHS* Arbitrator thoroughly analysed a number of cases and discussed the jurisdictional issues at length. However, it seems that the Tribunal's pre-existing views on this issue might have determined the selection and analysis of the cases more than these cases having influenced the Tribunal's decision.

For example, in addition to the cases mentioned above, the Tribunal touched upon *PSEG*,[5] *Alcoa Minerals*,[6] *Mihaly*,[7] and *SGS* v. *Pakistan*.[8] It dismissed the latter three as 'not of significant assistance'. However, this does not seem very persuasive regarding *Alcoa* and *SGS* v. *Pakistan. Alcoa* was excluded because the Tribunal in that case had stated that Alcoa Minerals of Jamaica had 'invested substantial amounts in a foreign State' (*MHS*, Award on Jurisdiction, para. 63). In contrast, the *MHS* Arbitrator was of the opinion that the amount invested by MHS could not be described as a 'substantial amount', without distinguishing further any of the facts of *Alcoa* from those of *MHS*.

SGS v. *Pakistan* was dismissed as 'not helpful' because the Tribunal in that case only focused on the meaning of 'investment' as defined in the Swiss-Pakistan BIT (11 July 1995, in force 6 May 1996) and there had 'arguably [been] no substantive discussion by the tribunal [...] on why the agreement was an 'investment' within the meaning within the ICSID Convention' (*MHS*, Award on Jurisdiction, para. 64). The *MHS* Arbitrator did not seem to contemplate that if the Tribunal in *SGS* did not feel the need to examine this, not having done so may in itself be a relevant fact. Indeed, the *SGS* v. *Pakistan* Tribunal was very much aware of the debate on the requirements of Article 25(1) ICSID Convention (*SGS*, Decision on Jurisdiction, para. 133):

> The ICSID Convention does not delimit the term 'investment,' leaving to the Contracting Parties a large measure of freedom to define that term as their specific objectives and circumstances may lead them to do so. In this case, the BIT between the Swiss Confederation and the Islamic Republic of Pakistan does contain a definition of 'investment.'

In the footnote to this sentence, the *SGS* v. *Pakistan* Tribunal acknowledges explicitly that the Parties' freedom is not unlimited, 'considering that 'investment' may well be regarded as embodying certain core meaning which distinguishes it from 'an ordinary commercial transaction' such as a simple, stand alone, sale of goods or services' (*SGS*, Decision on Jurisdiction, para. 133, n. 153). Apart from this rock bottom meaning of investment as different from a sales transaction, the *SGS* Tribunal thus saw no reason to read several criteria into Article 25(1) of the ICSID Convention. This is something quite different from a decision that is 'unhelpful' because it does not touch upon the same legal questions.

In other instances as well, some of the MHS Arbitrator's conclusions seem to rely strongly on precedents that do not go quite as far as what they are quoted in support for. In finding support for the Tribunal's statement that the contribution to the economic development must be significant, it cites *Bayindir* since it 'also endorsed the general view that a contribution had to be significant' (*MHS*, Award on Jurisdiction, para. 115). However, *Bayindir* (*Bayindir*, para. 137), referred to both a ruling that had supported a separate requirement of 'significance' (*Joy Mining*, para. 53) and to one that had not supported this separate requirement (*L.E.S.I.*, para. 13 (iv)), the Tribunal in *Bayindir* seems to conclude that if there is such a requirement, it might well be fulfilled by other conditions. Moreover, the parties were in agreement on this issue in the case before it so there was no need to go into this further. To draw from this the conclusion that the *Bayindir* Tribunal meant to subscribe to the 'general view'[9] that the contribution of the economic development of the host state *must* be (i) examined separately, and (ii) 'significant', seems to overstate its value as precedent.

Subsequently, the *MHS* Arbitrator stated that 'in *CSOB*, the tribunal stated that there must be significant contributions to the host state's economic development' (*MHS*, Award on Jurisdiction, para. 125). However, *CSOB* mentions the significance only once: 'This undertaking involved a significant contribution by CSOB to the economic development of the Slovak Republic.'[10] If a tribunal mentions the mere fact that an investment is a 'significant contribution to the development of the host State', it is not possible to logically deduce from this statement that the 'significance', or even the 'contribution to the development', was a *necessary* requirement for the tribunal to reach its conclusion.

In sum, any arbitrator is naturally entitled to his or her own opinion on points of law and preferences in structuring an award. A tribunal does not even have to base its decision on precedent.[11] However, if a tribunal does rely on case law to support its opinion, it is only fair to assume that these cases should indeed support the legal statement that is made. In the *MHS* Award on Jurisdiction, it is at times hard to distinguish between those instances where the case law is analysed objectively, and those where the Arbitrator's own pre-conceptions or views seem to prevail. This can contribute to a sense that the cited case law is not always used properly and that its value as precedent for certain statements may be overstretched.

The effect of this 'mixed' analysis becomes clear when a tendentious interpretation of case law earlier in the Award becomes the legal basis for seemingly objective legal conclusions afterwards. For example (*MHS*, Award on Jurisdiction, para. 131):

> '[. . .] the Tribunal finds that the Contract did not benefit the Malaysian public interest in a material way or serve to benefit the Malaysian economy *in the sense developed by ICSID jurisprudence, namely that the contributions were significant*.' (emphasis added)

Contrary to the Tribunal's analysis of several arbitral awards, there is arguably very little precedent in support of the standard of a 'significant contribution to the economic development'. Even the ad hoc Annulment Committee in *Patrick Mitchell*, which supported the criterion of a contribution to the economic development of the host state, stated explicitly that this condition's existence:

> does not mean that this contribution must always be sizable or success-ful; and, of course, ICSID tribunals do not have to evaluate the real con-tribution of the operation in question.[12]

Consequently, the *MHS* Arbitrator's reference to 'previous ICSID jurispru-dence' – as if it were a generally accepted or at least a common interpretation – seems hard to justify.

Additionally, the Arbitrator not only considers creating 'internal' signi-ficant economic value within the enterprise as a requirement, but also takes into account the purpose for which that value is used – that is, how the eco-nomic activity is used 'externally' in the national economy. Large scale con-struction projects or mining concessions seem to be acceptable. However, the Arbitrator seems to believe that it is inherent in a salvaging operation that it cannot significantly contribute to the economy, regardless the value of the operation. Separate from the debate on whether an investment *should* contribute to the economic development, this approach introduces another requirement, namely the *purpose* of the created economic value. Since this requirement touches upon the policy decision of the government to engage in this contract, it seems unsuitable as a criterion. Bearing in mind existing legal uncertainty in this field, to contribute even more unpredictable con-ditions to the debate on the scope of an 'investment' does not seem to be desirable either for investors or for host states.

9.3 The MHS annulment decision

9.3.1 *The majority decision*

The majority, formed by Judge Stephen M Schwebel (USA) and Judge Peter Tomka (Slovak Republic), found that the Arbitrator had manifestly exceeded his powers and consequently annulled the Award on Jurisdiction. Already in the first few paragraphs of the ad hoc Committee's analysis, a seemingly minor but fundamental difference in perspective compared to that in the Award is made clear. Where the Arbitrator interpreted the 'object and purpose' of the ICSID Convention to be 'economic development',[13] the Annulment Committee considers it to be 'to promote the flow of private investment to contracting countries'.[14] The Arbitrator relied for his conclu-sion on the Preamble of the Convention, the Report of the Executive Dir-ectors, the *CSOB* Award and a leading commentary (Schreuer, 2001). The ad hoc Committee instead based its conclusion on the purpose as it was described in an earlier draft of the Convention.[15]

The ad hoc Committee, for convincing reasons, disagreed with the Arbi-trator's Award on Jurisdiction. This illustrates the stark disagreement on the role of development for an ICSID 'investment', even amongst the world's most respected lawyers. It is remarkable that the disagreement between the ad hoc Committee and the Tribunal, but also that between the Committee and the Dissenting Opinion, focuses predominantly on what the outer limits of the ICSID Convention are in light of the consent of the parties. This is reminiscent of the criticism raised against the Annulment Decision in *Patrick Mitchell*. This ruling had also focused on the 'development' requirement, and had considered this to be an 'essential' characteristic of an investment. The decision sparked a commentator to state that:

> given the fact that the notion of investment was a controversial notion, difficult to appreciate, it can be asserted that the annulment is a severe remedy. Deciding to annul an award because the tribunal did not apply criteria and an approach that is not unanimously adopted can be seen as an attempt by the members of the committee to impose their own views.
>
> (Hamida 2007: 302)

Considering the mostly undisputed character of the understanding of a 'two key' test of ICSID jurisdiction, it is surprising to see the amount of criticism directed against the decision of the Sole Arbitrator not to consider the BIT as the other one of the two requirements as soon as he concluded that one of them was not fulfilled. If the two are indeed cumulative requirements, this seems a perfectly justifiable logical step.

It seems that sometimes annulment tribunals see their role more as akin to a *cour de cassation*, as exists for example in France. In addition to overturning (or literally, 'breaking') an appeals judgment because of a violation of fundamental rules of procedure, the *cour de cassation* can also annul a judgment because the appeals court has erred in law (for example, by misinterpreting a concept in a statute). Consequently, it has an important role in safeguarding the uniformity of interpretation of the law. However, on this last point, a *cour de cassation* and an ad hoc annulment committee should differ fundamentally. While the convenience of a *jurisprudence constante* can be tempting for ad hoc Committees, the annulment mechanism is not designed to bring about consistency in the interpretation and application of international investment law (*MCI Power Group*, Decision on Annulment, para. 24).

The heart of the analysis of the Annulment Committee in the *MHS* case is clearly the interpretation of the notion of investment. Regardless of the merits of the points raised by the Committee, it seems doubtful that a different interpretation of the word 'investment' falls under the very limited ground for annulment of Article 52 of the ICSID Convention. Moreover, it is not self-evident to square this with the ground the Committee invoked to annul the Award, namely 'that the Tribunal has manifestly exceeded its powers'.[16]

The restricted nature of the annulment procedure is aptly pointed out in the *MCI Power* Annulment Decision. The ad hoc Committee stated that 'the role of an ad hoc committee is a limited one, restricted to assessing the legitimacy of the award and not its correctness' (para. 24). Also, the recent Annulment Decision in *Fraport v Philippines* underscored the limited role of the Committee:

> The task of the Committee is not to pronounce itself on which interpretation is better or more plausible. If the Committee were to proceed in this way, it would have been treating, as the International Court of Justice observed, 'the request as an appeal and not as a *recours en nullité*.'[17]

However, if a tribunal fails to apply the applicable law completely, ad hoc committee decisions recognize that a tribunal's failure to apply the applicable law may constitute a manifest excess of powers pursuant to Article 52(1)(b).[18] Nonetheless, the *MCI* ad hoc Committee highlights the important distinction between the *non-application* of the proper law, which may be sanctioned by Article 52(1)(b), and the *erroneous or incorrect application* of the proper law, which is not a ground for annulment.[19]

Consequently, a distinction should be drawn between, on the one hand, *what* was decided by the tribunal, and, on the other hand, *how* it was decided by the tribunal. The first potentially concerns a manifest excess of powers, the latter in principle escapes the scrutiny of annulment under Article 52(1)(b) as it concerns the reasoning of the tribunal (*MCI Power Group*, Decision on Annulment, para. 42). As pointed out in the Dissenting Opinion, numerous other ad hoc committees have also emphasized the narrow character of their annulment powers.[20]

In the *MHS* case, the ad hoc Committee deemed it necessary to annul the Award on the ground of manifest excess of powers for the following reasons:

a   it altogether failed to take account of and apply the Agreement between Malaysia and the United Kingdom defining 'investment' in broad and encompassing terms but rather limited itself to its analysis of criteria which it found to bear upon the interpretation of Article 25(1) of the ICSID Convention;

b   its analysis of these criteria elevated them to jurisdictional conditions, and exigently interpreted the alleged condition of a contribution to the economic development of the host State so as to exclude small contributions, and contributions of a cultural and historical nature;

c   it failed to take account of the preparatory work of the ICSID Convention and, in particular, reached conclusions not consonant with the *travaux* in key respects, notably the decisions of the drafters of the ICSID Convention to reject a monetary floor in the amount of an investment, to reject specification of its duration, to leave 'investment' undefined, and to accord great weight to the definition of investment agreed by the Parties in the instrument providing for recourse to ICSID.

(*MHS*, Decision on Annulment, para. 80)

With the preceding observations on the role of the annulment process in mind, it is interesting to examine these three reasons for annulment more closely.

First, the Committee considered that the Arbitrator in the *MHS* Award on Jurisdiction had 'not applied' the UK–Malaysia BIT but had instead focused entirely on the criteria found in Article 25(1) of the ICSID Convention. If so, this could indeed be a ground for annulment since it concerns applying the proper law. However, it is one thing to not even consider the BIT; it is quite another to decide that a different instrument takes precedence over the BIT and that there is consequently no need to discuss it further. Whether this interpretation is erroneous or not, it cannot be equated with simply not applying the applicable law. If it would be seen as such, any decision of a tribunal on the applicability of a legal instrument would by definition fall under the scrutiny of the annulment procedure.

Second, the Committee took issue with the Arbitrator's analysis of the criteria as jurisdictional conditions and the 'exigent' interpretation of the contribution to the economic development of the host state. If it is accepted, as argued above, that it is not the task of an ad hoc Committee to scrutinize the interpretation of the applicable law by the Arbitrator, it is difficult to see how this interpretational disagreement between the Arbitrator and the Committee makes the Arbitrator guilty of a manifest excess of powers.

Third, and arguably most contentiously, the ad hoc Committee alleges that the Arbitrator did not take into account the preparatory work of the ICSID Convention and so reached conclusions which contradict the *travaux préparatoires*. The Tribunal had indeed relied strongly on the object and purpose of the Convention as set out in its Preamble. Not only does the Committee consider the Award's interpretation of the ICSID Convention as a reason for annulment, it moreover criticizes the way in which the Tribunal came to this interpretation. First, with respect, it seems unlikely that a disagreement on the weight given to one or the other means of interpretation can constitute a manifest excess of powers or any other ground for annulment. Second, case law and commentary do not at all seem to be in agreement on the prominence of the *travaux* compared to other means of interpretation (Arsanjani and Reisman 2010: 599–604).

In the rules on interpretation in the Vienna Convention on the Law of Treaties (VCLT, 1969) in Article 31 and 32,[21] the *travaux* are merely seen as a 'supplementary means of interpretation' (or '*des moyens complémentaires*', in the equally authentic French text). However, this hierarchy of sources of interpretation should not be interpreted too strictly (Villiger 2009: 466–7). Nonetheless, this distinction is intended to ensure that the supplementary means do not constitute an alternative, autonomous method of interpretation divorced from the general rule (Sinclair 1984: 116). The means of interpretation used by the *MHS* Arbitrator is a source of interpretation that is part of the 'General rule of interpretation' in Article 31 of the VCLT. The second paragraph of this Article specifically refers to the preamble as a part of the 'context' in which a treaty should be interpreted. Moreover, the preamble is the 'natural place' in which to look for a treaty's object and purpose.[22] The ad hoc Committee solely bases itself on the *travaux*, a supplementary means of interpretation as set out in Article 32 of the VCLT. These means of interpretation should be resorted to in order to 'confirm the meaning resulting from the application of Article 31', or if the meaning determined by application of Article 31 VCLT is 'ambiguous or obscure' or 'manifestly absurd or unreasonable' (Article 32 VCLT).

The *MHS* Arbitrator's determination that the economic development of the host state is the object and purpose of the ICSID Convention should not be regarded as highly contentious. Yet his subsequent conclusion that this objective can introduce a jurisdictional bar to certain transactions is much more controversial. The ad hoc Committee clearly did not share this opinion. However, since this is an annulment procedure, it should not matter whether the ad hoc Committee agrees with the *MHS* Arbitrator on this point. The relevant question for annulment remains the following: is the fact that the *MHS* Arbitrator (according to the Committee) 'reached conclusions not consonant with the *travaux* in key respects' a ground for annulment? With the above-mentioned rules of the VCLT and the case law on the annulment procedure in mind, it is difficult to answer this question positively.

On the other hand, there might be grounds for annulment that the Committee did not touch upon, namely 'that the award has failed to state the reasons on which it is based' (ICSID Convention Article 52(1)(e)). The *MHS* Arbitrator stated that:

> The Tribunal considers that these factors indicate that, while the Contract did provide some benefit to Malaysia, they did not make a sufficient contribution to Malaysia's economic development to qualify as an 'investment' for the purposes of Article 25(1) *or Article 1(a) of the BIT*.
> (*MHS*, Award on Jurisdiction, para. 143, emphasis added)

The *MHS* Arbitrator did not state any reason why the benefits provided do not amount to an investment in the sense of Article 1(a) of the applicable BIT. The entire preceding motivation for a specific interpretation of an 'investment' pertained only to Article 25(1) of the ICSID Convention as it was built up of arguments specific to the ICSID Convention. Surprisingly, in its conclusions, the Arbitrator nonetheless extended its reasoning to the BIT. It has to be remembered that the *MHS* Arbitrator was of the opinion that once a 'transaction' is not an investment under the ICSID Convention, there is no further need to examine the BIT. Consequently, in the *MHS*

Arbitrator's defence, it can be submitted that there was no need to even address the BIT in the sentence quoted above. However, the *MHS* Arbitrator did extend its conclusions to the BIT and so presumably did attach consequences to this finding. Because no reason was given, this could possibly be considered as a ground for annulment.

9.3.2 *The dissenting opinion by Judge Mohamed Shahabuddeen*[23]

From the outset of his Dissenting Opinion, Judge Shahabuddeen explicitly positions himself amongst the arbitrators and commentators who weigh the objective elements in ICSID's notion of 'investment' more heavily than the state parties' consent as expressed in, for example, the BIT. The Dissent states that if the objective criteria of the Convention do not mark clearly the 'outer limits' of ICSID jurisdiction regardless of the parties' consent, there is nothing to separate an ICSID investment from any other kind of investment and ICSID arbitration would be indistinguishable from other kinds of arbitration (*MHS*, Decision on Annulment, Dissenting Opinion of Judge Shahabuddeen, paras 30, 32).

The way in which the Dissent is formulated on this point is unfortunate. Basing itself on commentary that the contribution to the development of the host state is 'the only possible indication of an objective meaning' of the term investment (Schreuer 2001: 116), the Dissent states that this can only be understood as a recognition that a contribution to the economic development of the host state is a condition of an ICSID investment. Yet that very commentator added in the second edition of his *Commentary* that the above-mentioned quote *cannot* serve as authority for the statement that a contribution to the host state's development is an obligatory requirement of an investment under ICSID (Schreuer 2009: 116; nr 121).

The Dissent also refers unconvincingly to *CSOB*,[24] which according to the Dissent stated that an international transaction which contributes to the promotion of the economic development may be deemed to be an investment in the sense of the ICSID Convention. This statement is then used in the Dissent to support the conclusion that contributing to the economic development of the host state is 'a condition' of an ICSID investment (*MHS*, Decision on Annulment, Dissenting Opinion of Judge Shahabuddeen, paras 25–6). As mentioned above, however, logically it is not possible to say that because all As are Bs, all Bs must be As.

Additionally, it is at times doubtful whether the cases cited in support of a statement can in fact be cited for this purpose. For example, the Dissent refers to *L.E.S.I.–DIPENTA* v. *Algeria* in a series of cases 'favouring the view that a contribution to the economic development has to be substantial or significant'. These paragraphs the Dissent referred to discuss only the importance of a contribution of resources and the duration; moreover, the Tribunal in *L.E.S.I.–DIPENTA* does not even consider it necessary to examine the contribution to the economic development as a separate characteristic. Consequently, it is unclear how it can be derived from this that development is a *necessary* requirement; and even more unclear how this Award can be cited in support for having a requirement of a 'substantial' contribution to the economic development.

9.4 A better balancing act?

9.4.1 *Development and investment*

The values envisaged by the Tribunal and the Dissenting Opinion, such as economic development and the need to keep frivolous or *mala fides* claims at bay, are essential considerations to the functioning of the investment dispute settlement mechanism. To maintain the legitimacy of the current procedures, such issues – documented in various legal and economic publications as well as by NGOs – will have to be acknowledged and addressed.[25]

It is remarkable that in the *MHS* cases, the arbitrators in favour of a central role for development in the jurisdictional phase, were nationals that were not from Europe or North America. The vast majority of ICSID arbitrators are nationals of these two continents.[26] Therefore, if only these arbitrators hold a certain opinion, it would easily be considered to be the mainstream in the case law. While this seems not to be the case at the moment, the *MHS* cases raise potential questions regarding legitimacy if a minority in the case law turns out to correspond consistently with a geographical rift amongst arbitrators. Aspiring to be a truly global system of adjudication, any such division could prove detrimental to its reputation.

However, it is important that in trying to address some concerns, other essential values in a fair dispute resolution mechanism are not overlooked. For example, these include 'equality of arms' and a level of legal certainty regarding the availability and accessibility of the dispute settlement procedure. Raising the benchmark for a protected investment ad hoc by reading a whole set of requirements in just one word does not seem to be a sound procedural approach. One has to remember that matters such as non-payment, unjust indirect expropriation and discriminatory treatment are unfortunately a reality. Protecting an investor against such actions is one of the core *raisons d'être* of investment dispute settlement.

This remains true where the investor happens to be an enterprise that does not inspire great respect because it is, for example, allegedly involved in corruption or other loathsome behaviour. Indeed, it is absolutely fundamental that any enterprise should be fully held responsible for any such harmful conduct. However, as in domestic civil or criminal law, unlawful or unwanted acts do not put the perpetrator *outside* the law. Such conduct should be sanctioned by bringing it *into* the procedure on the merits, not by declaring perpetrators outlaws. If it would be proven in the jurisdictional phase that the investor is involved in some form of harmful conduct, this does not automatically exclude the possibility that the investor may also have justified claims against the host state. If this is accepted, it would mean that the host state's claims are dealt with in the jurisdictional phase while the investor's claims are dealt with only at the merits stage, if there is one. Consequently, a successful claim from the host state would pre-empt the investor from ever having a ruling on the merits of its claims. In the allocation of costs and damages in the award on the merits, when the claims of both sides have been considered, mechanisms such as setoff can then be applied to the result.

Unfortunately, while the procedural law of international investment arbitration is developing fast, many aspects are not well-developed. Principles such as good faith and *nemo auditur* are of course known to arbitrators as general principles and are at times also applied, but there is not yet a significant and developed body of case law dealing with their specific application in investment disputes. Consequently, the apparent fear of certain tribunals that without their restrictive view on investment, the floodgates for unmeritorious claims would be opened, might not be totally unfounded. Because host states and arbitrators do not see how else to address above-mentioned legitimate concerns, it seems their sense of justice at times justifies reasoning that stretches the procedural rules possibly beyond their breaking point. However, it seems more constructive to address the underlying concerns in a structural way so that host states and arbitrators do not longer have to resort to thinly stretched logic to address their often legitimate concerns.

Evidently, the BITs and investment agreements play a crucial role here. Whichever specific criteria the host state considers as essential in an investment, it can introduce it in the negotiation of the BIT. Instead, Respondent States nowadays mention those criteria only as a defence in the jurisdictional phase of a dispute, resulting in varying degrees of success and legal uncertainty. Moving the emphasis away from interpreting a variety of jurisdictional conditions into the notion of investment towards a pragmatic 'ordinary meaning' supplemented by detailed provisions of the BIT seems to be the best guarantee for a better balance between investors and host states.

9.4.2 A different focus on 'investment'?

The legal issues surrounding the delineation of a protected 'investment' are particularly pronounced in the *MHS* cases, but it is clear that they are by no means an exception. Considering the well-reasoned but perpendicular opinions, reflection on this subject at a more fundamental level is needed. Otherwise, it is unlikely there will soon be an end to the current status quo, with some tribunals supporting certain criteria and other tribunals supporting a different number of different criteria. Moreover, even where tribunals formally choose to use the same characteristics of an investment, the interpretation and application of these characteristics can be as diverse as the different interpretations of 'investment' itself.

The debate centres around which conditions characterize an investment. Instead of trying to fine-tune the conditions superimposed on a *prima facie* investment, it could be suggested that the debate should not so much focus on the arbitrators' criteria of an investment, but on which economic operation should be taken into consideration. Instead of the government *contract*, the *local enterprise undertaking this contract* can arguably be more relevant.[27] Applied in the *MHS* case, this would mean not focusing the analysis on the properties of the salvage contract, but on the company itself (MHS, Sdn, Bhd) as the potential 'investment'. A focus on the established enterprise is arguably more in line with the 'ordinary meaning' of the term 'investment'[28] and with some of the early cases and commentary.[29]

This does not have to mean that the same unsolved questions on characteristics will simply shift and remain. Because of its inherent properties, the existence of an enterprise is more easily ascertained. Whichever characteristics out of the list of usual suspects (contribution, duration, risk, regular profit and return and contribution to the economic development of the host state) that are chosen by a tribunal in case it wants to apply them, none of these will likely elicit fierce discussion when it is the established enterprise itself – not its contract – that is the object of discussion. There is no reason that this should be a formalistic approach since, looking at the ordinary meaning, the form of enterprise or incorporation does not matter. Subsidiaries, branches and associates and both publicly and private owned corporations all qualify as investments. Unless, that is, the investment agreement would impose certain limitations.

This then raises the question whether any owner of shares or interests can bring a claim or whether there is a need a cut-off point. Theoretically, possibly all shareholders can bring a claim against the host state.[30] While the cost of arbitration proceedings will in practice mostly be prohibitive for very small shareholders, there is a potential of having a large number of claims brought before multiple tribunals. A starting point for this could be the standards used by UNCTAD (2009: 15–18), which identify minimal participation percentages for the different types of enterprise. In any event, this seems to be a matter in which the provisions of the investment agreement will be essential. Many current BITs include 'shares' and do this without any further requirements.

This approach will also not necessarily have a limiting effect on the scope of jurisdiction. Having established that there is an enterprise, that is, an economic presence, in the host state, a tribunal will not have to examine the particulars of its government contracts. After all, it is not those contracts which make the economical presence in the host state a protected investment; it is the fact that an enterprise was established in the host state that matters.

The common concern of a clash between the definitions of investment in BITs versus that in the ICSID Convention could maybe also be largely averted. Definitions of an investment in BITs are generally very broad, such as 'any asset or claim to money'. This, however, arguably does not mean that any home state national that owns 'any asset' in the host state, or has any outstanding claim against the other state, has an 'investment' in the sense of the BIT. Indeed, when the BIT so stipulates, 'any asset or claim to money' will be protected, but in the sense that it is *a contribution* to the investment. As stated in one of the draft definitions of an investment: 'any contribution of money or other asset of economic value [...]'.[31] All movable and immovable goods, all shares, interest in property, claims to money, intellectual property, goodwill, business concessions and so on can all be protected in the BIT. However, this is not merely because it are assets present on the territory of the host state that are owned by a foreign national or foreign enterprise, but because these assets are part of an enterprise in which the foreign investor has invested. This is to be contrasted with an enterprise that deals with a foreign state from its home office abroad and merely has a 'claim to money' against that state, for example as the result of non-payment in a contractual relationship.

Consequently, the wording of the BIT is relevant when it comes to determining which assets of the investment are protected, not to determining what an investment is or is not. The interpretation through the ordinary meaning should resolve differences in interpretation between the ICSID Convention and a BIT but also means that 'investment' cannot mean any good any national of the home state has purchased in the 'host' state.[32] However, the BIT may determine that, for example, its protection does not extend to 'any claims to money that arise from the extension of credit in a commercial contract'. This does not determine the character of the enterprise as an investment; only that from all the assets the enterprise comprises of, these specific claims to money do not benefit from the protection of the BIT. The issue is neither about how much material a foreign enterprise manages to drag into the host state for the execution of a government contract, nor about what the purpose is of that contract. It is the fact that a foreign national or enterprise has a 'foot on the ground', in economic terms, that determines whether there is an investment or not.[33]

The distinction between an investment and (what is often seen as its antipode), the 'ordinary commercial transaction' becomes less important. As long as an enterprise is established in the host state, it does not matter that it, for example, deals with the government of that state in the form of a simple sales contract. In case of complex, long-term or financially important transactions in a state where the foreign investor does not have a local enterprise, the investor may well prefer establishing a local subsidiary, branch or associate.

The investment dispute settlement regime has come under increasing scrutiny for a perceived pro-investor bias and for ever expanding its reach into transactions that are further and further removed from the 'ordinary meaning' of an 'investment'. While the role of consent of the host state is often emphasized, many of the transactions that are now deemed to be 'investments' were arguably not in the host state's mind when it consented to the investment agreement. Taking the enterprise, that is the legal entity operating within a country, and not the contract as the benchmark for an investment will not solve all issues, but it is a perspective that can provide more clarity in situations where the current case law gives very diverse answers. After all, it is in the interests of both the host states and investors to know, when making the investment, what is a protected asset or claim to money and what is not.

Notes

1 The BIT is available at www.unctad.org/sections/dite/iia/docs/bits/uk_malaysia. pdf (last visited 12 February 2011).
2 *Malaysian Historical Salvors, SDN, BHD* v. *Malaysia*, ICSID Case No. ARB/05/10, Decision on Jurisdiction (17 May 2007); Decision on Annulment (16 April 2009).
3 *Black's Law Dictionary* (2004: 862). In the case of the Sole Arbitrator in the Award, this was later made explicit in Michael Hwang and Jennifer Fong Lee Cheng (2010: 123): 'A criterion of "significant contribution to the economic development" would help to sieve out vexatious and de minimis claims, reducing the financial cost to states of defending such claims.' However, no matter how legitimate, there is a long road from 'concern' to 'law' and the tempting shortcut of interpretation only goes so far.
4 *Salini Construtorri S.p.A. and Italstrade S.p.A.* v. *Morocco*, Decision on Jurisdiction, ICSID Case No. ARB/00/4 (2001); *Joy Mining Machinery Limited* v. *Egypt*, Decision on Jurisdiction, ICSID Case No. ARB/03/11 (2004); *Jan De Nul N.V. and Dredging International N.V.* v. *Arab Republic of Egypt*, Decision on Jurisdiction, ICSID Case No. ARB/04/13 (2006); *Consortium Groupement L.E.S.I.-DIPENTA* v. *Algeria*, Award, ICSID Case No. ARB/03/08 (2004); *Bayindir Insaat Turizm Ticaret Ve Sanayi A.S.* v. *Islamic Republic of Pakistan*, Decision on Jurisdiction, ICSID Case No. ARB/03/29 (2005); *Ceskoslovenska Obchodni Banka* v. *The Slovak Republic*, Decision of the Tribunal on Objections to Jurisdiction, ICSID Case No. ARB/97/4 (1999); *Patrick Mitchell* v. *Democratic Republic of the Congo*, Decision on the Application of Annulment, ICSID Case No. ARB/99/7 (2006).
5 *PSEG Global, Inc., The North American Coal Corporation, and Konya Ilgin Elektrik Uretim ve Ticaret Limited Sirketi* v. *Turkey*, Decision on Jurisdiction, ICSID Case No. ARB/02/5 (2004).
6 As cited in Sanders (1979: 206 *et seq*).
7 *Mihaly International Corporation* v. *Sri Lanka*, Award, ICSID Case No. ARB/00/2 (2002).
8 *SGS Société Générale de Surveillance S.A.* v. *Islamic Republic of Pakistan*, Award, Decision on Jurisdiction, ICSID Case No. ARB/01/13 (2003).
9 It is noteworthy that the *Bayindir* Tribunal only cited one case, *Joy Mining*, in support of its view what ICSID Tribunals 'generally' consider.
10 *Československa obchodní banka, a.s.* v. *Slovak Republic*, Decision on Jurisdiction, ICSID Case No. ARB/97/4 (1999) para. 88.
11 However, this is increasingly common in international investment arbitration, perhaps because this is a relatively new area of law. See, for example, Kaufmann-Kohler (2007); Crina Baltag (2007).

12 *Patrick Mitchell* v. *Democratic Republic of the Congo*, Decision on Annulment, ICSID Case No. ARB/99/7 (2006), para. 33.

13 *MHS*, Award on Jurisdiction, paras. 66–8. Compare generally Ranjan, Chapter 10 in this volume.

14 *Malaysian Historical Salvors Sdn Bhd* v. *Malaysia*, Decision on the Application for Annulment, ICSID Case No ARB/05/10, para. 57.

15 '[T]he purpose of this Convention is to promote the resolution of disputes arising between the Contracting States and nationals of other Contracting States by encouraging and facilitating recourse to international conciliation and arbitration.' in ICSID (1968: 16).

16 *MHS* Annulment, para. 80, referring to Article 52(1)(b) ICSID Convention.

17 *Fraport* v. *Philippines*, ICSID Case No. ARB/03/25 Decision on Annulment, 23 December 2010, para. 76, referring to *Arbitral Award of 31 July 1989 (Guinea-Bissau* v. *Senegal) I.C.J. Reports 1991*, p. 69, para. 47.

18 *M.C.I. Power Group L.C. and New Turbine Inc.* v. *Republic of Ecuador*, ICSID Case No. ARB/03/6, Decision on Annulment, 19 October 2009, para. 37, citing the Decisions on Annulment in *Klöckner (I)*, para. 59; *Amco I*, paras. 23 and 95; *MINE*, para. 6.40; *CMS* v. *Argentina*, para. 49; *Soufraki* v. *UAE*, paras. 37 and 85. Interestingly, this ad hoc Committee included Judge Peter Tomka, a member of the *MHS* ad hoc Committee.

19 *M.C.I. Power Group L.C. and New Turbine Inc.* v. *Republic of Ecuador*, ICSID Case No. ARB/03/6, Decision on Annulment, 19 October 2009, para. 42, citing *Soufraki* v. *UAE*, para. 85; *Klöckner (I)*, para. 60; *Amco I* para. 23; *MTD* v. *Chile*, para. 47; *CMS* v. *Argentina*, paras. 49–52. See also *Wena Hotel Limited* v. *Arab Republic of Egypt*, ICSID Case No. ARB/98/4, Decision on Annulment, 5 February 2002, para. 22.

20 *MHS*, Annulment Decision, Dissenting Opinion, para. 52, 56–8, referring to *Wena Hotels Limited* v. *Arab Republic of Egypt*, ICSID Case No. ARB/98/4, Decision on Application for Annulment, 5 February 2002, para. 25; *MTD Equity Sdn. Bhd. & MTD Chile S.A.* v. *Chile*, ICSID Case No. ARB/01/7, Decision on the Application for Annulment, 21 March 2007, para. 47; *Repsol YPF Ecuador S.A.* v. *Empresa Estatal Petróleos del Ecuador (Petroecuador)*, ICSID Case No. ARB/01/10, Decision on the Application for Annulment, 8 January 2007, para. 36; *Amco Asia Corporation and others* v. *Republic of Indonesia*, ICSID Case No. ARB/81/1, Decision on Jurisdiction, 25 September 1983, para. 22.

21 *MHS* Annulment Decision, para. 57, citing, amongst others, *Kasikili/Sedudu Island (Botswana/Namibia)*, Judgment, *I.C.J. Reports 1999*, p. 1059, para. 18. The ad hoc Committee confirmed that VCLT does not as a treaty apply to the ICSID Convention's interpretation but that the rules on interpretation are in any event applicable as customary international law.

22 Sinclair (1984: 128), citing Fitzmaurice (1957).

23 Signed 19 February 2009.

24 *Československa obchodní banka, a.s.* v. *Slovak Republic*, Decision on Jurisdiction, ICSID Case No. ARB/97/4 (1999) para. 64.

25 See, for example, Vandevelde (2000: 483); E. Aisbett (2009: 422).

26 71% overall and 75% in 2010, *The ICSID Caseload – Statistics*, Issue 2011–1, available at http://icsid.worldbank.org/ICSID/FrontServlet?requestType=ICSIDD ocRH&actionVal=ShowDocument&CaseLoadStatistics=True&language=English 11 (accessed 25 February 2011)

27 The term enterprise refers to a legal entity operating within a country, UNCTAD (2009: 15).
28 'An expenditure to acquire property or assets to produce revenue; a capital outlay': *Blacks Law Dictionary* (2004: 844).
29 '[T]he tribunal noted that Alcoa's operations in Jamaica fit within the ordinary meaning of 'investment' as a contribution of capital.' See Schmidt (1976: 99).
30 *CMS Gas Transmission Company* v. *Argentina*, ICSID Case No. ARB/01/8, Decision on Jurisdiction (2003) 51.
31 A History of the Convention on the Settlement of Investment Disputes between States and Nationals of Other States (1968: 623).
32 See *Romak, S.A.* v. *The Republic of Uzbekistan*, UNICITRAL Awards, 26 November 2009 (Switzerland/Uzbekistan BIT).
33 *Contra*: Consortium Groupement L.E.S.I.–DIPENTA v. Algeria, Award, ICSID Case No. ARB/03/08 (2004) II, 14 (i): '*De même est-il fréquent que ces investissements soient effectués dans le pays concerné, mais il ne s'agit pas non plus d'une condition absolue.*'

Bibliography

Aisbett, E. (2009) 'BITs and FDI: Correlation versus Causation in the Effect of Treaties on FDI', Sauvant, K.P. and Sachs, L.E. (eds), *The Effect of Treaties on Foreign Direct Investment*, Oxford: Oxford University Press.
Arsanjani, M.H. and Reisman, W.M. (2010) 'Interpreting Treaties for the Benefit of Third Parties: The "Salvors' Doctrine" and the Use of Legislative History in Investment Treaties', *American Journal of International Law*, 104: 597.
Baltag, C. (2007) 'Precedent on Notion of Investment: ICSID Awards in MHS v. Malaysia' *Transnational Dispute Management*, 4(5).
Fitzmaurice, G. (1957) 'The Law and Procedure of the International Court of Justice 1951–4: Treaty Interpretation and Other Treaty Points', *British Yearbook of International Law* 33: 203.
Hamida, W.B. (2007) 'Two Nebulous ICSID Features: The Notion of Investment and the Scope of Annulment Control – Ad hoc Committee's Decision in Patrick Mitchell v. Democratic Republic of Congo', *Journal of International Arbitration*, 24: 296.
Hwang, M. and Fong Lee Cheng, J. (2011) 'Definition of 'Investment' – A Voice from the Eye of the Storm', *Asian Journal of International Law*, 1: 99.
ICSID (1968) *History of the ICSID Convention: Documents Concerning the Origin and the Formulation of the Convention on the Settlement of Investment Disputes Between States and Nationals of Other States*, Vol. I.
Kaufmann-Kohler, G. (2007) 'Arbitral Precedent: Dream, Necessity or Excuse?', *Arbitration International*, 23(3): 357.
Sanders, P. (1979) (ed.) *Yearbook Commercial Arbitration*, Vol. IV, Deventer, Netherlands: Kluwer.
Schmidt, J.T. (1976) 'Arbitration Under the Auspices of the International Centre for Settlement of Investment Disputes (ICSID): Implications of the Decision on Jurisdiction in *Alcoa Minerals of Jamaica, Inc* v. *Government of Jamaica*', *Harvard International Law Journal*, 17: 90.
Schreuer, C. (2001) *The ICSID Convention: A Commentary*, Cambridge: Cambridge University Press.

Schreuer, C. (2009) *The ICSID Convention: A Commentary*, 2nd edn, Cambridge: Cambridge University Press.

Sinclair, I.M. (1984) *The Vienna Convention on the Law of Treaties*, 2nd edn, Manchester University Press.

UNCTAD (2009) *UNCTAD Training Manual on Statistics for FDI and the Operations of TNCs*, Vol. II. Available at: www.unctad.org/en/docs/diaeia20092_en.pdf (accessed 9 February 2011).

Vandevelde, K.J. (2000) 'The Economics of BITs', *Harvard Journal of International Law*, 41: 469.

Villiger, M.E. (2009) *Commentary on the 1969 Vienna Convention on the Law of Treaties*, Martinus Nijhoff Publishers.

10 The 'object and purpose' of Indian international investment agreements

Failing to balance investment protection and regulatory power

Prabhash Ranjan

10.1 Introduction

In recent times, a number of Investor-State Arbitration (ISA) disputes have emerged between foreign investors and host states involving a wide array of host states' sovereign regulatory measures such as environmental policy,[1] privatization policy,[2] urban policy,[3] measures to protect water services,[4] monetary policy,[5] taxation[6] and many others (Dolzer and Schreuer 2008: 7–8; Kaushal 2009: 511–12). This is not to suggest that in each such dispute regulatory measures have been found violating the International Investment Agreement (IIA).[7] In fact, limited empirical work done in this area shows that that the number of cases decided in favour of host countries are more than cases decided in favour of foreign investors (Franck 2007), and that statistically there is no evidence to show that the outcome of the ISA cases is dependent on the development status of the respondent state or the presiding arbitrator (Franck 2009). However, inconsistent legal conclusions and reasoning of arbitral tribunals (Spears 2010),[8] adjudication of such wide range of sovereign regulatory measures by ISA tribunals and award of substantive damages to foreign investors in some high-profile cases[9] have generated an intense debate about limits to regulatory power of the host state to adopt measures for pursuing non-investment objectives due to their IIA obligations,[10] in both the developing and developed world. For example, South Africa is reviewing its entire IIA programme,[11] Bolivia and Ecuador gave up their membership of the International Centre for the Settlement of Investment Disputes (ICSID),[12] the Russian Federation decided to terminate the provisional application of the Energy Charter Treaty in July 2009 (Salacuse 2010: 470), the United States and Canada adopted new model IIAs.[13]

Some scholars have argued that uncertainty regarding investment protection versus the regulatory power of the host state is the result of an expansive interpretation given to IIA treaty provisions by arbitrators (Sornarajah 2009: 283–91; Karl 2008: 234–6; Subedi 2008: 139–40). Some hold the adjudicating nature that exists in the form of ISA responsible for this (Van Harten 2007), while some emphasize on creation of an appellate court to correct legal errors made by ISA, which might otherwise stifle legitimate regulatory action (Franck 2005).

On the other hand, this uncertainty can be seen as arising due to the broad nature of the substantive law that arbitral tribunals apply, that is, the IIAs themselves (Alvarez and Khamsi 2009: 472–8; also see Ghouri 2009: 921). The provisions in the majority of IIAs are vague and lack clarity and thus become suitable candidates for broader interpretations of investment protection.[14] Furthermore, many IIAs espouse investment protection as the primary aim of the treaty, relegating other non-investment regulatory objectives as secondary in nature (Ortino 2005: 245) and do not explicitly recognize the host state's duty to pursue non-investment objectives (Alvarez and Khamsi 2009: 472). Thus, one needs to carefully look at the substantive law in the IIAs that the arbitral tribunals interpret.

In this regard, arguments have been made that countries need to draft IIAs in order to clarify the meaning of vague and open ended terms like fair and equitable treatment (FET), have developmental goals in the preamble, and to have more clarity about rights of competing stakeholders (Gross 2003: 899; Wiltse 2003: 1184–7; Muchlinski 2008: 1–44). In fact, some countries have amended their model IIAs to make investment protection standards more precise (Clodfelter 2009: 165). Some new IIAs now contain provisions aimed at balancing investment protection with the host state's regulatory power (Spears 2010).

In this light, this chapter will look at the balance between investment protection and India's regulatory power to pursue non-investment objectives in Indian IIAs by focusing on the substantive law in these treaties. Regulatory power, in the context of this chapter, means the ability of India to adopt laws, policies, and measures to achieve a variety of non-investment policy objectives such as safeguarding the interests of backward communities, addressing public health concerns, dealing with situations of economic turbulence, tackling imbalances in the development of different regions in the country, and so on. India is a huge country with a multi-ethnic and multi-religious population requiring a large number of regulatory objectives to be pursued. In case of India one cannot look at the debate between investment protection and India's regulatory power as a host state through arbitral jurisprudence because there is no arbitral jurisprudence involving Indian IIAs. India has been involved in only one ISA, the *Dabhol Power Project case*,[15] which was settled 'out of court'.[16]

This chapter does not interpret each substantive law provision in Indian IIAs. It is limited to determining the 'object and purpose' of the Indian IIAs. According to Article 31 of the Vienna Convention on the Law of Treaties (VCLT; 1155 UNTS 331) a treaty has to be interpreted in good faith by giving ordinary meaning to the terms of the treaty in their context and in the light of the object and purpose of the treaty (Buffard and Zemanek 1998: 311). Thus, finding the object and purpose – the aims of the treaty – is extremely important to shed light on the ordinary meaning of the terms,

especially when the terms used in the treaty are capable of different interpretations.[17] In such situations, finding the object and purpose helps in
adopting the meaning which promotes the aims of the treaty. Many ISA tribunals have interpreted IIAs in light of the object and purpose – by looking
at the preambles.[18] For example, the *Enron* tribunal in deciding whether
Article XI of the US–Argentina IIA is self judging looked at the object and
purpose of the US–Argentina IIA.[19] The tribunal held that since the object
and purpose of the IIA is to apply in situations of economic difficulties
requiring the protection of international guaranteed rights of the foreign
investors, holding Article XI self judging would be inconsistent with the
treaty's object and purpose.[20]

In this regard, it is also important to mention the cautionary note given
in *Plama* v. *Bulgaria*, where the tribunal (quoting Sir Ian Sinclair) said:

> risk that the placing of undue emphasis on the 'object and purpose' of a
> treaty will encourage teleological methods of interpretation [which], in
> some of its more extreme forms, will even deny the relevance of the
> intentions of the parties.[21]

One agrees that undue emphasis should not be placed on the object and
purpose of the IIAs. Nevertheless, due emphasis on object and purpose is an
integral part of treaty methodology warranted by Article 31 of the VCLT
and thus cannot be ignored (Shaw 2008: 933).

In any case Article 31 of the VCLT, in addition to identifying the object
and purpose of the treaty, provides to the treaty interpreter other tools as
well like context, subsequent agreements, and any other rules between the
parties. The treaty interpreter can also have recourse to the supplementary
means of treaty interpretation given in Article 32 of the VCLT. Furthermore, object and purpose cannot be relied upon to counter a clear substantive provision in the treaty (Gardiner 2008: 197–8; Aust 2007: 235).

Similarly, in the context of IIAs, it has been argued that determination of
object and purpose may be deceptive because IIAs commonly contain pream-
bular statements that their purpose is investment protection (McLachlan
2008: 371). In other words, the argument is that simply because preambles
have a broad language focusing on promoting and protecting investment, it
should not be interpreted to mean that there is a general preference to
protect investor interests over the interest of host state.[22] One concedes that
this conclusion should not be reached solely on the basis of the preamble
and, thus, one will have to look at the title and more importantly read the
treaty as a whole, which will provide a fuller indication of the object and
purpose of the IIA (Gardiner 2008: 197). Thus, this chapter aims to deduce
the object and purpose of the Indian IIAs by studying the title, preambles
and the text of 69 Indian IIAs. However, before doing that a brief description of the Indian IIA programme and the policy objectives behind entering
into IIAs is important to provide the broader context (Section 10.2). This

will be followed by discussing the title and the preamble in 69 IIAs (Sections 10.3 and 10.4 respectively). Section 10.5 discusses the key treaty provisions in Indian IIAs, and Section 10.6 presents the concluding remarks.

10.2 India's IIA programme

India started its IIA programme in the early 1990s as part of its overall economic liberalization. Since 1994, India has signed IIAs with 78 countries, out of which 69 are already in force and nine are yet to be enforced or ratified.[23] Further, in the past few years, India has entered into Comprehensive Economic Cooperation Agreements (CECAs), containing a chapter on investment, with Korea,[24] Singapore, Japan[25] and Malaysia.[26] CECAs are comprehensive economic agreements covering trade and investment liberalization, competition policy, trade facilitation, rules of origin and intellectual property rights. The investment chapters in these CECAs, along with provisions on investment protection, also contain market access provisions which do not exist in any of the existing standalone IIAs, which deal only with post-establishment.

Apart from this, India is negotiating CECAs with investment chapters with Indonesia, Mauritius and New Zealand;[27] a free trade agreement (FTA) with the European Union with a chapter on investment;[28] an IIA with the US;[29] and has concluded negotiations on an IIA with Canada.[30] Thus, India's IIA programme is on two legs: standalone IIAs and investment chapters in CECAs/FTAs.

This chapter studies 69 IIAs that have been enforced (including the Indian Model IIA[31]). All the standalone IIAs that India has entered into are for a ten-year period and are deemed to be automatically extended after this period unless either state gives notice in writing to terminate the treaty. Further, even if the treaty is terminated, the protection for the existing investments made in India will continue to apply for next 15 years. So far, India has not terminated any of its IIAs.

India's IIA programme can be seen as part of an overall attempt to signal to the world about India's makeover from a country where Transnational Corporations like IBM and Coca-Cola had to exit in the 1970s due to certain state regulations to a country that is now more open to foreign investment. This policy objective is clearly evident in the forewords written by different Indian finance ministers from 1994 to 2009 in compendiums of Indian IIAs that the Indian Finance Ministry regularly publishes. So far, eight such compendiums have been published.[32] In the first such volume (published in 1996–7), Finance Minister P. Chidambaram wrote that after the adoption of liberal economic policies in 1991, India initiated the process of entering into IIAs with a view to provide investor confidence to foreign investors (Chidambaram 1997). The same view of India entering into IIAs to protect foreign investment has been repeated in all the subsequent volumes, by different finance ministers belonging to different governments (Vols 2–8:

see Sinha 1999, Mukherjee 2009). None of these forewords talk about the relationship of investment flows with other non-investment issues, nor do they recognize that investment protection should be balanced with other legitimate non-investment objectives.

Further, this researcher's meetings and interactions with Indian government officials revealed that notwithstanding the global debate on IIAs, in India, IIAs are still seen primarily as instruments aimed at promoting and protecting investment; their relationship with regulatory power has not yet been fully realized. Indeed, these policy objectives have influenced India's Model IIA, which is heavily inspired from the model developed by Western capital exporting countries. However, given the increase in number of investor-state disputes, of late, there are signs of some change.[33] For example, the Indian government is planning to revise its model IIA; and there are some recent IIAs that have provisions aimed at preserving India's regulatory power (such as stating that non-discriminatory regulatory measures are outside the purview of expropriation) – though this practice is not consistent. Also, investment chapters in India's CECAs/FTAs with Singapore, Korea, Japan and Malaysia contain provisions that better balance investment protection with regulatory power.

Since no foreign investor has challenged an Indian regulatory measure in ISA (barring one solitary case as mentioned above), the belief, in Indian establishment, is that India's ability to exercise regulatory power is unaffected due to IIA obligations. There is also a lack of adequate understanding about the actual impact and working of IIAs across different government departments, resulting in domestic policies being adopted oblivious to the significance of IIAs.[34]

It is true that the past two decades (coinciding with the Indian IIA programme) have seen a massive increase in foreign direct investment (FDI) flows to India. They rose from US$393 million in 1992–3 to US$5549 million in 2005–6.[35] After 2005–6, FDI inflows to India showed a remarkable jump and stood at US$15,726 million[36] and US$24,579 million[37] for the years 2006–7 and 2007–8 respectively. FDI inflows continued their upward movement in the year 2008–9 and stood at US$27,309 million.[38] In 2009–10,[39] these inflows only marginally came down, to US$25,888 million.[40] However, there is no evidence to show that the increase in FDI inflows into India is due to IIAs or to what extent IIAs have contributed to attracting foreign investment. The reason is a lack of research on this issue (Ranjan 2010a). In the absence of any such evidence, the assumption of the Indian government is challengeable.

It is clear from these numbers and facts that India is vigorously pursuing its IIA programme even if the actual benefits and implications on regulatory power remain unknown. Furthermore, as India is fast integrating with the global economy due to high FDI inflows, the likelihood of regulatory disputes with foreign investors is ever greater than before. The recent tax dispute with *Vodafone BV International* (Vodafone's Dutch entity)[41] and disputes related to regulatory issues with *Posco Steel* (a Korean steel company)[42] are clear pointers in this regard. Although these disputes are national level disputes and not IIA disputes; they capture regulatory conflicts between India and foreign investors quite well. Notwithstanding this, apart from a few articles (Krishan 2008; Ranjan 2008), not much work has been done to analyse and understand Indian IIAs. Thus, implications of Indian IIAs on India's regulatory power are unknown and uncertain. It is in this light that this chapter makes the first-ever attempt to determine the object and purpose of the Indian IIAs by studying the title, preamble and the text, as a whole, of 69 Indian IIAs.

10.3 The titles

The title of the IIA can be one important indicator of the object and purpose of an IIA (Gardiner 2008: 180–1). For example, the tribunal in *Plama* v. *Bulgaria* deduced the object and purpose of the IIA by referring to the preamble and also the title of the IIA, which referred to 'mutual encouragement and protection of investments'.[43] Similarly, in *SGS* v. *Philippines*, the tribunal on finding out the object and purpose said that 'the BIT is a treaty for the promotion and mutual protection of investments'.[44] The tribunal said: 'It is legitimate to resolve uncertainties in its interpretation [provision on 'umbrella clause'] so as to favour the protection of covered investments.'[45]

The study of 69 Indian IIAs shows that, barring two, all IIAs have the following words in their title: 'promotion and protection' of investment. The only slight variation is that some IIAs, such as those with Kuwait and Saudi Arabia, use words like 'encouragement' instead of 'promotion'. Thus, according to the title of these 67 IIAs, all of them are 'An agreement for the promotion and protection of investments'.

There is nothing in the title of these 67 IIAs to show that these IIAs are also about a host state's power to regulate (given the proximity between investment protection and regulation) or to balance investment protection with the host country's regulatory power. Only two IIAs, India–Singapore and India–Korea, have a different title. The titles of these two IIAs are: 'comprehensive economic cooperation agreement' and 'comprehensive economic partnership agreement' respectively. 'Economic cooperation or partnership' is broader than 'investment protection and promotion'. However, the title of the IIA, on its own, cannot be conclusive to ascertain the object and purpose; one will also have to study the preamble and other provisions of the treaty.

10.4 The preamble

The preamble of the Indian Model IIA states the following objectives:

a   Desiring to create conditions favourable for fostering greater investment by investors of one State in the territory of the other State;

b   Recognising that the encouragement and reciprocal protection under International agreement of such investment will be conducive to the stimulation of individual business initiative and will increase prosperity in both States;

An identical preamble is to be found in 46 out of the 69 IIAs studied. Thus, close to 68 per cent of Indian IIAs have the same preamble as the model IIA. Out of the remaining 23 IIAs, four have a few different words from the model preamble. The objectives given in the preamble of these four IIAs is the same as that of the other 46 IIAs. Further, there are three IIAs that, apart from the investment promotion objectives, also recognize that FET regarding investment will help in fostering investment and in intensifying cooperation between the enterprises of the two countries. This is important because tribunals have relied on the presence of FET in the preamble to interpret FET as a treaty provision giving precedence to investment protection.

The preambles in all these 53 IIAs focus on creating conditions favourable for encouraging investment flows; and recognizing that encouragement and protection of investment will stimulate business activity and increase prosperity. Although all these preambles also talk about 'stimulating business initiative' and 'increase in prosperity' in both the countries, these objectives are not self-standing, but are linked to encouragement and protection of investment. According to these preambles, encouragement and protection of investment will result in increased prosperity in states and will stimulate individual business initiative.[46]

To understand this better, it is useful to compare the preamble in these IIAs with the preamble to the WTO treaty, which states:[47]

> *Recognizing* that their relations in the field of trade and economic endeavour should be conducted with a view to raising standards of living, ensuring full employment and a large and steadily growing volume of real income and effective demand, and expanding the production of and trade in goods and services, while allowing for the optimal use of the world's resources in accordance with the objective of sustainable development, seeking both to protect and preserve the environment and to enhance the means for doing so in a manner consistent with their respective needs and concerns at different levels of economic development...
>
> *Recognizing* further that there is a need for positive efforts designed to ensure that developing countries, and especially the least developed among them, secure a share in the growth of international trade commensurate with the needs of their economic development,...

This preamble provides that trade relations between countries should be conducted, among other things, in accordance with the objective of sustainable development. Further, it recognizes as a self-standing goal the need to take efforts to ensure that developing countries and LDCs secure a share in the growth of international trade, which is proportionate with their economic development needs. Relying on such a preamble, one can argue that the object and purpose of the WTO treaty is not just trade promotion but trade promotion in accordance with other important goals.[48]

The preambles of 53 Indian IIAs do not contain other regulatory objectives, nor do they mention that the objectives of investment protection and promotion should be balanced with regulatory power of the host state. They only contain the objectives of investment promotion and protection.

Very few Indian IIAs contain more values in the preamble apart from investment promotion and protection. For example, India–Singapore and India–Korea treaties refer to multiple values such as 'rights to pursue economic philosophies suited to their development goals'; 'rights to realise their national policy objectives'; and 'optimal use of natural resources in accordance with the objective of sustainable development, seeking both to protect and preserve the environment'.[49] On similar lines, the preamble in the India–Australia IIA provides that 'investment relations should be promoted and economic relations strengthened in accordance with the internationally accepted principles of mutual respect for sovereignty, equality, mutual benefit, non-discrimination and mutual confidence'.

10.5 Treaty provisions

Let us now turn to the key treaty provisions in these 69 Indian IIAs to determine the overall object and purpose. The discussion on different treaty provisions is not with the aim of interpreting these provisions but for the purpose of collectively assessing them to finding out the object and purpose of the Indian IIAs.

10.5.1 Definition of investment

Of the 69 IIAs studied, 68 contain a broad asset-based definition of investment. In these 68 IIAs, it is stated that investment means every kind of asset. These assets do not need to fulfil any other criterion to qualify as foreign investment under the IIA, such as that an investment should be of a certain economic value to the state or that investments should have completed a certain duration of operation before becoming eligible for treaty protection. This broad definition is then followed by an exclusive or non-exhaustive list of assets, which includes direct investment, portfolio investment, intellectual property rights, rights to money or to any performance under contract having a financial value, and business concessions conferred under law or contract. This shows that treaty protection extends to an extremely wide range of foreign investments. Of the 68 IIAs that provide a broad asset-based definition of investment, only the India–Korea IIA states that in addition to investment being every kind of asset that the investor owns or controls, it should have the characteristics of an investment like commitment of capital or other resources, the expectation of gains or profits or the assumption of risk.

There is only one Indian IIA (India–Mexico) that does not state that investment means every broad asset. It gives an exhaustive list of assets that qualify as an investment, with exceptions in the list such as stating that debt security of maturity period less than three years is not an asset that will qualify as an investment. Apart from this, under this IIA, like the India–Korea IIA, only those assets that involve a commitment of capital, expectation of gain or profit or an assumption of risk will qualify as being eligible as foreign investment.

The only semblance of regulation in the definition of investment in all these IIAs is that the assets established have to be in accordance with national laws. This gives regulatory power to India to refuse treaty protection to those investments that have been made in contravention of or which are illegal under Indian law.

10.5.2 *Promotion and protection of investment*

The Indian model IIA states that each contracting party 'shall encourage and create favourable conditions for investors of the other Contracting Party to make investments in its territory'. The same provision is present in 66 of the 69 Indian IIAs studied. Thus, all these IIAs, apart from mentioning this in the preamble, also provide in the text that investment promotion is an important objective of the IIA and that India will take steps towards creating suitable conditions for fostering investment. Furthermore, 34 Indian IIAs state that foreign investments shall be given full protection and security. None of these IIAs explain what is meant by full protection and security, barring the India–Korea IIA which states that 'full protection and security' does not require treatment in addition to or beyond that which is required under customary international law (CIL).

10.5.3 *Fair and equitable treatment*

The FET provision is often used by foreign investors to challenge host state's regulatory measures and has been labelled as 'an almost ubiquitous presence' in ISA (Dolzer 2005: 87). Sixty-six of the 69 Indian IIAs studied contain the FET principle. Out of these 66 IIAs, close to 90 per cent do not define the normative content of the FET, thus leaving it to arbitrators to supply this. Only in a handful of IIAs a reference is made to a minimum standard of treatment. For example, the India–Korea IIA states that FET does not require treatment in addition to or beyond that which is required by the CIL minimum standard of treatment of aliens. It therefore gives some guidance to the arbitral tribunal how to interpret the FET provision.

10.5.4 *Most favoured nation and national treatment*

Barring two IIAs, all Indian IIAs contain the most-favoured nation (MFN) principle. This principle is also broadly worded, making it possible for foreign investors to borrow beneficial treaty provisions from other treaties.[50] The only exception to the MFN principle is for the purposes of taxation and obligations imposed by FTAs or custom areas. Similarly, national treatment protection to foreign investment is offered in a broad manner. Barring a few IIAs like the India–Mexico IIA, the national treatment provisions in the majority of Indian IIAs do not contain the 'like circumstances' clause, which requires that in order to find out whether national treatment has been provided or not, only investments in 'like circumstances' need to be compared. This arguably broadens the national treatment protection to foreign investments.

10.5.5 *Expropriation*[51]

All 68 IIAs contain provisions on expropriation very clearly stating that investment shall not be nationalized or expropriated (direct expropriation) or subjected to measures having 'effect' equivalent to expropriation (indirect expropriation) unless or until there is a public purpose, and further that in such cases fair and equitable compensation should be promptly paid to foreign investors. Further, 56 IIAs out of these 68 do not provide any indication to arbitrators on how to identify indirect expropriation barring the focus on 'effect' on investment. In other words, in these 56 IIAs a large number of regulatory measures could be challenged as expropriation as long as they have an 'effect' equivalent to expropriation. Whether such challenges will succeed or not is besides the point here. Germane to our discussion is that the plain reading of the expropriation provision in 56 Indian IIAs shows that by focusing solely on 'effect' on investment and not mentioning the relevance of the 'purpose' behind the measure, the highest priority is attached to investment protection.[52]

Only 12 Indian IIAs contain provisions that could be relied upon to say that the expropriation provision, along with investment protection, also recognizes the importance of host state's regulatory power. These 12 IIAs contain certain indicators for the tribunal on how to determine indirect expropriation. For example, they require taking into account the character of the measure, including their purpose and rationale along with the effect of the measure on foreign investment. Further, these IIAs state that non-discriminatory measures designed to protect legitimate public welfare objective do not constitute expropriation – except in rare circumstances.

10.5.6 *Monetary transfer provision*

Once investment has been made in the host country, Monetary Transfer Provisions (MTPs) in IIAs regulate the transfer of funds related to investment in and out of the host country. Inflow and outflow of capital can have certain macro-economic consequences for the host country. For example, substantive increase in inflows can result in appreciation of the currency of the host country, adversely affecting its exports. To make sure that transfer of funds related to investment does not have such an adverse impact on the currency of the host countries, some IIAs contain exceptions. For example, Article 17 of the Korea–Japan BIT states that notwithstanding their obligation to let investors freely transfer funds related to investment, either of the countries can adopt measures to prohibit such transfers in the event of serious balance of payments problems.[53]

All the 69 Indian IIAs studied contain a MTP: 65 of these guarantee the investor transfer of 'all funds related to investment'. This is followed by an inclusive list of funds that can be transferred, which means that even those funds that do not appear on the list can be transferred provided they are funds related to investment. Further, more than 60 IIAs provide that these transfers should be without delay; either in the currency in which the investment was made or in any convertible currency; and at the prevailing market rate of exchange. For the purpose of preserving India's regulatory power, only 12 IIAs qualify the right to transfer funds related to investment. Of these 12, five subject this right to domestic laws. In seven IIAs, this right is qualified by stating that countries can adopt measures to prohibit transfer of funds related to investment in order to achieve certain monetary and non-monetary policy objectives. In the remaining 57 IIAs (82 per cent), the MTP does not contain any exception to the right of the foreign investor to transfer funds.

10.5.7 *Treaty exceptions*

Even if an IIA contains broad provisions with investment promotion and protection as its primary objective, a general exceptions clause can be used by the host state to adopt regulatory measures, temporarily, in situations that warrant giving precedence to non-investment objectives over investment protection. Article XX of GATT is a good example of such a general exception which has often been used to balance trade with non-trade values. Examination of 69 Indian IIAs reveals that in more than 60 IIAs these exceptions are very narrowly formulated. They allow deviations from the treaty only in situations of 'essential security interest' or in 'circumstances of extreme emergency'. These grounds require a very high threshold and hence India will be able to deviate from investment protection only for limited regulatory objectives. Very few IIAs allow deviation from investment protection on potentially very significant grounds such as 'public order', 'health' or 'environment' or on grounds such as 'to boost certain domestic industries' or 'domestic industries in economically backward regions' (Muchlinski 2008: 23). The India–Korea IIA is one such example, which states: 'India reserves the right to adopt or maintain any measure that accords rights or preferences to economically backward regions or groups in the interest of balanced development of the economy and maintenance of social equality' – as an exception to national treatment.

10.5.8 *Investor-state dispute resolution*

All the 69 IIAs studied contain investor-state dispute resolution mechanisms, including ISA. Investors can bring disputes against India before international arbitral forums without exhausting the local remedies. Further, in the majority of IIAs, the award has to be based on the provisions of the agreement, which means the IIA. However, it is important to mention that though Indian IIAs provide for submission of disputes to ICSID, this option cannot be exercised by the investor against India because India has not yet joined the ICSID Convention. Thus, the option available with the investor is to either use the ICSID Additional Facility Rules or to have an ad hoc arbitration tribunal based on the UNCITRAL Arbitration Rules subject to the modifications given in the IIA.

10.6 Conclusion

A collective examination of the title, the preambles and text shows that a large majority of Indian IIAs emphasize investment protection by:

- limiting the title of the IIAs to investment protection and promotion;
- containing investment promotion and protection as primary objectives in the preamble;
- providing treaty protection to every asset owned or controlled by foreign investor irrespective of duration, risk or economic benefits;
- having broad formulation of the enforceable and strong substantive provisions with no or limited deviations; and
- having narrowly defined treaty exceptions.

In other words, the object and purpose of a large majority of Indian IIAs is investment protection. The preamble and the substantive provisions in only a handful of Indian IIAs contain provisions aimed at preserving the host state's regulatory power, thus showing that the IIA is concerned about investment protection but also mindful of India's regulatory power. This does not mean that all the substantive provisions in Indian IIAs shall always be interpreted in favour of investment protection. How substantive provisions will be interpreted will depend on a number of factors including the facts before the arbitral tribunal, and the actual formulation of the provision, not just the object and purpose of the IIA.

Nevertheless, any ambiguity in the interpretation of investment protection could be resolved in favour of investment protection given the object and purpose of a large number of Indian IIAs, as some tribunals have done in the past with other IIAs. This will adversely affect India's regulatory power. If that is to be preserved, there is a need for India to renegotiate its existing IIAs and have new IIAs with the object and purpose of protecting investment by being mindful of regulatory power. Of late, India has shown some inclination to have provisions in its IIAs that will preserve its regulatory power. However, India's treaty practice has not been consistent in this regard.

A final point that needs to be dealt with is that even if the object and purpose of India's IIAs is investment protection and if this comes in way of India's regulatory power; India could still adopt regulatory measures under CIL. For example, India can use the doctrine of necessity given in Article 25 of the International Law Commission Articles on Responsibility of States for Internationally Wrongful Acts 2001. However, the Argentina cases have demonstrated[54] that given the extremely stringent nature of this exception it will be exceedingly difficult for India to invoke this defence.

Further under CIL India has the right to adopt 'non-discriminatory', 'good faith' regulation in public interest without attracting any international liability. This principle has been supported by ISA tribunals.[55] However, there is no consensus on how broad or narrow these 'police powers' are or which public interests can the state pursue by adopting such regulatory measures under CIL.[56] The *Saluka* tribunal said that since there is no consensus on which regulatory measures are permitted, this has to be determined by the adjudicator.[57] Instead of leaving such complex questions to ad hoc arbitration tribunals, countries as 'law-makers' should take up the responsibility to have clear and unambiguous rules as far as possible. Some new IIAs have been drafted in a manner that better balance investment protection with regulatory powers (Spears 2010; Clodfelter 2009).[58] Such drafting will not only play a crucial role in giving more specificity to a substantive law provision but also more scope to argue that the IIAs' object and purpose is not just investment protection; but protection in accordance with country's regulatory power.

Notes

1 *Metalclad Corporation* v. *United Mexican States* (ARB(AB)/97/1, 2000); *Santa Elena* v. *Costa Rica* (Final Award, Case No. ARB/96/1, 17 February 2000).
2 *Eureko B.V.* v. *Republic of Poland* (ARB/97/3, 2005).
3 *MTD Equity Sdn. Bhd. and MTD Chile S.A.* v. *Republic of Chile* (ARB/01/7, 2005).
4 *Biwater Gauff (Tanzania) Ltd* v. *Tanzania* (ARB/05/22, Award, 24 July 2008).
5 *CMS Gas Transmission Co.* v. *Argentina* (ARB/01/8, 2005 (ICSID)); *Enron Corporation* v. *Argentina* (ARB/01/3, 2007 (ICSID)); *Sempra Energy International* v. *Argentina* (ARB/02/16, 2007 (ICSID)); *LG & E Energy Corporation* v. *Argentina* (ARB/02/1, 2006 (ICSID)); *Continental Casualty Company* v. *Argentina* (ARB/03/9, 2008 (ICSID)).
6 *Occidental Exploration and Production Co.* v. *Republic of Ecuador* (U.N. 3467, 2004 (LCIA)).

7 The term 'IIA' in this chapter means Bilateral Investment Treaties (BITs), investment chapters in FTAs and in CECAs. It does not include Double Taxation Avoidance Agreements. In India, IIAs are called 'Bilateral Investment Promotion Agreements' (BIPAs). The text of Indian IIAs, referred to here, is taken from the eight compendium volumes of India's investment agreements published by the Ministry of Finance, Government of India (on file with the author).

8 For a detailed discussion on such inconsistent decisions, see Franck (2005: 1558–82).

9 For example in *CME Czech Republic B.V.* v. *Czech Republic* (Final Award, UNCITRAL Arbitration, 14 March 2003), the Czech Republic paid US$355 million to CME as damages for violating the IIA on account of adopting a regulatory measure.

10 For various nuances on the debate see Choudhary (2008); Franck (2005: 1521); Van Harten (2007: 63); Newcombe (2007: 357); Ruggie (2009); Spears (2010); Muchlinski (2008: 10–44); Sornarajah (Chapter 13 in this volume); Paulsson (2006).

11 Department of Trade and Industry, Republic of South Africa, Notice 961 of 2009 available at www.info.gov.za/view/DownloadFileAction?id=103768 (accessed 8 February 2011).

12 List of Contracting States and other Signatories to the ICSID Convention (as of 7 January 2010) available at http://icsid.worldbank.org/ICSID/FrontServlet?request Type=ICSIDDocRH&actionVal=ShowDocument&language=English (accessed 8 February 2011).

13 Alvarez and Park (2003: 383–6); Vandevelde (2008); Spears (2010: 1038). See also the Australian Productivity Commission Report, available at www.pc.gov. au/projects/study/trade-agreements (accessed 8 February 2011), and Nottage (2010).

14 Alvarez and Khamsi (2009: 472–8); Karl (2008: 238–40); Clodfelter (2009). Also see Brower and Schill (2009), who argue that the IIA provisions are not as broad as some suggest.

15 *Capital India Power Mauritius I and Energy Enterprises (Mauritius) Company* v. *Maharashtra Power Development Cooperation Limited* (Case No. 12913/MS, International Court of Arbitration of the ICC, 27 April 2005), available at http://ita. law.uvic.ca/documents/Dabhol_award_050305.pdf (accessed 8 February 2011). It is important to note that this one dispute gave rise to multiple IIA claims raised by foreign investors under different IIAs. However, these claims were not pursued after a mutual settlement was reached between the parties.

16 'GE settles Dabhol Issue', available at www.indianexpress.com/oldStory/73760/ (accessed 18 December 2010).

17 Also see Gardiner (2008: 190). *USA, Federal Reserve Bank* v. *Iran, Bank Markazi*, Case A28, (2000–02) 36 Iran–US Claims Tribunal Reports 5 at 22, para. 58.

18 See, for example, Dolzer and Schreuer (2008: 32). *Siemens A.G.* v. *Argentina*, (decision on jurisdiction, 3 August 2004), paras 80–1; *CMS* v. *Argentina*, above n. 5, para. 274; *Eureko* v. *Poland* (Partial Award, 19 August 2005); *Azurix Corp* v. *Argentina* (Award, 14 July 2006, para. 307); *Saluka* v. *Czech Republic* (Partial Award, 17 March 2006 under UNCITRAL rules, paras 299–300); *Enron* v. *Argentina*, above n. 5, paras 331 and 332; also see discussion in *Continental* v. *Argentina*, above n. 5, para. 258.

19 *Enron* v. *Argentina*, above n. 5, para. 331.

20 Ibid, paras 331 and 332.
21 *Plama Consortium* v. *Bulgaria* (ARB/03/24, 27 August 2008 (ICSID), para. 193), referring to Sinclair (1984: 130). See also Salacuse (2010: 146–8).
22 See also Kurtz (2010: 351); and *Saluka* v. *Czech Republic*, above n. 17, para. 300.
23 This list of 78 IIAs include the India–Singapore and India–Korea CECA that contain a chapter on investment (*India's Bilateral Promotion and Protection of Investments*, Volume VII, Ministry of Finance: Government of India: March 2009: 65–8). The India–Japan CECA has not been considered in this chapter.
24 The India–Korea CECA (containing the chapter on investment) was signed in 2009 and became effective from 1 January 2010. However, India also has an IIA with Korea signed in 1996. This IIA has not been repealed so both the BIT and the investment chapter of the CECA are in existence. However, this paper has left out the India–Korea IIA of 1996 and has included the investment chapter of CECA signed with Korea in 2009 as India–Korea IIA. India–Japan and India–Malaysia CECAs have also been left out because they are yet to be enforced.
25 FE Bureau, 'India–Japan CEPA to boost bilateral trade to US$25 billion' (17 February 2011), available at www.financialexpress.com/news/indiajapan-cepa-to-boost-bilateral-trade-to-25-bn/750965/ (accessed on 23 February 2011). See also generally Hamamoto, Chapter 3 of this volume.
26 India already has an IIA with Malaysia.
27 Department of Commerce, India, see http://commerce.nic.in/trade/international_ta.asp?id=2&trade=i (accessed 15 March 2010). India already has IIAs with Indonesia and Mauritius.
28 European Parliament, 'EU-India Free Trade Agreement', www.europarl.europa.eu/oeil/FindByProcnum.do?lang=en&procnum=INI/2008/2135 (accessed 10 January 2010).
29 G. Srinivasan, 'US Keen to Push for Bilateral Investment Treaty', 26 October 2009, available at www.blonnet.com/2009/10/26/stories/2009102651830100.htm (accessed 18 November 2009).
30 Background on Canada-India Foreign Investment Promotion and Protection Agreement, available at www.international.gc.ca/trade-agreements-accords-commerciaux/agr-acc/fipa-apie/india-inde.aspx?lang=en (accessed 18 November 2009).
31 There is some ambiguity regarding the Indian model text. The author has access to two model texts. The first was available on the website of the Finance Ministry until March 2010. However, later this text was replaced by a different text: http://finmin.nic.in/the_ministry/dept_eco_affairs/icsection/Indian%20Model%20Text%20BIPA.asp?pageid=2 (accessed 8 February 2011). The differences seem only minor – the new one contains a provision on 'denial of benefits', for example, and has an asterisk mark on the expropriation provision saying that the expropriation provision will be interpreted on the basis of the Annex to the treaty. (Yet there is no Annex provided on the website.) This author's efforts to clarify this ambiguity remain unsuccessful.
32 See also Arsanjani and Reisman (2010).
33 Saxena (2010). Also see the IISD Report on the Fourth Annual Forum of Developing Country Investment Negotiators, available at www.iisd.org/pdf/2011/dci_2010_report.pdf (accessed on 10 March 2011).
34 For example, the domestic FDI policy is made by the Commerce Ministry of India whereas it is the Finance Ministry that deals with IIA negotiations. The

domestic FDI regulations issued by the Commerce Ministry do not mention anything about the IIA obligations. See further Ranjan (2010b), and compare generally the situation in Indonesia outlined by Sitaresmi in this volume.

35 'Fact Sheet on Foreign Direct Investment (FDI) from August 1991 to March 2006', available at http://dipp.nic.in/fdi_statistics/india_fdi_mar06.pdf (accessed 8 February 2011).

36 'Fact Sheet on Foreign Direct Investment (FDI) from August 1991 to March 2007', available at http://dipp.nic.in/fdi_statistics/india_fdi_march2007.pdf (accessed 8 February 2011).

37 'Fact Sheet on Foreign Direct Investment (FDI) from August 1991 to March 2008', available at http://dipp.nic.in/fdi_statistics/india_fdi_March2008.pdf (accessed 8 February 2011).

38 'Fact Sheet on Foreign Direct Investment (FDI) from August 1991 to March 2009', available at http://dipp.nic.in/fdi_statistics/india_FDI_March2009.pdf (accessed 8 February 2011).

39 This is up to 31 March 2010. In India the financial year is from 1 April to 31 March.

40 'Fact Sheet on Foreign Direct Investment (FDI) from August 1991 to March 2010', available at http://dipp.nic.in/fdi_statistics/india_FDI_March2010.pdf (accessed 8 February 2011).

41 T.P. Ostwal and M. Solanki, 'The Vodafone Tax Dispute – A Landmark Judgment of the Bombay High Court', November 2010, available at http://wwww.bcasonline.org/articles/artin.asp?961 (accessed on 15 February 2011).

42 Dilip Bisoi, 'Posco Plans Hit Hurdle in Orissa High Court', 15 July 2010, available at www.financialexpress.com/news/posco-plans-hit-hurdle-in-orissa-high-court/646681/0 (accessed on 10 February 2011).

43 *Plama* v. *Bulgaria*, above n. 21, para 193.

44 *SGS* v. *Philippines* (ICSID, Case No. ARB/02/6), para 116.

45 Ibid.

46 In this context, see also Alvarez and Khamsi (2009: 470) where the argument on the preamble in the US–Argentina IIA is that 'greater economic cooperation' and 'economic development' are not self-standing goals but possible outcomes of protecting foreign investment, which is the object and purpose.

47 Preamble to the Marrakesh Agreement Establishing the World Trade Organization, available at www.wto.org/english/res_e/booksp_e/analytic_index_e/wto_agree_01_e.htm (accessed 8 February 2011).

48 For example in the 'Shrimp Turtle' case, cognizance was taken of the preamble to the WTO agreement to adopt a more balanced interpretation of the GATT provision – *United States-Import Prohibition of Certain Shrimp and Shrimp Products, Report of the Appellate Body, WT/DS58/AB/R, 12 October 1998.*

49 The preamble in these two agreements is for the entire treaty and not just the investment chapter. More generally on 'development' in the context of ISA, see the Malaysian Salvors case and other materials analysed by Coppens, Chapter 9 in this volume.

50 *Maffezini* v. *Spain* (ICSID Case No. ARB/97/7); *MTD* v. *Chile* (ICSID Case No. ARB/01/7); *Bayindir Insaat* v. *Pakistan* (ICSID Case No. ARB/03/29).

51 Given the ambiguity on the expropriation provision in the two model texts available with the author, as mentioned above n. 31, the Model IIA is not included in the discussion on expropriation.

52 It will also be interesting to compare the expropriation provisions in Indian IIAs with the 'right to property' jurisprudence that has emerged in India in the past 60 years first as a fundamental right and later just as a legal right since it was stripped of its 'fundamental right' status. For more on this jurisprudence see Singh (2008: 273–301, 845–6).

53 Salacuse (2010: 267–8); Hamamoto and Nottage (2010: 32); see also Waibel (2009); Kolo and Wälde (2008).

54 For detailed discussion on these cases, see Alvarez and Khamsi (2009).

55 *Methanex Corporation* v. *Mexico* (NAFTA Award, 3 August 2005); *Tecmed* v. *Mexico* (ICSID Case No. ARB/AF (00)/2).

56 Mostafa (2008: 272–3); Fortier and Drymer (2004: 299); Gudofsky (2000: 287–8); Weiner (2003) also see Subedi (2008: 164–72) and Newcombe and Paradell (2009).

57 Ibid, *Saluka Investments* v. *Czech Republic*, above n. 17, paras 263, 264.

58 For example see the 2009 ASEAN Comprehensive Investment Agreement; India–Singapore and India–Korea IIAs.

Bibliography

Alvarez, J. and Khamsi, K. (2009) 'The Argentine Crisis and Foreign Investors', *Yearbook of Investment Law and Policy*, 1: 379

Alvarez, G.A. and Park, W.W. (2003) 'The New Face of Investment Arbitration: NAFTA Chapter 11', *Yale Journal of International Law*, 28: 365.

Arsanjani, M.H. and Reisman, M.W. (2010), 'Interpreting Treaties for the Benefit of Third Parties: "The Salvors Doctrine" and the Use of the Legislative History in Investment Treaties', *American Journal of International Law*, 104: 597.

Aust, A. (2007) *Modern Treaty Law and Practice*, 2nd edn, Cambridge: Cambridge University Press.

Brower, C.N. and Schill, S.W. (2009) 'Is Arbitration a Threat or a Boon to the Legitimacy of International Investment Law', *Chicago Journal of International Law*, 9(9): 471.

Buffard, I. and Zemanek, K. (1998) 'The Object and Purpose of a Treaty: An Enigma', *Austrian Review of International and European Law*, 3: 311.

Chidambaram, P. (1997) 'Foreword', in *India's Bilateral Investment Promotion and Protection Agreements*, Vol. I, New Delhi: Ministry of Finance.

Choudhary, B. (2008) 'Recapturing Public Power', *Vanderbilt Journal of Transnational Law*, 41: 775.

Clodfelter, M.A. (2009) 'The Adaptation of States to the Changing World of Investment Protection through Model BITs', *ICSID Review: Foreign Investment Law Journal*, 24: 165.

Dolzer, R. (2005) 'Fair and Equitable Treatment: A Key Standard in Investment Treaties', *International Lawyer*, 39: 87.

Dolzer, R. and Schreuer, C. (2008) *Principles of International Investment Law*, Oxford: Oxford University Press.

Fortier, L.Y. and Drymer, S.L. (2004) 'Indirect Expropriation in the Law of International Investment: I Know it When I See It, or Caveat Investor', *ICSID Review: Foreign Investment Law Journal*, 19: 293.

Franck, S. (2005) 'The Legitimacy Crisis in Investment Treaty Arbitration: Privatizing Public Law through Inconsistent Decisions', *Fordham Law Review*, 73: 1521.

Franck, S. (2007) 'Empirically Evaluating Claims About Investment Treaty Arbitration', *North Carolina Law Review*, 861–88.

Franck, S. (2009) 'Development and Outcomes of Investment Treaty Arbitration', *Harvard International Law Journal*, 50(2): 435.

Gardiner, R.K. (2008) *Treaty Interpretation*, Oxford: Oxford University Press.

Ghouri, A.A. (2009) 'Investment Treaty Arbitration and the Development of International Investment Law as a 'Collective Value System': A Synopsis of a New Synthesis', *Journal of World Investment and Trade*, 10(6): 921.

Gross, S.G. (2003) 'Inordinate Chill: BITs, non-NAFTA MITs and Host-State Regulatory Freedom – An Indonesian Case Study', *Michigan Journal of International Law*, 24: 893.

Gudofsky, J. (2000) 'Shedding Light on Article 1110 of the North American Free Trade Agreement (NAFTA) Concerning Expropriations: An Environmental Case Study', *Northwestern Journal of International Law and Business*, 21: 243.

Hamamoto, S. and Nottage, L. (2010) 'Foreign Investment In and Out of Japan: Economic Backdrop, Domestic Law, and International Treaty-Based Investor-State Dispute Resolution'. Available at http://papers.ssrn.com/sol3/papers.cfm?abstract_id=1724999

Karl, J. (2008), 'International Investment Arbitration: A Threat to State Sovereignty', in Shan, W., Simons, P. and Singh, D. (eds) *Redefining Sovereignty in International Economic Law*, Oxford: Hart Publishing, p. 225.

Kaushal, A. (2009) 'Revisiting History: How the Past Matters for the Present Backlash Against the Foreign Investment Regime', *Harvard International Law Journal*, 50: 491

Kolo, A. and Wälde, T. (2008) 'Capital Transfer Restrictions under Modern Investment Treaties' in Reinisch, A. (ed.) *Standards of Investment Protection*, Oxford: Oxford University Press, p. 205.

Krishan, D. (2008) 'India and International Investment Law' in Patel B.N. (ed.) *India and International Law Volume 2*, Leiden/Boston: Martinus Nijhoff, p. 277.

Kurtz, J. (2010) 'Adjudging the Exceptional at International Law: Security, Public Order and Financial Crisis', *International and Comparative Law Quarterly*, 59: 325.

McLachlan, C. (2008) 'Investment Treaties and General International Law', *International and Comparative Law Quarterly*, 57: 361.

Mostafa, B. (2008) 'The Sole Effects Doctrine, Police Powers and Indirect Expropriation under International Law' *Australian International Law Journal*, 15: 267.

Muchlinski, P. (2008) Policy Issues in Muchlinski, P. *et al.* (ed.) *Oxford Handbook of International Investment Law*, Oxford: Oxford University Press, p. 1.

Mukherjee P. (2009) 'Foreword' in *India's Bilateral Investment Promotion and Protection Agreements*, Vol. VII, New Delhi: Ministry of Finance.

Newcombe, A. (2007) 'Investment Treaty Law and Sustainable Development', *Journal of World Investment and Trade*, 8(3): 357.

Newcombe, A. and Paradell, L. (2009) *Law and Practice of Investment Treaties*, Hague: Kluwer.

Nottage, L. (2010) 'Australia's Productivity Commission Still Opposes Investor-State Arbitration'. Available at: http://blogs.usyd.edu.au/japaneselaw/2010/12/isapc.html (accessed 8 February 2011).

Ortino, F. (2005) 'The Social Dimension of International Investment Agreements: Drafting a New Model BIT/MIT Model'. Available at: www.oecd.org/dataoecd/45/51/40311350.pdf (accessed on 5 December 2010).

Paulsson, J. (2006) 'Indirect Expropriation – Is the Right to Regulate at Risk?' *Transnational Dispute Management*, 3(2): 1.

Ranjan, P. (2008) 'International Investment Agreements and Regulatory Discretion: Case Study of India', *Journal of World Investment and Trade*, 9(2): 209.

Ranjan, P. (2010a) 'Indian Investment Treaty Programme in light of Global Experiences', *Economic and Political Weekly*, 45(7): 68.

Ranjan, P. (2010b) 'Fissures in FDI Regulatory Framework', Business Standard, Available at: www.business-standard.com/india/news/prabhash-ranjan-fissures-in-fdi-regulatory-framework/383116/ (accessed 10 December 2010).

Ruggie, J.G. (2009) *Report of the SRSG, Business and Human Rights: Towards Operationalizing the 'Protect, Respect and Remedy Framework*, A/HRC/11/13, para. 30.

Salacuse, J. (2010) 'The Emerging Global Regime for Investment', *Harvard International Law Journal*, 51: 427.

Saxena, P. (2010) 'Evolving Investment Treaty Practice and Regional Perspectives, Second Symposium on International Investment Agreements'. Available at: www.oecd.org/dataoecd/14/3/46770126.pdf (accessed 1 January 2011).

Shaw, M. (2008) *International Law*, 7th edn, Cambridge: Cambridge University Press.

Sinclair, I. (1984) *The Vienna Convention on the Law of Treaties*, 2nd edn, Manchester: Manchester University Press.

Singh, M.P. (2008) *V N Shukla's Constitution of India*, 11th edn, Lucknow: Eastern Book Company.

Sinha, Y. (1999) 'Foreword', in *India's Bilateral Investment Promotion and Protection Agreements*, Vol. III, New Delhi: Ministry of Finance.

Sornarajah, M. (2009) 'The Retreat of Neo-Liberalism in Investment Treaty Arbitration', in Rogers, C.A. and Alford, R.P. (eds), *The Future of Investment Arbitration*, Oxford: Oxford University Press, p. 273

Spears, S. (2010) 'The Quest for Policy Space in New Generation of International Investment Agreements', *Journal of International Economic Law*, 13(4): 1037.

Subedi, S. (2008) *International Investment Law*, Oxford: Hart Publishing.

Van Harten, G. (2007), *Investment Treaty Arbitration and Public Law*, Oxford: Oxford University Press.

Vandevelde, K.J. (2008) 'A Comparison of the 2004 and 1994 US Model BITs: Rebalancing Investor and Host Country Interests', in Sauvant, K. (ed.) *Yearbook on International Investment Law and Policy 2008–2009*, New York: Oxford University Press.

Waibel, M. (2009) 'BIT by BIT – The Silent Liberalization of the Capital Account' in Reinisch, A. (ed.), *International Investment Law for the 21st Century – Essays in the Honour of Christoph Schreuer*, New York, Oxford: Oxford University Press, p. 497.

Wiltse, J.S. (2003) 'An Investor State Dispute Mechanism in the Free Trade Area of the Americas: Lessons from NAFTA Chapter Eleven', *Buffalo Law Review*, 51: 1145.

Weiner, Allen S. (2003) 'Indirect Expropriations: The Need for a Taxonomy of "Legitimate" Regulatory Purposes' *International Law FORUM du Droit International*, 5: 166.

11 The evolution of Korea's modern investment treaties and investor-state dispute settlement provisions[1]

Joongi Kim

11.1 Introduction

Over the past two decades, Korea has aggressively concluded a vast range of international investment agreements (IIAs) in the form of free trade agreements (FTAs) or bilateral investment treaties (BITs). Tracing how Korea's investment treaties have evolved over the years is significant also for other emerging countries, particularly given Korea's rapid economic development and transition from primarily a net capital importer to a capital exporter. An analysis of the major transformations in Korea's investment treaties, especially in light of its recently signed FTAs with the US and the EU should help other countries that hope to gain insight from Korea's development experiences. This chapter therefore critically assesses Korea's investment treaties and suggests how the present legal regime, especially the dispute resolution provisions, should be further enhanced to provide more effective protection and security for investors.

11.2 Korea's investment treaties

As a developing country rising from the ashes of war, Korea did not enter into its first IIA until 1964, when it signed one with Germany that entered into force in 1967. Thereafter, Korea remained slow to seek new partners for IIAs, with only four entering into force in the 1970s and two entering into force in the early 1980s. The vast majority of Korea's IIAs became effective from 1988, the watershed year when full-fledged democratization was finally achieved. After Germany, Korea's initial counterparts continued to hail from the developed countries of Western Europe such as the Netherlands (1975), UK (1976) and France (1979), befittingly given their status as leading capital providers. The next series of contracting parties primarily came from Asia – including Sri Lanka (1980), Bangladesh (1988), Malaysia and Thailand (1989), Pakistan (1990) and Mongolia (1991) – largely reflecting Korea's transition from a country primarily receiving capital into a country investing overseas. In the 2000s, this trend continued as Korea expanded its sphere of IIA partners and focused its attention on countries from South and

Central America, Africa, Asia and Eastern Europe. Korea made a noticeable shift in its trade policy when it commenced its first negotiations for an FTA, including an investment chapter, in 1999. This FTA was successfully concluded with Chile and entered into force in 2004.[2]

At present, in terms of geographic distribution, Korea has IIAs with 29 Asian countries (including Middle Eastern countries), 15 countries in Western Europe and North America (including Australia and New Zealand), 15 Latin American and Caribbean countries, 12 countries in Eastern Europe (including Russia and Ukraine) and nine African countries.[3] Currently, Korea has signed IIAs with five African and three Latin America countries that are awaiting entry into force.[4]

As of January 2011, Korea has 90 BITs or FTAs with investment chapters in force and together they apply to 95 countries. In terms of absolute numbers, Korea has the tenth most BITs in the world and second most in Asia after China (UNCTAD 2009). More recently, in 2010 Korea became the first country in Asia to sign FTAs with both the US and the EU, with both agreements seeking ratification in 2011. The KORUS FTA (2010) in particular garnered enormous interest in Korea concerning the investment-related dispute settlement provisions (contained in Chapter 5). Other noticeable FTAs with investment sections include the Korea–Chile FTA (2003, Chapter 10), the Korea–Singapore FTA (2005, Chapter 10), Korea's FTA with India called CEPA (2009, Chapter 10), the Korea–ASEAN FTA (2009, Article 18) and Korea–EFTA with the European Free Trade Association (2005, Article 16).

Encompassing a diverse range of issues, Korea's FTA with the US in particular not only represents one of the most comprehensive IIAs, it also deserves special attention given its significance for other countries pursuing similar arrangements with the US. Initial negotiations were concluded in 2007 under enormous nation-wide protest, and the agreement will be examined in detail. The Korea–EU FTA, on the other hand, does not contain provisions concerning investor protection because the EU's competence to negotiate them on behalf of the entire EU remains undetermined.[5] The Korea–EU FTA thus only covers pre-establishment investment that relate to activities before the actual investment is made, and investment liberalization commitments.[6] By contrast, post-establishment investor protection between Korea and European countries is governed through Korea's individual BITs with 22 of the 27 EU countries.[7]

11.3 FDI inflow and outflow

On an annual basis, FDI inflow into Korea has fluctuated between US$5 billion and US$10 billion over the past ten years, averaging US$7.3 billion, and peaking during the post-Asian Financial Crisis period of 1999–2000 after Korea made a painful but miraculous recovery. In recent years, the amount of declared FDI has increased but the actual amount of FDI inflow received has been marginally declining. In absolute numbers, the recent declining trend in FDI inflows over the past five years raises some concerns. But the cause is more likely a reflection of the aftermath of the Global Financial Crisis (GFC), particularly given that Korea's relative standing as a destination for FDI on a global basis has remained similar, ranking as the sixth largest destination for FDI inflows in Asia and 40th globally in both 2008 and 2009.[8] Overall, in terms of the overall composition of foreign investment into Korea, 80 per cent derives from indirect investment through portfolio investment and debt and the remaining comes from direct investment (Korea–US FTA Private Task Force 2006: 2).

Most of the FDI inflow into Korea has focused on the service sector, reflecting Korea's maturing economy as the proportion of its service sector outweighing the manufacturing sector continues to grow. Financial and insurance services, in particular, consistently attract the most FDI, with wholesale and retail distribution usually comprising the next largest segment. The manufacturing sector still manages to receive a steady stream of FDI as well, despite continuing challenges such as increasing labour costs and foreign competition. Electrical and electronic manufacturing, chemical engineering and transport machinery manufacturing are the primary recipients of FDI. Electrical, gas and waterworks construction received noticeable amounts of FDI in the early 2000s, but have dwindled significantly in recent years.

In terms of the sources of the inflow of FDI, a noticeable shift has emerged in terms of regional origins. Over 2001–4, the Americas reigned as the primary providers of FDI to Korea. Then, over 2005–9, Europe consistently displaced the Americas to become the largest direct investors. Europe's contribution, however, has been steadily declining particularly following the GFC. Instead, Asia-Pacific based FDI has rapidly increased during the same period, with American FDI also recovering. Most noticeably, FDI inflow from the Asia-Pacific region increased significantly in 2010, almost doubling that of 2009, and for the first time this region became the largest source of FDI for Korea – surpassing Europe.[9]

At the same time, in recent years, Korea has gradually emerged as a significant presence in terms of its investment overseas, largely a natural consequence of its economic growth and development. In Asia, Korea quite consistently ranks as the third largest country in terms of FDI outflows behind China and Japan, although India has begun to surpass Korea in recent years. Globally, Korea ranks as the 22nd largest in FDI outflow as of 2009. Asia has been the dominant destination for Korean overseas investment, with North America and Europe consistently following. In terms of industry, while the manufacturing sector remains the primary draw card for Korean direct investment its portion has been declining, over the past five years, the mining sector has quickly become the second most important attraction for Korean capital. Wholesale and retail, finance and insurance, and real estate and leasing form the next group of sectors that receive the most Korean FDI, although between them some variation exists from year to year.

11.4 Investor-state dispute provisions in Korea's IIAs

Essentially, Korea's IIAs almost all specifically require that investors receive basic protections such as national treatment, most-favoured nation (MFN) status, and fair and equitable treatment. Furthermore, most of the IIAs that Korea has ratified have investor-state dispute settlement (ISDS) provisions for private investors and also provisions for contracting parties to bring claims on behalf of investors. However, some IIAs – most notably the Korea–Germany BIT (1964) – only allow the governments to bring a claim.[10] To date, Korea has been involved in only one ICSID dispute, but it was not based upon a BIT and eventually settled before an award was issued.[11]

Eleven of Korea's BITs and all of its FTAs include some form of safeguard-type exception to its commitments in case of financial crisis.[12] All the BITs concluded since 2003 that have included such a provision provide that the safeguard applies in the case of 'serious balance-of-payments and external financial difficulties or threat thereof' or 'in exceptional circumstances, movements of capital cause or threaten to cause serious difficulties for macroeconomic management ... [such as] ... monetary and exchange rate policies'.[13] Prior BITs only contained simpler and more general language allowing parties the right to impose reasonable restrictions in cases for its 'balance of payments' or for 'exceptional financial or economic' situations.[14] Ultimately, such a provision has been added to all of Korea's FTAs, beginning with its first with Chile (in 2004) and including most notably the KORUS FTA (2010) and Korea–EU FTA (2010).[15] Previously, even in the Korea–US IIA (1998) concluded in 1998 during the aftermath of the Asian Financial Crisis, such safeguards were not included, and most other BITs do not have such provisions.[16] Nevertheless, Korea has never resorted to such safeguards even during the depth of the Asian Financial Crisis or the GFC, in the end making the provision more symbolic than necessary.

Most recently, experts have expressed concern because local and regional governments are engaging in fierce competition to attract foreign investment without fully taking into account the potential ramifications of Korea's investment treaty obligations (Lee 2010). The major FTAs to which Korea is a party all have provisions that specifically include regional governments.[17] In addition, the Korean Supreme Court has expressly held that regional rules and regulations must also comply with Korea's treaty obligations.[18] Hence, regional government actions could trigger investment state dispute provisions.

In terms of language almost all of the IIAs have been executed, at a minimum, in English, Korean and the language of the other contracting states.[19] Notable exceptions include the IIAs executed with France, Senegal and

Tunisia, which agreed upon French versions instead of English, and the IIAs executed with Bangladesh, Pakistan and The Netherlands, which only provide for English and excluded Korean. The most common third languages are (in descending order) Spanish, Arabic, German, French and Russian, while the IIAs with Mauritania and Tajikistan provide for four language versions. Most IIAs include a provision that stipulates that the English version will prevail with regard to disputes over interpretation and application between different versions, but several IIAs such as those with the UK, US, France, the Philippines and the Netherlands do not include such provision. Albeit not specifically in the context of large investment arbitrations, some observers have suggested that when multiple language versions exist then by implication it might be 'unavoidable' that the arbitration hearings should also be conducted in all of the languages of the agreement, unless the parties agree otherwise.[20]

Several BITs and all of the FTAs that Korea has entered into provide limitation periods under which one can bring claims based on the dispute settlement provisions. Most require that claims be brought within three years of the date that the investor 'first acquired or should have first acquired knowledge of the breach' or 'has incurred loss or damage'. The Korea–EFTA FTA provides the longest period: five years.[21] In terms of the knowledge standard, some IIAs provide a 'became aware or should have reasonably become aware' threshold to be met.[22] Under this standard, arguably, instead of actual acquisition of the knowledge, a mere awareness would be sufficient. Thus, a lesser degree of knowledge might suffice.

A number of Korea's IIAs have unclear dispute settlement (arbitration) provisions, and some even harbour some prickly potential issues. Among the more problematic IIAs, several do not properly stipulate who will decide which method of arbitration should be used should a dispute arise when several options exist and both parties can choose.[23] The Korea–Kazakhstan BIT (1996), for instance, provides in Article 9(3): 'Should the Parties fail to agree on a dispute settlement procedure provided under paragraph (2) of this Article, the dispute shall be referred to international arbitration *upon the request of either Party*' (emphasis added). Unlike most IIAs, where only the investor has the right to choose among the methods of arbitration that are provided, this BIT allows either party to make a request.

A problem could arise when the parties cannot agree to one of the particular methods of arbitration that are stipulated and each insists upon a different method. The arbitration options that are stipulated in the Kazakhstan BIT are, for example, ICSID Rules, the ICSID Additional Facility Rules or the ad hoc arbitration under UNCITRAL Rules. The ICSID option is available only if both parties are members of the ICSID Convention. It is not clear how such a stalemate should be resolved. One interpretation would be that the ICSID option should prevail if both parties are members to the ICSID Convention and other options would be available if both parties are not members. This interpretation can be challenged as well. The condition that 'if both parties are members of ICSID' may just modify the option to choose ICSID, and may not mean that other options should be excluded. Furthermore, even under this interpretation, it remains unclear what should be done if both parties are not members or only one party is a member of ICSID because two options, either to the ICSID Additional Facility or ad hoc arbitration, still remain. Another interpretation would be that the choice of whoever initiates the arbitration first should prevail since both parties did agree to the various arbitration methods as options. This interpretation, however, could lead to a 'race' to arbitration. Disputes could potentially arise as to who commenced first and, even worse, as to what was to be done if both parties filed at the same time. Of course, given the rarity in which states initiate actions this might be a more technical issue.

Korea's BIT with Argentina (1994) has a similar provision that requires the parties to agree to the method of arbitration. In this case, in contrast, the IIA includes a solution for the stalemate situation by stipulating that the parties will use ICSID if agreement cannot be reached within three months (Article 8(4)(c)). Similarly, the Korea–Hungary BIT (1988) provides for either the investor or host country to submit to ICSID, but this is offered as the only option for claims of expropriation or nationalization.[24] In a different light, allowing the host country to initiate arbitration itself can also be problem.[25] In the end, such treaties as the one with Kazakhstan must be carefully addressed to rectify such issues. Korea's BIT with Greece (1995) uniquely provides for the option of arbitration or conciliation, with the investor getting to decide if the parties cannot agree as to which option to choose.[26]

Almost all IIAs required a mandatory consultation or negotiation period before parties can seek formal dispute resolution.[27] Ten IIAs have periods of three months; one IIA, nine months; three IIAs, 12 months; and Korea's IIA with Argentina, 18 months; but 59 IIAs provide for six months.[28] Korea's BIT with Thailand contains the only IIA without a mandatory consultation period. However, it does not apply because Thailand has yet to ratify the ICSID Convention. After the consultation period, many IIAs then provide the option or require that parties seek resolution through local tribunals or courts. The question then arises as to whether an IIA containing an MFN clause could be applied to alter the consultation period, following the *Maffezini* case.[29] The KORUS FTA is the first IIA that specifically provided that the dispute settlement provisions should be excluded from the benefits of MFN. The KORUS FTA, however, did not make this exclusion in the treaty itself but by mutual agreement it was recorded in the negotiating history (Byun 2010: 62). Observers have noted that this type of stipulation should be explicitly recorded in the text of the treaty itself (Byun 2010: 62; Chung 2008: 159).

In five of Korea's IIAs, the *situs* or venue of the arbitral tribunal's hearings is specifically limited to only those countries that are members of the 1958 New York Convention on the Recognition and Enforcement of Foreign Arbitral Awards.[30] This includes Korea's FTAs with Chile and the US and

Korea's BIT's with Mexico, Vietnam and Kuwait. While the exact reason for this provision is unclear, it appears to be more common in Korea's more expansive and comprehensive IIAs such as those with the US, Mexico and Vietnam. The BITs with Mexico and Vietnam most likely included this provision because they were carried over from their respective IIAs with the US.[31] All Korea's other IIAs do not include such an explicit limitation. As part of its preference for the Permanent Court of Arbitration (PCA), the IIA with Qatar also specifies the venue for the arbitration to be the PCA at The Hague.

Three IIAs specifically stipulate that punitive damages cannot be awarded by a tribunal, notably Korea's IIAs with the US, Mexico and Vietnam. Again, as with the provision on venue mentioned above, the BIT with Mexico most likely has this provision because it was carried over from its respective IIAs with the US.[32] Since most IIAs do not specially mention anything about punitive damages the question remains as to whether they could be allowed if not specifically permitted. But given the rarity, controversy and lack of consensus over punitive damages in international arbitration, few tribunals would even contemplate such an award.

Most of Korea's IIAs do not clearly provide that pre-investment expenditures should be included in the scope of investment that should be covered.[33] Without any express authorization, the conservative view would hold that such expenditures therefore should be excluded (Hornick 2003; Chung 2008: 330 *et seq.*; Byun 2010: 24–9).

11.5 Institutional versus ad hoc arbitration

Most of Korea's IIAs strongly favour institutional arbitration through ICSID, with 68 of the IIAs providing for ICSID-based arbitration if both parties are members of the ICSID Convention. Thailand, Cambodia, Libya and Tajikistan are among those that are not member states of the Convention but have agreed to its application once they have joined.[34] Among the 12 IIAs that do not provide for ICSID arbitration, the most prominent include China, France, Germany, Russia, Uzbekistan and Greece. The rules governing the Additional Facility for the Administration of Proceedings by the Secretariat of the ICSID Centre have also been designated as a method for the IIAs with various developing countries, the notable exception among developed countries being the US.[35]

The next most frequently chosen option is ad hoc arbitration through the UNCITRAL Rules, which can be found in 32 BITs and five FTAs. At the same time, nine BITs provide for ad hoc arbitration without specifying the rules. Furthermore, many IIAs do not designate a particular institution, but instead allow the parties to decide upon which institution they prefer. Finally, five BITs specifically state that single arbitrators are allowed as well.[36]

Another interesting point revolves around how the chair of an arbitration tribunal should be appointed if the party-appointed arbitrators cannot reach an agreement within a certain period of time. The options vary from utilizing the Secretary General of ICSID, to the President of the International Court of Justice, to the PCA (Qatar and Iran), to the unique case of the BIT with France which designates the Chair of the International Chamber of Commerce (ICC), a private institution, probably reflecting France's comfort with the ICC whose headquarters are located in Paris. Lebanon and the Commonwealth countries of Guyana, and Trinidad and Tobago similarly agreed to the ICC Court of Arbitration as the forum to resolve their disputes regarding the chair.

11.6 Korea's most comprehensive and specialized IIA: KORUS FTA[37]

Among Korea's IIA, the investment chapter of the KORUS FTA contains some of the most comprehensive investment dispute settlement provisions that Korea has entered into to date. The US–Korea BIT currently in effect will remain applicable until the KORUS FTA is ratified but is limited to disputes between states and focuses only on investment into Korea from the US through the Overseas Private Investment Corporation.[38] Even from the US perspective, the final KORUS FTA – with its wide-ranging provisions – differs significantly from the 2004 Model BIT that serves as the benchmark when the US negotiates investment-related provisions (Korea–US FTA, p. 22).

Various provisions throughout the KORUS FTA seek to accommodate the various concerns of Korea regarding the dispute settlement process. The KORUS FTA, for instance, is the only IIA that Korea has entered that provides that (if the parties cannot agree otherwise) the official languages to be used in the entire arbitration proceedings, including all hearings, submissions, decisions, and awards may be conducted in both English and Korean (Article 11(20), para. 3). This appears to amount to a significant negotiating accomplishment from Korea's perspective, particularly given that the counterpart was a superpower – the US – and the agreement was by far the largest IIA in Korean history. Korea was concerned about 'procedural disadvantages' and the expenses that would arise from being required to translate all material into English (Chung 2008: 252). Nevertheless, it also raises various issues attendant to any multilingual arbitration, including added expenses, practical and logistical difficulties, and time delays (Blackaby *et al.* 2009: 3–54). Given that efficiency and expedient resolution should be the priority and also that Korea now has many international arbitrators proficient in the English language, the benefits of multilingual proceedings again might only be symbolic.[39]

Unlike Korea's prior IIAs, extensive transparency provisions explicitly provide that all of the hearings of the tribunal will be conducted openly to the public (Article 11(21)(2)).[40] Furthermore, subject to certain conditions, the responding state must disclose the notice of intent and arbitration,

pleadings, memorials and briefs submitted to the tribunal, minutes or tran-
scripts of the hearings and orders, awards, and the decisions of the tribunal
not only to the non-disputing home state but also to the public at large
(Article 11(21)(1)).[41] This reflects the desire to quell public anxiety surrounding proceedings, as required under US law (Gantz 2004: 747–9).
Another special provision explicitly allows the tribunal to determine the
location of the arbitration proceedings (Article 11(20)(2)). This provision
addresses the concerns that in an ICSID-based dispute such proceedings
would gravitate toward Washington, where ICSID is headquartered, and
therefore amount to an unfair disadvantage to Korea (Chung 2008: 251).

The KORUS FTA also represents the only IIA signed by Korea that
explicitly includes a provision on allowing *amicus curiae* briefs.[42] Article
11(20)(5) provides: 'After consulting the disputing parties, the tribunal may
allow a party or entity that is not a disputing party to file a written amicus
curiae submission with the tribunal regarding a matter within the scope of
the dispute.' The provision provides detailed guidelines on how the tribunal
should take the *amicus* submissions into consideration. This provision largely
replicates ICSID Arbitration Rule 37(2) and restricts *amicus* submissions to
written material and by implication excludes oral statements (Levine 2011;
Chung 2008: 255).

In a similar light, another unique provision covers the conditions under
which expert reports can be requested (Article 11(24)).[43] At the request of a
party, the tribunal may appoint one or more experts to report to it in writing
on any factual issue concerning environmental, health, safety, or other sci-
entific matters raised by a disputing party. Furthermore, a tribunal may
appoint experts at its own initiative as long as both parties do not disap-
prove. However, the provision specifies that experts can be appointed
through the applicable arbitration rules.

Under Articles 11(20)(6) and 11(20)(7), the KORUS FTA also provides
procedures under which the responding country can seek a decision from the
tribunal for preliminary issues before deciding on the merits.[44] Paragraph 6
gives the responding country the right to challenge that as a matter of law
the claimant's claim cannot be sustained. Paragraph 7 allows tribunals to
issue summary awards on claims for lack of jurisdiction. The tribunal must
decide on an expedited basis an objection under paragraph 6 and an objection that the dispute is not within the tribunal's competence. The tribunal
must then suspend all proceedings on the merits and issue a decision or
award on the objections within 150 days of such a request.

After an award has been issued, the agreement stipulates that parties
cannot seek immediate enforcement. For an ICSID award parties must wait
at least 120 days; for an ICSID Additional Facilities Award, ad hoc award or
other arbitration, at least 90 days must elapse (Article 11(26)(7)). Korea's
other IIAs do not provide for such a separate delay. This period is to allow
for parties to seek a revision, setting aside or annulment, of a tribunal award
and perhaps to encourage one last chance at post-award settlement.[45]

Finally, in the case of the KORUS FTA, pre-establishment investors must be guaranteed non-discriminatory treatment such as national treatment and MFN status and are thus subject to the ISDS process (as also under the Korea–Japan BIT). Pre-investment expenditures most likely will be included as well, based upon the definition of investor as provided under Article 11(28) which includes those that 'attempts to make, is making' or has made an investment (Byun 2010: 19–20).

11.7 Conclusion

Over the past 20 years, Korea has aggressively expanded its IIA portfolio and now maintains agreements with most major countries responsible for FDI outflows and inflows. The characteristics of Korea's IIAs cover a wide spectrum given their diversity in coverage, length, obligations, and conditions. Most IIAs have reached a substantial level of sophistication. Recently, as Korea continues its trade policy of focusing its attention on FTAs, FTAs increasingly have become the preferable method of entering into an IIA instead of the traditional mechanism of a BIT.

For the future, Korea needs to become more involved in promoting reforms to improve IIAs. Korea still maintains a relatively weak infrastructure in terms of investment arbitration, which needs to be strengthened. To the author's knowledge, for instance, few law schools in Korea offer a course that focuses on international investment law. Korea desperately needs more informed practitioners who can advise investors or states about the rights and obligations under investment treaties, as well as potential problems. Given the continued expansion of inbound and particularly outbound investment, more concerted efforts must be devoted to educate practitioners, businesspeople, investors, policymakers and academics alike about this important subject area.

Notes

1 The author is grateful for helpful comments from Luke Nottage, Jae Hoon Kim and research assistance from Sangho You. Unless otherwise noted, Korea refers to South Korea or the Republic of Korea.
2 As with Japan (Hamamoto and Nottage 2010), the shift to FTAs coincided with the lack of progress at the WTO to finalize a new round of multilateral negotiations.
3 Geographic distribution is based upon the five United Nations Regional Groups: the US is included in the Western European group, and Turkey and Israel are included in the Asian group.
4 Tanzania (1998), Democratic Republic of Congo (2005), Congo (2006), Rwanda (2009), Mozambique (2010), Brazil (1995), Uruguay (2009) and Colombia (2009).
5 Article 7(14), fn. 18. With the Lisbon Treaty on the Functioning of the European Union entering into force in December 2009, however, the EU has now

assumed exclusive competence regarding investment policy overall (Article 207(1)). However, the extent to which investment protection is covered has yet to be mandated and thus was not incorporated into the Korea–EU FTA.

6 Footnote 11 of Chapter 7 on Trade in Services, Establishment and Electronic Commerce in the Korea–EU FTA, for instance, provides that '[i]nvestment protection, other than the treatment deriving from Article 7(12), including ISDS procedures, is not covered by this Chapter'. Footnote 18 similarly provides that '[t]he obligation contained in this paragraph [on MFN] does not extend to the investment protection provisions not covered by this Chapter, including provisions relating to investor-state dispute settlement procedures' (Byun 2010: 30).

7 As of January 2011, Korea does not have IIAs with Cyprus, Estonia, Ireland, Malta or Slovenia.

8 Statistics are drawn from UnctadStat (on file with author). As of 2008, Korea, had the third lowest stock of inward FDI as a percentage of GDP among OECD countries – 8 per cent – ahead of only Turkey and Japan (OECD 2010: 33).

9 Nevertheless, rules of origins of foreign investment remain deceptive. For instance, one primary reason Asia-Pacific foreign investment increased in 2010 was due to seven investments from Samoa, a tax haven, which totalled more than US$2 billion. This made it the second largest foreign investor in Korea, but the investment most likely originally derived from another region. (These statistics are drawn from www.mke.go.kr, on file with the author.)

10 Other exceptions include Korea's BITs with Bangladesh (1986), Pakistan (1988) and Tunisia (1975). Korea's original BIT with Switzerland (1971) also was constructed this way but was replaced by Korea's IIA with EFTA (2005). The Korea–Thailand BIT (1989) includes an ISDS provision if Thailand becomes a member of ICSID, but as of March 2011 it had not yet ratified the Convention.

11 *Colt Industries Operating Corporation* v. *Republic of Korea* (ICSID Case No. ARB/84/2). Settlement was agreed by the parties and the proceeding discontinued at their request (Order taking note of the discontinuance issued by the Tribunal on 3 August 1990 pursuant to Arbitration Rule 43(1)). The dispute involved a US arms manufacturer and technical and licensing agreements for the production of weapons. See http://icsid.worldbank.org/ICSID (accessed 17 March 2011). Publicly available data is often limited due to the largely confidential nature of international arbitration, even in ICSID proceedings.

12 Korea's BIT with Switzerland (1971) contained such a provision but has been subsumed under Korea's FTA with the EFTA.

13 Korea–Japan BIT (2002) Article 17(1); Korea–China BIT (2007) Article 6(4); Korea–The Netherlands BIT (2003) Ad Article 4; Korea–Slovakia BIT (2005) Article 6. The EU–Chile FTA (2003) Article 166 contains a similar provision: Han *et al.* (2003: 248). See also Hamamoto and Nottage (2010: 32).

14 Earlier examples can be found in the Korea–Germany BIT (1967) Article 4; Korea–UK BIT (1976) Article 6.

15 Byun (2010: 262–72). The others include Korea's FTAs with Chile, EFTA, Singapore, India and the EU.

16 For discussion on background negotiations on whether to include such a provision in the KORUS FTA and Korea–US IIA, see Lee *et al.* (2006: 31–5).

17 KORUS FTA, Article 11(1); Korea–India CEPA, Articles 10(3) and 10(8); Korea–China BIT, Article 10; Korea–ASEAN FTA. See Lee (2010: 108–10). On the difficulties created by the expanded legislative autonomy given to local

governments in Indonesia, for example, see Chapter 6 by Butt and Chapter 7 by Sitasresmi, in this volume.

18 2004 Chu 10, Judgment of 9 September 2005, Korean Supreme Court. See also Lee (2010: 132).

19 Korea's practice contrasts with Japan's, where IIAs are all in English: Hamamoto and Nottage (2010: 28 fn. 72).

20 Blackaby *et al.* (2009: 2.81): 'It is both customary and logical for the language of the arbitration to be the language of the contract.... Sometimes a contract is made in two languages, each to be of equal authenticity. In such cases, simultaneous translations at the hearings of the arbitration may be unavoidable.'

21 KORUS FTA, Article 11(18); Korea–Chile FTA, Article 10(20)(2); Korea–EFTA, Article 16(6).

22 Korea–ASEAN FTA, Article 18(7)(a), CEPA Article 10(21)(5)(a), Korea–Singapore FTA, Article 10(19)(4)(a)).

23 Korea's IIAs with Kazakhstan (Article 9(3)) India (Article 8(3)), South Africa (Article 8(3)) and Ukraine (Article 9(3)) are leading examples.

24 Korea–Hungary BIT, Article 10(3). For non-expropriation or nationalization claims, both parties must agree if they want to proceed to use ICSID: see Article 10(4).

25 Some old Chinese BITs and Japanese IIAs apparently have the same issue: see Hamamoto and Nottage (2010: 27 fn. 68) and Shen (2010: 404). Concern has been raised that host states might seek to use this right to try to create *res judicata* effect: Hamamoto and Nottage (2010: 27 fn. 68).

26 Korea–Greece BIT, Article 9.

27 Compare the situation in Japanese IIAs: Hamamoto and Nottage (2010: 34).

28 IIAs that do not provide ISDS provisions and only allow state-state disputes have been excluded.

29 *Emilio Agustín Maffezini* v. *Kingdom of Spain* (ICSID Case No. ARB/97/7).

30 In Asia, notably, North Korea, Yemen, Bhutan, Myanmar, Tajikistan, Turkmenistan, Taiwan and Papua New Guinea have not signed the New York Convention, although Taiwan effectively recognizes its provisions since most of them are included in the Taiwan Arbitration Law: see also Pryles (2007). Korea signed the Convention in 1973 when it also entered into force with the reservation that it required reciprocity and that it would only apply to differences arising out of legal relationships, whether contractual or not, that are considered commercial under Korea's national law.

31 NAFTA, Article 1130; US–Vietnam Bilateral Trade Agreement (2001), Chapter IV, Article 4(5).

32 NAFTA, Article 1135(3).

33 Para. 48, *Mihaly International Corp.* v. *Democratic Socialist Republic of Sri Lanka* (ICSID Case No. ARB/OO/2), reproduced in 17 *ICSID Review* 142 (2002).

34 Similar provisions existed with Bolivia, Brunei, Kyrgyzstan, Mongolia, Nicaragua, Latvia, Laos, Lithuania, Peru, Poland and South Africa; they all subsequently became parties to the ICSID Convention.

35 Unlike in the treaty practice of some other countries, the main national arbitration centre (being, in Korea, the Korean Commercial Arbitration Board) has not been designated an option in any IIAs. For examples for some other countries, see Nottage and Miles (2009).

36 That is, BITs with the Czech Republic, Argentina, Trinidad, Guyana and Lebanon.

37 The final modifications made to the KORUS FTA that were reached through negotiations concluded in December 2010 did not include anything concerning the investment chapter or its dispute provisions.
38 Investment Incentive Agreement between the Government of the Republic of Korea and the Government of the United States of America (30 July 1998). KORUS FTA, Article 11(14)(2) provides that this prior BIT will remain 'compatible' with the KORUS FTA.
39 From the late 1980s, Indian, Korean and Chinese parties have become frequent users of ICC arbitration in Asia as well as other parts of the world: see Fry and Morrison (2009).
40 Such an explicit disclosure provision does not exist even in NAFTA. This also contrasts with the 'closed model' approach of FTAs that Korea and many other Asian countries adopted in their FTAs with ASEAN: see Lim (forthcoming 2011).
41 A similar requirement also exists in the Australia–Chile FTA (2009): see Nottage and Miles (2009).
42 For further discussion on *amicus curiae* briefs in NAFTA and other IIAs, see Van-Duzer (2007).
43 This provision is identical to NAFTA, Article 1133: Jimenez (2001: 250). ICSID Additional Facility Rules Article 43(c) and UNCITRAL Arbitration Rules Article 27 also contain similar provisions.
44 ICSID Convention Article 42(2) and the Australia-Chile FTA (2009) Article 10(20) contain similar provisions: see Nottage and Miles (2009).
45 For ICSID cases the 'setting aside' language is not used.

Bibliography

Blackaby, N., Partasides, N., Redfern, A. and Hunter, M. (2009) *Redfern and Hunter on International Arbitration*, Oxford: Oxford University Press.
Byun, P. (2010) *Korea's Investment Treaty Commentaries: Focusing on BITs and Recent FTAs*, Ministry of Justice, Seoul: Sungjinsa.
Chung, S. (2008) *Research on the Korea–US FTA's Investment Chapter, Ministry of Justice*, Seoul: Moonjung.
Fry, J.A. and Morrison, J. (2009) 'International Arbitration in South and East Asia – Opportunities, Challenges and the ICC Experience', *The Asia Pacific Arbitration Review*, London: Law Business Research Ltd.
Gantz, D. (2004) 'The Evolution of FTA Investment Provisions: From NAFTA to the United States–Chile Free Trade Agreement', *American University International Law Review*, 19: 647.
Han, C., Lee, and You, Y. (2003) *Korea–Japan Investment Treaty Commentary*, Seoul: Korea Institute for Industrial Economics and Trade.
Hamamoto, S. and Nottage, L., (2010) 'Foreign Investment in and out of Japan: Economic Backdrop, Domestic Law, and International Treaty-Based Investor-State Dispute Resolution' *Sydney Law School Research Paper No. 10/145*. Available at: http://ssrn.com/abstract=1724999 (accessed 21 February 2011).
Hornick, R. (2003) 'The Mihaly Arbitration: Pre-Investment Expenditure as a Basis for ICSID Jurisdiction', *Journal of International Arbitration*, 20: 189.
Jimenez, M.R. (2001) 'Considerations of NAFTA Chapter 11', *Chicago Journal of International Law*, 2: 243.

Korea–US FTA Private Task Force (2006), *Korea–US FTA, The Choice for the Future*, Seoul: Korea International Trade Association.

Lee, S., Kim, K., Lee, J. and Hyun, H. (2006) *Issues and Assessment of the KORUS FTA Investment Chapter*, Seoul: Korea Institute for International Economic Policy, Research Material 06–06.

Lee, J. (2010) 'Local Governments' Competition to Host Foreign Investment and International Investment Disputes', *Korea International Law Yearbook*, 55(2): 99.

Levine, E. (2011) 'Amicus Curiae in International Investment Arbitration', *Berkeley Journal of International Law*, 29: 101.

Lim, C. (forthcoming 2011) 'East Asia's Engagement with Cosmopolitan Ideals Under its Trade Treaty Dispute Provisions', *McGill Law Journal*, 56.

Nottage, L. and Miles, K. (2009) ' "Back to the Future" for Investor-State Arbitration: Revising Rules in Australia and Japan for Public Interests", *Journal of International Arbitration*, 26(1): 25.

OECD (2010) 'Economic Survey of Korea'. Available at: www.oecd.org/document/24/0,3746,en_2649_34569_45393816_1_1_1_1,00.html (accessed 17 March 2011).

Pryles, M. (2007) 'The Recognition and Enforcement of Taiwan Arbitral Awards in Australia', *Vindobona Journal*, 11: 25.

Shen, W. (2010 'Is This A Great Leap Forward? A Comparative Review of the Investor-State Arbitration Clause in the ASEAN–China Investment Treaty – From BIT Jurisprudential and Practical Perspectives', *Journal of International Arbitration*, 27(4): 379.

UNCTAD (2009) 'Recent Developments in International Investment Agreements (2008–June 2009), IIA Monitor No. 3. Available at: www.unctad.org/en/docs/webdiaeia20098_en.pdf (accessed 21 February 2011).

VanDuzer, J.A. (2007) 'Enhancing the Procedural Legitimacy of Investor-State Arbitration through Transparency and Amicus Curiae Participation', *McGill Law Journal*, 52: 681.

12 Legal issues in Vietnam's FDI law

Protections under domestic law, bilateral investment treaties and sovereign guarantees

Hop Dang

12.1 Introduction

Since the start of the *Doi Moi* (reform) policy in 1986, the Vietnamese economy and society have undergone fundamental changes. An important part of such changes has been the growth of the FDI sector, which now accounts for almost 20 per cent of the total GDP of Vietnam (FIA 2011). According to the Foreign Investment Agency of Vietnam (FIA), Vietnam had licensed over 12,000 FDI projects by the end of 2010, with the total investment capital registered exceeding US$190 billion (FIA 2011). These FDI projects have created millions of jobs, enabled the transfer of modern technology and management skills, produced new goods and services, and have had many important indirect effects on the Vietnamese economy and society.

The development of the Vietnamese legal system has played a critical part in the formation and growth of the FDI sector. In 1987, Vietnam enacted a short and simple Law on Foreign Investment which recognized for the first time the legality of FDI in Vietnam. From that starting point, Vietnam has now developed a comprehensive and sophisticated domestic legal framework to regulate FDI activities, comprising over 10,000 pieces of legislation dealing with almost every aspect of trade and commerce (Dang 2010). Government institutions and the court system have gained much more experience in dealing with foreign investment related matters. Arbitration is also developing as a means of alternative dispute resolution. As a result, the existing legal framework and institutions are now able to address many legal uncertainties and problems for which there were no answers in the 1990s.[1]

In addition, Vietnam has entered into the 1958 New York Convention on Recognition and Enforcement of Foreign Arbitral Awards. It concluded its first bilateral investment treaties (BITs) in the early 1990s and now has 55 BITs with countries from all continents. Most of these BITs provide for the usual protections for foreign investment, including no expropriation without adequate compensation, NT and MFN status, free conversion and repatriation of income, and resolution of investor-state disputes by international arbitration. In 2000, Vietnam entered into a bilateral trade agreement with the US, which includes a chapter on investment promotion. It joined the WTO in 2007 and it signed the ASEAN Comprehensive Investment Agreement in 2009. All these international agreements have supplemented the domestic legal framework to constitute an increasingly favourable legal environment for foreign investors in Vietnam.

However, at the same time, foreign investors have had to confront many legal issues in Vietnam that impede FDI activities. Apart from general issues such as uncertainties and inconsistencies in legislation, the level of discretion retained by government authorities, problems with the court system and enforcement of court judgments and arbitral awards (Dang 2010), foreign investors may face many specific legal issues in their particular investment projects. As an illustration, this chapter will discuss some specific legal issues for foreign investors in Vietnam including nationalization, changes in law, foreign exchange control, dispute resolution, choice of law and mortgages of land use rights. This chapter will discuss how these problems have arisen and how domestic law and BITs can be combined to give investors the necessary protection. Where investors find the protection afforded by domestic law and BITs inadequate, this chapter will show how investors have sought further protection by obtaining sovereign guarantees specifically for their projects. As such, domestic law, BITs and sovereign guarantees are three important sources of legal protection for foreign investors in Vietnam. This chapter will now discuss how they operate in the context of each of the issues below.

12.2 Nationalization

Protection against nationalization under domestic law for foreign investors in Vietnam lies in the nationalization provisions of the Vietnamese Constitution and the Law on Investment. Article 25 of the Constitution states that foreign invested enterprises shall not be nationalized. The same words were repeated in the Law on Foreign Investment (repealed in 2005). Article 6 of the Law on Investment now provides that there shall be no nationalization, except for reasons of national security, defence and national interest, in which case compensation is required to be paid based upon market value.

Such protection under domestic law is often perceived by foreign investors as having limited value in practice. Apart from the risk that the Constitution or the Law on Investment may be changed, the reality is that no investor in Vietnam has ever mounted a claim in a Vietnamese court alleging nationalization of its assets, notwithstanding the occurrence of events that may arguably constitute nationalization. There are several reasons for this. First, labelling an action of a Vietnamese authority as nationalization may bring undesirable political consequences. Thus, an investor would be very reluctant to frame an action as one of nationalization before a local court. Second, there is no legislative or judicial guidance in Vietnam on the meaning of 'nationalization' or on the calculation of compensation. This would create difficulties for an investor attempting to prove that nationalization has occurred, especially 'creeping nationalization'. Third, the circumstances of Vietnam may mean that it is difficult for an investor to succeed in a claim against the Vietnamese government for nationalization. One important reason is that the court system has no experience in these matters and may not be independent enough to find against government authorities on these issues (Dang 2010; Nicholson 2003).

In light of this, it is not surprising that no claim of nationalization has been brought before a Vietnamese court, even though events which arguably constitute expropriation or nationalization of assets have occurred. Two examples may be mentioned. The first is the action in 2004 brought by Phu My Hung Joint Venture Company, a joint venture owned by a Taiwanese investor operating a real estate complex in Ho Chi Minh City, against the Ministry of Planning and Investment for having amended the investment licence of Phu My Hung to increase the applicable profit tax rate from 10 per cent to 25 per cent. Phu My Hung asked the Court of Ho Chi Minh City to quash this decision of the Ministry of Planning and Investment on the grounds that it was inconsistent with the spirit of the foreign investment regulations which was meant to protect investors and stabilize their rights and interests. The claim however was never framed as one of nationalization. This claim was eventually dismissed by the Ho Chi Minh City Court as being out of time (Tuoi Tre 2004).

The second, and more recent, example is the action brought in 2010 by Vinametric Ltd, a foreign joint venture company owned by a Singaporean investor and operating a hotel in Ho Chi Minh City, against the Taxation Office of Ho Chi Minh City for imposing an amount of tax on Vinametric higher than the rate specified in its investment licence. The Ho Chi Minh City People's Court at first instance found for the Taxation Office, holding that the correct tax rate was stated in the tax regulations invoked by the Taxation Office, rather than the rate stated in Vinametric's investment licence. This is another case which arguably could have been framed as one of nationalization but was not. As long as Vinametric continues to operate its hotel in Vietnam, in the present circumstances, it will be unlikely to make a claim of nationalization against the Vietnamese government in a Vietnamese court. Therefore, the value of the protection under Vietnamese law against nationalization is rather limited in practical terms.

On the other hand, if the investor is from a country which has a BIT with Vietnam, the BIT could provide more realistic protection by allowing the investor to make a claim of nationalization against the government in a neutral forum under the BIT. For example, both the BIT between Vietnam and Taiwan (applicable in the *Phu My Hung* case) and the BIT between Vietnam and Singapore (applicable in the *Vinametric* case) contain protections against nationalization, combined with a right of the investor to bring arbitral proceedings against the State of Vietnam in a neutral venue if a nationalization dispute arises. Therefore, if the foreign investor in Phu My

Hung or Vinametric had wanted to, they could have brought an action against the State of Vietnam on the basis that the increased taxation amounted to nationalization.[2] Putting aside whether the investor would have won on the merits, the important point is that an action was possible and this could have had an influence on the State of Vietnam. A precedent for this was an action brought in 2003 by a Dutch investor (of Vietnamese origin) named Trinh Vinh Binh against the Government of Vietnam for having confiscated his assets in breach of the BIT between Vietnam and the Netherlands (IISD 2005). A tribunal was constituted under the UNCITRAL Arbitration Rules to hear this matter, but the case was eventually settled in 2007 (IISD 2007). This illustrates how a BIT may offer useful protection to an investor in the event of nationalization.

Nevertheless, the protection available under a BIT may not be adequate for some investors. BITs are typically valid for only a limited period and thereafter may be terminated by the Vietnamese government. Such limited periods may not be sufficiently long to protect investors who have their investment in Vietnam for 30, 50 or even 70 years. Consequently, investors in such projects often seek project-specific sovereign guarantees from the Government of Vietnam to protect them throughout the life of their projects. Invariably, these sovereign guarantees will provide for resolution of disputes between the investor and the Government of Vietnam by international arbitration. This will be an objective and neutral forum in which the investor may openly seek redress in case they have a dispute with the Government of Vietnam concerning nationalization.

There is another point on which project-specific sovereign guarantees can offer investors the protection which domestic law or BITs cannot give. This is in relation to the quantum of compensation for nationalization. At the moment, the Law on Investment provides for compensation at market value at the time of the announcement of the nationalization (Article 6). This is arguably inadequate because the investment may lose its value once the nationalization has been announced. On the other hand, BITs often provide for compensation at market value at the time immediately prior to the nationalization becoming public (BIT between Vietnam and Australia, Article 7). That would be a more appropriate point in time to value the assets of the investor. However, such protection under a BIT may not be adequate in projects where investors require that, if nationalization occurs, compensation must be a fixed amount to be calculated on the basis of a pre-agreed formula, which may not necessarily be the market value of the nationalized assets. Investors require such fixed compensation because they need certainty regarding compensation, which is particularly important for projects in which lenders insist that they must recover their debt and interest fully in case of nationalization, regardless of the market value of the nationalized assets (Cooper 2004).

Sovereign guarantees (often referred to in Vietnam as 'Government Guarantees and Undertakings Agreements' or GGUs) are not easy to obtain. The foreign investor needs to be in a significantly strong bargaining position in order to request, negotiate and obtain a GGU from the Vietnamese government. At the moment, it seems almost impossible, unlike the position ten years ago (Cooper 2004), to obtain a commitment from the Vietnamese government that it will not nationalize an investment. Instead, the government only seems prepared to undertake that a fair amount of compensation shall be paid upon nationalization. The precise formula for compensation will have to be negotiated on a case by case basis. So far, only about five energy projects have obtained GGUs in a form satisfactory to investors and lenders. These include the Nam Con Son Gas Project (Magennis 2003), Phu My 3 BOT Power Project (Cooper 2004) and KNOC Gas Project (EnergyPedia News 2005). However, it is expected that more sovereign guarantees will need to be given by the Vietnamese government in the next few years when it needs more energy and infrastructure projects to be financed.

In addition to the GGU, in order to make a project 'bankable', i.e. financeable by international banks, an investor may also need to seek further protection in the form of a legal opinion from the Ministry of Justice (MOJ) stating that the GGU is legal and enforceable under Vietnamese law. This is because certain provisions in the GGU may arguably be inconsistent with Vietnamese law and therefore illegal. For example, where a GGU provides for 'no nationalization', this may be inconsistent with the Law on Investment which allows nationalization in certain situations. As another example, where a GGU provides for a fixed amount of compensation which may exceed market value, this may be inconsistent with the Law on Investment which only allows for compensation based on market value. Such inconsistency with Vietnamese law may give rise to a risk of illegality and unenforceability of the GGU, even when the GGU is governed by a foreign law (typically English law). Therefore, investors would feel more comfortable if they had a legal opinion of the MOJ stating that the GGU is legal and enforceable under Vietnamese law. In practice, the MOJ has given such an opinion in projects which are considered very important to Vietnam. Investors often believe that this MOJ opinion renders the risk of illegality practically non-existent from both political and legal perspectives. First, once the MOJ has opined that the transaction is legal, it is very unlikely that any Vietnamese authority will subsequently challenge the legality of the transaction. Second, even where this is challenged, there is a precedent that such an opinion will preclude the government from raising the defence of illegality.[3] Such a precedent is likely to be followed in international arbitration, the forum where a dispute under a GGU will be resolved.

12.3 Changes in law

In reality, changes in law represent a much greater risk to foreign investors than nationalization. The Vietnamese legal system is constantly evolving and changing (Dang 2010).[4] After its enactment in 1987, the Law on

Foreign Investment was amended several times before it was eventually repealed and replaced by the Law on Investment in 2005. While the system is becoming more mature and stable, further changes are inevitable. This represents a serious risk for investors because a change in tax law or environmental protection law, for example, may result in drastic changes to the economic viability of the project, possibly rendering the project much less feasible as originally envisaged.

Protection against changes in law is available under the domestic law of Vietnam. A guarantee against changes in law was first introduced into the Law on Foreign Investment of Vietnam as early as 1992. This guarantee has been maintained and expanded upon in Article 11 of the Law on Investment, which essentially states that an investor may enjoy the benefit of changes that result in a more favourable treatment while being protected against unfavourable changes causing an adverse effect compared to its original position. Article 11 is as follows:

1   If a newly promulgated law or policy contains higher benefits and incentives than those to which the investor was previously entitled, then the investor shall be entitled to the benefits and incentives in accordance with the new law as from the date the new law or policy takes effect.

2   If a newly promulgated law or policy adversely affects the lawful benefits enjoyed by an investor prior to the date of effectiveness of such law or policy, the investor shall be guaranteed to enjoy incentives the same as the investment certificate or there shall be resolution by one, a number or all of the following methods:

   a   Continuation of enjoyment of benefits and incentives;
   b   There shall be a deduction of the loss from taxable income;
   c   There shall be a change of the operational objective of the project;
   d   Consideration shall be given to paying compensation in necessary circumstances.

3   Based on the provisions of the laws and commitments in international treaties of which the Socialist Republic of Vietnam is a member, the Government shall make specific provisions on guarantee for interests of investors in the case where a change in laws or policies affects adversely the interests of the investors.

The protection given by Article 11 is both broad and narrow. First, it is broad as it protects investors against adverse changes in both law *and policy*. 'Law' is defined in the Vietnamese Law on Promulgation of Legal Instruments as pieces of legislation issued by state authorities and having generic application. Policy is potentially wider than law and could include actions targeted at specific cases or expressed in documents other than legislation. A

typical example is an administrative decision such as an investment certificate issued by a state authority to approve a specific project. A change in an
investment certificate is unlikely to be considered a 'change in law' but could
qualify as a 'change in policy', and the affected investor would therefore be
entitled to the protection granted under Article 11. In that sense, the protection given under Article 11 is quite broad and highly conducive to
encouraging foreign investment. It should be noted that the term 'policy'
was not present in the equivalent provision in the Law on Foreign Investment (Article 21a) and so its addition in the Law on Investment means substantial further protection for investors in this area.

On the other hand, the protection is narrow in that, if one reads paragraph 2 of Article 11 carefully, one will see that the protection given by it is
quite limited. Only 'incentives' (such as a low tax rate or exemption of land
rent, often recorded in an investment certificate) are stabilized (the opening
paragraph of Article 11(2) and clause (a)). Thus, the Vietnamese government
may validly impose changes on a project, such as a new tax, while still maintaining its 'incentives'. But the new tax alone may be enough to make the
project unviable. In this case, the investor will be entitled to protection in
the form of the deduction of the loss from its taxable income (paragraph
2(b)) or a change to the objective of the project (paragraph 2(b)). However,
neither of these protections may be useful or desirable for the investor as the
project may have no taxable income (because of the losses suffered due to the
change in law) or a change in the objective of the project will render it
uneconomic. Most importantly, paragraph 2(d) states that consideration will
be given to paying compensation in some necessary circumstances. This
effectively renders the protection illusory for many investors as they may
prefer financial compensation. If compensation is optional and subject to the
discretion of the Vietnamese government, the protection seems highly inadequate for many investors.

BITs that Vietnam has concluded do not explicitly provide for protection
against changes in law. It is possible that when Vietnam changes its law or
policy and damages the interest of a foreign investor, it may constitute an
act of nationalization or denial of 'fair and equitable treatment' and so may
give rise to a claim under a relevant BIT. To that extent, BITs may provide
some protection to investors against changes in law or policy. However,
making out these claims under a BIT may not be easy.

Accordingly, investors in large projects often seek further protection from
the government in the form of a GGU. How much protection the government gives the investor in the GGU depends on the investor's bargaining
power and negotiation skills. Some investors have obtained a guarantee that
there shall be no changes to the legal or tax regime applicable to their projects (Cooper 2004). Such a commitment is now impossible to obtain from
the Vietnamese government. More commonly, investors may obtain a commitment from the government that they will be compensated in the event of
an adverse change to the law but the guarantee of compensation may be

expressed in different ways. For example, the government may only agree to compensate once the damage exceeds a certain threshold. The government may also insist that, in order to obtain full compensation for any unfavourable change in law, the investor must return to the government all or part of any benefits it obtains from any favourable change in law. In other cases, a change in law resulting in a certain loss may trigger the right of the investor to terminate the investment and claim from the government an amount of compensation calculated according to a pre-agreed formula (Cooper 2004).

A possible issue here is that, in those cases, the firm commitment to full compensation for changes in law obtained by the investor may arguably go beyond what Article 11(2) contemplates – that is, compensation to be determined at the discretion of the government. If so, the guarantee is inconsistent with Vietnamese law and the risk of unenforceability may arise, as discussed above. Investors may, however, rely on Article 11(3), which may be construed to reserve to the government the ability to agree, for important cases, a fixed amount of compensation for changes in law which may go beyond the discretionary compensation in Article 11(2). It should be noted that Article 11(3) is new and was not present in the 'change in law' provision in the Law on Foreign Investment. Therefore, it is possible that Article 11(3) has been deliberately added to give the Vietnamese government the power to agree on a fixed amount of compensation for change in law in some special cases. If this interpretation is correct, this represents a positive improvement in the Law on Investment for the benefit of both investors and the government.

12.4 Foreign exchange controls

Foreign exchange is an important issue for foreign investors in Vietnam. Every investor has the ultimate objective of making profits and remitting such profits out of Vietnam in freely convertible currencies, typically in US dollars. Except for those in export oriented projects, most foreign investors, having made the investment in foreign currencies, will earn income in Vietnamese dong. Under Vietnamese foreign exchange regulations (Ordinance on Foreign Exchange Control), all prices must be denominated and paid in dong. Therefore, it is important for an investor to ensure that it will be able to convert its revenue into foreign currencies and remit such revenue out of Vietnam and, most importantly, that there will be sufficient US dollars to convert the dong revenue into. The three key words therefore are *conversion*, *remittance* and *availability*.

Protection under domestic law on this issue may not be sufficient, especially for investors who have invested large amounts of capital. While expressly allowing foreign investors to convert their revenues into foreign currencies and remit such foreign currencies offshore (Law on Investment, Article 4), Vietnamese law contains strict foreign exchange control regulations. In order to convert dong into US dollars, for example, an investor will need to prove its legitimate needs such as the need to pay foreign parties for goods or services (contracts and invoices must be shown) or the need to repatriate profits (documents showing required taxes have been paid and the business actually generates profits must be produced) (Ordinance on Foreign Exchange and Decree 160 of 2006).

The paperwork required in this conversion and remittance process makes many foreign investors concerned that delay may occur, especially at times when the market is volatile and foreign currency is scarce. In such circumstances, a short delay is sufficient to cause the foreign investor a significant loss. In addition, a real concern for investors in capital intensive projects is the shortage or unavailability of foreign currencies in the Vietnamese market, especially if it is caused by a government foreign exchange control measure. For example, in a tight market such as in early 2011, the government may order that available foreign currencies will be prioritized for certain key industries and facilities (Government Resolution 11/NQ-CP dated 24 February 2011). In that case, investors in other industries will have a real problem.

BITs may offer some stronger protection in that they explicitly require Vietnam to allow the investor to convert and repatriate their investment and income (for example, the BIT with Australia 1991, Article 9). However, some BITs require that this be done in accordance with the law of the host state (Singapore BIT (1992), Article 10; Philippines BIT (1992), Articles 7 and 8). Thus, it may be difficult for an investor to have a claim under a BIT if it is unable to convert or remit its revenues due to the generically applicable law or policy of Vietnam or because there is a shortage of foreign currency in the domestic market. In addition, most BITs provide for conversion at the market rate or official rate announced by the government of the host state upon the date of conversion (Singapore BIT, Article 9; Thailand BIT (1991), Article 8). This will expose the investor to the risk of currency market volatility between the time the income is obtained and the time it is converted.

For these reasons, the protection afforded by BITs will be inadequate for investors with large amounts of investment in US dollars and large income streams in dong. Such investors will often require, as part of the GGU, a special foreign currency regime applicable to their own projects (Cooper 2004; Magennis 2003). Under this regime, the investor and the government and a relevant commercial bank agree upfront the procedures and paperwork required for conversion and remittance of revenue, in order to avoid any dispute or delay regarding required paperwork. In particular, in this regime, the government guarantees the availability of foreign currency so that if the converting bank runs short of US dollars, the government guarantees to supply sufficient US dollars to meet the requirements of the foreign investor. This guarantee is crucial because, if there are no US dollars available, the right to convert and the right to remit will be meaningless. In addition, investors often require as part of this regime that the government guarantee the conversion at a fixed rate such that the investor does not have to take the risk of the exchange rate fluctuations.

Although some investors have secured such agreements from the government and some are continuing to negotiate for them, they are very difficult to obtain. This is because Vietnam, as a developing country, is constantly concerned about its foreign exchange reserves. Any foreign currency guarantee for investors may reflect negatively on its balance sheet. In the worst case scenario, when a shortage actually arises, the government may wish to reserve the scarce foreign currency for its key industries, rather than to pay it to a foreign investor to repatriate profits offshore. If such a project-specific foreign currency regime is not given, an investor must continue to live with the current stringent foreign exchange control regulations of Vietnam and attempt to hedge the risks of the currency market through financial means. In the current economic and financial climate, where the availability of foreign currency is increasingly limited, these concerns of investors become even greater.

12.5 Dispute resolution

It is the desire of all foreign investors in Vietnam that any dispute they have with a Vietnamese counterparty or with the Vietnamese government will be resolved in a fair and objective forum, and that the decision of that forum will be enforced. Such a wish, however, seems difficult to realize in Vietnam due to the fact that both court and arbitration systems in Vietnam are still developing and that foreign arbitral awards are hard to enforce in Vietnam.

Under Vietnamese law, where a foreign investor has a dispute with a Vietnamese counterparty or the Vietnamese government, the dispute may be resolved in a Vietnamese court, by arbitration in Vietnam or arbitration offshore (Dang 2007). Obviously, arbitration is only possible by agreement, either in a specific agreement entered into by the investor or, in the case of investor-state arbitration, an indirect agreement under a relevant BIT. In the absence of such agreement, the dispute will have to be resolved by a Vietnamese court. Vietnamese law does not allow, or contemplate, the possibility of an investment dispute being resolved by a foreign court. As foreign court judgments are difficult, although not impossible, to enforce in Vietnam, this is not a commonly chosen forum.

Foreign investors often try to stay out of Vietnamese courts. The court system of Vietnam is overloaded and judges may be inexperienced in cross-border commercial matters (Dang 2010). Therefore, foreign investors often negotiate for arbitration agreements in their project contracts, especially where the contract is with a state authority, in which case international arbitration is an absolutely critical requirement. The real choice for foreign investors therefore is between arbitration offshore in a neutral venue (typically Singapore, Paris, London or Switzerland) or domestic arbitration in Vietnam.

Two real differences exist between foreign arbitration and domestic arbitration in Vietnam. First, the arbitral process in Vietnam is not yet adequate for complex cross-border commercial disputes. The arbitration system in Vietnam, including both law and supporting institutions, is still developing. The 2003 Ordinance on Arbitration had quite a number of restrictions on arbitrators and the arbitral process (Dang 2007). Arbitrators are also not experienced in resolving complex cross-border disputes. On top of that, the courts are not always supportive of arbitration and may set aside awards on technical grounds. Therefore, Vietnam is not preferred as the seat of arbitration for foreign investors, compared with more established arbitration seats such as Singapore, London or Paris. The 2010 Law on Commercial Arbitration is expected to improve the arbitration environment in Vietnam but that improvement has yet to materialize.

On the other hand, arbitration in Vietnam offers an advantage over foreign arbitration in that arbitration in Vietnam results in a domestic arbitral award which is directly enforceable without an application to a court to recognize and enforce it (Law on Commercial Arbitration, Article 66). If the losing party does not take steps to have the award set aside, the winning party may take the award directly to the relevant Judgement Enforcement Department to ask it to take enforcement action. By contrast, an arbitration overseas results in a foreign arbitral award which cannot be enforced in Vietnam unless a Vietnamese court recognizes it. To achieve this, the winning party must submit an application to the MOJ, which will then forward the documents to the relevant court; the court will then examine the case and decide whether to recognize the award.

Notwithstanding the fact that a small number of arbitral awards have been enforced, the general perception is that Vietnamese courts are very slow in recognizing and enforcing foreign arbitral awards, as shown in *Tyco Services Singapore Pte Ltd v Leighton Contractors (VN)*.[5] This is the result of the Supreme Court of Vietnam taking a narrow view of 'commercial transactions' (a reservation Vietnam made in acceding to the New York Convention – namely, that it would only enforce awards arising out commercial transactions) and an expansive view of 'public policy' which is a ground for refusing to recognize an award under the New York Convention. There has been little indication that these views of the Vietnamese courts have changed since then.

Therefore, foreign investors are caught in a dilemma. If they arbitrate in Vietnam, the award is directly enforceable but the arbitral process may not be adequate. On the other hand, if they arbitrate outside Vietnam, the arbitral process may be adequate but the award may not be enforced. This has become a serious concern for many foreign investors. The Law on Commercial Arbitration in 2010, drafted by taking into account the principles in the UNCITRAL Model Law on International Commercial Arbitration (as revised in 2006), will hopefully improve the arbitral process in Vietnam so foreign investors may feel more confident in choosing to arbitrate in Vietnam. It is therefore useful to provide a brief summary of the main new points in the 2010 Law on Commercial Arbitration to illustrate this potential (see Table 12.A).

It is also hoped that the new features of the Law on Commercial Arbitration will enhance the quality of arbitrators in Vietnam and cause the court to adopt a more supportive approach to arbitration. If so, foreign investors will have more confidence in arbitrating in Vietnam.

Disputes between a foreign investor and the Vietnamese government, however, will need to be arbitrated outside Vietnam in order to ensure absolute neutrality. Such arbitration may be conducted on the basis of an arbitration agreement between the foreign investor and the Vietnamese authority (for example, in the GGU) or on the basis of the arbitration provision in a relevant BIT. Most BITs concluded by Vietnam provide for international arbitration of investor-state disputes, typically by ad hoc arbitration

Table 12.A Differences between Vietnam's 2003 Arbitration Ordinance and 2010 Law on Arbitration

No.	Issue	2003 Ordinance (repealed)	2010 Law on Arbitration
1	Nationality of arbitrators	Only Vietnamese	Foreign arbitrators allowed
2	Qualification of arbitrators	University education plus five years of practical experience in the field of study	Any person with special knowledge may arbitrate
3	Language	Vietnamese as default language if parties do not agree	Tribunal can determine the language, unless parties agree otherwise
4	Choice of law	Tribunal shall apply the law chosen by parties provided it is not inconsistent with basic principles of Vietnamese law	Tribunal shall apply the law chosen by the parties
5	Choice of arbitrators in institutional arbitration	An arbitration centre may only appoint arbitrators from its panel	An arbitration centre can appoint any person, in or outside its panel
6	Choice of arbitrators in ad hoc arbitration	If parties do not agree on an arbitrator, the courts shall make the appointment	Parties may agree on a neutral appointing authority to make the appointment if parties cannot agree
7	Interim relief	Only courts may order interim relief	Arbitral tribunals may order interim relief

(Philippines BIT (1992), Indonesia BIT (1991) and Singapore BIT) or, less commonly, institutional arbitration such as ICC (Taiwan BIT (1991)) or ICSID Additional Facility (Korea BIT (1993)). These BIT arbitrations will result in foreign arbitral awards which will need to be enforced against Vietnam under the New York Convention. There has been no practical experience of this but it is likely that enforcement of such awards will need to take place outside Vietnam as Vietnamese courts will be very slow to enforce such foreign arbitral awards, as discussed above. Finally, it is necessary to mention that Vietnam has not signed the Washington Convention 1965 to become a member of ICSID. It was reported in 2010 that the Ministry of Planning and Investment had submitted to the government a proposal for Vietnam to join ICSID (US Commercial Service 2010). However, at the time of writing (March 2011), the government has not made any decision on this.

12.6 Choice of law

Where a foreign investor has a contract with a Vietnamese counterparty, it often wishes to choose a foreign law to govern that contract, in order to avoid the uncertainties and other problems of Vietnamese law as an evolving legal system. The concern for many investors is that such a choice of foreign law is not permitted under Vietnamese law so this may affect the validity of the contractual terms, as well as the enforceability of any award or judgment that may be rendered regarding the contract.

Vietnamese law allows choice of foreign law for contracts with foreign parties (not one amongst two Vietnamese entities) but subject to an important proviso that the application of the foreign law must not contravene Vietnamese law or its fundamental principles (Civil Code, Article 759(4) or the Commercial Law, Article 5(2)). As it is not clear what the content of the fundamental principles of Vietnamese law are, the actual scope of the applicability of foreign law to the contract is unclear. It is quite possible that a choice of foreign law must be subject to provisions of Vietnamese law and, if so, there will be little value in a choice of foreign law for the contract. More uncertainty is added to this by other provisions of Vietnamese law that potentially relate to choice of law but may not. For example, Article 5(4) of the Law on Investment states that:

> Applicable to foreign investment activities, where the law of Vietnam does not yet contain any provision, the parties may agree in the contract on application of foreign law and international investment custom, if application of such foreign law and international investment custom is not contrary to the fundamental principles of the law of Vietnam.

While this arguably refers to choice of governing law for investment contracts, it seems more likely that this refers to rules relating to the performance of the investment activities such that, for example, where Vietnamese law does not prescribe a particular construction standard, parties may agree to apply a foreign construction standard if it does not violate fundamental principles of Vietnamese law. However, this is far from clear and may also mean that foreign law may only govern an investment contract where Vietnamese law is silent. Such uncertainty makes the issue of choice of law in Vietnam even more confusing.

The removal of the proviso relating to fundamental principles of Vietnamese law would bring more certainty to the choice of law issues in Vietnamese law and give foreign investors more comfort in choosing foreign law to govern their contracts in Vietnam. This has been done in Article 14(2) of the 2010 Law on Commercial Arbitration which requires arbitral tribunals, in resolving a dispute with foreign elements, to apply the law chosen by the parties. Importantly, Article 14(2), for the first time in Vietnamese legal history, omits the proviso that foreign law must not be inconsistent with Vietnamese law or its fundamental principles. This means that where the contract is governed by English law, for example, an arbitration tribunal will simply decide the dispute based on English law without the need to refer to Vietnamese law or its fundamental principles (except for relevant mandatory rules that the tribunal may be obliged to apply). However, there remains the risk that if the award is inconsistent with fundamental principles of Vietnamese law, it may be set aside by a Vietnamese court.

12.7 Mortgages of land use rights

Many foreign invested projects in Vietnam need to raise loans from international banks by way of project finance. For lenders to loan money, they require a strong security package, which in most cases includes a mortgage of the land use right (effectively the land for the duration of the project) and the assets on the land. In the event that the investor as the borrower defaults on the loan, the lenders or its nominee may step in, foreclose on the mortgage and take over the land and assets on land and run the project to repay the debt.

The problem under Vietnamese law is that companies may only mortgage land use rights and assets on land in favour of banks authorized to operate in Vietnam (Law on Investment, Article 18). This includes mostly Vietnamese banks and a small number of foreign banks having commercial presence in Vietnam. However, in the case of a large project finance deal, the syndicate of commercial banks often includes many banks with no commercial presence in Vietnam. Therefore, it is legally impossible for them to have a mortgage of the land and assets on land in this sort of case.

In some projects, a practical solution has been devised whereby the land and assets on land are mortgaged in favour of an 'onshore security agent' –a foreign bank with a commercial presence in Vietnam, which then holds such security on behalf of all the lenders pursuant to a separate agreement between them. Given the uncertainties regarding the enforceability of this arrangement under Vietnamese law, lenders often require the MOJ to give an opinion that such a mortgage agreement is lawful under Vietnamese law.

A slightly different situation arises with respect to projects that are considered especially important, where the government grants an exemption to the project from the obligation to pay land rent. This is an 'incentive' for the investor which is meant to encourage the investor to invest in Vietnam and make the project more commercially feasible. However, this has given rise to a serious legal difficulty for these projects, because this incentive puts the investor in the category of those 'exempted from land rent'. Under Vietnamese land regulations, these land users are not permitted to mortgage the land to anyone (Decree 17 of 2006). The reason for this is that land rent exemption traditionally is only granted to professional, academic or other non-profit institutions. These institutions are not supposed to conduct business and therefore they cannot mortgage land to borrow money. However, when the government adopted the policy to exempt land rent for important investment projects, these land regulations had not yet caught up. By receiving an 'incentive' from the government, these investors find themselves unable to mortgage the land to lenders, which makes them unable to raise loans.

The practical solution to this has been for the investor to pay a nominal rent to the government to take it out of the categories of those 'exempted from land rent'. Alternatively, the government may explicitly state that the investor is to be regarded as having paid up all the rent up front. That will also take the investor out of the categories of those 'exempted from land rent' and therefore able to mortgage the land. However, these are practical solutions and it is uncertain whether this may be treated as 'avoidance schemes' and therefore may be unenforceable under Vietnamese law. Again, lenders and investors will require an opinion of enforceability from the MOJ and, once such opinion is given, lenders often treat the risk of unenforceability as acceptably small. However, it would help if this aspect of Vietnamese law were also amended to remove this peculiar legal difficulty.

12.8 Conclusion

This chapter has described and discussed some legal issues that foreign investors, especially those in large scale projects, have confronted in Vietnam and how these issues have been addressed by Vietnamese domestic law, BITs, project-specific sovereign guarantees or all of them in combination. It shows that while the Vietnamese domestic legal system, supplemented by the BITs, has come a long way to address issues for foreign investors, many other issues remain and Vietnam must continue improving its laws and institutions to remove them for the benefit of foreign investors. In particular, developing the court system, the arbitration environment and enforcement mechanisms for domestic and foreign arbitral awards will send positive signals to the international community and help Vietnam to attract more foreign investment at a lower cost. Otherwise, foreign investors and their lawyers will continue to have to spend significant amounts of time and resources to address those legal risks and seek project-specific sovereign guarantees, ultimately at the expense of the Vietnamese government and its people.

Notes

1 For general overviews of legal reforms in Vietnam, see for example Gillespie (2006); and Gillespie and Chen (2010).
2 It has long been recognized that increased taxation can amount to an act of nationalization. See, for example, *Revere Copper and Brass* v. *Overseas Private Investment Corporation* (1978) 56 ILR 258.
3 *Marubeni & South China Ltd* v. *Government of Mongolia* [2004] 2 Lloyd's Rep198.
4 Compare also the situation in Indonesia, outlined by Butt in Chapter 6 of this volume.
5 Judgment No. 02/PTDS dated 21 January 2003 (Court of Appeal of the Supreme People's Court of Vietnam). For details see Garnett and Nguyen (2006).

Bibliography

Cooper, B. (2004) 'Project Financing a Vietnam Power Project', *Journal of Structured and Project Finance*, 10(1): 34.

Dang, H. (2010) 'The Vietnamese Legal System: The Past 25 Years, the Present and the Future', in Bell, G. and Black, A. (eds) *Law and Legal Institutions in Asia*, Cambridge: Cambridge University Press, p. 185.

Dang, H. (2007) 'Towards a Stronger Arbitration Regime in Vietnam', *Asian International Arbitration Journal*, 3(1): 80.

EnergyPedia News (2005) 'Vietnam: Foreign Companies sign offshore development deal'. Available at: www.energy-pedia.com/article.aspx?articleid=110628 (accessed 15 March 2011).

Foreign Investment Agency, (2011) 'FDI Report for the Year 2010'. Available at: http://fia.mpi.gov.vn/News.aspx?ctl=newsdetail&p=2.44&aID=1043 (accessed 15 March 2011).

Garnett, R. and Nguyen, K.C. (2006) 'Enforcement of Arbitral Awards in Vietnam', *Asian International Arbitration Journal*, 2(2): 137.

Gillespie, J. (2006) *Transplanting Commercial Law Reform: Developing the Rule of Law in Vietnam*, Aldershot, UK: Ashgate.

Gillespie, J. and Chen, A. (eds) (2010) *Legal Reforms in China and Vietnam: A Comparison of Asian Communist Regimes*, London: Routledge.

IISD (2005) 'Investment Law and Policy News Bulletin, May 27, 2005'. Available at: www.iisd.org/pdf/2005/investment_investsd_may27_2005.pdf (accessed 15 March 2011).

IISD (2007), 'Investment Treaty News, March 27, 2007'. Available at: www.iisd. org/pdf/2007/itn_mar27_2007.pdf (accessed 15 March 2011).

Magennis, B. (2003) 'Petroleum Law and Contracts in Vietnam', *AsiaLaw*. Available at: www.asialaw.com/Article/1972429/Search/Results/Petroleum-Law-and-Contracts-in-Vietnam.html (accessed 15 March 2011).

Nicholson, P. (2003) 'Vietnamese Jurisprudence: Informing Court Reform?' Paper presented at the conference 'Law and Governance: Socialist Transforming Vietnam', Melbourne, 13 June 2003.

Tuoi Tre Newspaper Online (2004) 'Court Dismissing Action by Phu My Hung', *Tuoi Tre*, 3 September. Available at: http://tuoitre.vn/Chinh-tri-Xa-hoi/47011/Toa-bac-don-kien-cua-Cong-ty-Phu-My-Hung.html (accessed 15 March 2011).

US Commercial Service Vietnam (2010) 'Investment Climate in Vietnam'. Available at: www.globaltrade.net/international-trade-import-exports/f/business/text/Vietnam/Investing-FDI-Investment-Climate-in-Vietnam.html (accessed 15 March 2011).

13 Review of Asian views on foreign investment law

M. Sornarajah

13.1 Introduction

Assuming that there is a collective Asian view on foreign investments, its foundations must be found in a common historical attitude towards economic exploitation during the colonial period and the later adoption of a more pragmatic vision that foreign investment, selectively admitted, may be harnessed to the goals of economic development that Asian states have adopted. A combination of a historical sense of hostility, nationalism that continues to dictate events, pragmatism and competition among themselves to attract foreign investment underlies the different policies of the Asian states.

India, Malaya, Indonesia, the Philippines, Vietnam and Myanmar had suffered direct colonial rule. China, Japan and Thailand were subjected to the practice of extraterritoriality through treaties.[1] Even in Australia and New Zealand, though the same degree of resentment may not have set in, there is a lingering sense of exploitation or cultural distance. These attitudes may have passed as later phases set in, erasing to some extent the distaste felt for foreign investment as a harbinger of domination, but the sense of unease still lurks in a corner.

There is again no common degree of distaste towards colonialism. Indonesia had to fight a long and cruel war against the Dutch to secure independence. Malaysia and Singapore were given it by a power that had grown too weak to hold onto colonies. Japan, though Asian, was an aggressor in Asia. Japanese atrocities on Asian people are still remembered, although their memory is fading. Attitudes therefore vary in degree as to the linking of colonialism with foreign investment. The extent of resentment did shape policies in the immediate post-colonial phase. Indonesia immediately after independence was hostile to foreign investment, nationalizing colonial companies and excluding new entry, but Thailand and Singapore never displayed open hostility. Quite early in the post-colonial phase, variations among Asian states had begun to emerge.

In the immediate post-colonial phase, Asian states were intent on supporting measures to recover control over their economies from the economic dominance of the multinational corporations from the metropolitan powers. Many sectors of the economy, particularly the plantation and the natural resources sectors, were in the control of foreign corporations. The first phase of recovering economic control was accomplished through a series of nationalizations in Asia, some of which were celebrated instances in international law.[2] It was during this period that Asian states spurred the effort to bring about a New International Economic Order (NIEO). The NIEO sought to change many of the rules of existing international law. The Charter of Economic Rights and Duties of States sought to establish the Calvo doctrine as a universal doctrine.[3] That is, the package of resolutions articulated appropriate compensation upon nationalization instead of the old formula of prompt, adequate and effective compensation, required settlement of disputes by local tribunals according to local law, and recognized the doctrine of permanent sovereignty over natural resources. China, India and Indonesia, as aspirants to Third World leadership, were in the forefront of these movements. Again, there was no absolute unity. Thailand and Singapore had emerged as states having a different viewpoint, refusing to support Article 2(2)(c) which asserted the right of exclusive local control over foreign investment.[4]

However, once this early nationalist phase ended, a pragmatic phase followed. The success of the smaller states (such as Singapore, South Korea, Taiwan and Hong Kong) in adopting a foreign investment led strategy of development led to rethinking. These successes were wrongly attributed to the adoption of neo-liberal policies, when in fact all of these states had a visible presence of the state in the running of industries. There were also a new set of leaders who had succeeded those who had led the freedom struggle; Soekarno, Nehru, Tunku Abdul Rahman and Mao had given way to a new set of leaders who took their states towards a view that accommodated foreign investment. It was a stage of pragmatism. There was no rolling out of red carpets to foreign investors, as in Singapore, but rather the making of local laws that would accept foreign investment on a carefully selected basis, having regard to the needs of the economy and incipient local industries. The announcement of the 'Open Door Policy' in 1979 by China was a turning point in attitudes. India was to follow some 13 years later.[5] A new phase in foreign investment had begun, but it would be wrong to assume that state intervention and regulation in foreign investment had disappeared. In the politics of Asian states, the state remained a strong presence. This was so in foreign investment as well. There may have been liberalization as a matter of theory, but in practice entry of foreign investment and its subsequent operation within the state always remained subject to controls devised to further economic goals.

One can see such patterns in the development of the laws on foreign investment of Asian states. The Foreign Investment Law (1967) of Indonesia preferred joint ventures as the mode of entry requiring progressive divestment of the foreigners' shares. The Thai law had divided sectors into categories, the first into which entry would be permitted fully, a second into which entry would be permitted through joint ventures and a third which was operated exclusively by local entrepreneurs. This was the early pattern in China as well, where the initial laws adopting the Open Door Policy permitted foreign investments but through joint ventures with state entities. The investment code of the Philippines likewise limited shares of foreign investments in companies through which they could operate. Whatever changes the Asian states made as to the image overseas of their investment laws, comparatively restrictive laws or at least practices have remained the pattern to this day. The norm of permanent sovereignty had entered into the constitutions of many Asian states. The vestiges of earlier phases cannot be easily erased. They have a tenacity to influence policies and can resurface when circumstances become appropriate for their emergence. Thus, during a phase of nationalism, which surfaces often in Asian life, there would be a hearkening back to ideas of older attitudes to foreign investment. These attitudes lie smouldering, and revive when circumstances become appropriate.[6]

In the pragmatic phase, however, there was competition for investment among the Asian states. Policies were mirrored due to the fear that investors might be attracted to the competing states. It is easy to see that every measure that was taken by an Asian state to attract foreign investment was matched or bettered by other states. It is very visible in the grant of tax incentives, despite warnings that such incentives do not attract foreign investment but instead have a negative impact by giving away what was not necessary. Another is the making of investment treaties. States make them as a response to other states which had given incentives, in the belief that if they do not go along foreign investors may have negative perceptions of them.

But the modern phase is one in which considerable ambivalence has arisen as to investment treaties in the light of experiences such as the Asian economic crisis of 1997 and the global economic crisis of 2008. Also, the Asian experience with investment disputes has not been an altogether happy one. In that context, investment treaties will be looked at with greater scepticism and we will see the introduction into them of greater safeguards for the interests of the state. This is easy for the Asian states to do for, unlike treaties in other areas based entirely on the neo-liberal assumption that foreign investment is uniformly good for the host state and will result in economic development, Asian states always showed a reluctance to accept models of investment treaties that worked on the basis of an absolute assumption that foreign investment was totally beneficial to the host state. As a result, the Asian states will easily fit in with the global scepticism that has come about regarding the usefulness of investment treaties.

The philosophy behind each treaty does differ according to the period in which the treaty was made. Thus, for example, the expropriation provision may identify expropriation expansively to include not only indirect expropriation but a category of expropriation that is tantamount to a 'taking', thus creating an impression that there is a wider array of state interventions in investment that would amount to takings under treaties. But, within a few years, a new phase of restricting expropriation eventuated, when the notion of regulatory expropriation came to be stated in the treaties, taking much of the wind out of the sails of expropriation laws under the treaties. The Indian treaties are an example of this evolution. Likewise, the inclusion of fair and equitable treatment was uniform, but when it came to be realized that the term is capable of expansive interpretation, states – including Asian states – restricted its meaning by tying it with the international minimum standard of treatment, again constraining any further development that arbitrators may attempt on the basis of this nebulous standard.

13.2 The paucity of Asian investment disputes involving treaty violations

Asian states have faced few investment arbitrations despite the fact that they are among the most prolific makers of investment treaties. The reasons for this lie primarily in the type of investment treaties that Asian states have signed.[7] The Chinese treaties, which include over 127 BITs, traditionally submit disputes to arbitration involving only the calculation of damages arising from expropriation. Though the 'new generation' treaties (such as those with Germany and Holland) are said to deviate from this older form,[8] the fact remains that the newer treaties still tend to insist on the exhaustion of local remedies. The other large state, India, has had only one dispute so far brought to arbitration. This related to the Dhabol project involving Enron, a company that failed spectacularly. The allegations of corruption involving politicians on both sides, as well as other factors, led to a settlement (Roy 2010). However, claims have been brought on the basis of Chinese and Indian treaties,[9] presaging a new trend of both countries as exporters of capital. This puts the shoe on the unintended foot. It could well be that the erstwhile developed states of Europe and the United States may begin to have second thoughts about making treaties with these two states.

The South-East Asian states have also been spared too many disputes under investment treaties. This is despite the fact that the states went through an economic crisis. The Argentinean experience with the economic crisis was that 45 different arbitration claims were filed on the basis that measures taken to curb the effects of the crisis amounted to violations of the investment treaty standards. Argentina, the home of the Calvo doctrine, had signed a treaty with the United States in 1992 containing pre-entry national treatment and strict standards of investment protection. Though Argentina has been able to reverse its initial defeats in these arbitrations to a significant extent, the experience of investment arbitration that Argentina had alerted other states to the problems of restrictions investment treaties impose on necessary regulatory measures that may have to be taken in times of national emergencies. This led to considerable disenchantment with investment treaties, particularly in Latin America, where a return to the Calvo doctrine is a distinct possibility.

The South-East Asian experience was in contrast. Unlike in Indonesia, where the prescriptions of the IMF were adopted as the means for recovery from the Asian economic crisis of 1999, Malaysia adopted its own measures of withdrawing internally and closing off all external transactions through strict controls on outflows of money including currency controls. These measures clearly violated investment treaties as repatriation of profits became forbidden. There were other possible violations as well. The one effort to bring a claim on the basis of these measures against Malaysia, *Grueslin* v. *Malaysia*, proved unsuccessful. The reason why the arbitration in Grueslin failed at the initial jurisdictional phase was that the Malaysian treaty, in common with most treaties made in South-East Asia, protected only approved investments. When the arbitration was commenced, Malaysia took up the objection that the investment had not been approved for purposes of protection of the UK–Malaysia Bilateral Investment Treaty (1988). This objection was upheld and jurisdiction was denied.[10] The need for approval is one of three further reasons why investment treaties do not bring about a significant number of investment arbitration in Asia. These three reasons deserved to be examined, in turn, more closely.

13.2.1 *The requirement that the investment is an approved investment*

This requirement is a consistently found in the investment treaties of South-East Asian states. The matter was considered in *Yaung Chi Oo* v. *Myanmar*, the only arbitration brought under the ASEAN investment treaty system.[11] The ASEAN treaty required that the investment must be specifically approved in writing for purposes of protection by the treaty. The claimant was unable to show that the investment was so approved. This proved to be a hurdle in securing jurisdiction. There is no record of any treaty having been approved for purposes of protection in South-East Asia. The present writer, as the lead counsel for the claimant in *Yaung Chi Oo*, asked every ASEAN member state to indicate its procedures for approval. With the exception of Singapore, no state was able to produce any formal process for the approval of any investment for the purposes of the ASEAN investment treaty or, for that matter, any treaty that any of these states had made with other states. Technically, therefore, these treaties had no value as on the basis of *Grueslin* v. *Malaysia* and *Yaung Chi Oo* v. *Myanmar*, it is safe to say that since no investment could have secured approval in the absence of any formal procedure for such approval, no investment was protected by any of the treaties that the South-East Asian states had made with their treaty partners. This may be different under the ASEAN Comprehensive Investment Agreement (2009). Probably in reference to the past lapses, this requires procedures for approval to be indicated by each party; but this Treaty is not yet in force.

If the above assessment is correct, it does have consequences for it indicates that most South-East Asian treaties were of little practical use. It indicates that no foreign investor has sought approval under them so that they could be put to use in the protection of their investment. This in turn indicates that foreign investors coming to South-East Asia did not care very much about whether or not they had treaty protection. The inference is possible that the existence or absence of treaties has no part to play on investment flows – the foreign investors who came to South-East Asia having shown no regard either to their existence or, if they did, to seeking investment protection by having their investments approved for protection. The largest investors in the region are from Japan and the United States. Neither country has significant investment treaties with South-East Asian states. Japan is a late-comer to this treaty practice.[12] In the context of the evidence that South-East Asia has to contribute, the linkage between flows of foreign investment and the existence of investment treaties would be difficult to make. South-East Asian states have the capacity to attract as much investment as they would have had there been no treaties. The treaties cannot have played any significant role in investment flows into the region. It could well be that richer states within the region, desirous of promoting investments to poorer states so that they could be used as their hinterlands, are desirous of such treaties. But, even so, the poorer states would not need treaties to attract such investments as investment flows are determined more by factors such as geographical proximity rather than by the existence of secure protection provided by these treaties.

13.2.2 The requirement of conformity with laws and regulations on entry and operation

South-East Asian investment treaties have generally contained a provision which subjects the protection of investment to the requirement that the investment should have conformed to the laws in existence at the time of entry. One would think that this means the satisfaction of the requirements of the law at the time of entry; but this does not appear to be so for, at the time of entry, the regulatory body that controls admission of investment could impose conditions as to the manner in which the foreign investor should conduct himself after entry. To that extent, what are controlled are not only the requirements for entry but also subsequent performance of the investment. Entry laws specify certain requirements such as proof of capital being brought from outside, operation through joint ventures, the export of a sufficient quantity of manufactured products, conformity with standards of environmental protection, obedience to labour laws and the employment of local personnel. These requirements concern not only events at the time of entry but at later stages of the working out of the investment process.

Frapport v. *Philippines* is an award in which it was held that an investment made in violation of the Anti-Dummy Law of the Philippines, which required a particular equity structure in the joint venture through which alone a foreign investment could be made, results in the removal of the investment from the protection of the investment treaty.[13] The formulation in the Germany–Philippines treaty required that the investment be made 'in accordance with the law and regulations' in the Philippines. The words 'from time to time in existence' appear in some treaties, making the restriction even more stringent.

13.2.3 The existence of exceptions

Asian treaties had regulatory exceptions earlier than treaties in other regions. The accent on the conservation of regulatory space was strong in a region which had substantial regulatory mechanisms controlling entry and subsequent operation of foreign investments. Thus, the inclusion of language similar to the exception in the General Agreement on Tariffs and Trade, relating to measures taken to conserve health and public welfare, can be seen in many Asian treaties. The inclusion of such exceptions is a later phenomenon in the treaties of other regions. The possibility that the measures may fall within these precluding circumstances may have kept investors from having ready recourse to arbitration as did happen in other regions. The trend of creating exceptions has increased in the newer Asian treaties, making it hazardous to predict outcomes of arbitrations based on such treaties. Foreign investors would be deterred by the cost of arbitration when they know that victory is not a certainty, as it would have been had there been no mention of circumstances precluding responsibility.

13.3 Negative experiences with investment arbitration

The paucity of investment arbitration in the Asian context has also meant that there have not been as many negative experiences with investment arbitration as in the case of some Latin American states like Argentina and Bolivia, or European states like the Czech Republic. Yet the few cases that have arisen have resulted in some concern with the states that have been affected. Among the Asian states, a pronounced reaction has been from the Philippines, which has indicated disfavour with investment arbitration in a clear fashion. This results from the experience of the Philippines in *Société Générale de Surveillance (SGS)* v. *Philippines*,[14] in which the 'umbrella clause' was used by a tribunal to found liability. The umbrella clause is a throwaway provision in an investment treaty, which requires that all commitments made to the foreign investor (such as contractual commitments from the host state) should be satisfied by the host state. Its existence had hardly been noticed until it was used in two cases, both involving SGS as claimants. SGS was a company that provided customs inspection of goods at the source of origin. Its activity could hardly be described as an investment, although there was the tenuous link that SGS was also establishing a computer system for the Philippines customs and providing training to customs officers of the Philippines. The issue was more properly one of non-payment on a contract for services. Yet the tribunal decided to exercise jurisdiction over the case and find the violation of the umbrella clause on the basis that there was a commitment to pay. It was a bad case decided badly by overzealous arbitrators who were intent on extending the scope of investment protection by finding a new cause of action by way of the violation of the umbrella clause.[15]

The absurdity of establishing a cause of action on the basis of an umbrella clause was explained by a tribunal presided over by a distinguished Philippines judge and international lawyer in a case involving the same claimant, SGS, against Pakistan.[16] The tribunal refused to hold that the umbrella clause could be the basis for founding a claim on the ground that this would not only convert contract claims into treaty claims, as contracts involved commitments, as it would also render otiose the basis of a carefully negotiated treaty. Why would states negotiate such detailed provisions when all that was required was to say in the treaty that commitments made should be honoured?

The sequel to the incident in the two cases was that the Philippines became disenchanted with investment arbitration. The disenchantment has manifested itself in several ways. The investment chapter in the free trade agreement between Japan and the Philippines (2006) does not contain a provision on investor-state arbitration. There is a caveat to the dispute settlement provision in the ASEAN Investment Treaty (2009) that, for the Philippines, there must be consent given by the state after the dispute had arisen – making recourse to unilateral investment arbitration not possible in the case of the Philippines. In the same period, Philippines had also faced *Frapport* v. *Philippines* which it won at the jurisdictional phase, but there is an annulment procedure brought against this award. The same dispute also went through an ICC arbitration process on the basis of a contract and the expenses involved were high. The latter case involved prominent politicians of the state and charges of corruption were freely made during proceedings. In a region noted for corruption, the washing of such dirty linen outside the state may cause embarrassment and would have an impact on the international image of the state.

Though the Philippines reacted to its experience in the manner indicated above, other states have also have had similar experiences which did not result in any manifest action indicating displeasure with the system of investment arbitration. Pakistan had several arbitration brought against it around the same time, provoking the Attorney General to observe that the total claims involved in the arbitrations exceeded the assets held in reserve by Pakistan.[17] It is little comfort to say that the arbitrations typically do not result in the full damages claimed, for the claims are akin to a sword of Damocles hanging above the state while they are pending and have to be fought by spending money. This aspect is seldom taken into account when

considering the benefits of investment treaties. Even if they lead to investment flows (and there is an absence of convincing evidence on this), they certainly result in the anxiety of having to defend arbitration claims and spend
money to do so, sometimes hiring expensive law firms to do so. There may
not be economic development flowing from the treaties but there is certainly
economic development for law firms and arbitrators as a result of these treaties, which is increasingly demonstrable.

Both Indonesia and Thailand have had contract-based arbitrations flowing
from investment related claims. Indonesia had a succession of three arbitrations involving several billion dollars as claims arising from the economic
crisis, the consequent fall of Soeharto, and the measures taken to contain the
economic crises which included the freezing of the investment contracts
made during the Soeharto regime. All of these arbitrations were attended
with controversy. The Indonesian courts used anti-suit injunctions to stop
these arbitrations taking place. In the *Himpurna* Arbitration, the tribunal
shifted venue from Jakarta to The Hague and made an award in controversial
circumstances. In the *Karaha Bodas* Arbitration, there was an award which
was subsequently enforced; but it is a much criticized award. The third
arbitration, the *Phaiton Energy* Arbitration, was settled. These were arbitrations which caused much displeasure in Indonesia (Wells and Ahmad 2007).
The Soeharto regime which had made the contracts was noted for corruption. The procedure followed in the arbitration invited criticism and the
method of calculation of damages has been criticized.

Malaysia won the *Grueslin* dispute but has had problems with the *Malaysian Historical Salvors* arbitration.[18] The latter was again a bad case, as it was
doubtful that there had been an investment. The dispute involved a contract
for services. The claimant was a small company providing salvage services.
He fulfilled the contract by salvaging historical artefacts at the instance of
the Malaysian Archaeology Department. There simply was not an investment. Nor was there an approved investment, as *Grueslin* had indicated.
These would have been sufficient jurisdictional grounds for dismissing the
arbitration for want of jurisdiction. Instead, the arbitrator went off on a long
discursion on the meaning of an investment. Prudence would have dictated a
short statement dismissing the award for want of jurisdiction on the basis
that a contract of services did not amount to an investment. The eventual
dismissal was challenged successfully through annulment procedures. The
case involved a small-time investor who hardly had funds to mount such
proceedings. Yet, for certain reasons, it went the whole distance giving rise
to complicated definitions of what would amount to an investment. The case
added to the list of cases demonstrating the division of opinion that has
arisen on fundamental aspects of investment law. It again is a situation that
brings about a negative image of foreign investment arbitration.

Similarly, in Thailand, the *Walter Bau* Arbitration resulted in displeasure
with decisions made that there would be greater scrutiny of foreign arbitration clauses in contracts of investment. The incident concerning the buying

of shares by Singapore sovereign wealth funds in telecommunications companies controlled by (former) Prime Minister Thaksin Shinawatra sparked a political crisis in the country. The possibility of protection of such ventures under investment treaties was fortunately not raised. But, in a similar situation where Singapore wealth funds acquired telecommunication interests in Indonesia and the Indonesian monopolies commission interfered with the merger, there was threat of arbitration against Indonesia. This threat did not eventuate. However, it can be seen from the last two episodes described that there is likely to be an increase in intra-regional disputes. Singapore, and possibly Malaysia,[19] would be the capital exporters seeking to make investments in the rest of the South-East Asian region. Such disputes may result more in political disputes rather than in investment disputes. Prudence may require them to be settled through political means than through legal means. Legal victories will prove ephemeral in such situations, poisoning relationships rather than bringing about amicable solutions. The great danger is that the richer states of the region – Singapore, Malaysia and possibly Australia – will seek to make use of treaties as a sword provoking negative reactions from the other states. This is a situation that needs to be avoided.

13.4 The global economic crisis and the end of neo-liberalism

Asia escaped the effects of the recent global economic crisis to a large extent because it had had an economic crisis in 1997–9 and had taken prudential measures to control financial services and flows of capital. It was well known that the sudden withdrawal of foreign capital from Asia precipitated the crisis. Consequently, there was not as great a belief in the merits of foreign investment as existed elsewhere. Thailand changed policies to generate internal growth rather than depend on foreign capital to spur its development, and to various degrees such thinking existed in other parts of Asia as well.

The belief in neo-liberalism had become dented in Asia during this period. The success of Malaysia in getting over the economic crisis without depending on the loans and prescriptions of the IMF further diminished the confidence in what had come to be known as the 'Washington Consensus', a set of neo-liberal rules which the World Bank, the IMF and the White House thought were necessary preconditions for economic development. The Malaysian experiment was in stark contrast to that in Indonesia, which chose to swallow the bitter pill of the IMF conditionalities – including free flow of foreign investment. Malaysia succeeded spectacularly in overcoming the effects of the economic crisis. Thereafter, the prescriptions of the Washington Consensus could not possibly be regarded as the panacea for the problems of economic development. In that context, it is unlikely that Asian treaty practice will get more intense in the making of these treaties, with an emphasis on the protection aspects of foreign investments.

13.5 Looking to the future

Nonetheless, investment treaties will continue to be made. What one sees in recent practice is the so-called 'balanced treaty' with protection standards spelt out with heavy exceptions and further exceptions contained in particular provisions. One recent example can be looked at briefly. The ASEAN Comprehensive Investment Agreement (2009) captures the significant features of the type of treaties that will be made. The requirement for approval in writing continues from old practice. The treatment standards are hedged in to prevent expansionist interpretations. National treatment is subjected to the restriction that discrimination alleged must be between like parties. Regulatory 'taking' is not expropriation. National security is a matter of subjective assessment. There are exceptions relating to measures taken to promote health, public welfare and the environment. One wonders whether an investor would be satisfied with a balanced treaty which erodes investment protection as the central theme of the treaty. The future of the new ASEAN Investment Treaty is not going to be any different from that of the experience of ASEAN's older treaties on investment. It will be an unworkable treaty – an ornamental document (compare Maxwell and Wegner 2009). It can hardly give comfort to foreign investors.

What is meaningful is that the Asian region has always attracted foreign investment, even without treaties. There is little evidence to show that the treaties have enhanced investment flows. As shown above, the treaties that were in existence seem to have been of little use in giving protection to foreign investors in any event. It may be best to move away completely from this charade of treaties and go back to the system of negotiated contracts, effective domestic laws affording protection of the domestic courts, and the old system of 'diplomatic protection' (with investors requesting their home state to bring a claim against the host state for alleged interference with their investments). The experience of investment treaties has been that they promote predatory lawyers and arbitrators who feather their own nests, and dependence on institutions which promote agendas that serve the states which support their existence. Economic development has not been shown to result. Instead, what results is expensive arbitration that exposes the states of the region to threats of heavy damages.

Notes

1 The historical sense of past exploitation is particularly strong in China: Bickers (2011).
2 The Indonesian tobacco nationalizations provoked litigation in Europe and considerable commentary (for example, McNair 1959).
3 Singapore and Thailand voted against Article 2(2)(c) of the Charter, which asserted the right of exclusive local control over foreign investment and thus universalized the Calvo doctrine. More generally on the doctrine, see Cremades (2006).

4 Years later, Singaporean efforts to buy telecommunications shares in Thailand set off the coup against Thaksin Shinawatra's government and prolonged instability in that country. Likewise, the attempt by Singapore to buy shares of Indonesian Telecoms provoked the intervention of the Monopolies Commission requiring divestment of the share. Despite later efforts to create free flows of foreign investment in the region, such problems that involve nationalism still remain strong. See 'Temasek Holdings Investment in Thailand Shaken', *Bangkok Post*, 5 February 2011.

5 See also its evolving treaty practice outlined by Ranjan, Chapter 10 of this volume.

6 An example is the triggering of the coup against Shinawatra in Thailand on the news that Singapore's government investment funds had acquired large shares in the telecommunications sector. A threat to national security was conjured up, leading to the ouster of the government.

7 Compare Nottage and Weeramantry, Chapter 2 in this volume.

8 Compare the chapters by Bath (Chapter 4) and especially Eliasson (Chapter 5) in this volume.

9 For two treaty claims brought by Chinese investors, see Eliasson, Chapter 5 in this volume. *Sancheti* v. *United Kingdom* was the first claim brought by an Indian national, under UNCITRAL Arbitration Rules on the basis of the India–UK BIT (1995). For an English judgment relating to the arbitral proceedings, see *Sancheti* v. *the Mayor of London* [2008] EWCA 1283.

10 (2000) 5 ICSID Rpts 483.

11 (2003) 42 ILM 540.

12 For Japanese treaty practice generally, see Hamamoto, Chapter 3 in this volume; for a case study of the Japan–Indonesia treaty (2007), see Sitaresmi, Chapter 7 in this volume.

13 ICSID Case ARB/03/25 (16 August 2007). The award has since been annulled.

14 ICSID ARB/02/06 (2004).

15 The tribunal backtracked after this finding, postponing the stage of assessing damages and then holding that damages were not payable.

16 ICSID ARB/01/13 (2004).

17 At that stage, Pakistan faced *Bayinder* v. *Pakistan* (ICSID Case No. ARB/03/29, 2009) and the *Hubco* Arbitration (Barrington, 2000) which arose from an investment contract.

18 ICSID Case No. ARB/05/10. See also Coppens, Chapter 9 in this volume, discussing the arbitrator's decision and its subsequent annulment.

19 As outlined by Farrar, Chapter 8 in this volume.

Bibliography

Barrington, L. (2000) '*Hubco* v. *WAPDA:* Pakistan Top Court Rejects Modern Arbitration', *American Review of International Arbitration*, 11(3): 385.

Bickers, R. (2011) *The Scramble for China*, London: Allen Lane.

Cremades, B.M. (2006), 'The Resurgence of the Calvo Doctrine in Latin America', *Business Law International*, 7: 53.

Maxwell, I. and Wegner, K.-J. (2009) 'The New ASEAN Comprehensive Investment Agreement', *Asian International Arbitration Journal*, 5(2): 167.

Lord McNair (1959) 'The Seizure of Property and Enterprises in Indonesia', *Netherlands International Law Review*, 6: 218.

Roy, A. (2010) 'Enron's Dhabol Power Project', *International Journal of Business and Globalization*, 5: 188.

Wells, L.T. and Ahmad, R. (2007) *Making Foreign Investment Safe: Property Rights and National Sovereignty*, New York; Oxford: Oxford University Press.

Index

Page numbers in *italics* denote tables.
Please note that page numbers relating to Notes will have the letter 'n' following the page number.

cronyism 168
cross-border investments 34, 48
Crouch, H. 170n
CSR (corporate social responsibility),
    Indonesia 116, 121, 122
culturalist thesis 30, 32–3, 34
customary/traditional law, Indonesia
    119
Customs Act 1967, Malaysia 158
Cyprus, case law 100, 109n, 194, 197,
    206n, 207n
Czech Republic, case law 47n, 48, 59,
    65n, 104, 109n, 110n, 204, 205n,
    206n, 208n

Dabhol power project dispute 46n, 193
Damian, E. 121
Dang, H. 225, 226, 227, 229, 234, 235
Daryono 119
Das, S.B. 166
David, R. 121
David Hey v. *New Kok Ann Realty Sdn
    Bhd* 159
Davies, K. 68
Decentralization Law, Indonesia 124
definitions of 'investment': BITS vs.
    ICSID Convention 175, 176, 186–7;
    Chinese investment treaties/BITS 93,
    94, 100–1, 105; Indian international
    investment agreements (IIAs)
    199–200; Japan–Indonesia EPA 136,
    142; jurisdictional approach 175;
    Malaysian Historical Salvors cases 176;
    'ordinary meaning' 186, 187; treaty
    definitions, and role of economic
    development 174–91; typical
    characteristics approach 174, 175; *see
    also Malaysian Historical Salvors* cases
delays, institutional barriers thesis 31,
    36, 38
denial-of-benefits provisions 103, 107
Denmark, bilateral investment treaties
    93, 136
deregulation 31
Deutsche Bank AG v. *Democratic Socialist
    Republic of Sri Lanka* 44
developing countries 9, 26, 217
devolution, Indonesia 122
direct costs 36, 37, 39

dispute resolution: Asia 14–15; China
    72–3; investor-state provisions 203,
    214–17; Japan–Indonesia EPA 141,
    147–8; negative experiences with
    investment arbitration 248–51;
    overview of, in Asia 14–15; potential
    causes of investment disputes 147–8;
    treaty violations, paucity of Asian
    investment disputes involving 245–8;
    Vietnam 234–7; *see also* arbitration,
    investment; ICSID Convention
    (Convention on the Settlement of
    Investment Disputes between States
    and Nationals of Other States) 1965;
    investor-state arbitration (ISA);
    investor-state dispute settlement
    (ISDS)
dispute resolution pyramid 28, 39
divestments, FDI 29
Dixon, C. 6
Doha Round (WTO) 55, 63n, 150n
Doi Moi (reform) policy, Vietnam 225
Doi, V. 163, 164
Dolzer, R. 2, 93, 117, 192, 200, 205n
Domestic Investment Law 1968,
    Indonesia 115
Double-Taxation Agreements, Malaysia
    158, 169n
Drysdale, P. 47n
Dutch law, Indonesia 119
Duval, C. 142

East Kalimantan v. *Kaltim Prima Coal
    and others* 45, 147, 151n
Economic Cooperation Framework
    Agreement (China–Taiwan) 69, 72
economic crisis 27; *see also* global
    financial crisis (GFC)
economic development: historical
    overview 5–9; Malaysia, pre-NEM
    154–7
economic downturns 28
economic partnership agreements
    (EPAs): vs. FTAs 56; Japan 53–61,
    62, 118; 'new generation' 3, 57–8,
    245; Philippines 58–9, 141, 143; *see
    also* JIEPA (Japan–Indonesia
    Economic Partnership Agreement)
Economic Planning Unit, Malaysia 156